The Folklore
of Worcestershire

The Folklore of Worcestershire

by

Roy Palmer

Logaston Press

LOGASTON PRESS
Little Logaston Woonton Almeley
Herefordshire HR3 6QH

First published by Logaston Press 2005
Copyright © Roy Palmer 2005

ISBN 1 904396 40 2

Set in Times by Logaston Press
and printed in Great Britain by
Biddles, King's Lynn

Contents

Introduction & Acknowledgements

Between 48 and 52 AD the Romans established an auxiliary fort, possibly taking over an earlier, iron age, strong point, at what is now Worcester. They named the place, *Vertis*, from the Latin 'to turn', referring to a bend in the river. Some time later they called it *Uueogorna civitatis*, after the local tribe, *Weogoran* or *Wigoram*. This was their version of Wyre, which in turn appears in the county's name, *Wireceastrescir*, first recorded in *c*.1040.

With peripheral changes the county continued for over nine hundred years until, to the dismay of many and the anger of some, it disappeared in 1974 into the newly-created hybrid of Hereford and Worcester. The ill-advised innovation lasted a mere 23 years before the two ancient counties regained their autonomy.

My book, *The Folklore of Hereford and Worcester* (1992), went out of print at roughly the same time. In 2002 I extracted, revised and augmented the Herefordshire material for a separate publication, and it is with great pleasure, especially since I now live in the county, to have been able to complete a similar exercise for Worcestershire. Anyone working on folk-lore is indebted to kindred spirits of the past: people like Jabez Allies (1787-1856), Lusley-born, whose major work, *On the Ancient British, Roman, and Saxon Antiquities and Folk-lore of Worcestershire*, appeared in 1852 and incorporated material from his earlier book, *On the Ignis Fatutus, or Will-o-the-Wisp, and the Fairies* (1846); and Edward Bradley (1827-89), born at Kidderminster, who managed only a fifth class degree at Durham (there were seven classes at the time), spent part of his time as a clergyman at Leigh, wrote articles on folklore under the pseudonym of Cuthbert Bede, contributed to *Punch*, and published some very successful novels. Then there is the solicitor, Edward F. Corbett, imprisoned for embezzlement in 1902, who wrote a lengthy series of columns on Worcestershire villages in the 1920s and '30s for the *Worcester Herald*. More recently, Lavender Jones (1900-97) published a very useful pamphlet, *Customs and Folklore of Worcestershire* (1970), and also *Contented with the Time* (1992), a charming account of her family's stay at Colletts Green, near Powick, during the 1940s. I was fortunate enough to interview Lavender Jones on a number of occasions, and she generously passed on to me her collection of notes and cuttings.

I am indebted to a very wide range of publications, as will be seen from my extensive bibliography. Many institutions have helped, especially Worcestershire History Centre and Worcestershire Record Office, but also

Birmingham Central Library, Bodleian Library, Cambridge University Library, Folklore Society, Library of Congress, Malvern Library, Stourport Civic Society, Vaughan Williams Memorial Library (Cecil Sharp House), Worcester Cathedral Library and Worcestershire Federation of Women's Institutes. For assistance and information I should like to thank David Beacham, Nick Berkeley, Margaret Bramford, Keith Chandler, David Chestney, Richard Churchley, Audrey Cooper, Bill Driver, Mr and Mrs B. Dudley, David Franklin, Stuart Hellier, Rev. T. Henderson, T. Howes, Pat Leighton, Maureen Martin, Charles Menteith, John Middleton, Mr John Morrison, Miss M.W. Oliver, Rev. S.G.F. Owens, Emma Palmer, Simon Palmer, Miss D.J. Porteous, Steve Roud, Sue Smith, Frances Timbers, Mrs J. Truscott, Mrs R. Vaughan Williams, Mrs Joy West (Wilden All Saints' First School), Mark Woolley and K. Stanley Yapp.

My greatest gratitude is to my wife, Pat. She not only accompanies me on expeditions, reads maps and takes photographs, but she transcribes tunes and inscribes fair copies. In addition, she is long-suffering over my long-standing penchant for archives, libraries and secondhand bookshops.

Acknowledgements for use of illustrations are as follows: Author p.229 (upper), The Bodleian Library, University of Oxford pp.40 (Ballad no. 25046, in *Wood 401 (171)*, 233 (*Harding A10 (10)*); Eric Bottomley p.131 (upper); Bob Etheridge pp.99, 143, 207 (lower), 319 (lower); David Franklin p.78; Roger Hall-Jones of First Paige p.292; Mr Austin Heeks p.207 (upper); Capt. Stuart Hellier, Bayton churchwarden p.88; Mrs E. Mitchell p.156; Pat Palmer pp.5 (lower), 7, 8, 9, 13 (lower), 25, 32, 35, 36 (upper), 37, 42, 45, 56, 57 (both), 71, 76 (right), 82, 86 (lower), 93 (both), 94 (all), 95 (both), 96 (lower), 100 (lower), 103 (both), 106, 108, 118 (lower), 122, 123, 130, 131 (lower), 133, 154, 159, 160, 162, 165 (both), 167 (left), 168, 169 (both), 171, 172, 173, 174, 176, 182, 185 (upper), 190, 192 (lower), 210 (lower), 229 (lower), 252, 267, 268, 269, 270, 295, 309, 325; Steve Roud p.243; Mrs B. Rhys, for items in the Wight Collection held in Herefordshire Record Office pp.13 (upper), 21; Society of Antiquaries p.245; Vaughan Williams Memorial Library at Cecil Sharp House p.265 (both); Mr Stewart Gilbert, Editor, *Worcester News*, p.28 (from *Malvern Gazette*), and from *Worcester Journal* pp.12, 22, 91, 114, 128, 178, 212, 213, 214, 221, 289, 290, 293, 308 (both), 311 (upper), 313 (upper), 314, 315, 318 (both), 319 (upper), 321, 322, 326; Worcestershire Record Office pp.107 (upper), 117 (upper), 134, 185 (lower); Mike Yates p.201.

Roy Palmer

Map of Worcestershire

CHAPTER 1

Places

Fierce local loyalty, sometimes turning into rivalry and even hostility, produced sayings and rhymes passed on by word of mouth. Place names gave rise to fanciful exercises in etymology. Standing stones had their stories, as did other features of the landscape: hills and caves, springs and rivers. Even single trees inspired allegiance, like the fields and forests in which they stood.

Pride and Prejudice

Sayings like 'All about Malvern Hill a man may live as long as he will' and 'Blest is the eye between Severn and Wye' certainly express local pride. So does the claim that something 'shines like Worcester agen Gloster'. Yet the ladies of Worcester were proverbially held to be 'poor, proud and pretty.'

The mention of several places—including Pershore—once elicited the invariable comment of 'God help us', a reference to the fabled poverty of the inhabitants. Tibberton, near Oddingley, had:

A stone church, a wooden steeple,
A drunken parson, a wicked people.

The Anchor Inn at Wyre Piddle, from an old postcard

One rhyme makes no comment; perhaps none is needed, so long as one knows that the Piddle is a stream, tributary of the River Avon:

> Naunton Beauchamp,
> Peopleton and Crowle,
> North Piddle, Wyre Piddle,
> Piddle in the Hole.

A variation on the rhyme begins with the words: 'There's Upton Snodsbury', and is shown on the postcard above. Another list simply enumerates the hamlets and villages between Inkberrow and Evesham whose names derive from the Old English, *hlenc*, meaning hill: 'Lenchwick, Sheriff's Lench, Atch Lench, Church Lench, Ab Lench and Rous Lench'.

Bad feeling between pairs of neighbouring settlements was once endemic. The people of Areley Kings, believing themselves a cut above their neighbours at Stourport on the other side of the River Severn, claimed that they themselves 'lived on Christian shores'. The notion may date back to the eleventh century, when Areley Kings was owned by Queen Edith, the wife of Edward the Confessor.

The inveterate hostility between the people of Kidderminster and Bewdley perhaps led to the latter to protest too much:

> For ringers, singers and a crier,
> Bewdley excelled all Worcestershire.

Even so, the sentiments expressed lack the strength of antipathy towards a Gloucestershire neighbour revealed in this rhyme:

> Worcester for beauty, Malvern for wit,
> Upton for liver and Tewkesbury for shit.

Some villages liked to emphasise their superiority over neighbouring towns. The little settlement of Dodderhill looks down on Droitwich both literally and figuratively:

> Who'er has been to Dodderhill
> And down on Droitwich gazed
> Will not, if he should go to hell,
> Be very much amazed.

The tower of Evesham Abbey

Church Honeybourne made the claim that:

> There was a church at Honeybourne
> When Evesham was but bush and thorn.

This leads us on from derogatory and congratulatory remarks to the derivation of place names. A thirteenth-century seal of Evesham Abbey shows a swineherd looking up at a vision of the Virgin Mary. The inscription beneath (translated into modern English) reads:

> Eoves dwelt here and his swine,
> Therefore call this Evesham.

The story is that a swineherd, Eoves or Eof, was tending his pigs by the River Avon where he heard celestial harmonies and saw a vision of the Virgin. He reported the experience to his master, Egwin, Bishop of Worcester (later canonised; see chapter 2), who hurried to the spot and saw the same vision. The Virgin told him to build an abbey there in what was the wilderness of Blackenhurst. The new church was dedicated in 714, and the place came to be called Eoveshome—later Evesham. In 2004 Wychavon District Council granted planning permission for a statue of Eof to be erected in the Market Place at Evesham. The ten or twelve-feet high figure, designed by a Worcester artist, John Mckenna, required funding of some £65,000, raised by public appeal.

Such attempts at etymology are often disputed by scholars. Kidderminster comes from Cydda's minster but that does not prevent a different—and no doubt tongue-in-cheek—explanation:

> King Cador saw a pretty maid,
> King Cador would have kissed her.
> The damsel slipped aside and said:
> 'King Cador, you have missed her'.

The pedigree of Oddingley is also far-fetched. Two Saxon giants, Odd and Dingley, fought on a common until the former was obliged to concede, with the words:

> O Dingley, O Dingley, spare my breath.
> This shall be called Oddingley Heath.

There may not have been a Dingley, but there was an historical Oddo or Odda, a Mercian nobleman who is buried in Pershore Abbey. Dudley and Doddingtree are both named after him, and so is Oddingley, which means 'clearing of the people of Odda'.

The name of Bromsgrove is supposed to stem from Boar's Grove, after the place where a legendary wild boar was slain. The man responsible, Sir Humphrey Stafford, was himself killed in 1450 during the rebellion of Jack Cade, and buried in Bromsgrove Church. Another version of the story—and there usually is another version—claims the victor to be Sir Ryalas Bolton, who was the subject of a ballad entitled *The Jovial Hunter* (see chapter 3). Until 1806 two stones weighing several tons stood in front of Bromsgrove Town Hall. When the road was paved they were too big to move, so great pits were dug and they were buried on the spot. Supposedly they were originally put there by the Jovial Hunter, who shook them out of his shoe because they were hurting his feet. Another explanation is that there was a disagreement between the Hunter and his rival, who lived at Malvern. They launched huge stones at each other—the Hunter from Lickey and the other from the Malvern Hills— and these collided in flight, to fall to earth in Bromsgrove.

Stones

The durability of stones made them useful as boundary markers. The Four Shire Stone near Moreton-in-Marsh shows where four counties—Worcestershire, Gloucestershire, Warwickshire and Oxfordshire—meet, or rather used to meet. It so happens that a battle was fought thereabouts in 1016 between the English under Edmund Ironside and the Danes under Canute. The English won after 'great slaughter'.

The Four Shire Stone, from a postcard

In the late eighteenth century four standing stones were being set up on one of the Clent Hills on the orders of Lord Lyttleton of Hagley, who wanted a picturesque vista from his house. Various beliefs about the stones quickly emerged: they were of druidical origin; they stood in memory of the Scots bard, Ossian; they marked the meeting of four counties—Staffordshire, Worcestershire, Shropshire and Warwickshire. Even today some people claim that the stones go down to the brook to drink when they hear the chimes of midnight.

In a hollow below the crown of Bredon Hill is a group of rocks twenty yards round called the Bambury or Banbury Stones. This was a single enormous

The Bambury, or Banbury Stones, Bredon Hill

5

stone until during the nineteenth century a movement of the ground caused it to split apart. Despite such bulk it, too, was said to go down to the Avon to drink when it heard a church clock strike midnight, or alternatively when it heard the bells of Pershore Abbey. The stone may have been used in prehistoric times as a sacrificial altar. More recently, it was customary for people to climb the hill on Good Friday and kiss the stone. The same custom also obtained at Pecket Rock in the Habberley valley near Kidderminster, near where a giant fell to his death over a cliff, and was buried where he lay.

On another part of Bredon Hill, above Westmancote, are the King and Queen Stones. Until the end of the eighteenth century the sessions of the manorial court were proclaimed here—the stones having been ceremonially whitewashed beforehand—and then adjourned to the Royal Oak in Bredon's Norton below. Until the late nineteenth century people were passed between the two stones in the belief that the ritual would charm away aches and pains and restore the weakly to good health. There is a suggestion that a baptismal rite for witches was carried out at the same spot. Not far from the King and Queen Stones, which like the Banbury Stones are part of natural rock formations at their respective sites, at Bredon's Norton, near Aldwick Wood, are monoliths which were probably moved there in Neolithic times to make a long barrow (burial chamber).

Hills

As well as having a secure place in folklore, Bredon Hill also appears in fiction, from Henry Fielding—in whose *Tom Jones* it is disguised as Mazard Hill—to John Moore and Fred Archer. The Malvern Hills, too, have many literary

Upton-on-Severn from Ryall, 1780, with a trow on the Severn and the Malvern Hills in the background

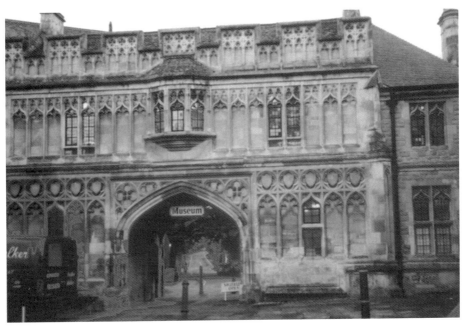

The Gatehouse of Malvern Priory

connections, starting as early as the fourteenth century with the Colwall-born—at Langlands Farm—William Langland and his vision in the poem *Piers Plowman*, of a 'fair feeld ful of folk' seen 'on a May morwenynge on Malverne hilles'. Langland could have been educated at either Great or Little Malvern Priory, and a room in the former's gatehouse (which still stands) was traditionally associated with him.

A later poet, Michael Drayton, referring to Bredon in *Poly-Olbion* (1613) says:

> And when great Malvern looks most terrible and grym,
> Hee with a pleased brow continually doth smile.

Yet Drayton calles Malvern 'mighty' and 'manly', and comments that 'Malverne (king of Hills) faire Severne over-lookes'.

Celia Fiennes, writing some eighty years later, in prose, but with some poetic licence, described the 'Mauborn hills, or as some term them the English Alps' as being 'at least 2 or 3 miles up and ... in a Pirramidy fashion on the tops', and added:

> I rode up upon the top of one of the highest, from whence I could discern
> the Country above 40 miles round, and noe hills, but what appeared like
> Burrows or Mole hills; these being so high nothing could limitt the eye
> but distance.

Little Malvern Church and Court (formerly the priory)

In 1888 Charles F. Grindrod published a novel entitled *The Shadow of the Raggedstone*. In it he tells the story of how a monk from Little Malvern Priory defies a vow of chastity and falls in love wth a local woman. As a penance he is made to crawl up Raggedstone Hill on his hands and knees each day. In his torment, just before dying, he utters a curse 'May all upon whom the shadow of this stone falls untimely die'. The story stuck, and has confidently been repeated ever since. During the First World War it inspired a poem by Wilfrid Gibson about a soldier and his sweetheart:

> As I was walking with my dear, my dear come back at last,
> The shadow of the Ragged Stone fell on us as we passed;
> And if the tale be true they tell about the Ragged Stone,
> I'll not be walking with my dear next year, nor yet alone.

According to Edwin Lees, writing in 1856, 'This legend was related by my friend, the Rev. W.S. Symonds [1818-87], ... and he found it in an old document to which he had access'. One can only say that such a provenance is dubious.

A version of the story claimed to be authentic concerns a dispute over land between the monks of Little Malvern and Sir John Nanfan of Birtsmorton. Nanfan enclosed land, some of which the monks claimed as theirs. One day Sir John found a monk on Raggedstone Hill, part of the area in contention, and ordered him off. The monk retorted that this was the monastery's land, and if Nanfan failed to restore it God's judgement would be called down on him. 'Do your worst', replied Sir John. The monk pronounced the formula of excommunication, and when Nanfan remained defiant, prophesied that whenever the

Birtsmorton Court

shadow of the hill fell on Birtsmorton Court the oldest son of the house would die within twelve months. As he spoke, the shadow fell on the house. Nanfan's oldest son died within the year.

The respective positions of the house and the hill mean that the shadow can only fall on a particular day in November, providing, of course, that the sun is shining, which is not necessarily the case every year. Nevertheless over the centuries unexpected deaths among Nanfan heirs—a fall from a horse, a casualty during the Civil War (the only Royalist to die in a skirmish in the Leadon Valley), a duelling victim after the Restoration—were attributed to the curse. In 1704 the elder branch of the Nanfan family was extinguished, and the malediction transferred to a junior branch which itself died in poverty at Worcester in the nineteenth century. Over time, other alleged victims of the curse included the wife of Henry VI, Margaret of Anjou, who died in poverty; Cardinal Wolsey, once chaplain to a Nanfan (though not in fact at Birtsmorton), and William Huskisson, the government minister killed by a train—the first known victim of a railway accident—in 1830, who was born at Birtsmorton Court.

The path worn on the hill by the monk in his penance can be seen, it is said, from as far away as Worcester, and even Hanbury. Another feature still visible along parts of the Malvern ridge, including the Raggedstone Hill, is a trench known as the Red Earl's Dyke. Malvern Chase, a tract of over 6,000 acres, mainly in Worcestershire, was granted to Gilbert de Clare, the Red Earl of Gloucester. Clare assumed that parts of of Eastnor and Colwall were included, but they belonged to the diocese of Hereford. Bishop Cantilupe protested to the

9

king, who referred the dispute to two local justices and a jury made up equally of Herefordshire and Worcestershire men. After visiting the hills, when earl and bishop also attended, they found in April 1279 for the latter. Clare, ordered to make a ditch to mark the boundary reputedly started digging in person, throwing the spoil on the Hereford side, so that deer could more easily jump into his land than out of it. His dyke was probably not completed until 1287, five years after Cantilupe's death. Over 700 years later, early in the twenty-first century, archaeologists were surprised to discover that Clare had merely renewed a boundary which had existed since the Stone Age.

On the Worcestershire Beacon towards the northern end of the ridge Macaulay tells us that a fire was lit in 1588 to warn of the Spanish Armada, and 'twelve counties saw the blaze from Malvern's lonely height'. In 2000 the millenium and in 2003 the jubilee of the queen's reign were celebrated by further beacon fires in the same place.

The Herefordshire Beacon, otherwise known as the British Camp, is reputed to have been the place in 50 A.D. of the last stand of Caractacus (or Caratacus), prince of the Atrebates, against the Romans. Some disagree. Henry Card, an early nineteenth century vicar of Great Malvern, nevertheless stuck in his writings to the British Camp as the site of Caractacus' last stand. So did the librettist of Elgar's choral cantata, *Caractacus* (1898). A plaque at the foot of the hill by the A4104 mentions the Red Earl but not Caractacus. Close to this point, which used to be called Burstners Cross, a gold coronet encrusted with precious stones was unearthed in 1650. Oddly enough it had probably belonged to a British prince who lived at the time of Caractacus.

The Clent Hills, which are within sight of the Malverns, have a furrow thought to run from Clent village to St Kenelm's Church. The groove was made, so it was said, by an old woman's plough when her oxen ran away in protest at being made to work on St Kenelm's Day (28 July; for Kenelm himself see chapter 3). A variant is that when the woman attempted to start ploughing on a Sunday she became blind and her oxen escaped. Her piece of land, somewhere in a hollow of hills, was believed to have grown unnaturally greener grass ever since as a warning to others.

Even quite small hills, especially when they rose inexplicably from level ground, presented a challenge to people's imagination. The devil often features in the aetiological stories which resulted. For example, he is vexed at the piety of Bewdley, so determines to dam the Severn and drown the town. He takes up a spittleful (spadeful) of earth and sets off towards Bewdley from Kidderminster. On the way he meets a cobbler carrying a bundle of worn-out shoes for repair, and asks him how far it is to Bewdley. The quick-witted cobbler, realising that his interlocuter means no good, replies: 'Well, I've worn out all these shoes coming from there'. The devil drops his spittleful in disgust—it is reassuring that he can be so easily deceived—and stamps off. The

The Devil's Spadeful

evidence can still be seen. The hill—duly called The Devil's Spadeful—is marked on the OS map close to the railway line at Blackstone Farm, about half way between Kidderminster and Bewdley.

George Griffith related the story in a poem of 1839, 'The Devil's Spadeful'. This subsequently appeared in Griffith's collection, *Ribbesford and Other Poems* (1868), and three years later formed the basis for a pantomime in a Kidderminster theatre. Griffith, who in 1833 married the daughter of the land-lord and landlady of the Mug House at Bewdley, had the tale from Severn boatmen among their customers, who claimed that the cobbler-hero had been a fellow habitué.

Below Ground

Real finds such as the one at Burstners Cross must have stimulated the many traditions of buried treasure, and of secret passages. The mediaeval hall at Cofton Hackett is said to be linked by a tunnel to the church. The Manor House at Ashton-under-Hill claims to have passages leading both to the church and to the monastery at Beckford, two miles away. White Ladies, a house in the Tything at Worcester, incorporates fragments of the nunnery founded in about 1250 by Bishop Cantilupe. (The nuns also owned land at the village which came to be called White Ladies Aston). Tradition held that the Worcester house had passages leading to the cathedral and also to Hindlip House. The likelihood seems remote, but there certainly was a passage of some kind for it was explored by the historian, Nash, who penetrated a hundred yards before foul air put out his lantern and forced him to retreat. Worcester Cathedral was also supposed to be connected by a secret passage to Malvern Abbey, despite the distance involved, not to speak of the obstacle presented by the River Severn.

Caves served both for concealment and for open occupation. Smugglers constructed an elaborate underground storage space in Worcester, approached by a narrow passage leading from South Quay through the grounds of St Andrew's Church. The cellar came to light when in about 1900 some houses were demolished in the street then called Birdport (now Deansway). Similar spaces, often naturally occurring in the first instance, were occupied by medi-aeval ascetics (see below) and later by ordinary people. In north-west Worcestershire the many rock houses usually consisted of living room, bedroom, pantry and store, with floors of brick or stone 'quarries'. 'A type of short pick called a "stocker"', writes L.T.C. Rolt, 'was the principal tool used in the excavation of these homes, and the men who practised this curious craft were known as "rock-stockers"'. Despite the occasional fatality caused by falls of rock, such dwellings were used until the 1940s at Blakeshall, Drakeslove and Wolverley; in the Habberley valley; at Kidderminster; and at Holy Cross, near Belbroughton. As late as 1971 at Wolverley, Bill and Gwen Pearson extended the accommodation of their house into the sandstone cliff

Birdport

below the church. Two years later, for business reasons they reluctantly sold 'Sleepy Hollow' and moved away. Perhaps they were the last rock house dwellers in Worcestershire.

Rock dwellings at Blakeshall (?1950s)

Remains of similar dwellings at Wolverley (2005)

Wells and Waters

Early peoples valued water for practical reasons but also felt it had a sacred dimension. Springs and wells connected the world of every-day life with a mysterious realm below the ground.

Great Malvern may owe its origin to the spring known as St Anne's Well, which was perhaps in the first place dedicated to Anu, a Celtic water Goddess. A Christian missionary, possibly in Saxon times, may have noticed the veneration in which Malvern water was held, and resolved to harness this to his own purposes by using the spring for baptism. Eventually, Anu became Anne (mother of the Virgin).

St Anne's Well was famous in mediaeval times. Its water healed skin and eye diseases, the spiritual element having acquired a literal dimension. The same power came from the water of the Holy Well and Eye Well (at present Malvern Wells), of which a homespun poet wrote in 1622:

> A little more I'll on their curing tell,
> How they help sore eyes with a new found well.
> Great speech of Malvern-hills has late reported
> Unto which spring people in troops resorted.

Later in the same century John Evelyn recorded in his diary:

> We set out towards Worcester, by the way (thick planted with Cider-fruit) we deviate to the holy Wells trickling out of a vally, thro a steepe declivity toward the foote of great-Maubern hills: They are said to heale many Infirmities, As Kings-evill, Leaprosie, etc: sore Eyes ...

St Anne's Well, Malvern, from a card postmarked 1903

In the eighteenth and nineteenth centuries the springs led to Malvern's prosperity as a spa town. They are still sought out by those who are dissatisfied with the quality of local tap water.

People 'dressed' wells—that is, decorated them with flowers—on various occasions. John Aubrey (1626-97) recorded that a solemn feast was 'yearly observed at Droit-Wich in Worcester-shire, where on the day [3 April] of St Richard the Tutelar Saint of the Well, that is, Salt-well, they keep Holyday, dresse the well with green Boughs and flowers'. A well in West Malvern known in Aubrey's time at St Thomas's Spring was later called the Royal Well. In 1870 William Ryland bought it and in gratitude for being cured of a life-threatening illness by its water presented it to the local people. Ryland's Fountain, as it was then styled, attracted an annual ceremony of dressing, when bands played and visitors took tea. This was one of a score of wells round Malvern—there were 88 springs, spouts, fountains and wells in the neighbourhood in all—which in the late twentieth century were again dressed. The ceremony became a firm annual fixture in connection with the May Day activities at Malvern.

St Peter's Well at Martley once served to baptise the faithful. Monks came from Worcester for the purpose, perhaps before the village had its own priest or church. At Shrawley the water of St Keyne's Well near the church was recommended to anyone who married. The explanation is that the first of a married pair to drink will obtain the mastery. One Cornishman—St Keyne is also the patron of the town bearing her name in Cornwall—left his wife at the church porch after the ceremony to rush to the well but found that his wife had already taken a bottle of the water to outwit him. The saint herself never married. Her story is told in Southey's poem, *The Well of St Keyne*.

Many wells have now disappeared or fallen into disuse. The Holy Well at Worcester's Henwick enjoyed the reputation of curing eye troubles. In the eighteenth century its water was used to brew beer, and during the nineteenth was sold at a halfpenny a can as the purest in the town. In the 1870s, though, it was bricked up.

On Bredon Hill some 300 yards east of the Banbury Stones is a spring traditionally associated with St Catherine of Alexandria. Close by stood a chapel where a yearly fair celebrated St Catherine's Day (25 November). After the Reformation the chapel was allowed to fall into ruin, and in 1871 the last stones were levelled. The holy well is still shown on today's maps but demand for its healing water has long ceased.

Water also achieves a powerful presence through the county's many rivers, of which the Teme, the Avon and the Severn are pre-eminent. As early as 1431 an Act of Parliament declared 'the king's highway of Severn' to be 'common to all the king's liege people to carry and re-carry all manner of merchandise as well in trowes and boats as in flotes [rafts], otherwise called drags'.

Describing the position some 350 years later, Thomas Telford wrote:

The barges and trows have masts, which can be lowered to go under bridges; the stream carries them down, with or without a sail, and they are towed up by men, assisted or not, in the same manner, according to the wind. The barges are from 20 to 80 tons burden, and trade very much between Shrewsbury and Gloucester. The trows are larger and belong to the ports lower down the Severn.

The tide reached upstream as far as Bewdley, and the famous surges known as bores could be seen at Blackstone Rock. River traffic had to contend with rock bars and shoals of gravel, and with floods and 'freshes' (sudden rushes of water) downstream. Up to 200 vessels are known to have congregated at times by Pool House, Upton, to wait for tides to take them up river, or freshes down. Some 200 yards below the bridge at Bewdley, a submerged sandstone ridge was known as Laxford: people used it to ford the river to Lax Lane. Boats travelling to Stourport with 17 or 18 tons of wood needed three feet of water over it, failing which part of their cargo had to be unloaded, carried ashore to Ribbesford, then re-loaded.

In the mid-nineteenth century the Severn Navigation Company began the work of canalising the river by constructing weirs and locks at Lincomb, Holt, Bevere and Diglis, so as to ensure a more or less permanent depth of ten feet

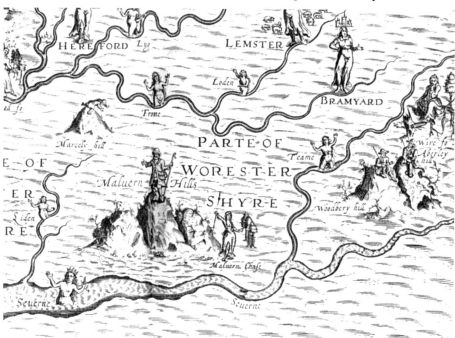

Map from Drayton's Poly-Olbion *(1613-22), showing the* 'Seuerne', *complete with scantily-clad nymph, and* 'Parte of Worester Shyre', *including the Malvern Hills but curiously omitting Worcester itself*

of water from Gloucester to Worcester, and seven feet from there to Stourport. Within the pounds thus created, rock bars were reduced by excavation, gravel shoals by dredging. In this way, many fords disappeared, and by 1939 only two remained, at Upper Arley and at Worcester's Dog and Duck.

In an earlier era the men who dragged vessels by main force over rock bars, where the depth of water seldom exceeded 18 inches, were called bow hauliers,

River traffic at Worcester in the eighteenth century.
The porcelain factory site is now occupied by riverside car parks

Worcester Bridge c.1820, with bow hauliers (bottom right)

The Old Mug House, Bewdley (1880)
and its current sign (below)

who sealed verbal contracts by accepting a mug off beer or cider at certain public houses on or close to the river. These were termed Mug Houses, and the bow hauliers' contract system may have given rise to the expression 'to be had for a mug'. Between eight and 20 men, depending on conditions, would be needed to tow a barge the 15 miles from Bewdley to Bridgnorth; their day's work would earn them 2s. 6d., two meals, and the ritual mug of drink. On average, during the 1790s a man pulled three tons a mile at a total cost of 3s., but a horse (introduced 20 years earlier) managed 18 tons for only 1s. The bow hauliers opposed a change which threatened their livelihood, and as late as 1832 went on strike:

> They nailed the gates up along the towing path, and assembled in great numbers to prevent any horses being attached to the vessels. The magistrates made several attempts to convince them of the unreasonableness and folly of their proceedings, but to no purpose. At last the Riot Act was read, and a troop of Scots Greys marched into Worcester from

Kidderminster. Under this escort the gates were opened and several vessels taken up the river, but not without determined opposition and much disturbance. Eight men were committed for trial to the sessions.

Two years earlier the steam tug, *Sabrina*, had begun working between Gloucester and Worcester, and by 1853 paddle tugs could tow several boats at once from Gloucester to Stourport in between 15 and 18 hours, half the time taken by horses. In 1930 came the first motor tug. Some of the tough and resourceful boatmen have published lively reminiscences. For example, B.A. Lane (born 1924) has written memorable tales of living off the river, when 'ducks, pheasant, hares, rabbits, and eels, lampreys, salmon and other fish were all fair game'. He also has a dramatic account of shooting Worcester Bridge when the level of floodwater seemed to leave insufficient headroom:

When I got through the railway bridge I had to pile all the power and speed on her. As the old river men said, she would still be making speed as she entered the bridge. I could not believe what happened next. As she entered, the bow started to go down, the after end lifted up, I could see through the balustrade, then the after end started to go down. By this time I was on my knees in front of the steering wheel. My mate took his photograph, then dived on to the deck. The crewman in turn threw himself down beside the engine-room casing. I was looking toward the bow, which disappeared above the arch of the bridge as it went out of the bridge hole. The underside of the arch was now just above my head. We came out of the bridge, she levelled off and we were away. It was only then that I broke out into a cold sweat. Once again the old river men had been right, for she had pushed the water out of the bridge hole to dip beneath the arch. I would never do that again, not even if someone offered me a thousand pounds.

The bow hauliers of the Severn, like their counterparts on the Avon, are long gone, but two mug houses still exist, at Bewdley and Claines respectively. The old stone bridge at Upton-on-Severn where the men 'waited on providence' for weather or work was replaced after sustaining heavy damage in the flood of 1872, but its fellow at Bewdley which dates from 1798 bears on its underside marks made by their ropes as they dragged vessels upstream.

Other river traffic included coracles. Those of Bewdley were made of cleft oak from the Wyre Forest and hides from the tannery (later sailcloth). The skill lasted at least until the 1930s. A far-fetched suggestion is that the use of coracles ended when a fisherman lugged aboard a huge salmon he had caught, and sank both himself and his frail craft.

Small ferries plied across both Severn and Avon, often at historic crossing points. Very few are now left. One takes people on request from the Bredon

Kepax Ferry, Worcester, from a card postmarked 1903

side of the Avon to the Fleet Inn at Twyning and back. Another operates—with proceeds to charity—to carry summer visitors over the Severn by Worcester Cathedral's watergate.

A mile or so upstream opposite the north-western end of the Pitchcroft King Stephen is reputed to have erected earthworks in the twelfth century on the river

Offenham Ferry on the River Avon in the 1940s

bank to protect the crossing. A house called King Stephen's Mount still occupies part of the site. Below, on the river bank was the Dog and Duck Inn which took its name from the so-called sport of loosing dogs to catch ducks whose wing tendons had been cut so that they could not fly away, and betting on the outcome. Public opinion ended this in the 1840s, and in the following decade the Portobello Pleasure Gardens adjacent to the inn succumbed to their unsavoury reputation. The Dog and Duck ferry, though, carried on until 1964.

Pixham is a hamlet on the Severn, opposite Kempsey. Simon de Montfort crossed here in 1265 with his prisoner, Henry III, on the way to death and defeat at Evesham. The Pixham Inn with its bowling green closed in 1903 but the ferry survived. Its charges 30 years later were: foot passengers, 2d., bicycles, 3d., and motors, 3s. Soon after this the big boat capable of carrying cars had to be abandoned, but a small craft operated until the great flood of 1947 damaged it beyond repair. In Lane's End on the Kempsey side stood the Severn Trow Inn, with ample stabling for the horses which towed vessels up-river. Its licence allegedly lost because of some smuggling imbroglio, it is now a private house.

A mile downstream from Stourport, the ferry was run by monks living in caves in the Redstone Rock who acquired a bad name for rapacity in levying payment. A main route from Wales to Worcester passed this way, via Astley Cross then down the east bank of the Severn. When Prince Arthur died at Ludlow in 1502 his body probably passed this way to be interred in Worcester Cathedral. People lived in the Redstone caves until late in the nineteenth century, by which time the ferry had ceased, for it ended with the opening of the bridge at Stourport in 1775.

The old ferry house at Redstone (now demolished), where travellers waited, sometimes for several days, to cross the Severn when it was in spate

Another sandstone cliff and another hermitage, though not another crossing. Blackstone Rock is downstream from Bewdley. High on its sandstone cliff is the entrance to some caves where hermits once lived. There is a tradition that the holy men regularly rescued from the river unwanted babies who had been set adrift at Bewdley. They brought up and educated the children, all of whom were given the surname of Severn.

The curious name of Delarivere Severne appears in Abberley church register for 1741 long after the time of monks at Blackstone, and Severns were recorded at Shrawley in the early sixteenth century. Local telephone directories in 2004 still showed several examples.

In the Blackstone hermitage Sir Harry Wade once lived while waiting to take his revenge. He was betrothed to Alice Clopton of Stratford-on-Avon, but the Clopton family was notoriously unlucky, and Alice seems to have been no exception. She was seized by a rival suitor, blindfolded, and carried away on horseback. Wade gave chase, and was about to catch up when the fugitive threw Alice into the River Rea at Deritend, in Birmingham. Wade naturally stopped to help her, but she drowned. He then tracked the murderer through Edgbaston, Hagley Wood, Blakedown and Kidderminster, but lost him when he took sanctuary in Bewdley. Wade, his patience matched only by his hatred, lived for ten years as a hermit at Blackstone Rock until the murderer at last ventured there for confession, only to be summarily thrown to his death in the river below.

The 'racy and peculiar folk' (in A.G. Bradley's phrase) who worked the river are no more. Traffic is now almost exclusively recreational, though there are plans to bring back freight for which speed is not of the essence. Whatever happens, the Severn's power and majesty will continue to enthrall us, as it did the veteran boatmen who took Wilfred Byford-Jones to Arley, and told him this story:

Floods at Worcester, December 1910

Five rivers rise in Mount Plynlimon. ... They are the Llyfinant, Mynach, Rheidol, Wye and Severn. These five streams, says the ancient legend, decided one day in a race from Mount Plynlimon to the sea. The Wye, with artful cunning, rushed off before the time that was fixed for the start, but gained nothing, for she was detained by rocks and had to take a tortuous course. The Severn, flowing more directly, reached the Bristol Channel first, and the Wye could only get there with the aid of Severn. The other three rivers, dallying about and then finding themselves late, took a short cut and plunged into the Irish Sea.

Smaller watercourses, too, sometimes have their stories. The Sapey Brook near Clifton-on-Teme was renowned for a series of circular marks on its sandstone bed. Two—at Jumper's Hole (for which, see also chapter 7)—were particularly clear, with other good specimens between Clifton and Stanford Bishop. Some of these were removed from the bed of the stream by Jabez Allies, and taken to Worcester Museum. Most scholars agreed that the marks were caused simply by the action of the water, though one argued that prehistoric beasts had left them. Tradition says that St Catherine of Ledbury and her servant, Mabel, had a mare and colt stolen one night as they were travelling this way. The thief led the animals along the brook to avoid leaving tracks, but Catherine prayed that their tread and that of the thief (who turned out to be a girl wearing pattens) should remain visible. Her request was granted. The animals were traced to Ledbury, and recovered. The marks remained. There were similar markings in the bed of the Dick Brook at Rock. In this case the explanation offered is that a church was being built on one side of the brook, but each night the stones were carried across to the other by a mare and foal which permanently imprinted the bed with their hooves.

Between Chaddesley Corbett and Bromsgrove runs a stream which can be seen from the M5 motorway. As a boy Edward Corbett was told that its water ran red with blood on the day of a battle, thus giving it the name of Battlefield Brook. The battle in question, Corbett claims, involved the defeat of a Roman force on Walton Hill during the first century A.D. If so, the power of oral tradition has been strong enough to carry the story for some 1,800 years.

What's in a name?

As well as of brooks, the names of fields and farms often convey glimpses of long-past events. Hangman's Cross is the name of a field off Lincomb Lane, Hartlebury, and commemorates a gibbet which stood nearby. Gibbet Lane and Gibbet Wood at Stourton recall a highway robber and murderer of 1812 who was hanged at Stafford, but whose body was brought back to be exhibited at the scene of the crime. This is said to have been the last instance of gibbeting in the Midlands. According to oral tradition at Abbot's Morton, Gibbet Butts took its name from the hanging there of a sheep stealer. In the same village

Parson's Coppice was remembered because of the melancholy clergyman who took his own life there.

Foxhall's Field at Tenbury bears the name of a farmer from Queen Anne's time. The man owed money to a neighbour, and to avoid repaying laid a charge that the neighbour had robbed him. The creditor in turn accused him of perjury. To avoid arrest Foxhall jumped into the River Teme and was drowned.

Deadland Furlong art Ripple was the site of a Civil War battle. Deadman's Ait (Island) in the River Avon near Offenham derives from an earlier battle, that of Evesham in 1265: wounded men fleeing the field are presumed to have died there, and human bones and scraps of armour and weapons have been found. Headless Cross near Redditch is said to take its name from executions carried out at the spot, after which blood flowed down what became called Red Ditch, and then Redditch. Unfortunately for the claim, the red of the name comes from the colour of the earth; and earlier spellings have Hedley's, rather than Headless, Cross.

The Devil's Bib is a field at Heightington in north-west Worcestershire. In the same parish is a Devil's Spadeful, which must have the same kind of pedigree as the hill mentioned earlier. Fields with an unsavoury reputation, whether because of a gloomy aspect or intractability for cultivation, were often associated with the devil. One of the roughest fields in the parish of Inkberrow was known as the Devil's Bowling Green. Elsewhere one finds the Devil's Den (Hanbury), Pitch (Abberley), Slether (the Lenches) and Hole (Hindlip).

Next to the old pound in the village of Wolverley is Knight's Meadow. A whole saga explains its name. One day a milkmaid, accompanied by an old dog, was crossing the field on her way to milking when she saw a man asleep on the grass. He was thin, ill-kempt, and in fetters. She was alarmed, but the dog seemed to recognize the man, who woke up and claimed to be Sir John Attwood. He was taken to Lady Attwood, who had despaired of her husband's return from crusading—this was in the fourteenth century—and was on the point of re-marrying. She could not recognize the man as her husband after so many years of separation but he produced the broken half of a ring which perfectly matched the half kept by his wife when they parted. The fetters were struck off, the new marriage was cancelled, and Sir John came home.

He explained that he had been miraculously transported from imprisonment abroad after praying and seeing a vision of an angel or the Virgin Mary. He travelled on the back of a swan, and as they were coming in to land his foot touched the top of the church steeple. In gratitude for his deliverance and in fulfilment of a vow he gave land at Wolverley to Worcester Cathedral. His funeral monument in Wolverley Church showed him with a swan as his crest and a dog (or possibly a lion) at his feet. When the old building was demolished in 1772 the effigy was removed to Wolverley Court. The fetters were also preserved; one account says at least until 1988.

The church at Wolverley with Knight's Meadow in the foreground

The story is full of well-known motifs. The faithful dog and impending re-marriage recall Ulysses' return to Ithaca. The obliging swan comes from northern mythology, the foot touching a pinnacle from oriental romance. The broken ring or token was a favourite theme in British traditional song until this century.

There was no English crusade during the fourteenth century but Sir John Attwood could have joined a group of knights on one of Bertrand du Guesclin's expeditions against Pedro the Cruel, King of Castile. He could have been taken prisoner, exhausted his fortune in paying a ransom, and then made his way home penniless and weary in 1368 or '69. One sceptic has suggested that the whole thing was made up by monks to explain how they had come into posses-sion of certain lands. Another has pointed out that it might be a fantasy based on the swan and the dog of the effigy. Nevertheless for many years there was a rent charge on the Knight's Meadow which went to pay someone 'who should keep the irons polished and show them to all who would like to see them'.

At Bretforton are to be found fields called Porridge Yats, Bull Butts and Pumbleditch. Victims of the Black Death of the fourteenth century are reputed to have been buried in Blackpit Field at Inkberrow, and Pestilence Lane at Alvechurch commemorates the same plague.

It is a great pity that many field names disappear. Sometimes they are simply lost as old people die and newcomers replace them. Sometimes the removal of hedgerows deprives fields of their names along with their identity.

The Tuppeny Cake is a small, triangular green at Bournheath, three miles from Bromsgrove. Until the 1930s tenants of the adjoining cottages had to pay an annual fee of twopence to its owner, the squire of Fockbury. Friday Street at Pebworth is said to be so called because Shakespeare liked to go and drink there on Fridays, and so many people came to join in the conversation that the street was very busy on that day of the week. In the rhyme which Shakespeare is supposed to have made about various villages in the locality, Pebworth came out as 'piping'—a reference to the pipe and tabor players who accompanied the morris dancers.

The word, Callow, occurs in a number of place and field names, including Callow End (near Powick), Callow's Piece (Martley), Callow's Lane (Stoke Prior), Callow's Grave (near Tenbury) and Callow's Leap (Alfrick). It derives perhaps from the Old English, *calu*, meaning bare, but a fertile imagination led to the tale that Callow was a mighty hunter whose feats included a fearless leap across the gorge of the Leigh Brook, and who was eventually buried near Tenbury. The term, end, may prosaically mean simply an outlying part of an estate. According to Vincent Waite, though, when land between the Malvern Hills and the Severn was forested, and charcoal burners worked there, the end in place names referred to a man's territory, at the end of a path. This gave us Picken End, Russell's End, Drugger's End (which often brings a smile to visitors who spot its signpost), Gilbert's End, Piper's End and Callow End. Someone's heated imagination has produced the story that Catchem's End at Bewdley was where law officers waited to tackle wanted men when they emerged from the town after taking sanctuary there. If this were so, the story would be very old, since Bewdley's status as a sanctuary town ended in 1544.

Trees

Even trees and woods had their stories. The famous Whitty Pear of the Wyre Forest is described in chapter 4. Until 1974 Kempsey had its Revolution Elm, the last of three planted on a bank on the south side of the churchyard in 1688 to mark the so-called Glorious Revolution which replaced James II by William of Orange. There are many Gospel Oaks (see chapter 3) and some Holy Thorns (chapter 10). A famous oak tree is supposed to mark the place where St Augustine met a synod of British bishops in 603, during the time of King Ethelbert. Five places in Worcestershire claim the honour of St Augustine's Oak: Alfrick, Martin Hussingtree, Stanford Bishop, Rock and Hartlebury. The name itself of Rock means 'at the oak'. A tradition at least ten centuries old when it was written down in 1670 claimed that a particular tree there was Augustine's. It stood till 1775, about a mile from the Hundred House on the road to Abberley. However, the Mitre Oak at Hartlebury, mentioned by Camden, claims to come from an acorn from Augustine's original tree. It stood beside the main Worcester road, and Queen Elizabeth I was met there on one of her progresses by the Bishop of Worcester and local gentry. It is possible that the tree was merely used as a landmark. Again, a mitre could have been hung

The Devil's Oak, Sherrard's Green, near Malvern

in the branches as an inn sign or the name could have arisen because of the tree's proximity to the Bishop's Palace.

By contrast, the Devil's Oak was to be found until the 1920s at Sherrard's Green, near Malvern. The name may have reflected the tree's grotesque, menacing shape, or derived from the tale of chimney sweeps who had sheltered from the rain in its hollow, and were taken for devils when they came out through the veils of an autumn mist.

A famous sweet chestnut tree spreads over a quarter of an acre at Kateshill House (once part of Tickenhill Manor) at Bewdley. Prince Arthur, who lived there,

The Bewdley sweet chestnut

Save Our Tree campaigners at Upton-on-Severn

planted the tree in 1501 to celebrate his marriage by proxy to Catherine of Aragon. Arthur died the following year and Catherine married his brother, the future Henry VIII.

The affection which venerable trees can generate was shown in 2004, when a 300-year-old oak came under threat at Upton-on-Severn. Local people petitioned and demonstrated against its planned felling, and succeeded in preserving 'Our Tree'.

CHAPTER 2

People

Of the great figures and events in history, some linger in memory for a generation or so, whereas others last for centuries. Queen Matilda, the wife of William the Conqueror, was long remembered for the worse in Worcestershire, Queen Elizabeth I for the better. Opprobrium, reinforced by the annual rituals of 5 November, clung to the Gunpowder plotters of 1605 and their associates. The protracted and deeply divisive events a few decades later of the Civil War cast a lasting shadow, with principal protagonists like Oliver Cromwell and Charles I and II remaining household names. More pacific figures also left a mark. Shakespeare is associated with various places in Worcestershire. Richard Foley, whose life overlapped with that of Shakespeare, succeeded through what we would now call industrial espionage, while in the following century Hannah Snell by other means of deception enjoyed a career as a female soldier.

Two Queens

In the Domesday Book only the first element of the name of Hanley Castle occurs, the second having been added only after 1206-13 when King John had a stronghold built there. The village retains its full title, though the castle is long gone. After being the seat of the earls (including the Red Earl) of Gloucester and Warwick, the fortress fell into decay towards the end of the Middle Ages, suffered damage from Parliamentary forces during the Civil War, and lost its last remnant, a tower, in 1795.

A Saxon holder of the manor of Hanley and of the forest of Malvern was Brictric, lord of Gloucester. As a young man he went to Flanders on an embassy from Edward the Confessor in about 1045 to the court of Baldwin V. Baldwin's fifteen year-old daughter, Matilda, took a fancy to him but he rejected her advances. Seven years later she married William, Duke of Normandy. The two were related in some way, and the pope declared their union incestuous but later relented when as penance they paid for the construction of a two abbeys in Caen.

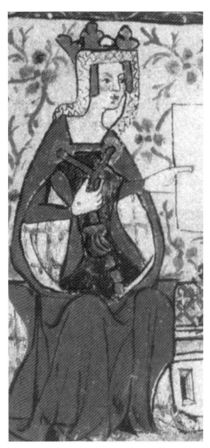

William the Conqueror's queen, Matilda

When William conquered England, Matilda, remembering Brictric's slight, demanded that his vast estates be confiscated and, says tradition, took Hanley — where Brictric had just completed a chapel consecrated by Wulstan, Bishop of Worcester—for herself. Gloucestershire people placed the humiliation of Brictric at Avening, where Matilda ordered a Saxon chapel to be torn down and a new church built. Both versions of the story agree that Brictric died in the 'noisome prison' in which William had ordered him to be confined at Winchester.

Wulstan was the only Saxon bishop to keep his place after the Norman conquest. Most Saxon noblemen were dispossessed, including Brictric, but his lands were first granted by William to the Earl of Hereford, William FitzOsbern, and only later (in 1074) to Matilda. After her death they reverted to William, who made Hanley part of a royal hunting preserve, Malvern Chase. The earliest part of Hanley Church dates from the twelfth century, and the claim for a Saxon forerunner rests precariously on a fragment of tombstone now preserved by the Lechmere family at Severn End. Some scholars assign this to the ninth century, though others place it 200 years later.

Even so, Worcestershire people continue to tell the tale of Matilda's malice. On the other hand, a queen of some five centuries later is remembered with affection. Queen Elizabeth's House, a half-timbered building in central Worcester, is probably the last survivor of the row of houses in Trinity Street endowed by Elizabeth I in the early years of her reign. It originally stood a few yards away on a different site.

During her visit to the city in 1575 the queen watched a pageant and addressed the people of Worcester from the house's open first-floor gallery and on the same occasion she is said to have plucked three pears from a tree growing at the Cross, and ordered that they be depicted thenceforth on the city's arms. (An earlier tradition claims that Worcestershire bowmen at Agincourt wore badges showing a 'pear-tree fructed'.) The tree, from an

'Queen Elizabeth's house' at Worcester,
bedecked with greenery (from a postcard)

orchard between the White Ladies' Convent and St Oswald's Hospital, had been re-planted by the Cross in the middle of Worcester. (The Cistercian nunnery founded in about 1250 by Walter de Cantilupe, Bishop of Worcester, was first called the House of St Mary Magdalene, then Whistons—from its building material, and finally White Ladies—after the dress of its occupants. The village of White Ladies Aston is still so called, thanks to land once owned by the nuns.) In memory of Queen Elizabeth's munificence her portrait hung outside the house bearing her name until 1877, and again from about 1908. Every year on the eve of Trinity Sunday (the first after Whit) it was decked with garlands prior to Trinity Wake.

Gunpowder, treason ...

Worcestershire owes its first written history to the plot of 1605. Thomas Habington of Hindlip was not directly involved but he sheltered wanted men at his house, where, incidentally, Elizabeth I had stayed in 1575. Habington was

Hindlip House, burned down
in the early nineteenth century

arrested, then released, on condition that he remain within the county's boundaries for the rest of his life. He spent the next 40 years in researching and writing, though his work waited until the 1890s to be published in full, under the title of *A Survey of Worcestershire.*

31

Hindlip House was replaced in the nineteenth century by the present building, Hindlip Hall. On the other hand, Huddington Court, which dates from the sixteenth century, is still there in all its grandeur. Starting in 1450, the Wintour (Wyntour or Winter) family lived there for generations. Robert inherited the house, together with a considerable fortune, at the beginning of the seventeenth century. He was an ardent Catholic, like his wife, Gertrude, daughter of John Talbot of Grafton Manor, near Bromsgrove. His younger brother, Thomas, and their cousin, Robert Catesby, inveigled him into joining the Gunpowder Plot.

As the Wintour brothers set off on their desperate errand to London, Robert told Gertrude that when they returned, if they waved their hats as soon as they saw the house it would signal success. The historian, Joan Simon, herself related to the Wintours, wrote in 1970 of a different family tradition:

> I remember my father telling us when we were children the little-known tale of how she [Gertrude] waited at an upper window of the house for the signal from her husband that was to tell her the result of the Plot. If it had succeeded she could expect to see a rider go by fluttering a white handkerchief, but if he gave no sign, she would know it had failed.

Either way, there was no hopeful sign. Robert and Thomas Wintour, together with their brother John, Robert Catesby and others, arrived on 6 November as desperate fugitives, only to set off again in the darkness of the early hours of the following morning. The Wintours were soon captured. Robert and Thomas were executed in London, John at Red Hill on the outskirts of Worcester.

Huddington Court in 2004

While Gertrude waited for news, first of the plot, then of the trial and execution, she paced the brookside close to Huddington Court. After her death she reputedly continued to appear there, and the place is still called Lady Wintour's Walk. (The courtesy title came to her in widowhood when her brother acceded to the title of Earl of Shrewsbury). She, like John Wintour, is buried in Huddington Church, though their graves are unmarked. Robert Wintour's spectral figure has also been reported from Huddington—headless, which is surprising since he was not decapitated but hanged, drawn and quartered.

Robert Wintour

Roundhead and Royalist

Well over 50 places in Worcestershire have connections with the Civil War. In September 1642 the first serious fighting of the war took place at Powick where after 'a confused and bloody mêlée' a Parliamentary force fled, leaving Prince Rupert master of the field. A tree known as Rupert's Thorn survived until 1860, when it was removed to make way for a house.

Mrs Mary Martha Sherwood, celebrated in her day as a children's novelist, lived at Lower Wick for a time at the beginning of the nineteenth century. Her recollection of the tree differed. She wrote in 1847:

Mary Martha Sherwood

> The rising ground from the bridge over the Teme had been defended against the Parliamentary army by Prince Rupert, who had made a stand under a yew tree, and turned on the enemy from the brow of a hill close to our house.

Militarily, perhaps, the battle at Powick was minor. Yet, as the historian, Austin Woolrych has written, 'Few actions involving only 2,000 men have been so written about as Powick Bridge, but its significance really was disproportionate to its scale'.

Rupert, deciding afterwards that Worcester's crumbling fortifications were inadequate, ordered Sir John Byron (the poet's ancestor), who was in the city guarding the king's treasure — chests of money and much of the plate of Oxford University and its colleges — to take it on to Shrewsbury. So, despite their defeat, Parliamentary soldiers entered Worcester the following day. Ignoring the orders of their commander, Lord Essex, they 'demonstrated their horror of superstition by urinating in the [cathedral] font, ripping down the organ, breaking every shrine in sight, and relieving themselves where and when they felt inclined'. In addition, they plundered nearby houses belonging to catholic gentlemen.

Attacks of this kind were endemic in Worcestershire for a decade. One September day in 1643 a band of men plundered the manor house at Castlemorton owned by Richard Bartlett, catholic and Royalist. The marauders, led by Captain Scriven, a Gloucester ironmonger, chose a day when they knew most Castlemorton people would be away at Ledbury Fair. They took £600, household effects, and an eaglestone for which £30 had been refused. (Such stones — hollow, with sand and tiny pebbles inside, were highly prized as amulets believed to help with pregnancy and childbirth).

In the same village on another occasion Roundheads are said to have besieged their opponents in the church and set fire to the tower in which they had taken refuge. One by one as the flames approached Royalists fell or jumped to their deaths. Castlemorton Church undoubtedly suffered from fighting, since the victorious Parliament in due course granted money for repairs.

Tradition has it at Shrawley that Richard Chylde defended the castle (now gone) and the Severn ford against Cromwell: unsuccessfully. The field on the far side of the river from which the Parliamentary artillery operated is still called Battle Meadow. The site of fortifications by the ford is now called Oliver's Mount. Just up the river Andrew Yarranton may have repaired or produced weapons for Cromwell's men at his forge on the Dick Brook, a tributary of the Severn.

Many miles downstream, Old Nan's Hill at Ripple may be a corruption of Ordnance Hill. From it in 1643 General Waller's guns fired on Prince Maurice's men, but had to fall back to the village, and then to Tewkesbury, leaving a number of casualties, some of whom drowned in the Severn as they attempted to ford it at Uckinghall. On 13 April each year the battle is re-enacted *in situ*.

In June 1644 Charles I with 6,000 men and 60 coaches and waggons passed over the Avon at Pershore on their way from Oxford. The king ordered the

Re-enactment in 2004 of the battle at Ripple

bridge's central arch to be destroyed to hinder pursuit. The work was bungled, and some 30 men died, crushed or drowned. Local tradition says that when the structure came to be repaired stone from the old castle at Elmley was used.

Even minor incidents of the Civil War were remembered for centuries, accurately or otherwise. Prince Rupert slept at the hall at Areley Kings, and no doubt in many other places. When Charles I spent the night in the vicarage, opposite Inkberrow Church, in May 1645 he left behind one of his map books, which is now kept in Worcestershire Record Office. He, or one of his men, also failed to recover the bag of money for soldiers' wages which remains buried somewhere in or near the village. Cromwell is reputed to have burned down the vicarage because it had sheltered Charles; the present building dates only from 1762. Charles also stayed at Pixham Court—or was it nearby, at Prior's Court? —after his defeat at Naseby in 1645. Both houses were reputedly owned by the Lane family, and Jane Lane was to render great service to Charles II (see below).

Memorials to the Blount family can be seen in the churches at Astley (see page 103), Kidderminster and Mamble. One branch lived at Sodington Hall, near Mamble, a moated mansion said to have been burned by Cromwellian soldiers when they were refused access to a forge there to make or repair arms. One of the Blounts—either on this occasion, or when he was challenged to a duel by a Roundhead—was so anxious to fight that he rushed out in his slippers, thus giving the local public house the name it still bears of Sun and Slipper—the sun and armed boot being the Blounts' device.

The sign of the Sun & Slipper at Mamble

Cromwell's decisive victory in the last important battle of the Civil War was partly achieved at Powick, though mainly in Worcester. The city had supported the king but surrendered to Parliament in 1646 after a siege. Its Royalist governor was Colonel Henry Washington, an ancestor of George, the first president of the United States. The family arms—three stars and five horizontal stripes—can be seen at Wickhamford Church on the grave of Penelope, the colonel's daughter. The design formed the basis for the flag of America, the Stars and Stripes.

In August 1651 the small Parliamentary garrison at Worcester retired on the approach of a large Royalist army, mainly composed of Scotsmen. Prince Charles—or King Charles II, for he had been so proclaimed a few weeks earlier at Carlisle—having spent the previous night at the Swan Inn at Tenbury, entered Worcester unopposed. He set up his headquarters in Sir Rowland Berkeley's house, a Tudor building on the corner of New Street and the Cornmarket which has been known ever since as King Charles's House.

Cromwell arrived outside Worcester in late August. He is known to have stayed at Evesham on 27 August (and again on 5-7 September). There are traditions that during the campaign he lodged at the Lygon Arms, Broadway; in the home of Mr. Justice Berkeley at Spetchley; at Moor (otherwise known as Hill

King Charles's House

Abutment of old bridge at Upton

Moor), between Fladbury and Throckmorton, on 28 August; and at White Ladies Aston in the half-timbered house (demolished in the nineteenth century) of his friend George Symonds, on 29 August. That morning, Cromwell went to Upton to thank Colonel Lambert's men for their achievement in entering the town. The Royalists had destroyed two arches of the Severn bridge, but left single planks across the gap for the convenience of local people who wished to cross, but omitted to remove them overnight. As the guard slept, reputedly after heavy drinking in the Anchor Inn, Parliamentary dragoons crept over the planks at dawn. The garrison, at last alerted, fought back, and the attackers were obliged to barricade themselves in the church. The Royalists set fire to the building but their opponents held out in the tower until reinforcements arrived, after fording the river. The Royalists were eventually driven off, with heavy casualties. As Cromwell spoke to his men by the church he looked across the road and saw a woman at her window. Impressed by her beauty and on learning her identity — she was a Miss Morris, he ordered that her brother, whom he had earlier ordered to be shot, should be pardoned. Only the tower of the old church (fitted with a cupola, and known as 'the Pepperpot') now remains, and a plaque on the house opposite records Cromwell's presence there in August 1651.

He presumably went on to Worcester, where his main force was drawn up on Red Hill, which is now a suburb off London Road to the south-east of the city. On 29 August 1,500 men sallied out from Worcester with the intention of making a surprise night attack on the camp and killing Cromwell. They wore white shirts over their tunics for mutual recognition in the darkness, but these also made them conspicuous to the Parliamentary troops. The Royalists suffered disastrous casualties because Cromwell had been forewarned of their plan by a Worcester tailor or cloth-worker, William Guise, who had climbed down the city walls by means of a knotted rope. News of his own expedition must have leaked out, for on his return he was arrested and summarily hanged from the signpost of the Golden Cross in Broad Street. Six days after the battle of Worcester Parliament voted his widow £200 a year for life.

Cromwell, it is said, delayed the main battle of Worcester until 3 September, the anniversary of his victory at Dunbar the previous year. He apparently spent the night before at Rous Lench Court, where the Rouses, who lived there from 1382 until 1721, were strong supporters of Parliament during the Civil War. Royalists seized one of the family in his own garden, says a local tale, and

Rous Lench Court

imprisoned him in Warwick Castle, where he died: his body came back to Rous Lench Church for burial alongside his ancestors. Richard Baxter was quartered at Rous Lench Court when he served as chaplain to Colonel Whalley's regiment during the siege of Worcester in 1646-7, and he stayed on afterwards to write much of his celebrated book, *The Saints' Everlasting Rest*.

On the eve of battle some of Cromwell's men fortified themselves with ale at the Ketch, an inn close to the confluence of the Teme and Severn. Ironically, the Strensham-born Samuel Butler later wrote part of his virulently anti-Roundhead poem, *Hudibras*, in the parlour of the same inn, overlooking the ferry. The Ketch is still there, just off the A4440, though the building is modern. Other troops were in less mellow mood. Soldiers passing through Tibberton on their way to Worcester seized, for unexplained reasons, a man with the Shakespearean name of Pescod, and hanged him by the neck from a pear tree.

When they left, half an hour later, villagers cut down the victim, and found to their astonishment that he was still alive. Pescod recovered, and in due course acted as guide to the fugitive Dr Warmestrey, who returned to Worcester after the Restoration as dean of the cathedral and master of King's School.

Cromwell's secondary force had assembled at Powick, threw pontoon bridges over the Severn and Teme and made the first assault. The Royalists withdrew, and Parliamentary troops were quickly transferred to Red Hill to support the main attack. By the evening Worcester had fallen. Some 2,000 Royalist troops were killed, and 6-7,000 taken prisoner, many of them held in the cathedral. Some 3,000 Scots cavalry escaped, but few got home given the many miles of hostile territory they had to pass through. Commonwealth losses amounted to under 200 killed.

Proclamation of a reward for the king's capture (1651)

At about 5 pm, realising that the day was lost, Charles had withdrawn into Worcester through the Sidbury Gate. He found the way blocked by an overturned ammunition wagon, so he dismounted and clambered over it. The incident seems to have given rise to the story that a man drew a cartload of hay across the gateway to shield the king from pursuit: he was called Moore, and came from Elmley Castle; at the Restoration, Charles gave him the farm at Kersoe which remained in his family for many generations.

Charles fled, pausing briefly at Rowland Berkeley's house where as Parliamentary soldiers were smashing down the front door he slipped out of the back to a waiting

The Royal Patient Traveller.

O R,

The wonderful Escapes of His Sacred Majesty King C H A R L E S the Second from Worcester-Fight; And his making a Hollow Oke his Roy-
all *Pallace. The* going in a *Livery* Cloak with Mis. Lane. And the
Discourse between the Kings Majesty, and the Cook-maid im-
ploying the King to wind up the Jack; but being not
used to do it, did wind it up the wrong way.

To the tune of,   *Chivy Chase,* Or,   *God prosper long our Noble King*

God hath preferred our Royal King
the second of that name,
And those that will not pray for him,
indeed they are to blame:
For thousands have against him spoke,
but I shall't disclaim,
And wish all others have a care
how they should do the same,
David we read had enemies
that did him sore annoy,
So CHARLES the Second had the same,
who is fair Englands joy.
In May it was the twenty nine,
King Charles of high Renown.
Being his birth-day (as 'tis known)
to London came to town.
But had you seen the triumph made
And Bonfires flaming high.
and all the people for to cry
God save his Majesty.
I will rejoyce at his happiness,
and pray he long may reign,
And of some passages he had
with honest Mistris Lane,
From Scotland he to Worcester came
though friends did look about,
Yet Cromwel came with a mighty Force
and did give him the Rout,

A journey long I am sure he had
with friends the loving Scot.
King Charles mounting himself so brave,
three times his Horse was shot.
The King did therefore for his safety,
make friends to have some pitty,
For so our Saviour he doth say
as I write in this Ditty:
If persecution being great,
of such then have a care,
So at that time tis very true
one did cut off his Hair.
His Princely cloaths he off did strip,
and did himself disguise,
So of King Alfred I have read,
that was a Prince most wise.
A Chain of gold that he had then,
worth hundreds without doubt,
He gave away unto a friend,
who lead him there about,
Into a wood where Inns was none
nor Lodgings there bespoke,
The best of Lodgings he could get,
was in a hollow Oke.
O happy Oke (saith Mistris Lane,
that ever I did see,
A Pallace for a Prince then wast
but he will go with me.

*Henry Jones, an Oxford street singer, wrote this ballad (of which part is
reproduced here) in 1660 to celebrate Charles II's escape after the battle of
Worcester and his restoration to the throne. The black-letter type used was
normal until the end of the seventeenth century*

horse. He decided to go north, leaving the city by St Martin's Gate. His long and difficult road to exile led initially to Ombersley, where he stopped at the inn now called the King's Arms. An alternative tradition places his meal in Hartlebury, at the White Hart. Either way, Charles went via Stourbridge to Boscobel in Shropshire, then set off on a tortuous journey to the south coast with a price of £1,000 on his head. His guide was Jane Lane, and he assumed the guise of her servant.

According to the king's account, taken down in shorthand by Samuel Pepys in 1680, 29 years after the events, he rode dressed as 'a serving man' from Moseley Hall, eight miles from Boscobel, to Long Marston in Warwickshire. Less than two hours into the journey his horse cast a shoe, so they were obliged to find a smith 'at a Scattering Village, whose name begins with something like Long ---'. Some have assumed this to be Long Marston, but they were only part of the way there. William Matthews in the collection of documents on the subject of Charles II's escape which he edited expresses the view that Bromsgrove was meant, from which it was still a ride of some 20 miles to Long Marston. This is Charles's version of his encounter with the blacksmith, transcribed from Pepys's shorthand:

> As I was holding my Horses Foot, I asked the smyth What Newes? He told me that there was noe newes that he knew of since the good newes of the beateing of the Rogues, the Scotts. I asked him whether there was none of the English taken that joyned with the Scotts. He answered that he did not heere that that Rogue Charles Stewart was taken, but some of the others he said were taken, but not Charles Stewart. I told him that if that Rogue were taken he deserved to be hanged more than all the rest for bringing in the Scotts. Upon which he said that I spoake like an honnest man, and soe we parted.

Some have placed the incident at the Black Cross Inn at Bromsgrove. Another tale makes Charles a shoeblack in the Talbot Inn at Knightwick. His escape to France, six weeks after the battle of Worcester, became a national legend which, as Woolrych observed, 'accreted a wealth of dubious detail, some it contributed by Charles himself, who never tired of recounting it'.

As for Sir Rowland Berkeley of Cotheridge Court, having either fought or assiduously avoided fighting—depending on which account one follows—at Powick, fled on his rather conspicuous horse to the farm of one of his tenants at Wick, closely pursued by Cromwell's troopers. The farmer, on the hasty promise that he would never be turned out if he helped, hid the incriminating horse and put in its place another mount of similar appearance. The troopers who arrived soon afterwards accepted that no one could have ridden from the field on so fresh a horse, so Sir Rowland was saved from arrest or perhaps

Whittington Tump

worse. He kept his promise, and the farmer's descendants were still in possession over 300 years later.

Cromwell was so delighted by the victory at Worcester that, according to a
story told in the 1920s to John Tooby at Colletts Green by his governess, Miss
Pearson, he called his soldiers together and ordered them to fill their hats with
soil. They then marched several miles to the east and emptied the soil to form
Whittington Tump close by the present junction 7 on the M5 motorway. The
tump is properly known as Crookbarrow Hill, the name of which derives from
the Anglo-Saxon *cruc* (hill) and *beorh* (mound). Roman coins have been found
there, and its existence goes back to a very long time before the Civil War. In
more recent times celebrations were held there: they are described in chapter 10.

Royalists claimed that Cromwell won thanks only to the help of the devil. On
the morning of 3 September, they asserted, he had met the devil in Perry (or
Pirie) Wood near Red Hill and offered his soul in exchange for victory. Cromwell
asked for a further twenty-one years of life, then tried for fourteen, and finally
had to settle for seven. He remarked to Colonel Lindsay, who witnessed the pact:
'Now, Lindsay, the battle is won and I long to be engaged'. In fact the meeting
between Cromwell and William Guise took place in Perry Wood, and for
Royalist propaganda the move from Guise to the devil was not difficult. An alter-
native scenario places the fateful encounter at White Ladies Aston, with Mr
Justice Symonds as the third person present. When the bargain was struck, and
Cromwell and his men left, according to 'a Worcestershire lady':

> Symonds turned round to the gentleman in black and requested him to
> inform him [of] the good luck in store for him, as he did his friend. He
> immediately replied in a deep, sarcastic tone:

The last of your race to Satan will be given,
And perish by the hangman's rope in 1707.

A strange coincidence. In 1707 a descendant of this Symonds, together with his brother-in-law (Palmer) and two other desperate villains named Hunt and Dunn, murdered a Mrs Palmer at Upton Snodsbury, she being the mother of Palmer, and mother-in-law of Symonds, and afterwards set fire to her house and hung her favourite dog in Bow Wood. These four villains used to meet at Bredicot Common, or Rough, as it was called by some people, and under a large oak tree swore to be true to each other, come what may, and also to plan this diabolical crime. They were all executed at Worcester, and afterwards gibbeted and hung in chains on Red Hill.

(The Tyburn-style triangular gibbet or triple tree stood on a site formerly marked by a perry pear tree in the garden of number 4, Whittington Road. Until at least the 1970s Hangman's Cottage remained in Walkers Lane behind a house called The Elms).

According to the same writer of 1892, in the Lovers' Walk a short distance from the Symonds mansion at White Ladies Aston, a Muriel Symonds used secretly to meet her lover, a Royalist killed at Naseby. 'The lady's mind was so affected by her lover's death that she used to walk in her sleep and talk to him (as she thought) the same as in his lifetime; and after her death it was believed

Cromwell's head on Worceseter Guildhall

that her ghost used to walk in this green lane '"in white satin"' every year on the eve of the battle of Naseby'.

For his part Cromwell did die seven years to the day after the battle of Worcester. The violent storms which swept the country were seen as proof by some that the devil was indeed taking his soul.

At Worcester, Oliver's Knoll, part of what remains of Perry Wood, now encircled by roads, still exists. The Guildhall has fine statues of Charles I and II but Cromwell's carved head is nailed by the ears over the doorway. The Sidbury canal bridge bears a plaque with Cromwell's summing up of the battle 'It is for aught I know a crowning mercy'. At Bredon rectory twin stone figures at either end the roof are supposed to represent Charles II and Cromwell. Local people say that if they ever come together the end of the world will be nigh.

Statues of Charles I and II by the entrance to Worcester's Guildhall

Shakespeare

When the playwright travelled to Worcester to obtain a marriage licence, there is a tradition that he stayed on the way there (or back) at Inkberrow and spent the night at the Old Bull Inn. No licence was normally required, since three readings of the banns sufficed, but Shakespeare was a minor and his wife to be, pregnant. In November 1582 'William Shagspere and Anne Hathwey of Stratford in the Dioces of Worcester maiden' were duly authorised to marry after a single reading of banns. The licence has not survived, though when its issue was recorded the bride appeared as 'Anna Whateley de Temple Grafton'. The Anna could be a clerical error, but Temple Grafton remains a mystery. The village church records of the time have not survived, and the place of Shakespeare's marriage is simply not known. One of several conflicting traditions claims it for St Martin's in Worcester. Curiously, although this church's marriage registers are extant, the relevant page has at some time been carefully and precisely cut out. If Shakespeare did marry in Worcester, then both he and Anne may have called at the Old Bull.

There is a celebrated verse about what became known as 'the Shakespeare villages':

> Piping Pebworth, dancing Marston,
> Haunted Hillborough, and hungry Grafton;
> With dodging Exhall, papist Witchford,
> Beggarly Broom, and drunken Bidford.

Of these, only Pebworth is in Worcestershire, and its epithet alludes to the place's passion for morris dancing, accompanied by the music of pipe and tabor. If, as is suggested, Shakespeare wrote the rhyme, then he is likely to have known Pebworth, as well as the Warwickshire villages mentioned.

Another of Shakespeare's alleged compositions, a scurrilous ballad on Sir Thomas Lucy, circulated orally until 1703, when it was noted from Thomas Jones, aged 'upwards of ninety', at Tardebigge. It begins:

> A parliamente member, a justice of peace,
> At home a poor scarecrow, at London an asse,

The Old Bull, Inkberrow

Other stories may be even less credible. R.H. Lloyd reports the belief that Shakespeare 'in his barn-storming days' took part in plays performed in the tithe barns both at Bredon and Bredon's Norton. Even wilder is the claim that in the late eighteenth century, despite the well known injunction on his tomb ('Good friend for Jesus sake forbeare / to digg the dust enclosed heare'), Shakespeare's skull was stolen from the church in Stratford by three men paid £3 each by a Dr Frank Chambers of Alcester. After having second thoughts the doctor ordered the men to return the skull, and they asserted that they did so. However, a few years later one of them, called Dyer, confessed that they had not done so: he stated that the skull was in the ossuary of a church 'in a remote parish' (Beoley, near Redditch), and produced a small piece of bone from the skull as identification. Chambers went to Beoley, found the Sheldon vault in St Leonard's Church, but could see no trace of a skull. Then he noticed a chamber off, which proved to be the ossuary, and retrieved a skull with a jagged hole in the forehead into which the fragment fitted as neatly as a piece in a jigsaw. 'The veritable skull of William Shakespeare was there', he remarked. Few have believed him.

Foley the Fiddler
The Foley Arms is not uncommon as an inn sign. The family, which still has members living in Herefordshire, owes its original prosperity to the iron trade,

and nailmaking in particular. The chief founder of the fortune was Richard Foley (1580-1657), who, the son of a nailer, born at Dudley later moved to Stourbridge. In 1627 he set up a mill at Kinver which mechanically slit the thin sheets of iron needed for nail-making, so replacing the laborious cutting by hand. Despite infringing the patent of a slitting-mill established in Kent 28 years earlier Foley was able to establish himself in a dominant position in the Midland nail trade.

A much more romantic account attributes the source of the Foley fortune to an instance of industrial espionage. Its earliest source seems to be a passage written in 1812 by the poet Samuel Taylor Coleridge, and repeated approvingly by Samuel Smiles in his book *Self Help* (1859), with the added information that the place in Sweden twice visited by Foley was Dannemora near Uppsala. This is Coleridge's version:

Foley, from Nash's Worcestershire *(17871)*

> The most extraordinary and the best attested instance of enthusiasm, existing in conjunction with perseverance is related of the founder of the Foley family. This man, who was a fiddler living near Stourbridge, was often witness of the immense labour and loss of time, caused by dividing the rods of iron, necessary in the process of making nails. The discovery of the process called splitting, in works called splitting mills, was first made in Sweden, and the consequences of this advance in art were disastrous to the manufacturers of iron about Stourbridge. Foley the fiddler was shortly missed from his accustomed rounds, and was not seen again for many years. He had mentally resolved to ascertain by what means the process of splitting bars of iron was accomplished; and, without communicating his intention to a single human being, he proceeded to Hull, and thence, without funds, worked his passage to the Swedish iron port. Arrived in Sweden, he begged and fiddled his way to the iron foundries, where, after a time, he became a universal favourite with the workmen;

and, from the apparent entire absence of intelligence or anything like ultimate object, he was received into the works, to every part of which he had access. He took the advantage thus offered, and having stored his memory with observations and all the combinations, he disappeared from amongst his kind friends as he had appeared, no one knew whence or whither.

On his return to England he communicated his voyage and its results to Mr. Knight and another person in the neighbourhood, with whom he was associated, and by whom the necessary buildings were erected and the machinery provided. When at length everything was prepared, it was found that the machinery would not act, at all events it did not answer the sole end of its erection—it would not split the bar of iron.

Foley disappeared again, and it was concluded that shame had driven him away for ever. Not so: again, though somewhat more speedily, he found his way to the Swedish iron works, where he was received most joyfully, and to make sure of their fiddler, he was lodged in the splitting mill itself. Here was the very aim and end of his life attained beyond his utmost hope. He examined the works and very soon discovered the cause of his failure. He now made drawings or rude tracings, and, having abided an ample time to verify his observations and to impress them clearly and vividly on his mind, he made his way to the port, and once more returned to England. This time he was completely successful, and by the results of his experience enriched himself and greatly benefited his countrymen. This I hold to be the most extraordinary instance of credible devotion in modern times.

Another version of the story relates that Foley was drinking one day in an alehouse when his wife came to tell him that the cow had been seized for rent. Richard went off in shame and returned three years later from Holland with the technique of the slitting mill. There he had played not the fiddle but the flute, and had disarmed any suspicions on the part of his hosts by pretending to be a fool.

By whatever means—and there is evidence in the Foley archives that he did travel to Uppsala—Richard undoubtedly made a fortune (largely by his exceptional organising ability) and established a dynasty whose wealth was displayed in imposing mansions at Great Witley and at Stoke Edith in Herefordshire (though, ironically, both were subsequently destroyed by fire). He lies buried in front of the chancel steps at Oldswinford Church, Stourbridge, (or, according to another source, at St Mary's, Stourbridge) having left a will which shows him to have been a deeply religious man. Perhaps he repented his wild years as Foley the fiddler.

The Female Soldier

Hannah Snell, the daughter of a hosier and dyer, was born at Friar Street, Worcester, in April 1723. Although she was one of six sisters she enjoyed playing at soldiers, inspired perhaps by stories of her grandfather and brother, both of whom had been killed in war. This account comes from her *Life and Adventures*:

> When she was scarce ten years of age, [she] had had the seeds of heroism ... implanted in her nature, and she used often to declare to her companions that she would be a soldier if she lived; ... she formed a company of young soldiers among her playfellows, of which she was chief commander, at the head of whom she often appeared, and was used to parade the whole town of Worcester. The body of young volunteers were admired all over the town, and they were styled 'Young Amazon Snell's Company'.

Hannah Snell, by Richard Phelps, 1760

After the deaths of her parents, Hannah went at the age of seventeen to live with her married sister at Wapping in London. In 1743 she herself married James Summs, a Dutch sailor who disappeared when she was seven months pregnant. Her child lived for only a few months. In 1745 Hannah dressed in a suit of clothes belonging to her sister's husband, assumed his name (which was James Gray), and set off in search of Summs.

First she travelled to Coventry and enlisted in a regiment which soon moved to Carlisle by means of a 22-day march. A Worcester carpenter called George Beck joined there but did not recognize Hannah who soon after this deserted over some grievance and spent a month in walking to Portsmouth. There she enlisted as a marine, in which capacity she made several voyages and also fought in India. During her travels she met a man who was able to tell her that James Summs was dead, having been executed aboard a Dutch ship for murder. Only on being discharged after almost five years' service did Hannah Snell reveal that she was a woman. For a time she went on the London stage, dressed as a soldier and singing 'humorous and entertaining songs':

> All ye noble British spirits that midst dangers glory sought,
> Let it lessen not your merit that a woman bravely fought;
> Cupid slily first enroll'd me, Pallas next her force did bring,
> Press'd my heart to venture boldly for my love and for my King.
>
> Sailor-like to fear a stranger, straight I ventured on the main
> Facing death and every danger, love and glory to obtain.
> Tell me, you who hear my story, what could more my courage move?—
> George's name inspired with glory, William was the man I loved.
>
> When from William Susan parted, she but wept and shook her hand;
> I, more bold (tho' tender-hearted), left my friends and native land;
> Bravely by his side, maintaining British rights, I shed my blood,
> Still to him unknown remaining, watch'd to serve and do him good.
>
> In the midst of blood and slaughter, bravely fighting for my king,
> Facing death from every quarter, fame and conquest home to bring.
> Sure you'll own 'tis more than common, and the world proclaim it too,
> Never yet did any woman more for love and glory do.

In 1750 a remarkable book was published under the title of *The Female Soldier or The Surprising Life and Adventures of Hannah Snell*. It is full of equivocation. As James Gray, Hannah Snell has an 'intimate acquaintance' with at least three women, one of whom wishes to marry him/her. On the other hand, fellow servicemen find James effeminate; on one ship he mends linen and is called 'Miss Molly Gray' by sailors 'for want of having such a rough beard as they'. Perhaps to compensate James joins in drinking sessions, displays 'as much skill and dexterity as any sergeant or corporal ... in the military exercise', and with 'wonted intrepidity' faces 'numerous hardships, fatigues and dangers'. He also frequently shares a bed with other men, normal practice for the time, without being unmasked. Even a spell in hospital after wounds in the legs and groin received during the siege of Pondicherry fails to reveal his true identity. What is more, so do two floggings, stripped to the waist.

The first of these is at Carlisle:

> At that time her breasts were but very small, and her arms being extended and fixed to the city gates, her breasts were towards the wall, so that then there was little or no danger of her comrades finding out the important secret which she took uncommon pains to conceal. At her second whipping on board the ship, when her hands were lashed to the gangway, she was in much greater danger of being discovered; but she stood as upright as possible, and tied a large silk handkerchief round her neck, the ends wherof entirely covered her breasts, insomuch that she went through the martial discipline with great resolution, without being in the least suspected. ... At this time, it is true, the boatswain of the ship, taking notice of her breasts, seemed surprised, and said they were more like a woman's he ever saw; and as no person on board ever had the least suspicion of her sex, the whole dropped without any further notice being taken.

Later Snell was married twice more, kept a public house, and received a government pension of a shilling a day. Eventually she became an out-pensioner of the Chelsea Hospital. She was committed an insane to the Bethlehem Hospital in London, and died there in 1792, aged 69. She was buried at the Chelsea Hospital, one of only two women ever to be accorded the privilege.

Hannah Snell's story was part of a great vogue for tales of female soldiers, sailors and highwaymen. Some may find it far-fetched—and undoubtedly it was embellished, but it contains many details which have been verified. Her life, with fact and fiction carefully disentangled, was re-told by Julie Wheelwright in the 2004 edition of *The Oxford Dictionary of National Biography*.

CHAPTER 3

Churches

The archetypal village scene shows a church, usually in a prominent position, with houses clustered round it as if for shelter. Such sites were chosen after debate and even dissension. The saint to whom a church was dedicated also called for a careful decision. The churchyard, often designated as 'God's acre', served both sacred and secular purposes, as burying ground for the dead and recreational space for the living. The building's fabric, with its wealth of objects in wood and metal, stone and stained glass, achieved iconic status. Its officers—lay or clerical—sometimes provided decades of blameless service, sometimes fell from grace. Parishioners sought social contact and spiritual solace. They also required the ceremonies appropriate to birth, marriage and death: these are examined in chapter 4.

Sites and Saints

Church sites were often chosen—or so persistent reports would have us believe—by supernatural means. The original intention at Kidderminster was to build St Mary's Church opposite its present position, on the other bank of the River Stour. When the first attempts at construction were made the stones erected were removed every night by an unseen agency to the present site, and the builders eventually followed suit. A carving on the tower showing an angel holding a piece of arch reminds us of the story. The rejected site is called Cussfield: cursed field.

At Inkberrow—model for the fictional Ambridge of the Archers—spirits called Arkbus took exception to the position first chosen for the church, and carried stones nearer the village every night until the masons conceded the point. Even so the Arkbus were unhappy at the disturbance which the church bells caused them, and made this lament:

> Neither sleep, neither lie,
> For Inkbro's ting-tangs hang so high.

Arkbus, otherwise rendered as Arkub or Aupuk, may be 'old puck'. At haytime the same mischievous spirits were thought to play in the fields at night, scattering the cut crop in all directions. The church's alleged original site has not been identified but the Domesday Book records a priest at Little Inkberrow, which is where the building could have been. The existing churchyard is almost circular, a phenomenon which can indicate the adoption of a pre-Christian sacred place.

An intervention of a different kind was made when the old church of St Mary was being built at Worcester soon after 960, where the present cathedral now stands. A huge square block of stone was noticed. Workmen were told to make use of it but were unable to move it. St Oswald prayed that the hindrance should become clear, and saw a little black devil sitting on the stone. He traced the sign of the cross, which made the devil flee, and the masons then easily lifted the block. Again in Worcester, when the church of St Clement was about to be rebuilt in the 1820s on the eastern side of the Severn an angel came at night and moved the foundation stone to the other bank where some land was unclaimed by St John's. The new church was built there, and the parish extended accordingly.

The builders of Rock Church, near Bewdley, originally chose a site beyond the Dick Brook. However, a mysterious mare and foal, inscrutably guided, each night carried the stones used during the day to the new position eventually adopted for the church. One wonders whether the primitive horse's head inscribed on masonry inside the building is intended as a reference to the story.

The horse's head carving at Rock

One saint in Worcestershire met a violent death, the place marked by a miraculous spring. On the death of his father in the early part of the ninth century Kenelm became king of Mercia. As an infant of only seven he was placed under the tutelage of his older sister, Kendrida. Wishing to take the crown for herself, Kendrida persuaded her lover, Askobert, to kill the child. Kenelm was taken from the royal palace at Winchcombe in Gloucestershire on a hunting expedition which led many miles to the Clent Hills. Knowing that he was about to die Kenelm planted his staff in the ground where it rooted and became a thorn tree. As he knelt to say the *Te Deum* his head was struck off by Askobert with a long-bladed knife. A white dove flew out of the head and made its way to Rome where it dropped a scroll on the high altar at St Peter's. The document bore a message which in modern English reads:

In Clent cow-pasture under a thorn
Of head bereft lies Kenelm, king born.

The pope ordered enquiries to be made in England. A procession of clergymen headed by the bishop of Mercia was led to Kenelm's grave by a ray of light or — in another version — by a cow which stood there without eating but still growing fat. As the body was disinterred church bells pealed of their own accord and a spring of water gushed forth from the ground. A dispute arose as to whether the churchmen of Worcestershire or those of Gloucestershire should have the body. Eventually the two parties agreed to lie down to sleep at Pyriford (possibly Pershore), the first to wake having priority. The Abbot of Winchcombe and his men woke first, and had secured a lead of several miles with the precious body before the Worcestershire men set off in pursuit. The Abbot of Winchcombe

Figure supposed to represent St Kenelm, exterior of south wall of St Kenelm's Church, Romsley

prayed, and as he put his crozier to the ground a spring came forth. Refreshed by its water the Gloucestershire men were able to outdistance their pursuers and carry their burden safely to Winchcombe.

The rest of Kenelm's story belongs to Gloucestershire, but at Clent the spring became a place of pilgrimage. A chapel was built and then in the eleventh century a small church with the spring inside. Another spring about half a mile from the church in a field called Cowbatch (the cow-pasture of the rhyme) also claimed to be St Kenelm's Well; its waters cured diseases of the eye. The one beneath the chancel, prized by lepers, was partly destroyed at the Reformation. Hugh Latimer, Bishop of Worcester from 1535 until 1539, campaigned against what he regarded as superstition. He resided occasionally at Alvechurch and discouraged pilgrims from visiting and bathing in the well at Clent. Nevertheless, visitors continued, albeit in smaller numbers. In the mid-nineteenth century the spring was diverted from the church into the brook but later re-opened a few yards from the east end, where it can still be seen.

The village of Kenelmstowe grew up near the church, with some 30 houses and an inn called the Red Cow after the beast which had stood by the thorn tree. The place was important enough for Henry III to grant a charter for an annual four-day fair starting on the eve of St Kenelm's Day (17 July, changed to 28 July after the revision of the calendar in 1752). However, the place—by then called Clent—went into a decline after the Reformation, and now only St Kenelm's Church and a single house remain some distance from the modern village.

At the risk of spoiling a good story one should point out that the historical Kenelm died before his father, possibly in battle with the Welsh, and was buried at Winchcombe Abbey. His sister, Kendrida, was the abbess of Minster in Kent. The first account of the legendary Kenelm was written by William of Malmesbury in the eleventh century. In his dictionary of saints D.H. Farmer acidly comments that Kenelm's legend 'is a good example of how a writer with a vivid imagination and some half-understood historical data produced a completely fictitious account of a prince who certainly existed but of whom virtually nothing is known'.

Something similar, no doubt, could be said about the biographies of many other saints, such as Helen, mother of the Roman emperor, Constantine, and revered as one of the finders of 'the true cross' (her church is in Worcester); and Barbara, killed by her father for becoming a christian, patron of architects, builders, metal workers, miners and gunners, including the Royal Artillery (a church dedicated to her is at Ashton-under-Hill). In the case of Edburga, with dedications at Abberton, Broadway Old Church and Leigh, we may be on slightly firmer ground. She was the daughter of Edward the Elder, king of Wessex, and his third wife, Edgifu. As a child of four, asked to choose from a handful of jewels, a copy of the gospels and a chalice, she took the last two. After her death at Winchester, where she was a nun, in 960, some of her bones were taken to Pershore Abbey, which, when it was re-founded some twelve years later, adopted the joint patronage of Mary, Peter, Paul—and Edburga.

St Helen,
from a fourteenth-century miniature

Other local saints include Egwin, bishop of Worcester from 693 until 711. At one stage enemies accused him of unspecified crimes, so he decided to go to Rome to appeal to the pope. Before setting out he had his legs chained and padlocked, then threw the key into the Avon close to where Evesham Abbey would later be built. He also proclaimed that only divine intervention would release him from the chains.

When Egwin arrived in Rome all the bells rang in welcome of their own accord, an auspicious start for him. He told his followers to wait by the Tiber while he went into St Peter's to pray. To while away the time they went fishing in the river and caught a salmon. As the fish was being prepared for the bishop's evening meal a key was found inside, which proved to be the one thrown into the Avon. Egwin was released from his chains, and the pope must have been suitably impressed for he acquitted him of the accusations which had been levelled.

Back in England, Egwin was given land by Ethelred, king of Mercia (to whom he may have been related) for the purpose of building an abbey at what came to be called Evesham. The miraculous choice of site is related in chapter 1. In 709 Egwin was again travelling to Rome, this time with Offa, who had succeeded Ethelred. In the Alps the party—perhaps surprisingly—was in danger of perishing from thirst. Egwin saved the situation by causing a spring to issue from the ground. At other times he made a dumb man speak, saved a friend from imminent shipwreck, and foretold the end of smithing in Alcester (some say caused it, so as to punish smiths for working on Sundays).

Egwin resigned his see in 711, and became the first abbot of Evesham. He died six years later. In 1077 monks from the abbey took some of his relics on a tour of southern England to raise money to buy wood and stone for a new church. Miracles were recorded at Dover, Oxford and Winchester. The abbey's arms until the dissolution depicted a lock and chain. Egwin remains the patron of churches at Honeybourne and Norton with Lenchwick.

Werstan has no dedication, and very little documentation. In the time of Edward the Confessor he fled from Deerhurst Abbey near Tewkesbury when it was sacked by the Danes. Thanks to angelic guidance he found a new site at

The martyrdom of St Werstan, after a window in the priory church, Great Malvern

Malvern—possibly where the house called Bello Sguardo now stands—and built a chapel there. The king gave his approval but the Danes arrived and cut off Werstan's head. All this is shown in stained glass in the priory church (bought for the parish at the Reformation) of Great Malvern, together with the foundation in 1085 of a new Benedictine abbey by Aldwyn, encouraged by Wulstan, bishop of Worcester, and encouraged by William the Conqueror. Wulstan himself was canonised. King John, who greatly admired him, chose to be buried in Worcester Cathedral between the tombs of Wulstan and Oswald. The two saints are now long gone, though John remains (see below).

Richard de Wych, born at Droitwich in 1179, studied canon law at Oxford, Paris and Bologna Universities, and later became a priest. He was successively bishop of Lyons (1245) and Chichester. He died in 1253 and was canonised only nine years later. John Leland described in 1538 how Richard came to the rescue of his native town:

There be at this present tyme three sault springs in the towne of Wiche, whereoff the principall is within a butt shoote of the right ripe [bank] of the river [Salwarpe], that there cometh downe, & this springe is double as profitable in yielding of sault liquour as both the other. Some say that this spring did fayle in the tyme of rich de le Wich Bishop of Chichester and that after by his inter-cession it was restored to the profitt of the ould course; such is the super-stition of the people, in token whereof, or for the honour that the Wichemen and saulters bare unto this Richard their cuntriman, they used of late tymes on his daye [3 April] to hang about this sault spring or well once a yeere with tapestry, & to have drinking games & revels at it. There be a great number of sault cotes or furnaces about this well, wherein the sault water is decoct & brought to the perfection of pure white sault.

Statue of St Richard de la Wyche in
Vines Park, Droitwich

Habington dismissed such stories as 'the traditions of old wyfes ... synce we

St Mary's, Hill Croome

Raised bed effect at Alvechurch

have ould recordes to testify the contrary'. Even so, some form of celebration (see chapter 10) still continues by the statue of St Richard erected in Vines Park at Droitwich in 1935.

Churchyards

Evidence of antiquity is shown in circular church-yards, ground levels raised by numerous interments, and the presence of ancient yew trees. Churchyards which are or were circular include those at Astley, Kempley, Hill Croome (where St Mary's sits on an eminence crowned by a venerable yew), Shelsley Beauchamp and Stockton-on-Teme. At Whittington, where the Victorian church was preceded by a very early chapel, is a 900-year-old yew, strengthened by iron bands fashioned by the village black-smith. In the 600 years of its exis-tence the churchyard at Claines has received between 15 and 20,000 bodies, which have caused it to rise. A similar result, with footpaths and even buildings finding themselves below high banks, can be seen in many other places, including Grimley. The raised bed effect at Alvechurch is another example. Only when permanent gravestones became common, from the seventeenth century onwards, did the inexorable rise of ground levels cease. Burying plots then had to be enlarged, or newly created.

Before that, corporate memorials were sometimes provided in the form of churchyard crosses. Earlier crosses, marking the site of a church before it was built, would be visited by peripatetic priests. When construction took place the building would be placed to the north of the cross lest its shadow fall on it, which was considered unlucky. Part of a ninth-century cross, with carvings of birds and beasts, has survived at Cropthorne. Later examples can be seen in many other places, including Alvechurch, Beoley, Clifton-on-Teme, Great Malvern and Shrawley. Mid-way between the porch and one of the churchyard entrances at Ripple are the base and stump of the mediaeval cross at which the Palm Sunday procession would have paused for prayers. There is a similar cross at Church Stoke.

Bromsgrove Church in the nineteenth century

Various oddities are also found in churchyards. In what was once the northern boundary wall of Bromsgrove churchyard people used to point out Tom Thumb's Monument, probably the lid of an old stone coffin. The unfortunate Tom had made a pact with the devil, to be repaid by the surrender of his soul after death, whether he were buried outside or inside consecrated ground. Tom cheated the devil by having himself placed beneath the wall, and therefore neither in nor out. In 1824, though, the churchyard was enlarged, so what had been the boundary wall fell inside. What happened to Tom's soul at that stage is not known.

A curious structure, known as the Norchard sundial or the Wizard's Pillar, stood in the churchyard at Areley Kings until it collapsed in 1912. One side showed the figure of death, dart and spade in hand, standing over a fallen human body; the other, Father Time with hourglass and scythe. The pillar, dating from 1687, was erected in his garden at Hartlebury by Master Fidkin, a reputed wizard thought to have the ability, until cockcrow brought his powers to an end, of keeping people wandering round the village all night. The pillar for some reason was moved to Areley Kings in the early nineteenth century, possibly after the death in 1819 of Robert Fidkin (aged 82) of Hartlebury.

Another oddity at Areley Kings are the words, a mixture of Greek, Latin and English, carved on the western wall of the churchyard:

LITHOLOGEMA QUARE:
REPONITUR SIR HARRY
(Why a stone monument?
Here lies Sir Harry)

Sir Harry Coningsby—either at Hampton Court, near Leominster in Herefordshire (where he was born himself) or at Weld Hall, Shenley, Hertfordshire, the record is unclear—was playing with his infant son and accidentally dropped him into the moat, where he drowned. Consumed with remorse, Coningsby retired to a small estate, the Sturt, at Areley Kings and spent the rest of his life there. When he died in 1701 he left provision for the inscription to be carved. In addition he arranged for three walnut trees to be planted close by so that every year boys could crack the nuts and, presumably, remember his carelessness.

A much more sinister memorial, a tablet now fixed to the wall to the right of the church porch, is still to be seen at Berrow, a tiny village half way between Ledbury and Tewkesbury, not far from the M50:

> Under this stone beneath this tablet
> Lie the remains of Edward Gummary,
> Elizabeth his wife and Ann their
> Daughter who were cruelly murdered
> at the cottage
> Known as the Murder House
> in the parish of Berrow
> on the night of May 7th 1780.

On 6 May 1780 the village wake at Berrow took place as usual, with dancing on the village green to the music of Thomas Chinn's fiddle. Afterwards Chinn went to spend the night at Cicil House, the home of his sister, Elizabeth, and her husband, Edward Gummery. People on their way to church next morning, Sunday, were surprised to see a ladder propped up by an open window of the house. Richard Shuter, a boy of ten or twelve at the time, recalled to the end of his long life how his father had climbed up, peered in, and called down: 'Why, Dick, my boy, if it ain't every one of them killed'. When his father went to raise the alarm Dick went to see for himself:

> I gets up to the window to have a look. It was the Lord's Day morning and the bells were going for church, so there was soon a crowd of people and the house was entered. There was blood running down the stairs and out of the front door, and in the bedroom lay the man and his wife and daughter, all lying dead on the floor. Their heads were all hammered and their bodies were hacked and hewn and cut across ... The fiddler was lying dead but was not hacked and hewn like the others.

The tiny green at Berrow on which the wake took place

The murders remained a mystery for some 50 years. The background lay in enclosures of common land round Malvern which aroused violent resentment. In 1777 thirteen people were charged with riot for attempting to stop a surveyor, John Andrews, from marking boundaries deriving from the parliamentary enclosure Act of the previous year, which had been promoted by Sir Charles Cocks, lord of the manor of Leigh, and other landowners. One of their number, Thomas Kemp, a labourer from Leigh, was sent to prison for six months. In the same year the fencing of new enclosures was pulled up, and Daniel Davis of Castlemorton was sentenced to three years in Bridewell. In January 1778 'malicious and evil disposed persons ... did pull up and prostrate some posts and rails, and quick [hedges], set up and planted upon part of [Malvern] Link Common', then made a bonfire of them. The fences were renewed, but in November the protesters, still angry at the loss of common grazing land, 'with their faces blackened, and being otherwise disguised, and arms with guns and other offensive weapons, ... did cut down, burn, and entirely destroy all the posts, gates and rails'. A single heavy post was left standing, bizarrely hacked and hewed, as a kind of warning.

The offer of a reward of £100 or a free pardon for anyone who would turn king's evidence produced no response. Then, on the Saturday of Berrow Wake in 1780 Elizabeth Gummery called at Leigh Court and asked to see Sir Charles Cocks. The butler, explaining presumably that the master was out, asked her to call again on Monday. Before then she was dead.

Some 50 years later an old man, whose name has unfortunately not been recorded, fell out of a tree and broke his leg. He worked on the Beauchamp Estate at Madresfield, and had been gathering mistletoe for the Christmas festivities. He was taken to Worcester Infirmary where he made a death-bed confession to a clergyman:

> I was one of the conspirators who pulled up the fences and burnt them on the common. We stood round the fire and took an oath of secrecy, and swore that whoever turned king's evidence, we would hack and hew him and his family as we had done the post. When the woman came to the Counsellor's [Cocks's] house, the butler, who had also joined the night's work, suspected that she had come to claim the government's reward and make a clean breast of it. We knew that all would be ruined if she told, so we kept the oath and killed her and her family. Since then, some of us have gone one way and some another, and I am the only one left.

People took to calling the place where the Gummerys and the luckless fiddler had died the Murder House. Bill Driver, whose grandfather lived in Berrow, told me that the place had a 'spooky' feeling, and that the two daughters of the last couple who lived there were brought out mad. The building, on the Tewkesbury road where the lane to Berrow turns off, was then abandoned, and allowed to fall down.

We value churchyards as oases of calm, both for the dead and the living. In the past they also served for recreation, sometimes to the dismay of the clergy. As early as the 1180s Gerald of Wales deplored the common people's 'irreverent custom' during saints' festivals of staying 'up late over vile dances, not only singing wicked songs but also disturbing the offices of the devout'. He went on to describe

> The example of a priest in the district of Worcester who one morning when he was dressed for mass in his priestly vestments and standing set apart at the altar for the greeting to the people, that is, 'The Lord be with you', spoke instead before everyone, chanting in a loud voice in the English language, in this way, 'Swete lamman dhin are'. The gist of this phrase might be 'sweet mistress, your lover begs your aid'. He put in that part of the song—which they call a refrain—because he had heard it all night long as the dances went round the church, the part to which they kept on returning. It came to him out of all the rest of his thoughts, for the mouth customarily speaks out of the fullness of the heart. Acting on the occurrence of this event, the bishop of that place, William de Northall, issued a public prohibition through the synods and chapters under threat of anathema that that song should not be sung henceforth throughout his diocese on account of the painful recollection which could recall the crime to mind.

Over 400 years later, Archdeacon William Swaddon was still anxious about churchyards. In 1615 he enquired of incumbents in the diocese of Worcester:

> are your Bels, Belropes, and Clocke, in good repayre, and well ordered? Is your Churchyard well fenced and decently kept? Is it not prophaned with fighting, brawling, chiding, gaming, dancing, playing, or with unlawfull Cattell, or otherwise; and how, and by whome, and in whose default?

St Giles's Church, Lulsley, was closed in 1972 and is now a private house. A report of 1719 observed: 'In the yard was a place made for dancing with an Harbour and a bank thrown up between the wicket [gate] and the north corner, a very improper place for revelrys usually held on Saturday night and too often continued till Sunday morning'.

Wakes (see below and also chapter 9) were originally held in churchyards, as were some full scale fairs. Pershore Fair managed to survive in the abbey churchyard until 1838. Fund raising by means of church ales (see below) took place in churches, in churchyards, and in some parishes—Areley Kings, for example—in permanent ale houses built on church land. People seem to have had no difficulty in accepting the co-existence of sacred and secular activities. When more or less permanent gravestones came in, the space available was progressively restricted, though areas such as the unpopular north side were the last to be filled and thus the last to be used for recreation. To this day there are almost no burials on the north side at Dormston, where in addition the north door is blocked.

Gone Before

Apart from being a prime source for family history in particular and social history in general, epitaphs are rich in human interest, with emotions ranging from grief to resignation, from despair to serenity. Verses often run on traditional lines, with recurring motifs and phraseology. A majority mentions, but fewer comment on, the trade or profession of the person commemorated. Most that do are masculine, with women appearing only as wives and mothers (see below). A lone houseproud woman is remembered at St Stephen's, Redditch:

> Beneath this stone a housewife lies,
> Who acted under no disguise;
> She neatness loved—avoided pride—
> Respected lived—lamented died.

A verse traditional for blacksmiths, found all over the country, turns up with variation at Norton (1795), Powick (1903), White Ladies Aston (1807), Claines (1831) and Shrawley (1845). The last instance reads:

My sledge and hammer lie reclined
My bellows, too have lost their wind;
My fire is spent, my forge decayed
And in the dust my vice is laid:
My coal is spent, my iron is gone,
My nails are drove, my work is done.
My fire dried corpse here lies at rest,
My soul, smoke-like, soars to be blest.

A member of the same craft at Droitwich avoided the stereotype:

This zealous blacksmith died of late,
And went up to Heaven's gate.
He did not call, he did not knock,
Because he meant to pick the lock.

The gravestone of Jonathan Cooke (died 1783) at Tardebigge shows the tools of his trade: plough, harrow, rake, haybond twister, flail, winnower, scythe and sickle. A Claines farmer, Edward Watton (died 1776, aged 42) has this inscription:

With sweat and toil I have long till'd the ground,
But in it now a resting place have found,
With hopes in Jesus Christ I trust
That I, like purest wheat, shall spring from dust,
And share the joyful harvest of the just.

Variations on the same theme occur at Claines and Wichenford. For John Wheeler at Alvechurch a different image serves:

Once I my fields with toil did till,
And did my barns with pleasure fill,
But I am gone and shall no more
In future ages lay up my store.

Another countryman, Thomas Cooke (died 1814), also has a fitting inscription on a tombstone at Shrawley showing a gamekeeper who shoots partridges which his dog retrieves:

He sleeps! no more at early Morn
To wake the woods with mellow Horn:
No more with willing Dog and Gun
To rise before the Sluggard sun;
No more beside the Social can

To-morrow's sport with joy to plan;
Death took his aim, discharg'd his piece,
And bade his sporting season cease.

Soldiers are appropriately recorded at Bromsgrove:

He now in silence here remains
Who fought with Wolfe on Abram's plains,
E'en so will MARY HILL his wife,
When God please to take away her life.
'Twas EDWARD HILL their only son,
Who caused the writing on this stone.
(Edward Hill, died 1800, aged 70);

at Dowles (now obliterated):

At Dettingen and Fontenoy [1745]
Death stared me in the face,
But gave me furlough and convoy
To meet him in this place.
(William Pitt);

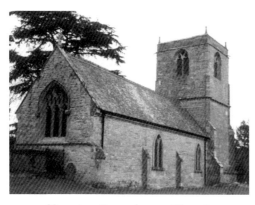

Naunton Beauchamp Church

and at Naunton Beauchamp:

Here lies
Retired from wordly deeds
An old officer of invalids
Who in the Army was born and bred
But now lies quarter'd with the dead
Stripp'd of all his warlike show
And laid in box of oak below
Confin'd in earth, in narrow borders
He rises not, till further orders.
(Captain Andrew Wambey, died
1820, aged 70).

If not sailors, certainly boatmen are suitably commemorated. John Oakes, a Severn waterman (died 1817, aged 52) and his son of the same name (died 1821, aged 27) are buried at Ribbesford, close to the river:

Boreas' blast and Neptune's waves
Have tossed me to and fro;
I strove all I could my life to save
At last obliged to go.

Now at anchor here I lay,
Where's many of the fleet;
But now once more I must set sail
My Saviour Christ to meet.

Another boatman has a more laconic, stoic epitaph:

My anchor's cast—
My rope's on shore—
And here I lie
Till time's no more.

Spectacular headstones in Bromsgrove churchyard were erected to the memory of two engine drivers—fatally injured when a locomotive's boiler exploded at Bromsgrove Station in 1840. The epitaph to Thomas Scaife (aged 28), like that of the blacksmiths, uses the appropriate occupational vocabulary to telling effect:

My *engine* now is cold and still
No *water* does my *boiler* fill:
My *coke* affords its flame no more.
My days of usefulness are o'er
My *wheels* deny their noted speed
No more my guiding hands they heed
My *whistle* too, has lost its tone

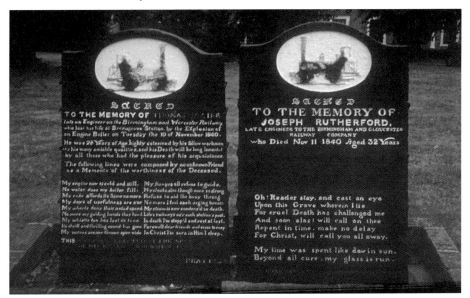

The memorials to the two engine drivers at Bromsgrove

Its shrill and thrilling sounds are gone
My *valves* are now thrown open wide
My *flanges* all refuse to guide
My *clacks* also, though once so strong
Refuse to aid the busy throng
No more I feel each urging breath
My *steam* is now condens'd in death.
Life's *railway's* o'er, each *station's* past,
In death I'm stopp'd and rest at last.
Farewell dear friends and cease to weep,
In Christ I'm SAFE, In Him I sleep.

A more mundane incident accounted for Charles Goode of Bewdley:

The Lord saw good, I was lopping off wood,
And down fell from the tree.
I met with a check and broke my neck,
And so death lopped off me.

Rather more light-hearted is the headstone at Holy Trinity Church, Belbroughton, which recalls Richard Philpotts (died 1766, aged 69) of the Bell Inn:

To tell a memory or a wond'rous tale
Over a chearful glass of nappy ale
In harmless mirth was his supreme delight,
To please his guests or friends by day or night.
But no fine tale, how well so ever told
Could make the tyrant Death, his stroke withhold;
That fatal stroke has laid him here in dust
To rise again once more with joy we trust.

Another publican receives more jocular treatment:

Beneath this stone in hopes of Zion
Doth lie the landlord of the Lion.
His son keeps on the business still
Resigned upon the heavenly will.

The establishment mentioned is the White Lion at Upton-on-Severn, where a series of episodes in Fielding's novel, *Tom Jones*, is set. The epitaph, too, may be fictional; an Upton writer of 1869 says it 'has been stated in Sunday magazines and newspapers to have existence in our churchyard (but) we can get no clear memory of its being here'.

Unsurprisingly, familial messages on gravestones heavily outnumber the professional. Survivors mourn deceased husband or wife, parent or child. Conventional—though not necessarily insincere—valedictions include:

Here lies lamented in his silent grave,
A tender husband and a parent brave;
Pale King of Terrors unkindly did destroy
The widow's hopes and her children's joy
(Thomas Harris, died 1794, aged 52, Feckenham).

Pale Death will hardly find another:
So good a wife, so kind a Mother.
In all her Actions, so discreet,
Was she who lies here at your feet
(Mary Hartwright, died 1753, aged 63, Claines).

More individual tributes include this, to Elizabeth Hart (died 1775, aged 35) of Martley:

Now in this grave my loving wife she's laid
If God had pleased with me she'd longer stayed
Oh that my eyes with hers had closèd been
Then I had not this time of sorrow seen.

Mary Read (died 1806, aged 80) received a fulsome endorsement at St James's Church, Defford:

An industrious woman here doth be,
A mother good to her dear family;
But now she's gone,
We hope her soul's at rest
And by God's goodness
Be for ever blest.

Frances Grove (died 1829, aged 50) is remembered more briefly at St Mary's, Hanbury:

She was — but words are wanting to say what;
Think what a mother should be — she was that.

Elizabeth Cupper (died 1724, aged 36) of Ombersley seems to have been another paragon:

Sharp was her wit,
Mild was her nature;
A tender wife,
And good humor'd creature.

Less harmonious relationships do at times emerge in epitaphs, though one wonders whether some of these were ever inscribed. Tom Sexton of Bredon had two (successive) wives, both of whom he outlived, and one of whom he memorialised:

Here lies the body of Sarah Sexton,
She was a wife that never vexed one;
I can't say as much for the one
At the next stone.

It is not clear whether a verse at Ribbesford was intended for the former parish clerk or his wife:

The children of Israel wanted bread,
And the Lord he sent them down manna.
Old clerk Wallace wanted a wife,
And the Devil he sent him Anna.

The parson-historian, Treadway Nash, wrote of an apparently apocryphal epitaph:

The following inscription is said to be in the church-yard at Upton upon Severn, but I never saw it:

Here lies the body of Mary Ford,
Whose soul, we hope, is with the Lord;
But if for hell she has chang'd this life,
It's better far than John Ford's wife.
N.B. John Ford was a bad husband to his wife Mary, and by direction of his neighbours put these lines on her grave stone.

A harmonious, complementary relationship is exemplified by the lines in the south aisle of the nave at Malvern Priory to Joseph Baylis, yeoman, and his wife, Elizabeth (died respectively 1728 and 1741):

They were so one, that none could truly say
Which of them rul'd, or whether did obey;
He ruled, because she would obey; and she,
In so obeying, ruled as well as he.

CHURCHES

On a stone at St Peter's Church, Besford, the dying thoughts of Mary Turnbill (aged 31 in 1782) turn to the children she is leaving behind:

Adieu, dear husband, for my time is past,
I ever loved you while my life did last;
Think on my children for my sake,
And ever on them pity take.

The death of young children arouses even more poignant feelings. In 1740 a widow at Tibberton mourned the loss not only of her husband, Edward Aries, but of six children:

Two sons, four daughters, and husband dear;
Seven tender friends lie buried here;
They departed in such dismal pain —
They died in hopes to live again.
They being dead cannot remain to me;
God fit me for my change that I may happy be.

A widower at Shrawley, in a verse reputedly written by William Wordsworth, reflected on the pain of loss and the consolation of life:

She Came Though Meek of Soul, In Seemly Pride
Of Happiness and Hope. A Youthful Bride
O Dread Reverse If Aught Be So Which Proves
That God Will Chasten Whom He Dearly Loves
Faith Bore Her Up, Through Pain In Mercy Given
And Troubles Which Were Each A Step to Heaven,
Two Babes Were Laid in Earth Before She Died
A Third Now Slumbers At The Mothers Side,
Its Sister Twin Survives, Whose Smiles Impart
A Trembling Solace To Her Fathers Heart
Reader If To Thy Bosom Cling The Pain
Of Recent Sorrow Combatted in Vain;
Or If Thy Cherished Grief Have Failed To Thwart
Time Still Intent Of His Insidious Part,
Lulling the Mourners Best Good Thoughts Asleep.
Pilfering Regrets We Would, But Cannot Keep;
Bear With Those Judge Those Gently Who Make Known
Their Bitter Loss By Monumental Stone;
And Pray That In Their Faithful Breasts the Grace
Of Resignation Find A Hallowed Place.

The wife was Mary Vernon, who died in 1831 at the age of 28.

Other epitaphs struggle to come to terms with grief, especially when they concern children. Daniel Ward died at Eckington in 1706, aged three years and six months:

> Sweet Pretty Babe
> Soon snacht away
> We trust to live
> With Christ in iay [joy].

At Hill Croome is commemorated Joseph, the son of John and Ann Howship, who died in 1840 at the age of eight months:

> Dear child farewell nor let a fathers grief
> Nor mothers tears dispair of heavens relief
> But wait for that solemn day that shall restore
> And prove their child not lost but gone before.

St Edburga's, known as 'the old church',
at Broadway

Those who devised epitaphs and those who chose them for their relatives frequently took the opportunity of making hortatory or admonitory statements. The message, ostensibly from beyond the grave, at St Edburga's, Broadway, starkly reads:

> As thow
> Art so was
> I as I am
> So shalt
> Thou BEE.

St Andrew's Church, Stockton-on-Teme

A parallel prediction, reinforced by the image of three skulls on one of the Walsh tombs in St Andrew's Church at Stockton-on-Teme, runs:

> Such as you are, once were we;
> But such as we are, even such
> shall you be.

John Collier (died 1671, aged 40) of Feckenham seeks to warn those still living:

Behold all you that pass me by,
As you are now so once was I;
As I am now so must you be,
When this you see then think on me
And serve the Lord, your lives amend,
And think upon your latter end.

At St Andrew's, Droitwich, Thomas Grainger (died 1724, aged 48) announces:

Weep not my friends and children dear,
I am not dead, but sleeping here;
My days are spent, my grave you see,
Wait but awhile, you'll be with me.

Elizabeth Bray (died 1820, aged 20) also craves the attention of posterity, at St Stephen's, Redditch:

The so-called Giant's Grave (front) at Ripple, with remains of the churchyard cross (see p.58) in the background

Stay, stranger, here, and cast an eye,
As you are now, so once was I;
As I am now, so must you be,
Therefore prepare to follow me.

As well as reminders of mortality, some epitaphs offer advice to the living. A tombstone in the churchyard of St Mary's, Ripple, marks what is locally known as the Giant's Grave. Here lies Robert Reeve, who died in 1626 at the age of 56. He was a powerful man, 7 feet 4 inches in height, who died of over-exertion—possibly what we should now call a heart attack—while engaged in a mowing contest for a wager in Uckinghall meadow. His epitaph is very simple:

As you passe be, behold my length,
But never glory in your strength.

There is a similar inscription in Welland churchyard.

Calls to repentance are common:

> Quick was the stroke destroyed my mortal day,
> Broke worldly ties and took my life away;
> Reader! reflect, what dangers around you fly,
> Repent in time, and well prepare to die
> (John Stone, died 1823, aged 73, Beoley).

Another theme is that of resignation, tempered by hopes of resurrection. An early example comes from the church at Lindridge, near Tenbury, which preceded the present Victorian building:

> This stone that covers earth and clay
> Long in the earth uncovered lay:
> Man forced it from my mother's womb
> And made thereof for man a tomb.
> And now it speaks and thus doth say
> The life of man is but a day:
> The days will pass, the night must come:
> Then here, poor man, is all thy room
> The writer and the reader must
> Like this good man be turned to dust:
> He lived well, and so do thou:
> Then fear not death, when, where or how
> It comes: 'twill end all grief and pain
> And make thee ever live again
> (William Pennell, died 1623).

A simpler, more direct inscription records the passing at Alvechurch in 1680 of Elizabeth Acton:

> Thy Soul & Body Running in a race
> Thy Soul held out, thy Body tyr'd apace,
> Thy Soul gain'd and left that lump of clay
> To rest it selfe untill the latter day.

Just as homely in language are these epitaphs from Aston Somerville and Abbot's Morton respectively:

> When he was here last
> In health a year past
> In this place he chose
> his bones to repose.
> God did him inspire

he hath his desire
disturb not his dust
hee'l rise with the iust
(Thomas Parry of London, died 1700, aged 26).

I choose this place myself,
Thinking it for the best;
I hope you will not me disturb,
But let me lie at rest
(John Husband, died 1786).

A touching certitude is revealed in the lines at Church Lench to Marris Hiatt (died 1714, aged 84) of Abberton and his wife:

Since thought may doubt whether dry bones may live
Faith doth answer to the Scruple give
It sayes they may nay more they must
Y^e dishonoured bodyes of the lust
Shall rise in glory even out of dust.

Beside such lofty sentiments jocularity sometimes crops up, as in this epitaph of 1690 at Knightwick in the graveyard of the old church:

Here lie the bones
Of JOSEPH JONES,
Who ate whilst he was able;
But, once o'erfed,
He dropped down dead,
And fell between the table.
When from this town
To meet his doom
He rises amidst sinners,
Since he must dwell
In Heaven or Hell,
To take him, which gives best dinners.

When Bishop Hurd of Worcester was visited by George III at Hartlebury the king's contingent had to pass through a tollgate at Worcester. (This was a roundhouse called the Barbourne gate—now a sweetshop—at the junction of the Ombersley and Droitwich roads.) The toll keeper, Robert Sleath, allowed the party through on promise of payment by an equerry. When the money was not forthcoming he refused to allow the king's party to pass on the return journey until both tolls, amounting to 27 shillings, were paid. When Sleath died in Birmingham in 1805 the incident was remembered:

On Wednesday last old Robert Sleath
Passed through the Turnpike Gate of death;
To him would Death no toll abate,
Who stopped the King at Wor'ster Gate.

The writers of epitaphs were not above making puns when the opportunity arose. At Bromsgrove the name of Knott was too good to miss:

Here lies a man that was Knott born,
His father was Knott before him.
He lived Knott, and did Knott die,
Yet underneath this stone doth lie;
Knott christened,
Knott begot,
And here he lies,
And yet was Knott.

An epitaph in punning Latin to a member of the Caldwall family in Clifton-on-Teme Church was translated in 1778 by Dr le Grosvenor of Bewdley:

Here lies old Caldwell whom nature did ease
With a wall of firm flesh quite as solid as brass:
Yet medical plaister this wall could not save.
It decayed, and at length tumbled into the grave,
Which swallows all walls both of flesh and of stone,
And in time will devour the walls of the sun.

Perhaps the most attractive verses are those combining simplicity of language with stoicism of sentiment. At St John's, Bromsgrove, Richard Carpenter (died 1681) has this inscription:

I did resist and strive with death,
But soon he put me out of breath.

Thomas Fisher, yeoman, of Eckington (died 1820, aged 70), also rests beneath a single couplet:

When death is come and life is gone,
Then well is he that well hath done.

Equally laconmic are the lines at St John's, Claines, for Thomas Mann (died 1848, aged 85):

A [*sic*] honest man and free from pride;
In credit lived, beloved he died.

Even this economy with words is bettered by another epitaph in the same churchyard which is no longer to be seen but was, according to W.J. Woodley 'referred to in the old records':

Honest John's
Dead and gone.

Bells, Ringers and Singers

As well as summoning the faithful to prayer or worship, church bells had secular uses. They pealed for victory in war and stood ready in peace to signal invasion or disaster. Bells once announced seedtime, harvest, gleaning; there was even an Oven Bell to proclaim that the lord of the manor's oven was ready to cook his tenants' dough—at a price.

St Martin's, Worcester, before it was demolished in 1768 and replaced by the present building

Many places had a Pancake Bell; at St Martin's, Worcester, a Plum Pudding Bell rang nightly several weeks before Christmas. Until 1801 at Bewdley the 5 a.m. bell which woke apprentices for their labour, schoolboys for study and people in general for work inspired understandable resentment against the ringer, expressed in a local rhyme:

Ye rascally ringers, ye merciless foes,
Who persecute every friend to repose;
I wish for the quiet and peace of the land,
You had round your necks what you hold in your hand.

The Day Bell as it was called at St Helen's, Worcester, rang for fifteen minutes every morning at 4, until about 1750. At Pershore the 5 a.m. bell was discontinued after a sexton called Blake on one occasion rang it five hours too early: he woke when midnight was striking but heard only the last five strokes,

William Bourne (left) and St Helen's, Worcester (right)

so dressed and rang what he thought was the five o'clock bell; some market gardeners, trusting him implicitly, got up, harnessed their horses and drove their ready-loaded carts off to market in Worcester, Birmingham or elsewhere. A similar mistake is related of William Bourne—otherwise known as 'Old Bill', 'Workhouse Bill' or 'Billy the Roman'—at Alvechurch, who for some 30 years lived in the church tower and rang all that time at 5 a.m. and 8 p.m. without missing a single day. (The 1851 census records him at Swan Street in Alvechurch).

Evesham's morning bell sounded at 4 a.m. throughout the year on Mondays, Thursdays and Saturdays only. 'Rumour vaguely ascribes the observance, wrote the historian, George May, in 1845, 'to the gratitude of a stranger, who at some unknown era had lost his way in the darkness of night till directed thither by an accidental peal, which he provided should be thenceforth perpetual'. The town's evening bell rang at 8 p.m., except on Saturdays, and also during the twelve days of Christmas, when it moved an hour earlier.

Pershore's curfew bell rung between Bonfire Night and Candlemas Day (2 February) until the 1890s. Goldsmith's well known line, 'The curfew tolls the knell of parting day', was once literally true. Even though the legal requirement for a curfew bell ended as long ago as 1100 the practice continued with many local variations until recent times.

St Helen's, Worcester, until 1939 had its own bell at 8 p.m. followed by as many strokes as days had elapsed in the month. The young Edward Elgar in the early 1870s sometimes deputised for the ringer when his rheumatism was too painful, and 'took a delight in adding occasionally an extra number or two to the actual date'. Other places with a curfew bell included Bewdley (until 1914), Bromsgrove, Clent (from Michaelmas until St Mary Day—2 February) and Stourport.

St Martin's, Worcester, had a special bell on December evenings to guide people through the darkness, and the ringing of its Pudding Bell (see above) may have originated in this way. The slim spire of St Andrew's Church, erected or re-built in 1751, is said to have owed its construction to a rich man grateful for being saved from walking into the Severn, one foggy night, when he heard the bells. Another traveller, returning to Kidderminster from St Luke's Fair in Bridgnorth—St Luke's Day is 18 October—ran into wild weather. At one point his horse simply refused to go a step farther. Straining his ears, the man heard the curfew bell at St Mary's in Kidderminster, and found his bearings: he was poised on the brink of a sheer drop from Jacob's Ladder at the head of Habberley Valley. He gratefully turned his horse's head away from the precipice, and later gave money to the church to support the bell ringing. To mark the event, a Kidderminster weaver called Noah Cooke wrote a lengthy poem, 'The Curfew Bell and St Luke's Fair'. Both Bockleton and Tenbury devoted rents from certain fields to providing light in the churches, and at Rochford the income enabled lights to be placed along the river bank road in the winter to stop people falling into the Teme.

The passing bell—where it is still rung—gives news that a death has occurred. Formerly it warned that death was imminent, to enable people to pray for the soul of the departing man or woman. The experience of hearing it must have been chilling for the person concerned. Until the 1920s St Mary's, Tenbury, had different numbers of rings for a man, a woman and a child. The custom at Offenham was for the number six bell—known for this reason as the 'death bell'—to be tolled at funerals. Three strokes for a man (two for a woman) were given in turn on the treble, second and tenor (third) bells, followed by as many on the tenor as the years of the person's age, after which the same bell was raised and tolled for five minutes. Bromsgrove also had three twos for a woman and three threes for a man. The saying, 'nine tellers make a man', survives from this practice, though it is often garbled into 'nine tailors make a man'.

A similar distinction between the sexes applied at Inkberrow, where in addition after a death a single bell would be tolled at each minute of the hour after sunrise and that before sunset. The tolling resumed for half an hour before a funeral, the pace gradually quickening as the cortège neared the churchyard, and continued for the same period afterwards.

Song on the casting of eight bells at St Helen's, Worcester,
a digitally enhanced copy of the original woodcut of the music,
first published in 1708

An ancient bell at Bretforton bore these words:

> Funera plango, fulgura frango, Sabbata pango,
> Excito lentos, dissipo ventos, paco cruentes.
> (I mourn [at] funerals, I break the lightning, I mark the Sabbaths,
> I hasten the slow, I disperse the winds, I calm the savage).

An inscription on the tenor bell at St James', Hartlebury, reads:

> For the living I do call,
> To the grave I summon all.

This or a closely similar message is shared with 13 more churches in Worcestershire. No fewer than 20 churches in the county have a bell inscribed 'Peace and Good Neighbourhood'. At Bretforton a bell proclaims:

> As Music Hath a Secret Charm
> We May the Atheist Soul Alarm.

While at Himbleton, Grafton Flyford and Severn Stoke the message is:

> All men that heare my rorin sound
> Repent before ye ly in ground.

An Evesham Abbey bell puts this in more measured language:

> I sound the sound that doleful is,
> To them that live amiss;
> But sweet my sound is unto such
> As live in joy and bliss.
> I sweetly tolling, men do call
> To taste on food that feeds the soul.

More prosaically, 'Prosperity to this Parish' (or a similar phrase) occurs on bells in another 15 churches, including those at Astley, Bransford, Little Comberton, Leigh, Powick, Ripple and Shelsley Beauchamp.

Great simplicity is shown on the bell of 1627 at Pensax which merely says: 'God is my hoop' (hope). In contrast, a new ring of bells installed at St Helen's Church in Worcester in 1706-7 had elaborate inscriptions marking English victories during the War of the Spanish Succession. In addition, a celebratory song, 'Sabrina's Bancks Rebound' was written soon afterwards by a Mr Henry Hall of Hereford. It is not known which of the two Henry Halls, father and son, successive organists at Hereford Cathedral, was responsible; probably the latter, who was also a prime mover in the foundation of the Tree Choirs Festival. Unfortunately, the bells of St Helen's were removed and melted down in 1951, leaving an empty tower and ringing chamber.

Discipline among the ringers seems to have been a perennial problem, and it is possibly reflected in the once-proverbial Worcestershire saying, 'Bellringer and psalmsinger, never was a home bringer'. A William Wathis of Worcester wrote indignantly in 1714 about an event at Eckington:

> Some young fellows upon ye occasion met and rung the bells, had 3s sent them to drink, but thinking that not sufficient they declar'd they would ring the bells backwd. Accordingly did, and allarum'd thereby the whole neighbourhood. I went into the church and demanded ye reason of it, and was answered that they had rung for a Roundhead's pleasure and were now ringing backwds for their own. I therefore ordered them to fall the bells, and dep't the church, both wch they refused to do, till I myself pull'd one of ye bells down that was set. The ringers whereof endeavrd to throw the rope about my neck, and said the gallows would be strong. After the falling of the bells and abundance of ill language they refus'd to go out of the church, declaring they would stay there all night if they pleas'd, and there I was forced to leave them.

Rules for ringers were sometimes set into verses painted on boards such as the example still in the ringing chamber at Ashton-under-Hill, which deals with the offence of overthrowing a bell through too strong a pull, which puts it out of action after breaking a restraining stave:

> A Table of Forfeits
> If First or Second bell you Fling
> One penny pay and that the thing
> If Third or Fourth turn by Chance
> Pay just the same, there's no advance,
> But if the Fifth you overthrow
> Then Two Pence to the Clark you owe
> And all these Forfeits he must have
> Before from hence you take your leave.

The notice at Ashton is dated 1785; that in the ringing chamber of the abbey bell tower at Evesham has no date but the 'forfeits' have significantly increased:

> Gentlemen Ringers far and near
> That are disposed to Ring here,
> Observe these Rules and note them well
> The Man that overturns his Bell,

> Unto the Sexton Sixpence pay,
> Before he passes hence away,
> And he that Rings with Spur or Hat
> Must pay likewise Fourpence for that
> Ropes cost Money, Oyl is dear
> Therefore make pay, or come not here.

A rather different board formerly hung in the chamber at Kempsey, with a valedictory verse to Stephen White, a bellringer who died in 1811, aged 85:

> Time and Stephen are now both even
> Stephen beat time and now time beats Stephen.

At Bromsgrove, rather more sedate lines were composed by a local poet, Waterson, in memory of Charles Ravenscroft who died in 1812, aged 46:

> Ay, CHARLES! thy ringing now is o'er
> Thou'lt call the merry peal no more,
> To Single not to Bob direct
> To give each Change its due effect,
> Nor teach the inexperienced youth
> The course to range with ease and truth.
> Of this no more, give up thou must,
> And mingle with thy parents dust!
> Into its place thy Bell is come,
> And Ruthless Death has brought thee home.

Still at Bromsgrove, printed rules dated 1875 were displayed in the belfry:

PARISH CHURCH BELLRINGERS' RULES

1. That the Society of Ringers consist of Ten Members and Two Supernumaries.
2. That the Ringers shall appoint from among themselves a Treasurer, to whom all Monies shall be paid, and by whom it shall be divided amongst the Ringers; and in case of any dispute, the matter shall be referred to the Vicar and Churchwardens, whose decision shall be final.
3. That no person shall be admitted into the Society except by the Vicar and Churchwardens, and that any Ringer guilty of misconduct, particularly of making use of bad Language, or of intoxication while engaged in his duties at the Church, shall be reported to the Vicar and Churchwardens, who will instantly dismiss such offender from the Society.
4. That the Ringers shall undertake to Chime on Sundays, and to perform all other duties connected with the Bells, except such as belong to the office of Sexton.

5. That the Ringers shall be required to appear in Belfry on the Sabbath Day in clean and decent apparel, or be the subject of a fine, the amount of which shall be determined upon among themselves.
6. That any Ringer frequenting a Public-house on a Sunday be expelled from the Society.
7. That all the Ringers attend Church regularly.

Ringing chamber at Badsey

Bromsgrove was clearly not alone in its anxiety about ringers' misdemeanours. A similar code at Badsey dating from 1888 forbade unseemly conduct and intoxicating liquor in the belfry; it also provided for a fine of sixpence for a ringer who failed to attend the service for which he had rung, yet only threepence if he did not turn up at all. Fines collected were shared out among the ringers at the end of the year in proportion to their attendances.

Perhaps the issue of regulations in Badsey was prompted by the kind of behaviour described by Arthur Savory, who lived in the manor house and farmed at Aldington from 1873 until the turn of the century, for much of which time he was a churchwarden at Badsey:

The parish must have been an uncivilised place in former times; there was an accusing record beneath the west window of the tower, in the shape of a blocked up entrance. I was told that the ringers, not wishing to enter or leave the tower through the church door during service, and also to facilitate the smuggling in of unlimited cider had, after strenuous efforts, cut an opening through the ancient wall and base some feet in thickness, and that the achievement was announced to the village by uproarious cheering when at last they succeeded. A door was afterwards fitted to the aperture, but the entrance was abolished later by a more reverent vicar.

The belfry was decorated with various bones of legs of mutton and of joints of beef, hung up to commemorate notable weddings of prominent parishioners—perhaps, too, as a hint to future aspirants to the state of matrimony—when the ringers had enjoyed a substantial meal and gallons of cider at the expense of the bridegroom.

As well as their perks from such events as marriages, ringers received fees for special occasions throughout the year. At Bishampton until about 1900 a muffled peal every 30 January marked the anniversary of Charles I's execution. Charles II's 'Crownenation day' in 1660 was worth two shillings to the ringers of Pirton, who were paid similar sums for bread and wine at 'Newerstite' (New Year's tide) in 1685, and for ale 'on ye day of rejoyceing for ye conkering of ye French fleett' in 1692. A century earlier the going rate seems to have been nine pence, the sum received by Bewdley ringers on several occasions, including 'for ringing the first of May' in 1596. John Glover there earned 20s. (£1) in 1612 'for ringing the schollers bell this two yeares ended at St Mary day last' (see above).

Miss Hemming, who kept a public house in the churchyard at Tardebigge was paid in 1800 for the ale she supplied to the bellringers when they rang for the anniversary of the 'Powder Plot'. Similar records exist in the churchwardens' accounts in many parishes.

On a very different occasion in November 2002 the sixteenth-century bell at St Andrew's Church in Worcester rang for the first time in 130 years to summon councillors to a meeting at the Guildhall. The All Saints' Church Society of Ringers was contracted to ring for eight such meetings a year at a fee of £80 after the bell had been restored and rehung. Their predecessors received two shillings a year.

Ringing in the new year at Inkberrow from the 1880s until the 1920s was lubricated by a jug of beer or cider for the ringers provided by Charles Knight, landlord of the Old Bull. Bells are still rung half-muffled to ring out the old year at Kempsey on 31 December: a leather pad is attached to one side of each clapper so as to deaden the sound, thus causing an alternation of loud and soft. Just before midnight the muffles come off, and the new year is welcomed with the bells' full voice. A similar procedure is followed at Worcester Cathedral. The ringers at Elmley Castle after pealing for the new year sing a carol at the churchyard gate, and in so doing follow a custom dating back to 1600.

Many ringing chambers contain boards showing details of peals such as the 2,040 grandsire triples rung at Bewdley in three hours and 20 minutes in 1782 and the 2,160 changes—Oxford Treble Bob, Kent Treble Bob and Plain Bob— rung at Belbroughton in 1862 in one hour 20 minutes. One special set of changes is known as the Hinton Surprise Major, after the village of Hinton-on-the-Green. Another spectacular effort was commemorated in a printed ballad entitled *A Song on the Famous Peal of 7308 Grandsire Cators Rung by the Society of All Saints Ringers, in Worcester, On the 28th of November, 1774*:

> Ye lovers of ringing now give your attention
> Unto these few words which my song it will mention:
> It is of Seven Thousand Three Hundred and Eight,

By the Youths of All Saints that was rung quite compleat:
In the year Seventy-four, now remark what I say,
In the month of November, the twenty-eighth day,
This peal was completed, which was to the fame
Of the Youths of All Saints, who shall still bear the name.

RICHARD PAINE to the Treble, I speak in his praise,
That I ne'er heard a bell better rung in my days;
For over the large bells he struck her quite clear,
And his compass at lead kept as true as a hair:
THOMAS HILL he the Second did steadily ring,
And in the Tittoms [a kind of peal] she sweetly did sing;
Though some seem to sneer at his prophetic dream,
Yet the Youths of All Saints they shall still bear the name.

JOSEPH STONE to the Third, he kept her stiff in hand,
And just at his own pleasure did her command;
Through the whole Seven Thousand Three Hundred and Eight:
THOMAS SPINNER the Fourth, for a solid hand's he,
And in ringing a length he rings quite steadily;
He marks his course bell, and sticks close to the same,
And the Youths of All Saints they shall still bear the name.

GEORGE ROE to the Fifth he did cheerfully stand,
And he struck her right well, both at back stroke and hand;
'There's Beauty!' he cry'd, and so smooth did he pull,
And smiled when the large bells at home they did roll:
At the Sixth RICHARD HERBERT, he look'd quite sharp,
And ne'er was observ'd in his course once to warp;
For to finish the peal, Sir, it was his whole aim,
And the Youths of All Saints they shall still bear the name.

WILLIAM KENDAL the Seventh, so smart a young lad,
I'd call the peal true, and he made each heart glad;
The Changes he plac'd in the Tittoms so tight,
And he told out just Fifty Times Nine, Seven, Eight:
JOHN BRISTOW, the Eighth, rang so solid and clear,
That no fault was discern'd by the most curious ear;
All his thoughts at that time he to ringing did frame,
And the Youths of All Saints they shall still bear the name.

To the Ninth THOMAS BARKER stood sturdy and stout,
And with hearty good-will he did swing her about;
Right boldly and bravely he stuck to her tough,
And he ne'er once faulter'd, or said he had enough:
To the Tenor GEORGE WAINWRIGHT stood like heart of oak,

And to this famous peal gave the finishing stroke;
When the clapper came out, which just answer'd the dream!
And the Youths of All Saints they shall still bear the name.

Four Hours and a Half and Six Minutes they were,
The people with watches in hand did declare;
And said the performers were worthy of praise,
For they ne'er heard a peal better rung in their days.
So here's a good health to those that wish us well,
And those that do envy us they cannot excell;
Those that wish us well, boys, we wish them the same,
And the Youths of All Saints they shall still bear the name.

There is an interesting footnote:

Thomas Hill dreamed three times, in one night, that he was ringing at All
Saints and each time awakened with the thought of the Tenor's Clapper
falling out at the end of the peal; which was verified this day, for as soon
as George Wainwright gave the finishing stroke, the clapper broke
through the middle.

A much less happy outcome to a ringer's prediction was reported from
Bretforton in 1806, where John Halford after a disagreement in the belfry
announced: 'I hope that next time I take hold of a bell-rope I shall fall down
dead'. Some time later he was threshing with a flail in a barn when news
reached him that an heir to the squire had been born. He rushed to the belfry,
begun to ring, and fell dead. He was 58. One does not know whether he
received a fitting epitaph, as did Samuel George, parish clerk and bellringer at
St John's, Hadzor, who died in 1774. His gravestone bears these words:

I have oft tolled the passing bell,
And dug the silent grave,
For many a neighbour dear.
Have oftimes sat beneath that yew tree shade,
As up the road was borne with solemn pace
The poor remains of some dear one deceased.
My mouldering body now in dust doth lie
Like theirs, awaiting for immortal day.

Once the bell ringers had called parishioners to church another team of
musicians took over: a band provided accompaniment for the choir and congregation before the days when organs became universal. Thomas Hardy in *Under
the Greenwood Tree* has left an affectionate portrait of a 'quire' of village musicians just before they were displaced by an organ.

A Village Choir, by Thomas Webster (1847)

Many churches banished musicians from the chancel to a gallery, usually positioned at the west end. Some of the west galleries in which such musicians played and sang still exist in Worcestershire, though they now often feature organs. They include churches at Defford, Grimley, Hanbury, Inkberrow,

The west gallery at Shrawley

Shrawley, Strensham, Tardebigge, Upton Warren, Wickhampton and Worcester St Martin's. Elsewhere, galleries came and went with changing tastes in ecclesiastical music and architecture. Kempsey, erected in 1759, was removed during the restoration of the church in 1863. St George's, Barbourne, built in 1829, had a west gallery in which 'one man and one or two children sang in unison with the addition of a bass viol' until they were displaced in 1848 by an organ. The gallery itself disappeared in 1894 when the church was demolished and replaced by a new building. In 1881 a harmonium replaced the village band in the west gallery at Rous Lench. Rev. W.K.W. Chafy remarked that 'Judging by the scores, the performance must have been of an ambitious nature. All that now survives [in 1901] is the head of the 'cello''. His note is tantalising

Grimley Church,
showing stair to west gallery

since no west gallery music from Worcestershire, either instrumental or vocal, has so far turned up.

The instruments were mainly employed to lead vocal parts. At St Mary's, Elmley Castle, a flute, clarionet and bassoon played by what W.G.S. Snow called 'self-taught village minstrels' accompanied a choir which used 'an old music book written by several different and obviously illiterate hands over a considerable period of years' in the eighteenth and early nineteenth centuries. The book seems to have been lost, though it is known to have contained hymns, metrical psalms, anthems for weddings and funerals, and Addison's *The Spacious Firmament*. An organ made its appearance in Elmley Castle Church in 1852, and a new music book followed. Rev. Lawson recalled the west gallery in the old church at Offenham (pulled down in 1861), where the choir was accompanied by a 'flute, clarionet and base [sic] viol'. At Ribbesford the choir occupied a dais at the west end while the instrumentalists—cornets, 'clarionet' and double bass—sat in the middle of the church.

Bromsgrove had a string and reed band, the latter instruments being used not only in church but outside by the waits (see chapter 9) at Advent and Christmas. Church Honeybourne was reduced to one violin and the ''oss's leg'

West gallery at Bayton Church before the restoration of 1905,
when it was removed

(a bassoon) when the players were replaced in the 1860s by a £5 Alexandre harmonium. Even the Methodist Mill Street Chapel at Kidderminster had fiddles, brass instruments and a serpent during the 1850s. (A serpent is an ancient bass instrument with three S-turns, made of wood covered in leather).

Longdon (until 1868) boasted a string quartet. A musician called William Smith played at Saintbury just over the Gloucestershire border near Broadway from 1834 until 1901, first woodwind instruments, then after the loss of his teeth the bass viol. He was succeeded by a Mrs Mason who played the harmonium for a mere 22 years, and then by Harold Andrews who was still using the same instrument in 1973 after half a century's service.

William Smith had a number of connections with Worcestershire. He sang at Broadway in 1840 when the new church of St Michael was dedicated at Broadway, and he owned a piccolo which had belonged to the last hayward at Honeyboume. He played in villages for miles round Saintbury at musical evenings and servants' balls. He also toured with the waits at Christmas, when 'it was the custom often to hire a non-player to go round with them to consume superfluous liquor, it not being etiquette to decline any offered'.

Band and choir at Tardebigge (male and female members of the latter entering by separate doors) were in the gallery, and during the hymns the congregation turned west to face them. The churchwardens' accounts between

1797 and 1818 show yearly payments of 5s. for strings for a viol and a bass viol. They then change to record annual payments of £1 to William Southwell, who had previously been in charge of the band, for 'turning the organ'—that is, a barrel organ. From 1835 the organ had a keyboard, and 'T. Suthall' (probably William's son) received 30s. a year for playing it. The barrel-playing mechanism remained in the instrument until 1879, when Nicholson's of Malvern renovated it but returned it to the chancel rather than the gallery.

The accounts at Wichenford, where the west gallery players survived until the mid-nineteenth century, include:

1831-2	A string for the Beas vile [bass viol]	1/6
1837	Paid for the base viol	2/6
1844	1st and 2nd viol strings	1/9
1845	Strings for violine	3/0
1847	Mrs Browning violin	£3/8/0

At Eckington a gallery was built at the west end of the nave in 1774, then enlarged in 1841 to accommodate both singers and a band of two violins, two cellos, one bass viol, flutes, 'clarionets', trumpet, trombone and bassoon. Items such as these appear in the church register:

1783	Paid for a Reed for the Musick	6s 6d
1786	Mending the Church Musick	5s
1825	Paid for Strings for the Church Musick	£1
1826	Bass Viol	£5. 19. 0

All of the Eckington musicians were supplanted in 1863 by a harmonium (which had to be repaired three years later at a cost of five shillings), and in 1887 the gallery itself was removed. In 1907 came the organ.

In June 1836 at Inkberrow Henry Whitfield signed a receipt to acknowledge 'that the Bassoon now in my possession dothe belong to the parish Churche and I holds the same for the use of the Church'. In the previous year the Frankley churchwardens paid 5s. 3d. for 'a set of strings for the bass viol and haring the bow' of the instrument used in the west gallery of St Leonard's. In 1949 they paid out 1s. 6d. for '2 yards of green baz for a bag for violoncello' and 1st and second string'. In 1850 the singers at Frankley were Jemima Taylor, Mary Connop (aged 18), Ruth Field (18), Sarah Nash, and Hezekiah Craddock (80). (The last of these also served as schoolmaster and clerk.) For singing they received £1 17s. 6d. between them for the year, paid at Easter. Three years later Field and Craddock remained, and were joined by James Taylor and James Follows. Each received 10s. for twelve months' singing. In 1854 the churchwardens engaged Herbert Smith of Halesowen to play the newly-acquired harmonium at a salary of £8 a year 'on each Sunday,

Christmas Day, Good Friday or Ascension Day'. Some singers may have resented the innovation, for only two remained: Taylor and Craddock, still paid 10s. apiece. In October 1854 Taylor replaced Craddock, who by then must have been at least 84, as clerk and leader of the singers. In 1857 he took over as harmonium player, but in the following year gave way to a Mr Shilvock. A new organ appeared in the nave in 1884 and moved to the west gallery in 1926, thus completing the cycle.

Frankley avoided the barrel organ stage, but at Bayton such an instrument was used both for services and dances. One Sunday morning the parish clerk forgot to change the barrel, and instead of the hymn announced by the parson, 'Let us sing in praise and glory of God', he cranked out 'The Keel Row'.

Personal recollections of west gallery music are rare. John Noake commented in 1851 on 'the orchestral performances' at Bishampton Church:

> The lad who presides at the flute would not be an inefficient musician if his fertile imagination were somewhat checked, and he were content with the ungarnished melody set before him; and with regard to the selection of tunes, I would recommend all choirs whatsoever to reject those nondescript, half-ball, half-latter-day-saint compositions which are so constructed as to render it necessary to divide one line in every verse into two parts. One of this class was sung at Bishampton on the day of my visit there ...

Noake went on to give an example: with repetitions, the line, 'Stir up this stupid heart of mine', became, 'Stir up this stu-, stir up this stu-, stir up this stupid heart of mine'. Another which I have heard myself is: 'I want a man-, I want a man-, I want a mansion in the sky'.

Rev. J.E.Vaux wrote in 1894:

> In my own youthful days it was a very common thing to have in village churches a band of rustics with fiddles to accompany the singing of Tate and Brady's Metrical Psalms. This was in the Midlands, where, if I mistake not, things ecclesiastical were often at a very low ebb. The men played, of course, with far more vigour than taste; a noise rather than melody seemed to be the thing aimed at. A clergyman has told me that when he went to Castle Morton, near Tewkesbury, the west gallery was occupied by a bass viol and three violins. I merely mention this to show that what I have heard called a 'Nebuchadnezzar band' in church was continued almost to our own time, and there are probably such things still in use. Barrel organs with, of course, an exceedingly limited selection of tunes, were, within living memory, by no means uncommon. A lady friend tells me ... the handle... was always turned very rapidly, but the music produced was slower than *legato*, and the singing was drawling to a ludicrous degree.

A photograph published in 1910 which shows the then late Mr White,
'the oldest Tradesman in Upton-on-Severn, member of the Church Choir
for 57 years'. He would have sung in both the old and new churches

The gallery built for players and singers in Castlemorton Church in 1724 was removed in 1879. In the same year the old church at Upton-on-Severn saw services transferred to the new building. Rev. E.A. Benson (1829-96) had memories which were reported by A.C. Bradley:

> The late Archbishop Benson has some entertaining recollections of this now abandoned church in his youth. The vocal music was absolutely a one-man performance, in the person of an autocratic clerk, a shoemaker, who wore a wig and large horn spectacles, a black suit and a white tie. The orchestra — flute, clarionet, violin and 'cello — were in gallery, and to their strains the clerk sang a strenuous but untuneful solo, not a soul in the church venturing to accept his invitation and sing 'in the praise and glory of God' either psalm or hymn.

Normally, west gallery music implied raw vigour of singing and bold harmonies. Over a century after its demise, the style was revived in Worcestershire in 1992 by John Williams and friends in Malvern who founded Vital Spark. The group of instrumentalists and singers performs in village halls and churches, especially those where a west gallery can still be used. They have issued recordings on compact disc, and their website is an example of modern technology used to further the music of yesteryear.

Object lessons

Green man from All Saints' Church, Evesham

Within churches are many items which express popular beliefs or have given rise to them. A favourite motif is the foliate head or green man, which some say symbolises sadness and sacrifice, death and ruin; others life and renewal, a potent force erupting from the collective subconscious. (The Green Man of inn signs is probably the Jack-in-the-Green of a spring ritual which dates back only to the eighteenth century). 'Most often', wrote Tina Negus in 2003, 'the Green Man has been connected with the concepts of rebirth, renewal, and regeneration. ... He has also been considered an archetype of the unity of humanity with the natural world. As such he has been adopted by the ecolog-

Green man from Worcester Cathedral cloisters

ical movement and become a powerful symbol of our times'.

There are examples of foliate heads carved in several Worcestershire churches. Palpably human heads with vegetation issuing from the mouth can be seen at Bredon on a coffin lid in the Milton Chapel; at Evesham All Saints' on wooden roof bosses in the north chapel; at Pershore Abbey in the bosses of the choir vaulting; and at Worcester Cathedral on bosses in the nave, in the south aisle, in the cloisters opposite the Chapter House door, and also on a misericord (see below). A similar profusion occurs at St Martin's,

Green man and dragon side by side on capitals by the south door at Holt Church

Holt, on a capital of the south door, on the twelfth-century font with its six grotesque heads, and on the nineteenth-century neo-Norman pulpit. The church at Rock has a green man on the capital of a column supporting the chancel arch, as well as a wide range of other extravagant carvings.

Cat heads replace those of humans, though still with foliage issuing, in carvings at Rous Lench on the eastern jamb of the niche with Christ in majesty over the south door, and in the remarkable lecterns, originally from Evesham Abbey, at Crowle and Norton (near Evesham). The former also shows St Egwin (see illustration on page 169).

Cat-headed figures on the pulpit (originally from Evesham Abbey) at Norton Church

Grotesque heads on the corbel table at Astley Church

A head on the church porch at Inkberrow

Fierce, caricatural heads apparently guard church exteriors at Astley, Holt, Inkberrow and elsewhere. Dragons, perhaps personifying evil, abound outside churches as well as inside, on fonts and furniture. Such motifs may seem strange enough in Norman buildings but it is even more surprising to find twin dragons or serpents on the clerk's desk which bears the date of 1635 at Stoke Bliss, near Tenbury. Other dragons look down from the nave roof at Eckington and appear on the font at Elmley Castle.

A thirteenth-century window at Kempley depicts the struggle between St Margaret and a dragon. St Margaret of Antioch's story was declared apocryphal by the pope as early as 494 but her cult flourished during the crusades, and at one stage over 200 ancient English churches were dedicated to her. At Bretforton the sculpture which curves round a pillar shows her swallowed by a dragon with a tiny human-like head at the end of its tail. She clings to her staff which with its cross has split open the dragon's body and allowed her head and neck to stick out, while her feet protrude from its mouth. Just above her head

Twin dragons on the clerk's desk at Stoke Bliss.
The words are: Roger Osland Churchwarden 1635

Dragons on the font at Elmley Castle

the cuff of a sleeve can just be made out, with the hand of God which has wrought the miracle of her deliverance.

Rather more amiable creatures on the tympanum over the south door at Beckford have been interpreted as the animal creation adoring the Trinity (represented by an eye), and alternatively as Celtic sacred beasts paying homage to the new religion represented by the cross. The carving in a similar position over the main entrance at Ribbesford has given rise to even more extensive speculation. Here, deer and salmon are shown together with an archer in the Norman tympanum admired by John Rushkin. The local explanation is that John Horshill, Lord of the Manor in the twelfth century, saw a hind coming

St Margaret and dragon at Bretforton

The tympanum at Beckford

down to drink on the opposite side of the Severn. He shot an arrow and killed not only the hind but a salmon which happened to leap at the critical moment. Sceptics say the carving simply showed the characteristic game of the area. Another—no doubt fanciful—theory is that it portrays Sigurd the Volsung, a hero of Teutonic mythology and Wagner's *Ring*.

Cuthbert Bede aired a 'more poetical version of the legend'. A poor but handsome hunter falls in love with a great lord's daughter. The pair meet in secret. The girl loses a prized ring with healing properties, and her father

The tympanum at Ribbesford

96

announces that the man who finds the ring will have his daughter's hand. The hunter shoots a leaping salmon, and presents it to the lord. When the fish is cut open the lost ring comes to light. The lovers marry. However, John Noakes dismissed the story as the recent 'invention of a local author', George Griffith.

Other powerful and evocative images are found in wood on misericords, of which Worcester Cathedral has a set of 37, dating from 1379. These were wooden brackets fixed to the underside of choirstall seats so as to give support to singers standing through the long services. Carvings in such a lowly position seem to have been left to the fantasy of craftsmen, so we find not only Biblical scenes but fabulous beasts, traditional sports, rough humour and vignettes from everyday life.

At Worcester the misericords show an old man stirring a pot, a flute player, an angel with a viol, a knight holding a dagger, a butcher slaughtering an ox, a circumcision, the presentation of Samuel, a woman writing, a sower, knights tilting, an angel playing a lute, a huntsman blowing a horn, a knight fighting two griffins, three reapers, three ploughmen, three mowers, Abraham and Isaac, the temptation of Eve, the expulsion from Paradise, Moses bringing the commandments, the judgement of Solomon, Samson and the lion, a man knocking down acorns, a lion and a dragon fighting, a knight hawking, a monster, a sphinx, a cockatrice, a naked woman riding on a goat, Adam delving and Eve spinning, a stag under a tree, and a dragon.

The misericords at Little Malvern Priory were hacked away during the Civil War, possibly by Parliamentary troops. A few handrests remain, one showing pigs with their heads in a trough, others grotesque human faces—perhaps caricatures of the monks who commissioned or the craftsmen who carved them. The priory church at Great Malvern (bought for the parish in the sixteenth century) fared better, and a score of misericords dating from 1480 survive

Harvesters on a misericord at Worcester Cathedral

Cockatrice or basilisk misericord at Malvern. The cockatrice was a mythical beast, part cockerel, part serpent, whose glance was fatal unless it could be confronted with its own reflection in a crystal

there. One series depicting the seasonal round of daily life includes such activities as weeding (April), mowing (June) and knocking down acorns to feed swine (October). Among domestic scenes, a man removes his wife's dirty boots while she belabours him with a distaff (February). There are mythical beings (mermaid and man, cockatrice and wyvern), and moral or satirical vignettes (three rats hang a cat, symbolising the world turned upside down; the figure applying a bellows to the posterior of a naked man has been interpreted as a woman driving away a demon or a monk expelling a devil from a man). Of

Naked man with bellows applied to the rear, at Malvern

98

The month of June: hawking, Ripple

three misericords added in the Victorian era, one shows a witch and broom-stick, with the flames of hell licking at her back, a motif too good to miss, even then. A further sequence at Ripple, dating from the late fourteenth or early fifteenth century, again portrays the monthly round, including Rogationtide (see below).

Funerary monuments have given rise to unofficial commentaries of various kinds. Ornate tombs, often adorned with life-like effigies of the dead, attracted a great deal of attention and exercised the popular imagination.

By far the most eminent of those buried in Worcester Cathedral was King John, who died in 1216 of a famous surfeit of lampreys. The original lid of his tomb, still in place, shows miniature representations, one on either side of him, of saints Oswald and Wulstan, just as he was buried between them in the hope that their sanctity would suffice for him, too. (Until the eighteenth century there was a solemn procession, every year on 19 January, the anniversary of Wulstan's death, to the tombs of the two saints, the whereabouts of which is now lost.) According to a popular belief, John made a further attempt to avoid recognition on the Day of Judgement and subsequent punishment for his crimes by having his body covered with the cowl and habit of a monk. However, kings, as the Lord's anointed, had the immemorial right to be buried in ecclesiastical garb. This was certainly the case with John, as the opening of his tomb revealed in 1797. Rather bizarrely, a workman appropriated one of John's thumbs on that occasion; the digit was later lost, though a plaster cast has been preserved in the cathedral library. It is possible that the discovery of John's religious robes in 1797 led to the traditional view of his motives.

The Little Crusader, Tenbury

Incised cross on door jamb at Defford Church

During the crusades, of which there were seven between 1095 and 1269, when knights died in the Holy Land their hearts were sometimes brought back for burial at home. The little crusader at St. Mary's, Tenbury Wells, is a miniature cross-legged knight of the late thirteenth century. The figure holds a heart. The small size of the effigy caused people to speculate that this was a child who had taken part in the children's crusade (of 1212) or gone with his father on a different expedition.

One of the arched tombs in the south wall of the Mitton Chapel at Bredon shows a shield with two arms holding a heart. According to local tradition, the heart of a knight killed during the crusades was indeed brought back for burial there. Another crusader, Sir John Atwode, is remembered at Wolverley (see chapter 1). The cross carved in the stone jamb of the church door at Defford is said to have been cut by a crusader as he left. On his safe return, he would have cut another on the opposite side.

The church of St Kenelm at Clifton-on-Teme has the effigy of a crosslegged knight of the fourteenth century, supposedly Sir Ralph Wysham. The conventional dog at his feet gave rise to the tale that as Sir Ralph was walking from Woodmanton to Clifton he fell dead under a yew tree where he was found lying with his legs crossed and the faithful animal at his feet.

The striking effigy of a knight in armour of the late fourteenth century at Alvechurch may represent Sir John Blanchfront. It has nevertheless given rise to the story of a nameless champion slain by an evil lord of Lickey who devastated the village, together with the palace of the bishops of Worcester (which existed there until 1780). Nash, who supports the identification of the effigy with Sir John Blanchfront, adds:

> Tradition assigns this monument to an unknown person, whom the inhabitants stile *the Knight of the Green*; who dwelt, they say, some ages since on Wetherock Hill. ... They affirm also that he made a causey at his own expence from thence to Alvechurch town, the ruins of which indeed are still visible.

In the north aisle of St John the Baptist's Church at Bromsgrove stands a fine alabaster monument to Sir Humphrey Stafford of Grafton Manor and his wife, Eleanor (though her name is incorrectly inscribed as Elizabeth). The story once circulated that Stafford, in about 1430, killed the extraordinary wild boar which was terrorising the neighbourhood from its den in an enchanted castle. In so doing, he released from a spell and from imprisonment the lady who became his wife. Alternatively he gained her hand because it had been promised to the man who rid Bromsgrove of the fierce wild boars which infested the woods round about.

Sir John Blanchfront at Alvechurch

The Staffords, of whom at least three generations lived at Grafton, had a boar in their crest, and it is possible that this gave rise to the stories (rather than the reverse). Sir Humphrey was killed at Sevenoaks in 1450 while fighting against the Kentish rebels led by Jack Cade. A ballad on the subject of his epic struggle with the boar circulated from the early seventeenth century until the early twentieth, on both sides of the Atlantic, with Sir Humphrey's name appearing as Egraball, Lionel, Rylas, Isaac-a-Bell, Abram Bailey, Branygwell, Old Bang 'em and Dilly-dove. The Worcestershire antiquarian, Jabez Allies (1789-1856), recalled hearing it in his 'juvenile days' from a carpenter called John Cole who in turn had heard it from an old man some 50 years earlier. However, Allies obtained a full version from Benjamin Brown of Upper Wick, who had learned it from 'a countryman' in about 1810.

The Jovial Hunter of Bromsgrove

Sir Robert Bolton had three sons—
Wind well thy horn, good hunter;
And one of them was called Sir Ryalas,
For he was a jovial hunter.

He rang'd all round, down by the wood side,
Till up in the top of a tree a gay lady he spy'd.

'Oh! what does thou mean, fair lady?' said he.
'Oh! the wild boar has killed my lord and his men thirty,
As thou be'st a jovial hunter'.

'Oh! what shall I do this wild boar to see?'
'Oh! thee blow a blast and he'll come unto thee,
As thou be'st a jovial hunter'.

Then he blow'd a blast full north, east, west and south,
For he was a jovial hunter;
And the wild boar heard him full into his den,
As he was a jovial hunter.

Then he made the best of his speed unto him,
Wind went his horn as a hunter;
And he whetted his tusks as he came along
To Sir Ryalas the jovial hunter.

Then the wild boar being so stout and strong
He thrash'd down the trees as he came along
To Sir Ryalas the jovial hunter.

'Oh! what dost thou want of me?' the wild boar, said he.
'Oh! I think in my heart I can do enough for thee,
For I am the jovial hunter'.

Then they fought four hours in a long summer's day,
Till the wild boar fain would have gotten away
From Sir Ryalas the jovial hunter.

Then Sir Ryalas draw'd his broad sword with might,
And he fairly cut his head off quite.

Then out of the wood the wild woman flew:
'Oh! thou hast killed my pretty spotted pig,
As thou be'st a jovial hunter'.

'There are three things I do demand of thee,
It's thy horn and thy hound and thy gay lady,
As thou be'st a jovial hunter'.

'If these three things thou dost demand of me,
It's just as my sword and thy neck can agree'.

Then into his locks the wild woman flew
Till she thought in her heart she had torn him
                                        through,
As he was a jovial hunter.

Then Sir Ryalas draw'd his broad sword again,
And he fairly split her head in twain.

In Bromsgrove Church they both do lie;
There the wild boar's head is pictur'd by
Sir Ryalas the jovial hunter.

*Memorial in Tardebigge
Church to Sir Thomas and
Lady Mary Cookes*

As late as the sixteenth century the funereal effigies of a gentleman who died on the battlefield would include the warlike symbol of a lion. In Astley Church, Walter Blount, who died in war in 1561, has a lion at his feet; Robert Blount, who died peacefully at home in 1575, has to make do with a dog. Women, too, were sometimes accorded a dog, though not the Blounts.

The church at Tardebigge contains a monument showing Lady Mary Cookes, who died in 1693, embracing her husband, Sir Thomas. She is shown with one breast bare, and this gave rise to the tradition that Sir Thomas was kept from starving in prison by his wife's milk. The red dagger shown in the family crest is explained as a symbol that he once killed his butler in a drunken rage. However, the stories seem to be entirely fanciful.

*Tombs in Astley Church of Walter Blount, with lion at his feet,
and Robert Blount (in background), with dog*

A plaque at St John's Church, Hagley, records the death in 1779 of Thomas, the second Lord Lyttleton, at the age of 35. The wicked Lord Lyttleton, as he was called, dreamed that a bird flew into his room, then changed into a white-robed woman and said: 'Prepare to die'. 'Not soon, I hope', he replied. 'Yes, in three days'. On the third day Lyttleton felt very well and promised that he would 'bilk the ghost' but as he was going to bed he 'put his hand to his side, sank back, and expired without a groan'. A friend, Miles Peter Andrews, said that Lyttleton appeared to him and said 'All is over' at what he later found to be the precise time of his death.

Parsons

'Your parsons are the happiest men alive', wrote the eighteenth-century poet, Robert Lloyd. Many must have been so, judging by the long periods they remained in place. In Worcestershire Rev. Hubert Parker officiated at Great Comberton for 57 years (1826-83), and Rev. Charles Dickins at Tardebigge for 62 (1855-1918). Both are outdone by Rev. H.M. Sherwood, who retired from duty at White Ladies Aston at the age of 96 after serving for 71 years of the nineteenth century. Inevitably, though, the ranks of the clergy included oddities and eccentrics, rogues and victims.

John Dee (1527-1608), imprisoned for attempting to cast spells on Queen Mary, and rehabilitated by Queen Elizabeth, to whom he gave lessons in astrology, was rector of Upton-in-Severn in 1553, though he may never have gone there. Edward Pearce, a clerk in holy orders at Inkberrow, was accused of being a 'common barrator [one who buys or sells ecclesiastical preferment], calumniator, curser, and stirrer up of strife'. He associated with publicans and sinners, went bat fowling in November 1603, and at Christmas played a game called 'fox, mine host', drank beers mulled with apples and herbs, and behaved to an alehouse landlady 'not quite like a clergyman'. Francis Rogers, curate of Dowles (near Bewdley), not only solemnised a marriage improperly, but in 1613 'rod uppon a bull at Areley [Kings] wake *contra decus et dignitatem clericalem*'.

In 1628 Rev. Henry Hunt in his twenty-ninth and last year as curate at Defford stood charged with being a 'malicious and contentious person' who used scandalous language 'without regard to time and place', and in church broke 'into violent swearing before quitting the pulpit'. He also threw stones on occasion at villagers and said one of them was a devil. Defford seems to have been unlucky in its ministers. The incumbent in 1687, 'a man of ill exemplary life', was 'much given to swearing and often debauched with much drinking'; and in 1708 Robert Griffiths, the curate, was 'several times drunk in a common ale house at an unseasonable time of night'.

Parishioners at Berrow protested in 1690 that their priest had 'not been in our church this seven weeks', with the result that 'We had a corpse lie in our church all night and have been forced to have a minister out of another county'.

The Crowle churchwardens complained in 1706 that Rev. John Matthew had neglected to read prayers on Ash Wednesday, Good Friday, Easter Monday and Tuesday, and Ascension Day. In addition, he had failed to beat the bounds. However, at the end of the same century the people of Tardebigge do not seem to have objected to the behaviour of Parson Richards (as he was universally known), the curate who for several decades ran the parish during the absence of a series of well-to-do but non-resident vicars. Richards, a keen sportsman and small farmer, would retire during the pre-sermon psalm to the vestry, and thence to fortify himself with a drink before preaching at the Magpie Inn, hard by the church, the site of which is now occupied by the village school. If only a small congregation turned up, he would say to the clerk, his brother-in-law: 'What, only these few? I shan't have a service for them. Take them into the public and give them a glass of beer apiece'.

Treadway Russell Nash, engraving by James Caldwell after a painting by S. Gardener

The levying of tithes often caused bad feeling between incumbent and parishioners. Collection in kind went on all the year round, but compounded tithes were traditionally paid on Ladyday (25 March) or settled after harvest, at the end of the farming year. The historian of Worcestershire, Rev. Treadway Nash (1725-1811), had a reputation for parsimony which inspired the rhyme:

> The muse thy genius well divines,
> And will not ask for cash,
> But gratis round thy brow she twines
> The laurel, Dr Nash.

At the same time he was very careful to collect what was due to him. After he became vicar at Leigh in 1792 he would drive there in a carriage and four from his house at Bevere, attended by servants. Each year shortly before the tithe audit fell due he preached a sermon on the text of 'Owe no man anything'. He died leaving £60,000 and estates at Droitwich, Kempley and Strensham.

At Oddingley near Droitwich the parson was the victim of a murder planned at the Speed the Plough public house in neighbouring Tibberton. The Rev. George Parker, a native of Cumberland, was presented to the living in 1793. His predecessors had agreed to accept £135 a year from each farmer in lieu of

*The Speed the Plough inn where the murder of the Rev. George Parker
was planned*

tithes; Parker wished to raise the sum to £150. Captain Samuel Evans of
Church Farm, which adjoins the churchyard on the north side, refused to pay,
and persuaded other farmers to follow suit. Parker then reverted to taking tithes
in kind, and after a few years the farmers, finding themselves worse off under
this arrangement, agreed to accept the earlier proposal. However, Parker then
asked for a collective payment of a further £150 to defray the expense he had
incurred in erecting a tithe barn. The farmers declined. Collections in kind
continued, accompanied by ill-feeling and punctuated by litigation.

On Midsummer Day in 1806 Parker was shot, then bludgeoned to death
with the butt of a gun. Immediately afterwards a Droitwich carpenter called
Richard Heming disappeared. The rumour circulated that he had committed the
murder, then escaped to America.

Not until 1830 was there any more news on the affair. In that year a barn at
Netherwood Farm by the road to Crowle was being demolished when the
remains of a body were found buried inside, together with a carpenter's rule
and other objects. Heming's wife identified the remains as those of her
husband. The inquest elicited a dramatic story from Thomas Clewes. Despite
being a magistrate Captain Evans together with three other farmers—Clewes
himself, George Banks and John Barnett—had instigated the murder of Parker
by Heming. Evans had then arranged for a Droitwich farrier called Joseph
Taylor to beat Heming to death in Clewes' barn and to bury his body there.

Taylor had died a few years after the murder, and Evans in 1829 (his family
vault is at St Peter's, Droitwich). The inquest jury brought in a verdict of wilful

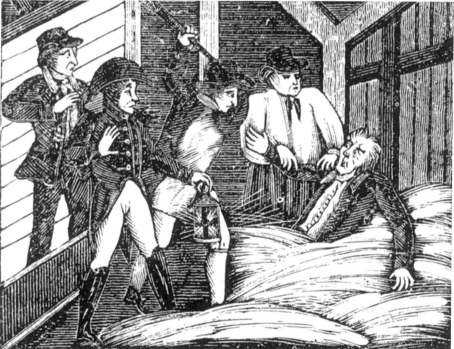

Contemporary illustrations of the murders of Parker and Heming
that accompanied ballad sheets printed in Birmingham

Broughton Hackett Church

murder in both cases against Clewes and Banks, and found Barnett an accessory before the fact. The three men were tried at Worcester but acquitted. The case was thrown out because the law at the time did not allow accomplices to be tried for murder after the death of the principal accused. To the fury of the new rector at Oddingley the news of the farmers' acquittal was greeted by the ringing of his own church bells. The new barn built at Netherwood Farm bore a stone with the discreet inscription '1806–1830'.

Even more scandalous stories, albeit lacking documentation, concern Broughton Hackett to the east of Worcester. A priest at St Leonard's Church there in the time of Queen Anne is said to have been tried, convicted and executed for baking his shepherd's boy in an oven. His motive has not been recorded.

Registers from the same church have pages missing; they were allegedly destroyed in an attempt to cover up a scandal. Apparently another cleric was having an affair with a farmer's wife. Together they murdered the man and buried his body beneath the parsonage stairs. Now the farmer had a brother who closely resembled him but had not been seen for many years. Having at last decided on a visit the brother arrived during a service and walked into the church. The parson, thinking the dead man had returned to haunt him, fell down in a faint. The story emerged and a savage punishment was inflicted. The parson was shut in a cage and suspended from a big oak tree near Churchill Mill, with food and water in sight but out of reach, and was left to starve to death.

In the seventeenth century, John Somers (whose son was to become William III's Lord Chancellor) fired a shot at Rev. Wybrough as he preached in the pulpit at Severn Stoke. Fortunately, he missed. His motive derived from religious fanaticism, on which a rhyme commented:

His satanical zeal at Stoke it was such
That he shot at the parson; you'll think it too much,
But he loved the Old Cause as his son loves the Dutch.

At the same period, Bishop John Prideaux, ejected from his cathedral at Worcester during the Civil War, was taken in at Bredon by his daughter, the wife of the rector. The bishop's income of 4s. 6d. a week proved insufficient for his needs; first he ate his furniture, then his books, and then even his boots. He remarked one day that he was turning into an ostrich (which are reputed to eat iron): he was on his way to sell some old iron to the blacksmith to raise a further small sum of money. He died in poverty in 1650. Perhaps his daughter and son-in-law, Henry Sutton, were

Bishop Prideaux

poor too: they had fifteen children, which rather gives the lie to Sutton's claim that he went blind after 40 years 'of almost uninterrupted reading'.

Another learned clergyman was William Tindal, rector of Worcestershire's Kington in 1792, later fellow of the Society of Antiquaries and chaplain of the

Bredon Rectory with the River Avon in the foreground

Tower of London. His history of Evesham won the praise of the twentieth-century novelist, Hugh Walpole, himself the son of an Anglican clergyman. As for Tindal, he shot himself at the Tower in 1804 during a fit of depression. Clearly, he lacked the serenity of his colleague from neighbouring Rous Lench, the splendidly-named Rev. Stanwix Whittingdale. When Whittingdale died in 1772 he left instructions that he should be buried immediately in front of the south door of the church, so that all who entered should tread over him. 'Popular rumour less gracefully says', wrote W.K.W. Chafy, 'that he gave out that he had been trampled upon in his life, and might as well be trampled upon in his death'. Whittingdale's successor, Rev. Charles Fortescue from Flyford Flavel, 'with a taste in cider and "most alarmin' fat"', was of a different stamp again.

Custom and Practice

Outside the church at Ashton-under-Hill is a fifteenth-century 'weeping cross', where erring parishioners were obliged to do penance for their sins. The punitive ritual continued in Worcestershire until perhaps the early nineteenth century. Examples include that of Joan Millard of Areley Kings, accused in 1633 of 'diverse scandal, opprobrious and diffamousious words against Mistriss Elizabeth Burrastone', and obliged to confess her offence and ask forgiveness in the presence of the church parson, Humfrey Walker, before doing penance. The precise form of words used on such occasions is preserved in a document in Ipsley Church, dating from 1664. Its use of the feminine gender underlines the system's bias against women:

> The said (penitent) shall come into the church aforesaid at the hearing of the first lesson at Morning Prayer arrayed in a white sheet over her wearing apparel, holding a candle ... and ... a white rod of an ell long in her hand and shall be placed in some eminent place near the minister's reading desk where she shall continue the time of Divine Service and Sermon and after the reading of the second lesson she shall make her humble confession unto Almighty God saying after the Minister as followeth ...

Then came the form of words to be used.

There is evidence that some women became restive at such humiliation. Ann Bach of Holt was in trouble in 1684 not merely for having a bastard child but 'for standing in a white sheet in our parish church rather in derision than like a penitent when she was publicly admonished by our minister'. Elizabeth Collins of Leigh, when she was charged in 1701 with 'antenuptial fornication'—having sex before marriage, as we should now say—'acted with as much confidence as though it had been as great a virtue as 'tis really a vice'. In 1728 Elizabeth Pudge of Hanbury was blamed not only for 'publishing and solemnly and frequently declaring that she hath been guilty of adultery with several persons' but for defiantly 'using much scandalous and opprobrious language' in the church court.

Nevertheless, the procedure continued. In 1766 (on 18 December) the *Worcester Journal* reported the rare instance of a man having to do penance:

> A few Sundays ago Mr M., of a certain parish not a thousand miles from Pershore, was married to Miss R., of the same parish, an agreeable young lady with a handsome fortune. That same morning Mr M., for a certain familiar transaction with his housekeeper, did penance in the same parish church in a white robe, immediately after which the ceremony of marriage between him and Miss R. commenced, she, with her own father, who gave her away, waiting in church while the penance was performing.

John Noake, writing in 1851 of an event 'some fifty or sixty years ago' at Elmley Lovett, described 'the penitential discipline' imposed by the church on a young woman who had given birth to an illegitimate child:

> The fair delinquent should, on a given Sunday, envelope [sic] herself in a sheet and proceed up the aisle to the seat where sat her seducer, so that he should be publicly put to shame as well as herself ... The penance was accordingly performed, but the disgrace was not publicly shared by the young man, some officious friend of his having given him such information as led him quickly to retrace his steps when within but a few yards of the church.

Noake adds a happy ending (as he saw it): 'The poor girl afterwards became a zealous Methodist, at Upton, and has not been dead many years'.

Penance could be ordered at any time but other practices recurred at particular points in the year. On the Sunday nearest to 6 January ploughs were taken to churches to be blessed: hence, Plough Sunday. On Candlemas Day (2 February) at Tenbury figures of the Virgin Mary were removed from the church and snowdrops scattered over the empty spaces. Rings of the flowers—alternatively known as Christ's flowers, Candlemas Bells or Fair Maids of February—were grown in the churchyard for the purpose. It was thought unlucky to pick them for any other reason.

Each February until 1986 the Nanfan Sermon was preached in Berrow Church. It originated, according to W.S. Symonds, in the time of Charles II when Sir Giles Nanfan of Birtsmorton Court killed the lover of his sister, Bridget, in a duel which took place in a field at Berrow thereafter called the Bloody Meadow. The grieving Bridget in due course bequeathed the field to the poor of the village, together with money to fund an annual sermon on the evils of duelling. Symonds claimed to have found the entry relating to the lover's burial at Berrow in a volume of the church registers which was afterwards lost. In fact the first Nanfan Sermon, endowed by Sir John Nanfan, seems to have been preached in 1745, but perhaps this merely renewed an earlier tradition, so Symonds could have been right after all.

Easter is a variable feast, falling between 21 March and 25 April, depending—curiously for a religious institution—on the first full moon after the vernal equinox. Women were expected to wear a new hat in church, or even a new outfit. Eggs, now usually of chocolate, have been associated with Easter for centuries, as a symbol of new life. Some suggest that real eggs were once donated to churches at Easter.

Forty days after Easter comes Ascension Day, and this is preceded by the four days—Sunday to Wednesday—of Rogationtide. From the eighth century onwards blessings were asked at Rogationtide (the Latin *rogare*, means to ask) on the coming corn harvest, and the beating of bounds—otherwise called processioning or bannering—took place. The parson would lead his parishioners round their boundaries, taking up his station to read from the Bible by strategic trees which came to be called Gospel Oaks. Sometimes the processions carried branches of trees which were stuck in the ground and occasionally took root. Other landmarks were stones (called liberty, or mere-stones), wells, and even public houses: the ancient Virgin Tavern in Tolladine Road at Worcester was a marker for Claines and St Martin's parishes.

Boys were beaten, bumped or ducked, or given buns or pennies for which to scramble, all to impress the boundaries on their minds so that they could testify to them for the rest of their lives if the need arose. For adults, eating and drinking were important parts of the proceedings, as we know from many records which have survived.

Rogationtide, from a misericord in Worcester Cathedral.
Similar scenes are shown on misericords both at Ripple and Great Malvern

The earliest recorded perambulation of Worcester city's boundaries took place in 1498. An early account from Eckington mentions a clergyman in post from before 1552 until 1578:

> yᵉ vickar of Eckinton called Sʳ James Colwall did in yᵉ company of most of his parishoners use in yᵉ Rogation week to goe yᵉ perambulation of yᵉ Parish of Eckinton and in yᵉ same did goe yᵉ Hamlet villadge and filed of wolashill [Woolas Hall] ... and did use to say a gospel at one Thomas Taylors gate ... and there commonly they had a drincking ...

We read that at Bromsgrove in 1573 the bellman was expected to 'waite on the Vicker or Curate in the Rogashun weeke to goe about ye Borders of ye Parish'.

Some reports in the following century feature bound beating as a thing of the past. In 1645 two octogenarians recalled how they had once taken part in the 'procession or perambulation, which, starting from the north door of the chapel [at Bordesley], went round the parish from gospel place to gospel place, so called because at each the gospel for the day was read'. On the other hand, one of the Worcester parishes seems to have been active enough:

> Holy Thursday, may 5, 1692, the minister, churchwardens and p'ish-ioners of ye p'ish of St Nicholas did goe ye perambulacon, and did remarke ye p'ticular places and bounds of ye said p'ish, viz., from the church to Mr Stirrop's parlour window in Angel Lane, over against a stone in Mr Savage's wall, from thence back again round by the Cross to Mrs Powell's house, widd., now inhabited by Nichs. Nash, mercer, at the hithermost part of the shop where the ground-sill of the house will show an old passage or dove case, at which place there was formerly an entry, and the p'ishioners in ye yeares '61 2 3 and 4 did passe throwe ye said entry, at which time one Mrs Cooksey lived there, to Mr Huntbache's, farther parte of ye house, then to that parte of ye house next the Crosse, being the backe parts of the White Harte, then down to the Trinity to a marke in the wall neare ye old goale, from thence throwe to Mr Blurton's garden, then to the joynt in Mr Blurton's malthouse, then up Sansome Field from that joynt, and soe throw to ye liberty post, then downe ye Salt Lane to the stile at St Marten's workhouse and soe back to the church.

At Rogationtide in 1732, after lunch in the Virgin Tavern (formerly in Newtown Road) the parishioners of Claines covered some ten miles: 'From Sandy Way, Martin Hussingtree, across to Warndon, from thence to St Martin's Gate [Worcester], on to Whiston, proceeding to the Severn opposite Hallow, up the middle of the river and continuing up the Salwarpe to Parker's Mill and linking up with Martin Hussingtree again'. In the same year, over two days at

Ascensiontide, Rev. Beresford Baker and his flock visited all Inkberrow's gospel places and boundaries, including Radford Bridge, Bag End Bower, Hollow Oak, Bank Lane Stone, the cross below Rush (now called Stud Farm), Mill Hopper, Brandard Brook, Red Field Cross, Hempstal Division, Astwood Division, Solomon's Bank, New Inn, Weegley Rush, Nunnery Wood, Thomas Burston's house and 'yᵉ end of yᵉ Kitchen Table at Thorn'. Back in Worcester, St Clement's recorded the expenditure in 1737 of 33s. 8d. at processioning, for cakes and ale (9s. 4d.), half a lamb (2s. 6d.), bacon and a leg of veal (4s. 3d.), 'pigg' (3s. 6d.), 32 quarts of ale (8s.), bread, greens and dressing dinner (5d.), cider (3d.) and 'carrying the bush' (1s.). St John's Church in 1818 spent £10 in three days of which 3d. was for 'putting up gospel bushes' and the rest for brandy, tobacco, pipes and 'a heavy wet'—a drinking session.

At Kidderminster, where the custom was called bannering, there were often fights between the men of adjoining parishes when they happened to meet on their rounds. One procession at least—in 1818—was peaceful. The town crier led the way, followed by 'javelin men' and a 'band of music'. Then came church dignitaries, followed by the people. The walk covered several miles, taking in Stourport, Wribbenhall, Trimpley, Shatterford and Wolverley. The party halted eleven times to hear readings from the gospel. A bough planting ceremony was carried out at the centre of the bridges at Mitton, Stourport and Bewdley; refreshments were taken at the Black Boy in Wribbenhall and two other places. The notables took dinner at the Lion at the end of the journey.

Dinner at the Swan was one of the attractions of the Chaddesley Corbett bound beating, held—unusually—over two days ending on Oak Apple Day (29 May). In 1827 Charles Throckmorton, lord of the manor, led the procession with Rev. Thomas Harwood. After that year instead of being held annually the event took place only once in each generation, and by 1891 it had lapsed. However, a revival in 1929 was photographed for Berrow's *Worcester Journal*.

Beating the Bounds at Chaddesley Corbett in May 1929

On 27 May 1854 the *Worcester Herald* carried this remarkable item, which is worth quoting at some length:

The ancient custom of 'processioning', or 'beating the bounds', on Ascension Day, it seems, has not yet become a dead letter in this city. The parishes of All Saints and St Clement are among the most determined upholders of antiquity in this respect; and although it is but seldom that either parish rejoices in these 'free-and-easy' carnivals, there are, nevertheless, a few jovial spirits left in each, who occasionally become so overcharged with a desire for practical fun and adventure that 'go they must', and straightway the venerable custom of 'beating the bounds' is as good an excuse as any other for indulging their appetite. The practice, we believe, has not been observed in the parish of All Saints for ten years past, till Thursday last, when it came off with all the *éclat* and superabundance of relish which had been accumulating during the interval of a decade of years.

The steeple [tower] being, of course, the rallying point, the party met in the morning in the vestry-room, from whence sallied the Rev. Dr Bartlett, the curate, Messrs H. Davis and E. Clarke, churchwardens, Messrs Hill and William Hole, overseers [of the board of guardians responsible for poor relief], and a party of about twenty parishioners, accompanied by a shoal of larkish striplings — a body which considerably augmented during the line of the route — *vires acquirit eundo* [gaining strength as it went]. Down Quay Street they went and down the steps towards a boat, but not without misgivings did the party cast their eyes aloft to the rough-and-ready customers assembled on the bridge, under the centre arch of which the 'processioners' were doomed to go. Two policemen had been impressed into the boat for purposes of defence, but what is a policeman more than any other mortal under the combined influences of a cataract of mud and water? And what avails a staff, sword, or dagger, when the enemy grins upon you from a perpendicular height of some twenty or thirty feet? Accordingly the party went through the ordeal with all the calm courage of victims whose only consolation is, that when custom sanctions, neither law nor personal comfort is accounted of the slightest consequence. On the whole they escaped as well as could have been expected, having encountered only a little water, mud, and a few et ceteras.

Thence they proceeded, and cast anchor in Dolday Bay, and after landing there, our informant assures us, 'the game was tremendous'. Six or seven shillings' worth of buns were scattered about to produce some scrambling among the boys, and the consequences, as might be supposed, were a considerable exhibition of juvenile activity ... Dolday and the Butts were passed, and the interior of eight or ten houses inspected, the wall of the Independent Chapel, Angel Street, scaled, and the Crown yard reached, when another drenching shower slightly damped the ardour of the borderers; but, like Cromwell's Invincibles, armed to the teeth with pluck, on they went, through Mr Loxley's house and back premises, down Powick Lane, through Tanner's yard, and so back to the vestry, where progress was duly recorded in the books. We should not omit to state that the chaplain, who accompanied the party, had done his best to turn the old ceremony to good account, by delivering appropriate addresses, &c., at various points on the line of route.

On again emerging from the vestry, a final salutation was given to the explorers by the assembled crowd, in which the policemen got thoroughly rinsed; a worthy Boniface [publican], known as 'The old fellow', was prostrated to the ground, in which position he shouted most piteously, 'Blow me if I ain't blinded'; and an overseer was so roughly handled, that his usual amiable temper became ruffled, and he swore a deadly oath, that if they gave him three months for it, he would punch the head of the first fellow he caught. The boys were treated to a scrambling for pence, and so ended the out-door performance. After the fatigues of the day, a jolly party of about twenty-five sat down to dinner at Mr Hill's, the Herefordshire House, Newport Street, whose admirable catering soon made them forget the mishaps of the morning, and a very pleasant evening was spent.

The St Clement's officials (Mr Bozward, churchwarden, Messrs Spilsbury and Fenn, overseers) and a number of the parishioners, armed with a flag and a bough of oak, took to the water like ducks, from Tearne's meadow, near the Dog and Duck, passed down the middle of the Severn to the Watermen's Chapel, where they landed to take in a part of the Cattle Market and the site of the old parish church; embarked once more, passed the Rubicon of the centre arch of the bridge, landed on the west side of the river, opposite the Cathedral, and performed all the remainder by land. The usual ablutions, debaubings, scramblings, and so forth, were not forgotten. Afterwards the party dined at the very comfortable hostelry of the Dog and Duck.

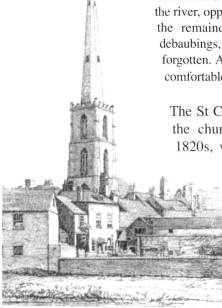

The St Clement's party would have started from the church in Henwick Road, erected in the 1820s, which replaced the mediaeval building which had stood at the junction of Dolday and Croft Road.

During what was probably the last perambulation of the bounds of St Andrew's parish in Worcester, beaters rowed up the Severn, pausing to prod the river bed with long poles. In the following year, choirboys were bumped at the farthest corners of St Helen's parish, again probably for the

St Andrew's Church, Worcester

Beating the bounds of St Helen's parish, Worcester, in 1912

final time. Even so, memories lingered. In the 1940s Rogation Day at Newland Green was recalled: children there marched with choir and clergy to a field where hymns were sung and crops blessed. At Hunnington a youth had to stoop at the Bannering Stone, 'his head protected by its hollow interior, while the person appointed administered chastisement'. At Alvechurch bound beating took place in 1896 and 1906, then lapsed until 1933, and was revived in 1951.

'A heavy wet', a decided attraction of bound beating, was also available at church ales, fund raising festivals once held in churches, then in churchyards, and finally in some cases in purpose-built houses on church ground where beer was brewed and consumed. One of these at Claines existed until 1773, when it was converted into almshouses which in turn were pulled down in 1866.

Beating the bounds at Alvechurch in 1896

Beating the bounds at Alvechurch in 1906

Another, half-timbered and perhaps mediaeval, still stands on the edge of the churchyard at Areley Kings.

William More was the last prior at St Mary's, Worcester, before the dissolution of the monasteries. As well as being a keen sportsman he had a liberal attitude to merry-makings and seasonal celebrations (see also chapter 10). Between 1518 and 1554 he granted small sums from priory funds to pay for ingredients for church ales at Crowle, Grimley (several times), Hallow,

Church alehouse at Areley Kings

Himbleton, Pensax, Stoke Prior and in Worcester at St Helen's and at St Michael's (which stood to the north of the cathedral, and was demolished in 1843). The occasions when the ales took place included Easter, May, September and October, with others undated. At least one entry in the accounts reads as though More attended in person: '1529-30 spend at the Churche Ale at grymley on blake Monday iijs. viijd.' (Black Monday signifies Easter Monday).

Other parishes raised their own money for materials. For example, at Badsey payments were regularly advanced from church funds for barley, some of them large: 38s. 8d. in 1537-8 alone. Church ales ran there from 1533 until 1585. At South Littleton records cover the period from 1548 until 1571. Many more such references could be found by trawling through churchwardens' accounts.

Puritanism brought an end to church ales, which were forbidden in 1603 in church, chapel or churchyard. William Stubbs, who strongly disapproved of the practice, wrote in his *Anatomy of Abuses* in 1583:

> In certain townes where dronken Bacchus beares swaie, against Christmas or Easter, Whitsontide, or some other tyme, the churchwardens of every parishe, with the consent of the whole parishe, provide halfe a score or twenty quarters of meult [malt], whereof some they buy of the churche stocke, and some is given them of the parishioners themselves, everyone conferring somewhat according to his abilitie, which mault being made into very strong ale or beere, is sette for sale either in the church, or some other place assigned for that purpose. Then, when this is set abroche, well is he that can gettethe soonest to it, and spend the most at it. In this kinde of practice they continue six weekes, a quarter of a yeare, yea, halfe a year together. That money, they say, is to repair their churches and chappels with; to buy bookes for service; cuppes for the celebration of the Sacrament; surplesses for Sir John [the parson], and such other necessaries.

In spite of the ban, a church ale is recorded at Elmley Castle in 1635, and a Whitsun ale three years later. The churchwardens made a profit of £4 for their funds in each occasion. According to Snow, Elmley's Whitsuntide wake was 'a lineal descendant of the old Church Ale.'

The day of a church's saint-dedicatee was marked by a vigil (or wake) of prayer, followed by more down to earth merrymaking. The second element gradually became indistinguishable from a pleasure fair, and is described in chapter 10. In some cases, a religious connection remained. To the intense annoyance of some parishioners at Claines, a fair with 'disgraceful scenes' continued in the churchyard on Wake Sunday until the mid-nineteenth century, though a hundred years before that at Tardebigge a similar event on the Sunday after St Bartholomew (24 August) lived only in the memories of the old.

An annual fair for the sale of goods, held probably in the space in front of St Kenelm's Church at Romsley (though far from much of the present village), was instituted in 1253, to take place on the eve and day of the saint (17 July) and the two days

St Kenelm's Church, from a card postmarked 1905

afterwards. As with other events, people added 11 days to compensate for the calendar change of 1752, and moved St Kenelm's Day to 28 July. William Timings of Clent, who attended as a child of 12 in 1784, claimed 'the fair was at its end soon after', but another Clent man, John Amphlett, writing in 1890, placed 'the last surviving remnants of this fair ... some fifty years ago', adding that 'shortly after the fair seems to have merged into a wake, which, becoming accompanied by great disorders on the hills, was soon suppressed, and the fair vanished with it, after existing nearly six hundred years'. This timing coincides with that of John Noake, who observed in 1856 that 'the custom of "crabbing the parson" was observed till lately at St Kenelm's chapelry'.

A far fetched local tale tells that, on his way to a service at St Kenelm's the parson stole, either from a farm or an inn, some dumplings which he hid in the sleeves of his surplice. During the service these began to roll out on to the head of the clerk, who sat below. (A painting by A.E. Everitt of the church interior in 1845 shows the three-decker structure which the parson and clerk would have used). 'Two can play at that game, master', said the clerk, and began to retaliate with crab apples which he had in his pockets. So began the tradition of crabbing which became extremely popular.

In fact, the custom has been recorded elsewhere, in connection with churches in Herefordshire, Oxfordshire and Somerset. At Romsley, not only was the parson pelted on Wake Sunday, but members of the congregation targeted each other, with sacks of ammunition deposited in advance. 'The substitution of sticks and stones for crabs led to the suppression of the practice', said Noake.

CHAPTER 4

Lives

Late in 2004 the Office for National Statistics published figures for the previous year which pointed to the decline of a long-standing moral taboo: 41% of births in England and Wales (over 50% in the latter country, taken separately) were out of wedlock. At the same time, paradoxically, marriages—perhaps stimulated by the modish minority's predilection for elaborate and expensive weddings—seemed to be on the increase, with a rise of 7.5% reported since 2001.

Proposals of marriage, sometimes after several years of cohabitation, are at times ostentatiously made, placarded on a hoarding or on the side of a doubledecker bus, while wedding and other anniversaries are marked by balloon-festooned public notices or announcements in newspapers. Deaths caused by mishaps inspire secular shrines at roadsides or outside buildings, with written messages, piles of flowers and, in the case of a child, heaps of toys and teddybears.

Few people are completely without superstitions, which are no doubt in inverse proportion to feelings of material well-being. Within recent memory the accidental breaking of a mirror or the sudden fall of a picture from the wall induced lasting anxiety, and even fear; people trod a careful path through potential pitfalls of ill-luck and ill-omen.

Good health was, as it remains, a major preoccupation. People's only recourse was often only to alternative practitioners and therapies, and even in an age of high-tech medicine various forms of complementary treatment continue to flourish. The desperate remedies of the past have rightly gone but other traditional recourses—to herbs, for example—have enjoyed new favour.

The moral health of communities has given cause for concern, with the fear that tolerance can become indifference. The crude rituals of the past by which communal disapproval was expressed are now largely gone, though Mike Foster, the anti-foxhunting Worcester MP, was burnt in effigy at least once in 2004 by hunt supporters. However, there is evidence that members of groups and communities have lost patience with anti-social behaviour, and are willing to support decisive action.

As they will always be, the beginning and the end of life are marked by rites of passage, and attended by many beliefs and practices. Some of these, past and present, are described here.

Birth

Until at least the 1930s people in Stourport—and no doubt elsewhere, too— believed it unlucky for a woman to wash her feet during pregnancy. It was considered unlucky—tempting fate, perhaps—to bring a child's cradle into the house before the birth. A cradle previously there would be stored elsewhere from the beginning of the pregnancy. A new cradle was unlucky in any case, so an old one would be handed down from generation to generation, usually on the male side. One farm at Tenbury Wells was let complete with a cradle passed on with the tenancy. As cradles fell out of use the superstitions associated with them passed to cots, and even prams.

To help a woman in labour sheep's lights were tied with string to her hands and feet, or a roasted mouse was laid on her stomach. At Broadwas-on-Teme in 1960 a midwife refused to allow a young woman to remove her shoes until after her child was born. The reasons remain obscure.

In the days of open fires—at least until the 1960s, to my personal knowl- edge—midwives would burn the afterbirth. Some believed that the number of times it popped would denote the number of children the mother would subse- quently have. There was a strange notion in certain places that if a woman died in childbirth the clergyman could demand that the infant be christened over its mother's coffin.

It was customary for new babies to be given something silver, such as a sixpence. When one of her children was born, at Colletts Green Farm, near Powick, in 1946, Lavender Jones received a visit from an old labourer, who knocked on the door and handed her 'a tanner for the babby'. She gave him a

Colletts Green Farm

slice of christening cake in return, whereupon he spat on it for luck and then put it in his pocket. Some households put a bowl out for contributions from visitors after a birth.

The first time a new baby is carried from the room in which it has been born it must be taken upstairs rather than down if it is to rise in the world. When Stanley Baldwin, a future prime minister, was born at Bewdley in 1867 his nurse was careful to follow this ritual. If no higher room existed someone would clamber on to a chair with the baby. Lest it grow up light-fingered the child would not have its nails cut, though they might be bitten short. There were different beliefs as to how long this should go on: only at the first trimming; until christening; for one year.

One of definitions of 'caul' offered by the *Oxford English Dictionary* is: 'The amnion or inner membrane inclosing the foetus before birth: *esp*. this or a portion of it sometimes enveloping the head of a child at birth, superstitiously regarded of good omen, and supposed to be a preservative against drowning'. A Mr C.C. Baines wrote to the periodical, *Folklore*, in 1950 to relate that a Worcestershire connection of his, born with a caul, went into the navy and only after his third escape from drowning (when, during the Second World War, his ship was torpedoed in a convoy to Malta and went down within ten minutes) discovered the existence of the superstition.

The strong disapproval of illegitimate births once widespread is exemplified by the remarks of a Woman's Institute member born in 1893 at Queenhill, near Upton-on-Severn. Her father worked for the Dowdeswells, who lived at Pull Court, and owned most of the houses in the village. They were keen to improve conditions for their workfolk, but 'mind you, they were strict and if a girl got herself into trouble and had a baby out of wedlock, the family were turned out'.

An early baptism was considered essential for a child's future well-being. An infant dying unbaptised would, according to an ancient belief, become a peewit—which might explain the bird's mournful cries. At the touch of the holy water at baptism it was lucky for the child to cry since this showed the departure of an evil spirit. Some churches—Holt, for example—would leave the north or devil's door open during the cere-mony so that an evil spirit could depart from the building after quitting the child.

The north door at Holt Church

If children of different sexes were being baptised at the same ceremony girls had to precede boys. A Worcestershire woman in 1856 who with seeming rudeness pushed past parents with boys so as to ensure that her baby girl was christened first offered this explanation:

> You see, sir, the parson bain't a married man, and consequentially is disfamiliar with children, or he'd a never put the little girl to be christened after the boys. And though it sadly flustered me, sir, to put myself afore my betters in the way I was forced to do, yet, sir, it was a doing of a kindness to them two little boys, in me a setting of my girl afore 'em. Why? Well, sir, I har astonished as you don't know. Why, sir, if them little boys had been christened afore the little girl, they'd have had her soft chin, and she'd have had their hairy beards—the poor little innocent. But thank goodness I've kep' her from that misfortin'.

On the other hand, the majority view seems to have been that at a multiple christening, boys should always precede girls. Such was the case, for example, at Hartlebury in the early years of the twentieth century. Other instances go back as far as almost a thousand years earlier.

A deep-seated belief among gypsy women required that after a child's baptism they should attend church services for three weeks. Mrs Mildred Berkeley reported in 1936 that after a Romany birth:

> Three Sundays running the party all came in in their picturesque attire, full skirt, gay handkerchiefs, and hatless. On the last Sunday I was surprised to hear a satisfied 'Now we're all right', as they left the church.

Choosing a Husband

Women were especially exercised by the search for a partner, as is evidenced by the wide range of rituals they observed. Writing in 1856, Edwin Lees commented that 'The following "love-spells" were communicated to me by a lady—(of course good authority)—as in actual practice within the last few years, and probably still so':

> Get a maiden-hen egg; carefully break it, and fill half the shell full of salt. Then eat the salt as you go to bed, *walking up-stairs backward*, and *backing* into bed also! Then keep silence, and you will dream of your lover. If he should (in the dream) offer a glass of water, he will be a poor man; if ale, a tradesman; but if a glass of wine, a gentleman.
>
> On some Friday night, going to bed, put your shoes under your pillow, crossing the left she over the right, and repeating while crossing this stanza:
>
>> On this blessed Friday night
>> I put my left shoe o'er my right,

In hopes this night that I may see
The man that shall my husband be;
In his apparel and in his array,
And in the clothes he wears every day;
What he does, and what he wears,
And what he'll do all days and years.
Whether I sleep or whether I wake
I hope to hear my true love speak.

Silence must be rigidly preserved until morning, and the lover is *expected* to appear in a dream.

In 1875 James McKay described some of the methods of divination employed by the 'merry maidens of the Malvern country':

> To this day, Worcestershire and Herefordshire girls bake a cake on New Year's Eve, and eat it in silence, meanwhile placing a clean chemise, turned inside out, upon the back of a chair, which is duly sprinkled with rosemary. The silence continues until the clock strikes twelve, when, if any one of them is to be married during the year, the prospective husband approaches and turns the linen. The charm is broken if any body speaks, and therein, no doubt, lies the mischief, which so often frustrates the experiment.

Orpine

Lavender Jones suggests that a rose, wrapped in paper on Midsummer Eve and opened on Christmas Day was, if it were found to be still fresh, worn to church, where the future husband would turn up and take it. A lover whose affections wandered could be drawn back by three roses, also picked on Midsummer Eve. The first of these had to be buried in the early hours of Midsummer Day under a yew tree and the second in a newly-dug grave, while the third remained for three nights under the woman's pillow, and was then burned. The woman would then haunt the erring lover's dreams until he returned to his allegiance. On the same day a woman could take two seedlings of the flowers called Orpine or Midsummer Men (*Sedum telephium*) and plant them in the house thatch, saying as she did so her own name and that of her sweetheart. If the flowers flourished a wedding would ensue; if not, the lovers would part. The same flowers were used for medicinal purposes.

A lover could be identified by this Hallowe'en ritual: 'If you'd see the woman you're to wed, / Touch with a lemon the posts of your bed'. On other occasions, according to an expedient noted at Hartlebury in 1900, a woman could address the moon:

> New moon, new moon, in the bright firmament, if --- is the name of my
> true love to be, the next time I see him, let his face be turned towards me.

Objects put in Christmas puddings were employed for divination until at least 1986 in Malvern. A portion found to contain a silver ring showed the recipient would marry within the year; a bone button—known as the bachelor's button—carried the message that the finder would remain single.

By contrast with such acute anxiety about a future husband the approach of men to their choice of partner was laconic and down to earth: 'Boy, you take a good look round the meadow before you find the gate'. Such good sense was echoed by at least one woman, who said 'There's more to marriage than four bare legs in a bed'.

The Wedding

In his book, *Cotswold Lad* (1960), Sid Knight affectionately remembered the Whitsun wakes of his young days in the village of Broadway. Others were less enthusiastic:

> Sometimes an embracing couple would vanish out beyond the sea of
> glaring lights, and towards Christmas there would be a hasty publishing
> of the banns in church, followed by a marriage of 'have to', as the
> country saying went. Either that, or there would be an ominous notice in
> the *Evesham Journal* calling upon the Whitsuntide lover 'to show cause
> why he should, or should not, deny the charge of paternity preferred
> against him by the complainant Miss Edith Lovewell'. If a sympathetic
> bench awarded the injured party a 'bastardy order' of 5s. a week, the rate
> for the job, then the village bloods agreed that it was far cheaper in the
> long run to marry the wench and get it over, they would be getting some-
> thing for their money; or, its popular alternative, slope off into the army
> where they couldn't touch you—and so the poor girl got none. Once,
> immediately after the ring was on the bride's finger, the bridegroom, best
> man, parson, and sexton were immediately called to deliver the happy
> bride in the vestry, while the blushing bridesmaid hovered excitedly in
> the porch waiting to know whether it was a boy or girl.

Some thought it unlucky to hear their own banns read. A Worcestershire woman reported in *Notes & Queries* in 1856 claimed that a young person 'who would insist in going to church to hear her banns "asked out"' went on to have six children who 'were in consequence all deaf and dumb'.

St Michael's Church, Worcester

Before Lord Hardwicke's Marriage Act came into force in 1754—it was this which made the reading of banns a legal requirement—couples could be married 'by consent', with few formalities. St Michael's Church at Worcester no longer exists (it stood close by the cathedral, to the north-east) but during the second half of the seventeenth century it enjoyed a reputation for providing quick marriages. The registers have entries for couples all over the Worcester diocese and as far afield as Westminster. Few questions seem to have been asked either by Rev. Joseph Severn at Birlingham, near Pershore. During the first 45 years of the eighteenth century 282 couples—mostly from outside the parish, and some even from Scotland—were married in his tiny church.

The old notion that the bride should wear something old, something new, something borrowed, something blue, is still widely held. The bride should not see her reflection in the mirror on her wedding morning once she is fully dressed for the ceremony; nor should she turn back on any account once she has set off from home for the church. It is also unlucky for the bride and groom to leave by a back door after their reception. That they should not see each other on their wedding day until they meet in church is also widely accepted, even by couples who have been living together for some years before deciding to marry.

Some weddings used to be timed to begin at five minutes past the hour so that the clock should not strike during the service, thus avoiding a bad omen. Another hazard was for the bride and groom to leave by the chancel door instead of following the custom of walking down the aisle and through the nave door. Only once had the aged inhabitant of one Worcestershire village known such a thing, and after it 'the bride was a widow before the twelve months was out'. It was a very bad sign if a ringer overthrew a bell when ringing a wedding peal or if a bellrope broke.

At Hanbury, and probably elsewhere, if a younger daughter married before an elder, the elder was made to dance in a pig trough on the day of her junior's wedding, which must have been a great humiliation.

Decorated tram car for a wedding party in Worcester in 1909

An unusual twist to the ceremony was reported by the *Worcester Journal* in 1775:

> A widow, being married again, to exempt her future husband for payment of any debts she might have contracted, went into one of the pews and stript herself of all her cloths [*sic*] except her shift, in which only she went to the altar, and was married, much to the astonishment of the Parson, Clerk, etc.

East of Worcester a group of villages including Abberton, Flyford Flavel, Naunton Beauchamp and Wick kept the custom of firing guns to give a nocturnal salute outside the house of a newly-married pair—this was in the mid-nineteenth century. Unfortunately:

> some parties at Wick were not long ago summoned before the magistrates for having participated in one of these popping bouts, but the indignation of the district was greatly aroused by their being mulcted in certain expenses and ordered to discontinue the practice, for it is believed to be nearly as 'old as Adam', and as indispensable a ceremony as the marriage vow itself.

Another case was reported by the *Worcester Herald* in March 1845:

> From time immemorial the custom has been ... to rejoice and be glad at a wedding, and ... to ring merry peals upon the church bells. ... But there are parishes and places where ... their churches never had bells. Among those unhappy districts may be reckoned Pensham, Pinvin, and other places in that neighbourhood, and to make up for the want of a merry 'ding dong', all the male residents, from the newly-breeched urchin to the ancient sire, tottering on the grave, who could command a firelock ... have assembled round the bridegroom's house, and kept up an irregular volley of blank cartridges. ... On Tuesday last, one George Gould was summoned before the magistrates of Pershore ... for shooting at the wedding of Miss Bright, of Pensham, and in so doing, damaged the door of Mrs Bright, her mother, in whose house the marriage feast was given. This serious offence was said to have been committed on Sunday evening se'ennight, and, in extenuation, George pleaded ancient usage and the custom of his fore-fathers. His plea did not avail him, as the right to blow holes in other people's doors, although they may have been unfortunate enough to get married, was not to be found in the common, or statute law. His offence, however, did not appear to be deemed a very heinious [*sic*] one, as he was let off on paying a fine of 6d. with 6d. damage and 6s. 6d. costs.

At Church Honeybourne when a couple with railway connections set off by train for a honeymoon fellow workers would place detonators on the line to mark their departure. The ringers at Offenham 'fire' the bells at a wedding: that is, the tenor bell leads but all the rest strike together. A quiet but more lasting commemoration can be seen at Little Comberton, where the outlines of hands on stone benches in the church porch are said to have been inscribed by newly-married brides.

Married Life

Tension in relationships lies behind sayings such as 'When rosemary blooms, missus is master', and 'When lavender flourishes, the woman rules'. Job Orton, landlord of the Bell Inn at Kidderminster in 1853, was so keen to steal a march on his wife, even after death, that he arranged to be buried upright so as to rise before her on Judgement Day.

Things did not necessarily run more smoothly for the well to do. Emma Vernon, heiress to Hanbury Hall and a notable beauty painted by Sir Joshua Reynolds, married, in 1776, Henry Cecil, Member of Parliament and scion of the aristocracy. Despite her privileged status she was unhappy, and turned for affection to the Hanbury curate, William Sneyd. The pair eloped and went abroad, but only four years later the ailing Sneyd (who had married Emma in the interim) was dead. Henry Cecil, meanwhile, had made a marriage—bigamous, but eventually regularised—with a miller's daughter from Shropshire. When he inherited both his uncle's title and mansion (Lord Exeter, Burghley House), his new wife came to be known as 'the cottage countess', and found her story celebrated by Tennyson.

Hanbury Hall remained uninhabited for many years, but after Cecil's death in 1804 Emma returned to live there with her third husband, John Phillips. When she died, 14 years later, she chose to be buried at the bleak northern edge of Hanbury churchyard, wrapped in the shroud which had been used for her lost love, William. Emma's position and fortune

Emma Vernon's grave

enabled her to override certain conventions but people at lower social levels were less fortunate.

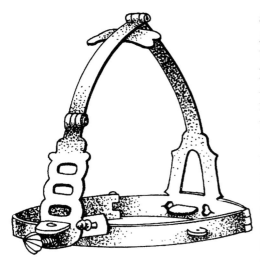

Scold's Bridle

A sanction directed not merely against wives but women in general was the 'scold's bridle', of which an example has been preserved in Worcester Museum. A spell in the iron gag with a framework which clamped round the head was inflicted on turbulent women such as Margaret Bache, the wife of a Chaddesley Corbett nailer. In 1603 she was excommunicated for 'misbehaving with her tongue towards her mother-in-law' at Bromsgrove, and twelve years later stood accused as 'a common scold among her neighbours' at 'the leate [leet] holden for the manor of Chaddesley'.

A more serious punishment was the gum or ducking stool which the magistrates could order not only for unduly sharp-tongued women but for tradesmen who gave short weight or sold adulterated food. It was used at Worcester, where the records have entries on 'making the gome stool' (1599) and on 'the money for whipping of one Rogers and for carrying of several women upon the gum stool' (1623). After being paraded through the streets, offenders were taken down a thoroughfare variously known as Cucken, Cooken or Cooking Street (called Copenhagen Street since Nelson's visit in 1802) to the Severn at the slip by the old Wherry Inn.

Alvechurch apparently lacked 'a cokynstole' in Tudor times but at Bewdley William Lake was paid fourpence in 1578 'for mending the gomestole'. The latter town's accounts for 1617 show £1 3s. 6d. for timber and iron 'for the pillory and gombell stowle', and a further 15s. 10d. for making the devices. On Woodrow Farm at Marlbrook, near Bromsgrove, Cuckold's Corner owes its name to the cucking stool used in the pool which once existed there. At Upton-on-Severn the stinking water of Gum Stool Pond at the bottom of New Street was

The 'gomestole' revived on carnival day at Bewdley (?1950s)

preferred to the river for duckings. The nearby Gum Stool Cottages were demolished only in 1882. The Leominster stool, a formidable structure originally used in Worcester, has survived and is kept in the Priory Church.

A sign of communal rather than judicial disapproval involved parading originally people and later effigies on poles, to the accompaniment of rough music. As early as 1572/3 an instance from Lindridge, east of Tenbury Wells, appears in the records. William Morton, 'one of them that caryed the coole staffe', was ordered to do penance one Sunday in the parish church, and the next at

Artist's impression of a ducking at Upton-on-Severn

Sign on a house which replaced one of the earlier Gum Stool Cottages at Upton

Evesham. He failed to turn up, so was suspended. The reason behind the use of the coolstaff is not given, nor is it in the case which came out at the Quarter Sessions in January 1614, though here the information is fuller:

> Iohn Hucke of Overmitton [Upper Mitton, near Stourport] in the counmtye of Worcester walker [fuller]
> Thomas ffrancklin of the same walker
> William Hardman of Hartlebury in the Countie of Worcester weaver
> These three with divers other uppon Wensdaye 20.October 1613 betwixt ix. And .x. of the Clocke in the night, beinge gathered together at the house of Thomas Hucke in Mitton tooke Mr Thomas Smithe Curat of Mitton and by violence putt him uppon a Cowlestaffe and Caried him up and down the towne and caused fidlers beinge then in company to play by them, and one range uppon A fryinge panne another blewe A horne, and the rest followeed makinge A great disorderly noise to the greate disturbance of all the neighborhood there about.

No information as to the outcome is available. However, at Worcester the community's disapprobation was aroused in about 1800 by a wife's beating her husband. Here, a man dressed as a woman rode on horseback behind the stuffed figure of another man and hit it upon the head with a ladle.

By this time the name given to the procedure was 'skimmington', and a description was offered in 1893:

a rough play got up for the annoyance of unpopular individuals. It usually consists of a procession, in which effigies of the objectionable persons are carried through the village accompanied by beating of tin kettles and other discordant noises. Under particular circumstances, certain articles of wearing apparel are carried on sticks, after the manner of flags or banners. The performance concludes with the burning of the effigies.

The writer, Jesse Salisbury, adds that Samuel Butler gives a description of such a performance in his poem *Hudibras*. Butler, the son of a farmer, was born in 1612 at Strensham where there is a memorial to him in the church. Local tradition holds that he wrote part of *Hudibras* at the Ketch Inn, Worcester.

Salisbury also says that 'a skimmington performance took place at Little Comberton at the beginning of 1893. Arthur Savory, who lived at Aldington, near Evesham, during the last quarter of the nineteenth century, described this 'demonstration of popular disapproval of the conduct of a woman resident, in matters arising out of matrimonial differences':

The entry in All Saints' Church marriage register concerning
James Grubb and Ann Hand.
The note concerning the 'sale' is at the bottom;
'Invalid' is written on the left-hand side

> The outraged neighbours collect near the dwelling of the delinquent, having provided themselves with old trays, pots and pans, and anything by means of which a horrible din can be raised, and proceed to serenade the offender. To be the subject of such a demonstration is regarded as a signal disgrace and a most emphatic mark of popular odium.

When relations between man and wife broke down completely the parties sometimes resorted to an unofficial form of divorce known as wife selling, which was believed (erroneously) to have legal force. On 12 May 1784 James Grubb, 'bachelor', and Ann Hand, 'widow', were married at All Saints' Church, Worcester. They made their marks in the register, and James Hand was one of their witnesses. Rev. Harrison of Crowle officiated, in the absence of the rector of All Saints', William Cleveland. On inspecting the register Cleveland later added a note : 'Invalid ... Ann Hand proved to be the Wife of James Hand, the Witness, not his Wid[ow]. He sold her'. Such a mention of a wife sale in a church register is most unusual, and probably unique. Most such cases are reported in newspapers. The handful from Worcestershire, beginning with an example at Bredon in 1766, are often mentioned in newspapers outside the county, but not in the local press. Some of them at least may therefore be fictional. However, there is no doubt about the document copied by the *Worcester Journal* on 22 July 1857:

> Thomas Middleton delivered up his wife Mary Middleton to Philip Rostins for one shilling and a quart of ale; and parted wholly and solely for life, never to trouble one another.
> Witness. Thomas **X** Middleton, his mark
> Witness. Mary Middleton, his wife
> Witness. Philip **X** Rostins, his mark
> Witness. S.H. Stone, Crown Inn, Friar Street.

As late as 1881 a woman produced in a police court at Worcester a stamped receipt for 25 shillings to prove that she was an honest woman, having been sold, and therefore divorced and re-married.

It has been suggested by Bill Gwilliam that Worcestershire custom permitted a man, if not to marry a deceased wife's sister or a deceased brother's widow, then to 'take a lease of her for life'. The children of such unions were not considered illegitimate.

Charms and Charmers
Horseshoes nailed to doors or fixed over bedsteads performed the double function of keeping away witches and bringing good luck. Some placed the points up, others down. The former configuration is associated with the horned moon, the latter with the Greek omega. Rowan—otherwise known as witty, wittan or

The Whitty Pear, drawn by George Jorden

wittern—also provided protection against witches, both as a living tree and as detached pieces. The Whitty pear, too, produced fruits valued for anti-witch powers. A famous specimen of the tree—in fact, a kind of rowan (*Sorbus domestica*) with edible, pear-like fruit stood in the Wyre Forest, where it was first noted in 1678 by a Worcester alderman, Edmund Pitt. A local poacher set fire to it in 1862 after serving a sentence imposed by a magistrate, Squire Childe of Kinlet in Shropshire, who had a particular liking for it.

Many villages once had a healer or charmer. Nanny Haines of Feckenham had the gift of second sight, and could foretell the future. The astrologer, herbalist and magician, Culpeper, is reputed to have lived at Astwood Court, Astwood Bank, in the sixteenth century. Useful herbs can still be found in the meadow adjoining the farm, and in a nearby field a circular depression where spirits came to do Culpeper's bidding is called

The shop kept by W. Meades, herbalist, in Blackwell Street, Kidderminster, from 1904 until 1908

Spirity Pit. At Upton-on-Severn a bonesetter called Beale had a great reputation in the early eighteenth century. Bonesetting is currently enjoying a new
lease of life, but those now engaged in the art call themselves chiropractors or
osteopaths.

Fladbury was noted for its female charmers. Elizabeth Billings lies buried
near the chancel door of Tardebigge Church. She not only owned land and kept
the Elbows Inn in the parish but practised as a herbalist and wise woman. For
some reason, the masculine equivalent was known as a cunning man. Thomas
Walshe, who died in 1729 after holding the manor of Stockton-on-Teme for 36
years, was termed 'the cunning doctor'. Once he discovered that a servant had
stolen apple grafts from his garden to use on trees of his own, Walshe secretly
substituted crab-apple grafts for them. He then confronted the man, and when
he denied the theft, predicted that his trees would bear only crabs. So it turned
out, and villagers attributed the result to the doctor's magic powers.

A charmer whose name has unfortunately not been recorded died in the
almshouse at Kyre, near Tenbury, in 1920. To cure a wart she put a pin in the earth
to rust. She also had a form of words which she was reluctant to divulge to a
woman: 'I mauna tell, for they must only be told to a mon', she said. However,
she was overheard, partly because the formula had to be repeated nine times:

> Out fire, in frost,
> In the name of the Father, Son and Holy Ghost.

These words were more usually employed to cure a burn.

According to Jesse Salisbury, the simple repetition of a verse from Ezekiel
(16:6) was thought an infallible remedy for a nose bleed: 'And when I passed
by thee, and saw thee polluted in thine own blood, I said unto thee when thou
wast in thy blood, Live; yea, I said unto thee when thou wast in thy blood,
Live'. Alternatively, for any form of bleeding, this verse could be tried:

> Jesus was born in Bethlehem,
> Baptised in the River Jordan;
> The water was wild and wood [mad],
> But he was just and good.
> God spake, and the water stood,
> And so shall now thy blood.

In south-east Worcestershire, as well as applying a dock leaf to a nettle
sting, people said:

> 'Ettle, 'ettle, 'ittle dock,
> Dock sh'll 'ave a golden smock,
> 'Ettle shaunt 'ave nerrun.

A child suffering from whooping cough would be taken to the miller, who would set his mill going and say: 'In the name of the Father, Son and Holy Ghost I grind away this disease'. The notion that such charms could have therapeutic powers seems ludicrous but apparently they often worked on the principle, no doubt, of faith healing. They embody a curious mixture of magical practice and religious faith, and must at times have been last ditch attempts at finding a cure when proper medical treatment was wanting.

Desperate Remedies

Certain substances were thought to have particular powers. Iron retained from primitive times a reputation for efficacity against witchcraft. The gold of a wedding ring blessed during the marriage ceremony could cure certain ailments (see below). Lead stolen from a church roof was doubly effective. Water left over in a font after a baptism was eagerly sought for its curative properties. The ceremony of baptism itself was considered a helpful step for a weakly or fractious infant, and consecrated wine was regarded as a useful medicine.

Personal amulets were widely carried. A double hazel nut or a potato carried in the pocket could ward off ill luck. A bloodstone gave protection against bleeding. The touch of some people, from dead man to living monarch, could also have therapeutic effects.

The principles involved in folk medicine range from faith healing to the use of substances now known to be chemically beneficial, such as cobwebs to staunch bleeding. They include would-be magical transference of disease to other people, animals, or objects. Some of the remedies, though, could have exacerbated rather than allayed disease.

Ague

Go to a tree grafter. Tell him what is the matter and then go away. When you are at home he will cut the first branch of a maiden ash and you will be cured. (The same technique was used for rupture). At Stourport the grafter said these words: 'Ague, farewell, till we meet in hell'.

According to Sid Knight, a dose of 'strong cordial distilled from the common "black" peppermint that grew wild in the bogs' cured him of ague, though Broadway villagers used it for 'everything from gumboils to gastritis'. He is probably referring to water pepper (*Polygonum hydropiper*), which was indeed widely used for sores, ulcers, swellings, toothache and jaundice.

Chilblains

As late as 1995 a Women's Institute member recalled the time-honoured treatment: 'Put your foot in the full "jerry", or rub snow on your feet'.

Cholera
Eat grated crumbs from bread baked on a Good Friday and kept till the following Good Friday. At Rock and elsewhere, small loaves of two to three inches in diameter were cooked on Good Friday to be saved, then ground to powder and mixed with hot water to be given for a variety of common ailments.

Danewort

Cramp
Wear an eelskin garter below the knee. Wear a ring made from a coffin hinge or a consecrated shilling. Alternatively, be christened or confirmed, as appropriate (also a cure for fits).

Dropsy
George Jorden (1783-1871) of Bewdley wrote: 'I have found *Sambucus ebulus* (the dwarf elder or danewort) and the common broom very useful in dropsies by using them both together in an infusion'.

Fits
Drink an infusion made from mistletoe growing on hawthorn. Wear on the finger or on string round the neck a ring made from sacrament silver—a coin given in collection at church, and blessed by clergymen. Parsons were frequently asked for 'sacrament shillings' for this purpose; the remedy, widely employed, was noted in 1840 at Hartlebury by Watson and in 1855 in Worcestershire generally by Noake. Jorden remembered as a child 'to have heard of people going to Bewdley Forest to cut chips from Buckley's Gibbet tree for fits, which were secured in a piece of silk and suspended from the neck'.

Jaundice
Take the inner rind of elder bark boiled in milk.

Piles
As its name implies, pilewort (*Ranculus ficaria*) or lesser celandine, was long thought to have particular properties. Culpeper wrote: 'It is certain by good experience that the decoction of the leaves and roots doth wonderfully help piles and haemorrhoids; also kernels by the ears and throat called the King's Evil [see under scrofula below], or any other hard wens or tumours'. Four centuries later, Knight's father was still using it at Broadway.

Quinsey

T.H. Packer noted, at the beginning of the twentieth century, that the people round Bredon Hill wore a crimson ribbon round the neck for quinsey. If the sufferer were a man, it had to be tied by a maiden.

Rheumatism

Carry a piece of alder wood in a pocket. Lay a hop pillow under the bed. (The latter remedy was prescribed for George III by a doctor at Reading). The cramp remedies also applied. Some people had themselves confirmed more than once in an attempt to deal with a recurrent problem.

Rupture

Slit a sapling; walk between the halves, then tie them up.

Scrofula

In 1666 the Chamberlains of the Worcester Corporation spent the large sum of £10 14s. in entertaining an Irishman called Valentine Greatorex, who claimed the ability to cure scrofula—otherwise called the king's evil. Greatorex, who served in the Parliamentarian army during the Civil War, discovered the therapeutic powers after the Restoration, and indeed cured a number of people. He failed, though, in an attempt to demonstrate his ability to Charles II, and retired to Ireland. In 1687 James II visited Worcester Cathedral for the purpose of touching sufferers. On other occasions people were given money to allow them to travel to London for the same purpose. In 1711, for example, the churchwardens of St Nicholas' Church, Worcester, paid 11 shillings 'for carrying of Walker to London to be touched'.

Shingles

Apply grease from the bearings of a church bell, preferably the tenor.

Sore eyes

Apply water from a holy well, or rainwater caught and bottled on Ascension Day. A sceptical Sid Knight, ordered as a boy by his mother to bathe his eyes in water from the Holy Well near Rookery Farm, Broadway, found to his surprise that the soreness was cured. George Jorden noted in his diary on 9 May 1849, Holy Thursday or Ascension Day: 'Showery, some holy water may be collected for sore eyes, which some people catch and have great faith in its curative properties and believe it will never spoil for keeping'. Almost a century later, in 1944, John Wood wrote: 'A few years ago basins were still being placed out of doors on Ascension Day at Elmley Castle to catch any rain that might fall, for the water thus collected was believed to be an unfailing specific for inflamed eyes'.

Sprains

In 1900 at Hartlebury a piece of red worsted was wound nine times round the affected limb.

Stye

Rub with wedding ring.

Viper bite (especially on the Malvern Hills)

Wrap affected part in a skin taken warm and reeking from a sheep. Or kill the snake, then make a paste of its liver and eat it. Adder skins were used to cure wounds made by thorns.

Warts

These are all different possibilities. Put a small pin in the earth to rust. Steal a piece of beef and bury it. Rub the warts with a black slug, then impale it on a thorn. Gather some ripe ears of wheat and cross the wart with them several times; then put the corn into a packet and drop it where three roads meet. Cut as many notches in a hazel stick as there are warts, and drop it where four roads meet. Secretly pinch out of a loaf of bread as many pieces as there are warts and bury them. Cut as many notches as there are warts in two sticks; lay them crosswise in the road, and the warts will be taken by whoever picks up the sticks. Make the sign of the cross and repeat *Gloria Patri* (Glory be to the Father)—though this can be done only by someone with the gift of charming. Sell them. (I met in 1990 a Bromyard doctor who said that he had often bought warts from patients). Two cases from the 1960s are supplied by Lavender Jones: 'Miss Phyllis Turner, aged about 64, told me that when a child she and her mother were walking down Hospital Lane, Powick, when she saw a small parcel under the hedge which she picked up and opened. It contained a piece of burnt wood. Her mother smacked it out of her hand to the ground. It was a wart cure and had been put there to remove someone's warts. Phyllis Turner by touching it had transferred the warts to her own hands. She said she subsequently had several warts. Mrs Leeke of Powick told me that her daughter Peggy had warts on her hand. Mrs Leeke put a grain of wheat for each wart into an envelope and took it to Worcester and dropped it at the Five Ways. This is an inn on the corner of Angel Street and the Butts where five roads converge. All the warts disappeared. It is essential that the person losing the warts should not turn round or look back after losing them'. Until the end of the twentieth century the water in which a blacksmith had cooled red-hot iron continued to be valued as a specific for warts.

Wen

Arrange for the wen, a lump or protuberance on the body, to be touched by the hand of a dead man.

Whooping Cough

Here again there are many different options. Eat bread and butter which has been placed in a dead man's hand. Take a pie dish filled with cider to the River Rea—this is mainly from Bayton; catch a trout and drown it in the cider, then fry the fish; the patient eats the fish and drinks the cider. Take 20 hairs from the nape of the patient's neck (or seven from the tail of a white horse) and put them between slices of bread and butter; give this sandwich to the first strange dog which passes, and say the Lord's Prayer; the dog will carry away the disease. Hold a frog in the mouth of the patient and cause him to breathe into its mouth; the frog will take away the disease. Inhale the breath of a piebald or skewbald horse. Pass the patient nine mornings running under the arch made by a bramble rooted at both ends; say the Lord's Prayer, eat some bread and butter, and give some to a bird or animal. Cause the patient to drink from a sacramental cup or eat from a bowl of ivy wood. Tie a string with nine knots round the neck. Find a married couple called Mary and Joseph and send them an unsolicited gift or ask the wife to lay her hands on the patient (the latter was recorded from Abbot's Morton in 1932). Find a woman successively married to two men of the same surname but of different families; ask her to cut bread and butter and give it to the patient. Find a woman with a second husband whose surname is the same as her maiden name; anything she suggests will produce a cure, though in practice bread and butter with sugar was usually recommended.

Weather Lore

Before the days of scientific weather forecasting people amassed a whole host of predictions, some general, some particular, which were the fruit of generations of knowledge. Many provide sound advice, particularly when they describe the sky itself, though none works all the time. For example, 'Rain before seven, dry before eleven' often proves true because most frontal rain bands last only a few hours; however, we can all remember occasions when rain has continued for a whole day or even longer. To take a different instance, the traditional view (see below) that January is the 'blackest' month is confirmed by scientific evidence that it is indeed, on average, the coldest month of the year in most places in the British Isles. On the other hand, the calendar changes of 1752 and also variations in climate such as the global warming we are experiencing affect the accuracy of traditional weather lore. The easiest observations to dismiss are those connected with miracle-working saints such as Swithin (for whom, see below).Weather lore was often cast into rhyme to make it easily memorable.

The moon was believed to be a very useful indicator. For example, the appearance of a new moon on a Saturday or a full moon on a Sunday would bring 20 days of wind and rain. Put another way:

The moon upside down, from a misericord at Ripple

> Saturday's new and Sunday's full,
> Allus wet and allus 'ull,

On the other hand, 'Sunday's moon comes too soon', that is, a new moon on a Sunday brings ill fortune. A moon on its back brings dry weather: 'Moon on its back holds water in its lap' but if the points are downward rain is indicated.

We are still preoccupied with rain, both in timing and in quantity, and there are probably more traditional sayings on this subject than any other. 'When the sun sets in a muddy mist, be sure that rain's at hand', is how one expression puts it. A local variant of the old shepherd's rhyme goes: 'A rainbow at night is the shepherd's delight'. A more elaborate verse runs:

> When the reds are out at night it's the shepherd's delight,
> But when out in the morning it's all day storming.

Particular landmarks feature in some predictive rhymes. One verse is still widely known:

> When Bredon Hill puts on his hat
> Ye men of the vale beware of that.
> When Bredon Hill doth clear appear
> Ye men of the vale have nought to fear.

Others must have been familiar to perhaps only a few hundred people. 'A mist round the tower, It'll rain an hour' refers to the folly built in 1800 on the hill above Broadway. Near Evesham, people who became aware of the carillon sounding in the abbey tower remarked:

> We be going to have some drier times,
> For I've been hearing E'sam chimes.

In addition they knew of a general warning:

> When it looks black in two places at once,
> And both should be drawing together,
> Go for shelter at once, for there's very soon here
> Some very, very hunkid [dreadful] weather.

Farmers with land by the Severn watched the tide:

> If it raineth when it doth flow,
> Then take your ox and go to plough;
> But if it raineth when it doth ebb,
> Unyoke your ox and go to bed.

The last time oxen were used in Worcestershire as draught animals was during the 1920s, so the rhyme may not have been heard for some years.

Still current, though, is the belief that the appearance of black beetles points to rain—and if they are killed it will be all the wetter. A cock's crow can also be significant:

> A cock crowing on going to bed,
> Sign he'll get up with a dropping [dripping] head.

The well known rhyme about the oak and ash is often thought to mean that we shall have rain either way, but a local variant makes clear that this is not so:

Oxen ploughing, 1803

> If the oak be out before the ash
> There'll only be a little splash;
> If the ash be out before the oak
> Then there'll be a regular soak.

Among the many ways of predicting rain in the vale of Evesham were these: clouds passing rapidly; a remarkably clear atmosphere; swallows flying near the ground; restless sheep; cows herding together; donkeys constantly braying; bees remaining close to the hive; frogs croaking and coming out onto the road; a smoky chimney; a taut clothes line; the closing of their petals by crowsfoot, speedwell, wood sorrel, scarlet pimpernel, anemone or stitchwort; damp bricks in a yard or path.

The best of the weather lore derived from a careful reading of the sky and the winds. 'Cruddledy [curdled] sky, cruddledy sky, not long wet, not long dry', says one forecast. Others predict 'Cloudy mornings turn to clear evenings' and 'Dew before midnight, next day will be bright'. The wind features in 'The weather's always ill when the wind's not still' and 'When the wind is in the east, there it will be for some days at least'. As winter approaches 'A storm of hail brings frost in its tail'. Even onions can provide predictions:

> Onion skins very thin,
> A mild winter coming in.
> Onion skins thick and tough,
> Coming winter wild and rough.

Most months of the year have their own lore. People were reluctant to settle bills on 1 January since they believed: 'Pay away money on New Year's Day, all the year through you'll have money to pay'. The same day had a rhyme about the lengthening of light:

> At New Year's tide a cock's stride;
> By Twelfth-tide another beside.

Twelfth-tide, or 6 January, was also known after the change of calendar in 1752 as Old Christmas Day; on this occasion one should rejoice if the sun shines through the branches of the apple trees.

On the whole January was not a popular month. 'As the days lengthen the cold strengthens' can still be heard, though perhaps not 'The blackest month of all the year, it is the month of Janiveer'. A mild January was thought to bring a cold May, though it was considered good time for planting at least one crop: 'Who in January sows oats, gets gold and groats'.

The weather on Candlemas Day (2 February) seems to have been very carefully watched for its predictive qualities. Wherever the wind was, especially in the east, it would blow for three months from the same quarter. Although snow would not linger after Candlemas,

> If Candlemas-tide be fine and clear
> Winter will surely re-appear,
> But if it be cold, wet and grey
> The worst of winter has passed away.

So ran a Bromsgrove rhyme.

The feeling that winter is not yet over is also reflected in:

> March will search and April try
> But May will tell if you live or die.

The winds of this month were regarded as significant:

> If the wind is in the east at noon on St Benedict's Day [21 March],
> It will neither chop nor change till the end of May.

Fruit growing is of great importance in Worcestershire. Evesham cider makers used to say:

> When the apple trees are in blossom in April and before May
> You can put all your barrels away,
> But if they are in blossom at the end of May and the beginning of June,
> You can get all your barrels in tune.

The cuckoo in Worcestershire was thought never to be heard before Tenbury Fair (20 April) or after Pershore Fair (26 June). Of the latter it is said: 'The cuckoo guz ter Parsha Fair, and then 'er 'ops it off from there'. If the cuckoo were heard after Pershore Fair (26 June) she had failed to buy a horse on which to ride away—merely another way of saying she was staying longer than expected.

'Easter come early, Easter come late, it's sure to make the old cow quake' gives warning that bad weather is still to be expected at this time of year. Another prediction seems to show that plenty will grow but little will be gathered in:

> If it rains on Good Friday and Easter Day,
> A good year of grass and a poor one of hay.

Or:

> If it's wet on Good Friday and Easter Day,
> The grass may be thick but there won't be much hay

To ensure successive crops runner beans should be planted on May Eve and June Eve. The classic formula for bean planting is:

> When elmen leaves are as big as a farden,
> Plant kidney beans in your garden.
> When elmen leaves are as big as a penny,
> Plant kidney beans if you mean to have any.

Apart from the lack of elm leaves to observe, this rhyme is now surely doomed to fall out of use through the disappearance of the farthing and the old penny.

The rhyme about the value of swarms of bees in different months remains very well known, but the one about thistles is less so:

> Cut thistles in May,
> They grow in a day.
> Cut them in June,
> That is too soon.
> Cut them in July,
> Then they will die.

The weather in May and June was rightly seen to have its effect on the coming harvest. 'Mist in May and heat in June will bring the harvest very soon', was one prediction. Contrariwise, another said 'A dry May and a dripping June always brings things in tune'. St Barnabas Day (11 June) signalled the beginning of haymaking. 'On Saint Barnabas put the scythe to grass'. Rain was expected on that day to christen the apples, though some areas applied this belief to St. Peter's Day (29 June).

Many country people still hold to the opinion that if rain falls on St Swithin's Day (15 July) it will continue for forty days. The belief has over a thousand years of history behind it, but no weight of metereological evidence. When Swithin died in 862 he left instructions that he was to be buried outside the west door of the Old Minster at Winchester. This was done, but about a hundred years later a decision was taken to move his remains inside the cathedral. On the day in question — 15 July 971 — miraculous cures were effected and heavy rain began to fall and lasted for 40 days.

Hops are still grown in the county, and this somewhat inscrutable saying comes from Knighton-on-Teme:

> St James's Day [25 July] has passed and gone,
> And there may be hops and there may be none.

The period from August to November seems less rich in weather lore, perhaps because after harvest at least the weather was not so important. Michaelmas (29 September) occasioned the wry reflection that plentiful supplies of apples would not last for ever:

> At Michaelmas or a little before,
> Half the apple's thrown away with the core.
> At Christmas time or a little bit arter
> If it's as sour as a crab,
> It's 'Thank you, master'.

In October farmers put rams to their ewes: 'At St Luke's Day [18 October] let tups have play'. In November signs of winter started to be seen:

> Ice in November to hold a duck,
> There follows a winter of slush and muck.

However, if the first snow of the season hung in the trees it was thought to show that the following year would be good for fruit. A similar sign was that if the sun shone through the orchard on Christmas Day a good year for apples would ensue. The same weather unfortunately predicted many fires in the year. Other signs were: 'Hours of sun on Christmas Day, so many frosts in the month of May' and 'If Christmas Day be bright and clear, there'll be two winters in the year'.

The day on which Christmas fell had its significance:

> If Christmas on a Thursday be
> A windy winter you shall see:
> Windy days in every week,
> Winter weather strong and thick;
> Summer shall be good and dry,
> Corn and wheat shall multiply.

An alternative was that if Christmas Day fell on a Sunday the following summer would be hot. Finally, and somewhat lugubriously, 'A green Christmas means a full churchyard'.

Signs

A large number of omens forewarned of possible misfortune. A portent of death was created if a person brought the first snowdrops of the season into the house, opened an umbrella there, shouldered a spade or dropped scissors so that they fell on one point. (To fall on the two together indicated a wedding).

Other tell-tale objects presaging misfortune were a clock falling, a church bell being rung as the clock strikes, a winding sheet—that is, an unburnt wavelet of wax curling away from the flame—on a candle, or a wick glowing long after it is extinguished, or a long run in black suits during a game of cards. Signs of death indicated by plants included the blooming of an apple tree twice a year or its bearing fruit and blossom at the same time, the dying off or shrivelling of a gooseberry or currant bush while it is fruiting, the death of ivy on a house, and the appearance of a rose with leaves between the petals. Certain animal behaviour was seen in a similar light—the howling of a dog, the coughing of a cat, rats' nibbling furniture, the entry to a house of a mole, frog or toad, the flight of a white bird against a window or the tapping of any bird at a pane.

The actions of birds were carefully watched. The flight of a bird over a sickbed signalled the death of its occupant. A robin's entering a house gave the same warning, though a bee's incursion meant a visit from a stranger. (So did a cock crowing in an open doorway, or a lid accidentally left off the teapot). Otherwise the robin was a lucky bird. As was the wren:

> Malisons, malisons, more than ten,
> Who kills the Queen of Heaven's wren.

It was considered unlucky to destroy a swallow's nest or kill an owl. The latter was favoured because it flew out of the oak tree not when Charles II hid in it but when searchers arrived, thus causing them to miss the fugitive. To see a raven was a bad sign. Magpies varied:

> One for sorrow, two for mirth;
> Three for a wedding, four for a birth.

A variant on this rhyme noted by Arthur Savory runs:

> One's joy, two's grief,
> Three's marriage, four's death,
> Five's heaven, six is hell,
> Seven's the devil his own sel'.

Two crows meant a wedding, and one a funeral, though a Worcester man thought the latter could be avoided by saying aloud the word 'break' on sight of the crow. The Seven Whistlers passing overhead at night portended disaster. There is uncertainty as to what these birds were, and this perhaps increases the fear. One possibility is the swift.

Despite its unpleasant habits the cuckoo does not bring ill luck. Some believed, though, that whatever one was doing on first hearing it would be one's main occupation through the ensuing year. Rain is predicted by the call of the stormcock (another name for the green woodpecker or yaffle), the bray of the donkey and the closing during daylight of the scarlet pimpernel.

A very long list of actions or omissions brings bad luck or unpleasant consequences. Kicking fungi leads to seven years' bad luck. The results of picking herb robert (*Geranium robertarium*) are shown in its local name Death-come-quickly. Ill luck comes of taking into the house snowdrops before the first chickens are hatched, or hawthorn before 1 May, or mistletoe or holly before Christmas. Elder wood should not be burnt at all, and no wood should be burnt green: 'Burn green, sorrow soon seen' except for pear: 'Pear dry, pear green, makes a fire fit for a queen'. Red and white flowers in the same bunch are considered unlucky, especially in hospitals, where they may point to blood on the sheets. Parsley should not be transplanted: 'Well, if you plants parsley you plants the Old Man' (the devil). The willow is cursed since the Virgin Mary whipped her son with it and caused him to say, in the words of the 'Bitter Withy' (see also chapter 9):

> Cursed be the sally tree which maketh me to smart;
> The sally tree shall be the first to perish at the heart.

How cricketers escape from this injunction is not clear, but there was a time when no countryman would hit an animal with a stick of willow.

A hare running down a village street showed that there would be a fire. A weasel crossing one's path was unlucky; so was the first lamb or colt of the season if it were seen facing away. Killing a ladybird was also unlucky, and so with many other things which people carelessly did or left undone.

Salt was a precious commodity, and also a symbol for immortality. Spilling it was decidedly unlucky: in Leonardo da Vinci's painting of the Last Supper Judas is shown overturning the salt, but the superstition may pre-date the picture. Returning borrowed salt was unlucky; so was putting salt on someone else's food, rather than simply passing it. Still at table, crossing knives led to a quarrel, but this could be averted if the lower of the two were withdrawn, and these words said: 'Blessed are the peacemakers'. Putting new shoes on the table is still considered unlucky by many.

A quarrel can again be caused when two people wash in the same water, unless the second spits in it first. Giving knives or scissors as a present leads to the end of a friendship unless something is given in exchange. However, the gift of a pin should not be repaid, even with thanks. A light should not be given at Christmas or the New Year, and being one of a party of thirteen was especially unlucky at Christmas.

Throwing out soapsuds on Holy Thursday (the Thursday before Easter) was unlucky, and hanging out clothes to dry on the same day would ensure that there would be a death in the family, with the corpse laid out in one of the items on the line. Good Friday was thought to be a special day for planting since this was 'the only day the devil has no right to the ground'. However, to leave soap-suds in a boiler over Good Friday will lead to a death in the house, and washing on the day brings bad luck for twelve months.

The phases of the moon were carefully watched, since planting had to be done as it waxed, and also the killing of animals and even the cutting of hair (at Hartlebury):

> Crop your head in the moon's wax,
> Ne'er cut it in the wane;
> And then of a bald head
> You shall never complain.

Pointing at a new moon (and also a rainbow) is unlucky; so is to see it first through glass. When it is seen in the open people should turn the money in their pockets and wish for a lucky month.

Certain days were unlucky, especially Friday—the day of the crucifixion—when fresh work should not be undertaken nor a journey begun nor a mattress turned. Cutting nails on a Sunday—a Friday in some versions—was to be avoided:

> Better had he never been born
> Than pare his nails on a Sunday morn.

Further ill luck came from saying goodbye over a stile or at a crossroads; treading on a piece of iron; meeting or passing someone on the stairs; going back over the doorstep for something forgotten (unless a person sits down and counts to ten to break the spell); passing beneath a ladder (unless bad luck is averted by crossing the fingers and thumbs); and even meeting a squinting woman (unless one speaks to her). When a fire was lit the devil was shamed when logs were crossed, and a useful tip was:

> One log can't burn.
> Two logs won't burn.
> Three logs make a fire.

Very few things seemed to bring good luck. A black cat crossing one's path is still very well known, but a fox's doing so at night is also lucky. Some farmers thought white cows lucky; others, a flock of sheep or a load of hay encountered on a journey. Certain omens were inescapable. A burning face indicates that someone is talking about the person. A shudder shows that someone is walking over the spot where one's grave is to be. An itchy foot will soon be treading strange ground; an itching ear portends news from the living; a nose, bad news or that 'You will be kissed, cursed or vexed, or shake hands with a fool'.

Death

A host of signs were thought to give warning of imminent death. 'Omens, or tokens of death, adhere to the popular belief to a more general extent than any other relic of superstition, perhaps one-third of the population attaching more or less credit to them'. So wrote John Noake in 1855, and instanced 'the howling of a dog, a winding-sheet in the candle, and the issuing of light from a candle after it is blown out'. Half a century later, W.H.D. Rouse heard from Joseph Pearce, a blind man living in Droitwich, that the fleeting appearance of a white rabbit, especially in an incongruous place such as an apple tree, betokened a death. Mrs Henry Wood (1814-87), the daughter of a Worcester glove manufacturer, claimed to have seen the phenomenon of a phantom coach coming at the time of a death to take away the departing soul; and she described it with due *frisson* in her novel, *The Shadow of Ashlydiat* (1863).

Those wishing for precise predictions could take ivy leaves, write on them the names of members of their family, and steep them in water overnight at Hallowe'en. Next morning the leaves corresponding with those members of the family who were to die during the ensuing year would bear the mark of a coffin. Some thought that if one listened on the same night at the door of the church the devil would be heard reading inside a list of the names of those due to die within twelve months.

The passing of a person close to death would be assisted by removing the pillow from beneath the head. All doors would be unlocked and opened so that the soul's departure would not be hindered. At Broadway, and no doubt elsewhere, a corpse lying unburied over a Sunday was thought to bring about another death a week later.

Bees had to be told of family events such as births, marriages and deaths. Arthur Savory wrote of his foreman and best worker at Aldington, Walter Bell, 'a clever and courageous bee-master' who '"took" all my neighbours' swarms as well as my own', that 'he firmly believed in the necessity of telling the bees in cases where the owner had died, the superstition being that unless the hive was tapped after dark, and a set form of announcement repeated, the bees would desert their quarters'. The same procedure, according to Stanley Yapp, remained current in Tenbury Wells at least until the 1980s. If the man of the house died his widow would 'tang' (rap) the hive three times with a front door key—a back door key would not do—and address the bees in one of several ways: 'Bees, bees, my husband is dead. Will you stay and work for me?'Or: 'Your master's dead but don't you go. Your mistress will be a good mistress to you'. Or: 'Bees, bees, your master's dead. You be gwain to have a new master'.

It was widely believed that if the ceremony were omitted the bees would either die or leave. The hive would sometimes be dressed with black crepe, and turned round as the corpse left the house.

Before a funeral procession left the house it was customary for the deceased's will to be read or to be passed over the coffin to the legatee. Some country solicitors still follow this procedure.

Coffins were sometimes carried long distances by relays of bearers, and it was not done to refuse a request to act as a bearer. Whether the route were long or short householders kept their curtains drawn along it until the coffin had passed. This was either a mark of respect or because it was unlucky to see a funeral procession through glass, or a combination of the two. When a coffin had to be carried from an isolated house across cultivated fields it was believed that a right of way would be created unless some payment, if only a few pence, were exacted by the landowner. Alternatively, a detour could be made to avoid private ground. 'One of these "corpse ways" as they were called', wrote Bill Gwilliam in 1991, 'is the Burial Way from Ham Green to Feckenham Church. It is an extremely primitive track, in most parts overgrown and impassable for vehicles. It has twists and turns and makes a final wide curve to reach its destination by the side of Feckenham Church'.

Another such path allegedly ran 23 miles from Castle Hill at Brailes (predating the church there) to Bredon Hill in Worcestershire. Some claim the route to be part of a ley line running from Banbury to the British Camp on the Malvern Hills. Perhaps it was simply a track on which people travelled for pleasure or necessity, for trade or war.

Corpses undoubtedly were carried long distances for burial. Although the church of St Michael and All Angels at Stourport dates only from 1791 a burial ground was consecrated there in 1625 so that the dead would no longer have to be carried to Kidderminster for interment.

Until 1864 people who died at Far Forest had to be buried at Ribbesford, three miles off. The bearers were in the habit of refreshing themselves on the way at eleven inns or alehouses: the Wheatsheaf, Plough, Blue Ball, Green Dragon, Royal Forester, New Inn, Mopsons Cross, Duke William, Tower Farm, Running Horse, Rose and Crown.

From Lower Moor the dead were carried by six bearers, each wearing a pair of new black kid gloves presented for the occasion, along the turnpike road to Fladbury and down to the church:

> The coffin made by the village joiner, Jim Hundy, was always delivered at night. Lying in bed, folk could hear the distant 'tramp, tramp, tramp' along the lane, and this told you that the coffin was being carried to the house of mourning. Wreaths and flowers were always taken after tea, for it was thought to be a more discreet time to call. Most folk called with

flowers. It was expected that the callers would wish to see the body which was usually clad in an ornately embroidered and lace-trimmed shroud. These special shrouds had been worked by the deceased, if female, and had been laid in black tissue paper awaiting this special day. Other ladies were laid to rest in their wedding night gowns which were also beautifully worked and lace trimmed. All the bodies wore long white stockings.

On the funeral day, village curtains were closed as a mark of respect as the funeral procession passed by to Fladbury. The burial ceremony over, most families observed the tradition of 'burying them with ham' or providing a 'spread' for the guests. 'Her's only going to have something to eat to hand round on a plate' was the comment upon simpler refreshments, and that was a great criticism by local standards. Funeral cards were always sent by everyone to close friends and relatives. Ornate and edged with black, 'Thy Will be Done' would be printed in gold lettering across the card. Some folk used to collect funeral cards and have them framed and hung upon their cottage walls. A bier on wheels relieved the situation in 1900. The money was raised by a fete complete with maypole dancing during the summer which paid for a wheeled bier complete with rubber tyres.

So wrote Mollie Carney.

In early times when Malvern Link belonged to the parish of Leigh, coffins in transit were rested at the boundary stone which stood at the crossroads just below where the station was later built. The bearers deposited a token coin in a recess in the stone before continuing the long haul to Leigh. After the mid-1840s burials were able to take place in the cemetery of the new church of St Matthias in the Link, and the ancient stone has now found a resting place there, too (see chapter 2). Shortly before reaching the church at Broadwas, bearers traditionally set down the coffin in the lane (Church Walk), formed a circle round it, and reverently bowed.

It was customary at Feckenham when a single woman or girl died for a garland to be carried before her

Malvern Link boundary stone

coffin and placed in the church. A similar practice obtained at Holt until the 1930s. Maidens' garlands—or 'crants', as Shakespeare called them—can still be seen in some churches, though not in Worcestershire. Until within living memory coffins were always carried through the village of Cookley for a funeral in the church. As the cortège passed, men and boys assiduously doffed hats and caps, as they did elsewhere when a hearse passed. In 1995 a Women's Institute member recalled the procedure at Heightington, near Stourport:

> Coffins were carried from the house to the church by four bearers, with four others walking behind so they could change over. However, they never changed places opposite a house, as that would have brought bad luck. All curtains were drawn in houses where deaths had occurred for up to four days. The coffin bearers had right of way across anyone's land. The church bell tolled seven times for a man, six for a woman and two for a child. The men all wore hard hats to the funeral but left them on the grass outside the church before going in.

Other bell ringing usages are described in chapter 3.

If at all possible bearers would avoid entering church or churchyard on the unfavoured north side. At Leysters, for example, funerals always entered the churchyard by the east gate and paused at a funeral stone from which the cortège would be read into the church by the vicar. The north or devil's side, reserved for suicides and strangers, was unacceptable for burials. T.H. Packer relates how the long-standing prejudice was broken at Elmley Castle when at her own request the deceased wife of the incumbent in the late nineteenth century—this must have been Rev. A.J. Rhoades—was buried on the north side of the church, previously the preserve of bad characters and malefactors. People were buried—as they still are—on an east-west alignment, looking towards the east from whence the resurrection would come.

By a cruel irony the name of resurrectionists was given to those who stole newly-buried bodies for dissection. In October 1822 a reward of £50 was offered for information on the resurrectionists who exhumed a body in Grimley churchyard but abandoned it as being too decomposed for them to sell. In the following month a body went from Broadway, and in November of the same year Bromsgrove's sexton, Joseph Rose, remarked on the theft of three more. In 1831 two bodies taken from St Mary's Churchyard at Hanley Castle were found in packing cases at the Anchor Inn, Upton, and restored to their graves.

Long after the Anatomy Act of 1832 legalised and regularised the supply of corpses for dissection, stories continued to be told of the hated resurrection men. Until the mid-nineteenth century Billy Bourne at Alvechurch (see also chapter 3) remained armed with sword and pistol ready to confront any resurrection men in a churchyard. At Shrawley one gravestone is politely inscribed:

'It is requested by John Beach that this stone be not removed 1850' — though this would surely not have restrained any body-snatchers.

During the 1930s Sir George Vernon of Shrawley fell out with the church and, scorning interment by 'prating priests', had himself buried in the grounds of his favourite cottage, in a wood, overlooking Middle Pool. The house is now ruined but the grave remains. A more serene end, that of George Barnes and his wife, Frances, was recorded in 1741 by James Brook, the vicar of Hanley Castle Church: 'Each of ym 84 years old and having lived in wedlock together 60 years, died ye same day and hour, and were buried in on[e] grave March ye 12th. A rare example of conjugal felicity'. The gravestone at Beckford of John Smith (died 1693) which shows his age as 202 is unlikely to be accurate, and even more so that of Sara Charlett at Cleeve Prior (also died 1693) which claims her to have been 609. Other examples of longevity seem more credible. Mary Lane died at Childswickham in 1741 at the age of 133; and Betty Palmer of Rock, who died in 1772 at the age of 113, had a mother, father and brother who were all centenarians. Thomas Laugher of Martley was 118 when he died in 1813.

Contented old age: octogenarians celebrating at Lenchwick, near Evesham in the late 1920s or early '30s

CHAPTER 5

The Supernatural

'What's happened to weird?' despairingly asked Sean Thomas in an article published in June 2004 which purported to investigate the mysterious death of the paranormal. The Society for Physical Research was reported as complaining of a shortage of ghosts, and the British Flying Saucer Bureau as having suspended its activities for want of sightings. Conversely, another journalist, Mark Gould, commented on the many hospital wards up and down the country 'where paranormal events can trouble clinical minds'. One 'clinical mind', Peter Fenwick, a neurologist from King's College, London, professed himself unable to offer an empirical explanation for many stories of odd events and perceptions near the time of death, and stated: 'As we move to a post-modern view of science, together with the recognition that, as yet, neuroscience has no explanation for consciousness, the possibility of transcendental phenomena around the time of death should also be considered'. Richard Wiseman, a psychologist at the University of Hertfordshire, suggested that hospital ghost stories were simply 'a way of passing the time. You have done the rounds, had a chat about East Enders or whatever, and so you start telling ghost stories because they are entertaining'.

Fairies are now exclusively the stuff of fiction and films, though belief among some adults lasted until a century ago. The devil, too, is dead, perhaps because of the overwhelming evidence provided by modern history of the all too human capacity for evil. Witchcraft as an elaborate form of charade ranging from commercialised Hallowe'en to histrionic Wicca may linger, but the wrinkled crone with maleficent powers is now confined to pantomime and creepy film.

The Wild Hunt
The ghostly hunt which rides through the sky on stormy nights is known in most parts of the world. Its appearance—even the mere sound of its riders and hounds—is thought to presage ill, and possibly disaster, for a community. One of the hunt's manifestations experienced in more recent years is the sound of

the Seven Whistlers in the night sky. To hear six of them is an ill omen; seven at once would signal the end of the world. No one can identify these birds, which have variously been taken to be swans, wild geese, whimbrels, curlews and swifts.

One phantom huntsman was known as Harry-ca-Nab. He kept his dogs at Halesowen—Hell's Own in popular etymology—and appeared on stormy nights mounted on a winged horse or wild bull to hunt boar across the Lickey Hills. To see this hunt would bring bad luck at best, death at worst.

Another hunter, Callow, frequented the Forest of Feckenham. He seems also to have appeared far from there, near Tenbury, where Callow's Grave is marked on maps. Hideous black dogs have been seen running round the spot at nights, and these also manifest themselves at Callow's Leap at Alfrick, where the hunter jumped down a precipice. The equally shadowy figure of Herne the Hunter also roamed in Feckenham Forest, where he killed a sacred stag belonging to the abbess of Bordesley. Shakespeare was well acquainted with such tales, and his own Forest of Arden was close to Feckenham. Indeed, there is a tradition that while waiting for some trouble to blow over at home Shakespeare spent eight months living in the Drainers' Arms—an inn which was burned down in 1892—at Earl's Common. He certainly mentions Herne in *The Merry Wives of Windsor*, though he transfers him to Windsor Forest.

Yet another ghostly huntsman was Sir Peter Corbet, who died in about 1300. He owned Chaddesley Corbett, together with a great deal of land at Alcester, and held a charter from King Edward I to kill wolves in the royal forests of five counties—Gloucester, Hereford, Worcester, Stafford and Shropshire. His pack of wolf hounds was kept in the Dog Kennels, a great stone pit close to Harvington Moat, and Corbet lived in Harvington Hall, or rather an earlier house on the same site.

An underground passage known as Bumble Hole ran from Dunclent to the hall, passing beneath the moat and ending in a dry well, with a branch joining the Dog Kennels. One night the restless baying of the hounds alerted a huntsman, who fetched Sir Peter. They witnessed a meeting between 'a gentleman from Wolverley'—his name is not given—and Sir Peter's daughter, and heard a further assignation made.

The following night the daughter was forcibly confined to her room, and the hounds were loosed. At the time appointed for the lovers' meeting a terrible uproar was heard, followed by silence. Next morning all that remained of the young man was his hands (which animals are said not to touch) and his feet (which were in his boots). On hearing the news the woman threw herself into the moat and was drowned. Sir Peter, filled too late with remorse, hanged all the dogs and sank their bodies in what came to be called Gallows Pool, a few yards from the pit. After his own death he was doomed to hunt the forest by night, accompanied by a spectral pack.

House Ghosts

Ghost guests, whether welcome or unwanted, reside in many a grand house, and also more humble dwellings. The licensees of public houses positively cherish their ghosts as commercial assets; and religious houses, both the 'bare ruined choirs' of yesteryear and the churches of today, have their share of spectral visitors.

Long after her death a Mrs Holland continued to frequent her library at Holland House, Cropthorne. In the same house a grey lady appears, as does a soldier in the dress of a Welsh regiment at the battle of Worcester (1651). On Cropthorne Heath at midnight a funeral procession is sometimes seen. The cortège, known as Old Dutton's Funeral, turns off at a particular gate and vanishes.

Little Comberton is considered one of the most haunted places on Bredon Hill. A.C. Smith wrote in 1932 of a young man who arranged to meet his sweetheart at Oxstalls Comer, just past Bricklehampton Hall on the way to Elmley Castle. As he drew near he saw she had already arrived. To surprise her he crept up, but when he slipped his arm round her waist 'it went clean through her body, corsets and all'. The shock (for which no explanation is offered in the narrative) so affected him that he went home, took to his bed, and, within a few days, died. Afterwards Oxstalls Corner enjoyed the reputation of being haunted by a beautiful swan or a dog, dragging a chain; and once a car stopped for a man in the middle of the road who turned out to be a phantom.

During the First World War two women were cycling home at night from Pershore. As they neared Marybrook Bridge on the way to Great Comberton, the lamp on one of the bicycles went out. The rider told her friend to ride on while she looked at it. She then noticed the figure of a man, and realised she

Marybrook Bridge near Great Comberton

Red House, Spetchley

Lightfoot's friends had mounted a rescue attempt but that they were all drowned when the horses drawing their coach unaccountably bolted and plunged into the lake.

Many houses have their stories. Mrs Jacqueline Taverner wrote of the 1960s:

> We lived in the Red House at Spetchley, near Worcester, when my children were small. During the seven years we lived there I saw a woman upstairs, and felt someone help me down from a step ladder in the dining room when there was nobody there. We all experienced something, even my mother when she visited us. Subsequently I met Mrs Mills, the doctor's wife from Callow End, and she said that during the war Joseph Conrad's son had lived at the house with his wife and family, and they frequently saw a woman on the stairs.

The owner after 1974, Mr Paul Ryder, experienced 'various strange phenomena' including the sound of footsteps from an empty bedroom. A frequent visitor, Mrs Rose-Marie Bradly, wrote in 1992: 'I have felt a "presence" from the very first time I entered the Red House'. She mentioned unaccountable 'feelings all around the house and also from the house to the barn', and added:

> I first noticed whenever I went up and down the stairs someone drew me into ... the dining room. Also I kept having 'flashbacks' of a family who I believe to be mother, father and daughter of about 8-10 years old. The child has strawberry blond long curly hair, the father is tall with very dark hair, the mother although I knew was there I couldn't see as clearly.

> I also get a very bad vibration up the flight of stairs towards the attic and I hate going in the one attic room. I'm sure some awful thing has happened there as I feel like crying if I go in. The steps to the cellar are also bad. I can go down there but I feel I need to mentally protect myself.

It remains a mystery how over a period of 50 years at least the Red House has stimulated such experiences in so many people. The answer may lie in its past—it was a dower house belonging to the Berkeley family, part of the estate at Spetchley Park.

In the attic corridors of Holt Castle a black-clad lady walked at night; whilst a raven materialised in the cellars and put out with its wings any candle that was lit there. The latter story is also told of Leigh Court, put about—it has been suggested—by servants who wished to frighten people away from the supplies of cider and ale kept in the cellar. Until the 1980s at least tales were told at Callow End of Prior's Court ghosts: a grey lady, a cavalier whose body is said to have been walled up in the house, and a butler of the 1920s who continued to welcome visitors long after his death.

At Bockleton, the shade of Sir Robert de Bockleton rides on certain nights around what was his estate. Another mounted ghost is that of a hard-drinking Georgian squire who still spurs over hedge and ditch on stormy nights at Ashton-under-Hill.

Ralph de Wysham lived at Woodmanton Manor, Clifton-on-Teme, during the fourteenth century. He happened to die under a great yew, and some villagers still feel a strange presence when they pass the tree. Clifton abounds with accounts of phantom horses, a white lady bending over a baby's cot, and soldiers of the Civil War heading down through steep woods to Ham Castle (which was in fact besieged by Parliament).

Echoes of the Civil War also linger at Holywell Cottage which, as the name implies, was built over a holy well, at Henwick. In 1991 Mrs Sue Spackman commented:

> Since we moved here four and half years ago both my husband and I, and one or two of our visitors, have seen the ghosts of a man and sometimes a woman, and on one occasion that of a little girl moving through from the front door to what was once the back door, although the back lobby has now been converted into a cloakroom. My husband until recently has always been very sceptical about ghosts and, whereas I never had any experience of them before, I certainly did not pooh-pooh the idea of their existence. On the occasion of our first sighting we both saw the same man, and our descriptions tallied exactly, and at the same time we experienced a cold feeling with the hair at the back of our necks rising. However, now we are used to them we experience no unpleasant sensations and they seem entirely benevolent, although by inclination I think

> I would have been a Royalist supporter and they are definitely Puritans
> by dress, the man in black and the females in grey.

A later conflict features in the account given to me in 2005 by Mrs Gwendoline Appleby of Malvern. During the Second World War she worked in radar in the premises of Malvern College (the school had been evacuated to Harrow). She became ill, and went to the sick-bay, which had been the boys' sanatorium, at a house called the Firs. She was put to bed overnight in a room alone, and told to ring the bell if at any time she needed help. At some point she became aware of a nurse by the door of her room, but realised that her cloak and uniform were bizarrely old-fashioned. Despite her fear, she got out of bed and took a few steps towards the figure, which then disappeared. She rang the bell furiously, but there was no response. She managed to get to sleep and the next morning felt almost ashamed of her experience. Although it remained vividly in her memory she did not mention it until perhaps many years later when she returned to Malvern after a long absence. She was then told that during the First World War the Firs had been used as a sick-bay for wounded soldiers. It is now divided into flats, which are apparently free of nocturnal visitors.

Several public houses and hotels were happily reporting strange phenomena in 2004. The Old Talbot (which prefers to style itself Ye Olde Talbot) in Worcester's Friar Street is haunted by a former employee, Mary Anne Elizabeth, who died there in a fire. Furniture moves, lights flicker, and doors slam, especially on the anniversary of the incident. A pub close by, the Cardinal's Hat, which is reckoned to be the oldest in Worcester, also claims the ghost of a young woman killed in a fire.

At the other end of the city, the Talbot Inn at Barbourne, according to the Worcester Paranormal Group, has the ghosts of a former landlady, a crying boy and a wife murderer. In January 2005, after visiting the former cells beneath Worcester's Guildhall, the same group reported seeing an Edwardian-style figure, hearing the sound of footsteps and smelling alcohol.

A little farther north, the Mug House at Claines, according to the landlady, Judy Allen, is occupied by spirits of the non-drinkable variety, those of soldiers from the battle of Worcester. Unexplained activity in the cellar includes objects such as cider barrels moved about behind a locked door.

At the Swan in Stourport the licensee between 1958 and 1972, Victor Mitchley, repeatedly saw a phantom bonnet-wearing woman. Different land-lords at the Bridge Inn in the same town saw in the 1970s and the 1990s respec-tively a crinolined lady. Within days of taking over a different Swan, at Upton-on-Severn—in December 2004, after a lengthy period of closure for refurbish-ment—the new managers heard a child sobbing on the stairs. Then the chef saw a figure passing which he took to be that of the landlady, Sian Murch, but when he checked with her he found that she had not been there at the time.

The Mug House at Claines

A ghost is thought to appear in the empty orangery of the Mount Pleasant Hotel in Malvern, though details are lacking. A guest in the main building in 1964, a Mrs Gillis, woke at 2.30 a.m. to see an old woman in a long black dress standing by the window. She felt not fear, but puzzlement, as the figure turned towards her, then vanished. At breakfast she related her experience to another guest, who confirmed that at about the same time she too had awakened, and

The Swan Inn, Upton-on-Severn

been paralysed with terror for some 15 minutes. The two women made enquiries, and found that the adjoining rooms they had occupied were once a single bedroom in which, many years earlier, a mother had smothered her young daughter.

The sixteenth-century Old House at Alvechurch was once an inn, the Bear. A vicar was unfrocked for unbecoming activities there, and a local tradition says that Shakespeare wrote part of *The Tempest* in one of the rooms. In 1873 the inn became a private house, and was occupied by successive doctors. Alastair Innes Dick moved there with his family in 1919 when he was nine. The village children soon told him that the house was haunted. His parents, who slept in what had been the inn ballroom, were awakened several times by knocking at the door, though no one was ever there. Young Alastair heard occasional rumblings above their ceiling which his parents put down to cats, though 'these were most uncatlike sounds'. In 1927 work began on converting the roof space into a box room, and a baby's skeleton immediately came to light. Medical opinion held that the child must have died over 50 years earlier, when the house was still an inn. People said that a servant girl could have disposed of an unwanted child. The bones were buried in the churchyard. Flowers appeared on the grave, and the rumour went round that the baby's mother, still alive, had secretly put them there. The identity of neither mother nor child ever came out, but after the burial the mysterious noises ceased in the Old House.

The rear of the Old House at Alvechurch in the 1920s

The ruins of Bordesley Abbey (left) and Guy, Earl of Warwick,
nicknamed The Black Dog of Arden (right)

The sufferings of monks displaced after Henry VIII's dissolution of the monasteries have been offered as an explanation for some phenomena. The phantom of a robber-monk called Benedict once appeared at Ashton-under-Hill. Monks expelled from Pershore Abbey have been linked with strange shapes seen at night in the shadows of Little Priest Lane. An old house at Badsey, once a *hospitium* (sanatorium) for Evesham Abbey was reputed to be haunted, and people told of 'the old fellows [monks] rattling about again' at night. Until the dissolution, Guy, Earl of Warwick, rested in peace at Bordesley Abbey, where he was buried in 1315, thanks to the money he left for monks to pray for him. When they left and their prayers ceased, Guy, true to his nickname of The Black Dog of Arden, came forth in the guise of a great black hound. One of his appearances shocked a mid-nineteenth-century party of archaeologists, and he continued to be seen at least until the 1950s.

Some villages seem more haunted than others, and Alfrick claims to have the most ghosts in Worcestershire. Its many apparitions include a black dog, a horseman, a wagon and horses, a crow, the persistent sound of a cooper's

Salwarpe Church

hammer, and a man, woman and dog walking from the old forge to the church of St Mary Magdalene.

Churches, churchyards and parsonages certainly seem to have their share of ghosts. The old church of St Michael at Abberley and the nearby rectory are visited by a grey lady. At Astley what is simply described as 'a presence' manifests itself at the former rectory and in the vicinity of the church. The churchyard at Salwarpe has its whispering monks, passing to and fro, together with a carriage which crosses the river from High Park to the church.

A Dowles man continued his feud with another until after the latter's death, and determined to desecrate his grave. One dark night he started digging, only to be alarmed by an apparition which came towards him from the western end of the church. He ran away towards Bewdley, pursued by the ghost. As soon as he reached the town he fell down on his knees and cried: 'Lord have mercy; forgive me and I'll never do it again'. At this point the ghost vanished.

A few years later, at the beginning of the nineteenth century, a French visitor, Louis Lefevre, riding near Childswickham encountered a hearse travelling at a furious pace—without a driver. He galloped after it and saw it stop by the churchyard gate, the black horses' heads nodding and harness jingling. Then it vanished.

A story heard by R.L. Brown in the Chequers Inn at Crowle in the 1970s concerns St John's Church. A gravedigger, Charlie Price, goes to Worcester to fetch a new spade. On the way back after nightfall—walking, of course—he is almost back to his home, a cottage on Crowle Court Farm, when someone steps out of the hedge and stops him with raised arm. He makes out the figure of a

The lectern at Crowle (formerly at Evesham Abbey), showing St Egwin

black-habited monk, and when it turns and beckons him to follow, despite being deeply afraid he feels a strange compulsion to obey. As they reach the church-yard the monk passes into it straight through the wall; Charlie clambers over. The monk points to the spade and to a place on the ground; Charlie digs. A foot or two down he strikes something hard and looks questioningly towards the figure but finds that he has disappeared. The next morning he goes back to the hole in the churchyard and digs out a stone object which turns out to be a lectern. This, later identified as originating from the Benedictine abbey at Evesham, now occupies a prized place in Crowle Church (see also page 93).

Brown also reported the experience of a woman who visited St Helen's Church in Worcester, before the period when it was used as the county record office. She was looking round when she saw a little girl on her knees in the aisle, searching for something, and sobbing. The woman offered to help but the child ran towards the door, and vanished before reaching it. When she spoke to the vicar he explained: 'For a number of years people have seen this girl in the church. She is always searching for something, and disappears on being spoken to'. He could offer no explanation for the phenomenon. The church has now been returned for use in occasional services and also concerts, and it seems that the sad little girl no longer appears.

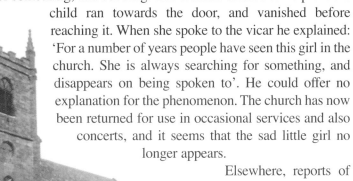

Hanbury Church

Elsewhere, reports of strange phenomena continue. One of my own sons, in about 1970 when he was still a teenager, went into Hanbury Church one day and

169

began to play the piano. After a very short time he was seized by an over-whelming feeling of terror, and his hair stood on end. All he could think of was to continue playing, and after a time his fear subsided. We later found out that workmen regularly refused to be inside Hanbury Church alone by day, and would not go there at all by night.

During the 1990s I visited many churches with the presenter, Mike George, of BBC Hereford and Worcester, to make recordings for a series of programmes. As we approached the secluded Huddington Church the unflap-pable Mike felt a sudden unease at the prospect of entering, and became distinctly alarmed inside when his tape recorder simply would not operate. At Broadway Old Church in 1997 the churchwarden's wife told us that the phantom figure of a woman, dressed in black and only between three and four feet in height, had been seen in the building. We visited the small Victorian church at The Hook, near Upton-on-Severn, after a telephone call from a Mr John Wall. He had been camping at Welland with his family, and on a sunny June day decided to walk to Upton by back roads. At The Hook he decided to go into the churchyard, where he saw, disap-pearing round the comer of the church, a bright green, shimmering, almost fluorescent object 'like the old-fashioned boa sometimes used by a cheap stripper'. He ran to the comer and looked round, but the object had gone. He had the lingering feeling that he had seen it somewhere before, possibly in childhood. Mike George and I were unfortunately unable to suggest any explanation.

Church at the Hook

Unquiet Spirits

The victims of injustice, murder and accident can, it seems, be reluctant to rest in peace. Multitudes of such events pass by without ghostly repercussions, while with no discernible principle of selection a few apparently provoke strange phenomena. At Salwarpe the cutting of the Droitwich Canal caused a big old house to be demolished. Its then owner is sometimes seen gliding down the embankment into the water, protesting in ghostly form. Many women must have been jilted; one of them grieved so cruelly that she haunted the Red House at Barnt Green, a short distance across the fields from the home of her faithless lover.

St Benedict's Pool in a field above Beckford Hall harbours the ghost of a beautiful woman who drowned there, perhaps by accident. Hidden treasure lurks there, too, in the shape of silver bells, golden candlesticks or even a golden bedstead. A curse protects it from any searcher.

According to a tradition at Offenham, William, one of the children of Lady Hoby, turned out to be a poor scholar. In the manner of the time, she beat him repeatedly: so much so that he died. Her remorse was so profound that after her death she walked, or rather glided, through the house at Offenham, wringing blood-stained hands in an effort to

Canal at Salwarpe

cleanse them. Centuries later, children's copybooks, much blotted, were discovered in the house. In childish script they bore the name of William Hoby.

Lady Hoby and her husband, Sir Thomas, are said to have been charged for a time by Queen Mary with the tutelage of Princess Elizabeth. This could not have been so. All the Hobys were strong Protestants, and therefore would have been distrusted by Mary. Thomas Hoby did not marry until 1558, the year Elizabeth came to the throne. (He was knighted by her in 1566). His second son, Thomas Posthumous Hoby, married Margaret in 1596, and she must be the Lady Hoby of the tale. She is the earliest known Englishwoman to have written a diary which survived. She and her husband lived at Hackness in the North Riding of Yorkshire, a further problem for the Offenham story.

At Broadway the ghost of a lady killed while out with the hunt rides along White Ladies Lane at the top end of the village. Broadway also has the ghost of a kennelman torn to pieces by his own hounds. Apparently he rushed out in the night when he heard them baying; they failed to recognise him in his night-shirt, and attacked him. His ghost appears in the same garment.

A very similar story comes from Church Farm, Besford, where an eight-eenth century kennelman went out at night after hearing a disturbance. He was not missed until the next morning. A search revealed only his jackboots with his lower legs and feet inside. It was never determined whether the dogs were

Church Farm, Besford

responsible or whether he had been killed by a stranger and fed to the animals. In later years, though, the boots with their jingling spurs were heard walking in what is still called Dog Kennel Place. A strange tail-piece to the story is that a skeleton was found in the field in 1930, intact save for the lower legs and feet. Later, more skeletons found at the same place were thought to be those of men killed in the battle of Worcester.

According to Robert Hunt and Ruth Jackson, the chroniclers of Inkberrow, 'many of the old houses are haunted, but only people who are psychic are aware of the fact and most of these live quite happily with their ghosts'. Suicide, though, is a different matter. At Salter Street crossroads the white ghost which comes flapping over the hedge is that of Joseph Mucklow, a pauper who was buried there in 1773 after hanging himself. Whether a stake was driven through his heart or not has not been recorded, though this often happened in such cases: certainly in that of Anne Hinton or Stinton, who lived at Boraston, near Tenbury, with her son, his wife and their children. For unknown reasons she tried to poison the children, then killed herself. She was buried, in about 1784, at Boraston Cross, and proceeded to haunt the spot.

A death of which the consequences have reverberated through six centuries took place at Wichenford Court. A Welsh army led by Owain Glyndwr and supported by a French expeditionary force was in Worcestershire in 1405. Some say the allies sacked Worcester, but they probably reached only the western suburbs before retreating to Woodbury Hill. Henry IV's army moved into position not far away, possibly at Abberley. A period of skirmishing, and even jousting, between the opposing camps then took place, after which the invaders, judging the time unripe for a major battle, withdrew.

Against this background stands the story that Margaret Washbourne of Wichenford Court killed a high-ranking Frenchman, even a prince. According

Wichenford Court

to one account she lured the leader of a raiding party into the house and stabbed him in the back with a dagger. In a more spectacular and better-known variation the Frenchman, captured by John Washboume and his men while crossing the River Teme during the allied retreat, was held for ransom at Wichenford. Washbourne then had to go away, leaving his wife in charge. During his absence she grew fond of the captive, and tried to seduce him. Incensed at being spurned, she gave him a sleeping draught and stabbed him. His blood left a stain on the floor, indelible over centuries, despite rebuildings of the house.

After the man's death 'Lady' Washbourne's regret deprived her of rest by day and sleep by night. When she died her spirit wandered through the house, a bloodstained dagger in one hand and a cup in the other. It invariably appeared on the eve (21 July) of St Mary Magdalene, patron of repentant sinners. In addition, the ghosts of French and Welsh soldiers drowned in the Fitcher Brook near the Court when a flood cut off their retreat were said to haunt the parish. Attempts to lay them failed because they could not understand the language used; on the other hand they must have been able to communicate if, as one account has it, they agreed to haunt only when the brook was in flood.

The Church of England still nominates one clergyman in each diocese to carry out exorcisms as required, within guidelines that set out best current practice. Many instances have been recorded in Worcestershire in the past.

'And Peaceful ever after slept old Colles' shade'—once a well known saying—referred to Edmund Colles, who lived at Leigh Court in the early seventeenth century. In an attempt to raise money, according to tradition, Colles

Leigh Church, with the Court on the left

waylaid a friend from Cradley who was riding home from Worcester with a large sum. Colles seized the horse's bridle but the man lashed out with his sword, and spurred on. When he arrived home he found a bloody hand still grasping the reigns, and on one of the fingers he recognised Colles's signet ring. (The theme, by the way, is well known. It was first printed in 1579 and still turns up in the form of stories about attempted thefts from motorists in contemporary Britain and America.)

Next day the Cradley man went to Leigh Court to confront Colles. He found him in bed nursing his wound, and forgave him. Even so, after his death Colles's spectre drove a coach pulled by four fire-breathing horses down the road at Leigh, up over the great tithe barn at the Court, and into the River Teme. Eventually twelve parsons assembled to conjure the apparition by a ritual Bible reading. Colles's ghost was conducted to a pool, which was then filled in. The family estate passed to trustees, who sold it in 1615 to Sir Walter Devereux, MP for Worcestershire and also owner of Malvern Link. Edmund Colles senior, who died in 1606, has a memorial in St Edburga's Church at Leigh; not so his son.

Since Biblical times the illegal moving of landmarks has been considered a great wrong. A mover of marks who went on to even worse things was Captain Thomas Bound of Upton-on-Severn, 'a desperately wicked man, very cruel and covetous and hard on the poor'. Bound moved the marker stones which are still to be seen on a meadow known as the Ham by the river so as to obtain more ground for himself. He married three wives in succession, and there were suspicions that he had done away with the first two. He lived at Soley's Orchard but moved to Southend Farm, which he secured by guiding the hand of a dying woman so that she bequeathed it to him. In retribution she haunted him. He in turn drowned himself in a pool by the Causeway, a raised path connecting Rectory Lane with Southend.

Bound undoubtedly existed. He was born in the time of James I, a member of an old Upton family. His handwriting as churchwarden can be seen in the church registers for 1640 and 1641. He was indeed married three times—to two Marys and a Margaret—with the first two both dying within twelve months of marriage. He owned Soley's Orchard, and leased Southend Farm from a Mrs Bromley. He served as a soldier for Parliament during the Civil War, which may explain the opprobrium in which local people clearly held him. On the day he died in late July 1667 a phantom cortège—black-draped coffin and black-cloaked men—was seen leaving the church.

Soon after Bound's death his ghost was seen at Soley's Orchard, Southend, the Causeway and Rectory Lane. An attempt to lay the unquiet spirit was made by a clergyman who dropped an inch of lighted candle into the fatal pool with the injunction to Bound to keep quiet until it was re-lit. This proved ineffective, and Bound grew so bold that he appeared in broad daylight on his grey horse. Three parsons next tried a ceremony in the cellar at Soley's Orchard, which was afterwards bricked up. They held hands in a ring, and tried to consign Bound to the Red Sea. One of them carelessly allowed his leg to move out of the circle. There was a 'whizz' and something hit him on the cheek; no hair ever again grew on that spot. Not surprisingly, Bound was soon seen again, sitting on a stone by the Causeway or riding up Rectory Lane with a land-measuring chain clanking behind him. To the terror of fishermen he would appear in early morning on the banks of the Severn, and as a further horror the spectral forms of his three wives were seen at Soley's Orchard.

Eventually the railway cut through what had been Bound's garden at Southend and the farm was demolished. The house at Soley's Orchard still exists, though it has been greatly modernised. Bound's grave and bones came to light in the mid-nineteenth century in the chancel of the old church at Upton. His skull was taken and turned into a macabre

Captain Bound's Stone on the Causeway

drinking cup. Bound's grim presence was long felt by timid people on dark nights in Rectory Lane, and it may be still.

Rev. Dr W.K.W. Chafy, rector of Rous Lench, wrote with some gusto of the predicament of a predecessor of his, Rev. Stanwix Whittingdale, who took up the post in 1746. Whittingdale's wife, Frances, lived for only eight years after their marriage, but she displayed 'a terrible posthumous vitality which nearly drove her husband out of his wits, and every servant out of the house'. She persisted in 'rustling in green silk' in rectory and churchyard, 'and, setting all well-established ghost-habits at defiance, incontinently started on her rounds before nightfall'. According to one tale, Whittingdale exorcised the ghost, 'but to his cost, for he did not live long afterwards'. Another claims that:

> she herself requested to be 'laid', indicating the duck pond as the place; whereupon several-parson-power was invoked, with 'Bell, Book, and Candle'—the number varies from four to a dozen, but the latter gets mixed with the candles—and 'they read, and laid her', though ... no sooner had she let out that they were safe so long as the last candle did not burn out, than they threw it into the water, where it 'went out with a fizz'.

Whittingdale died in 1772, aged 62 (see also page 110).

Late in the eighteenth century a farmer called Dee was living with his wife and daughter at a farm in Little Malvern. Dee's brutal treatment of his wife finally killed her, though not before she had threatened to haunt him if he proved unkind to their daughter. For a time he behaved well but then his old cruelty returned, and his daughter, then aged 12 or 14, resolved to drown herself. She went to a pool, but just as she was about to jump her mother rose from the water with arms outstretched to stop her.

Underhills (formerly Gough's) Farm, Little Malvern. The pool still exists just to the right of the track in front of the building

The girl ran back to the farm, where she found that her mother had also appeared. Indeed, she continued to do so, standing with arms akimbo, doing a kind of jig, or springing six feet from the ground, her glassy eyes staring at Dee. Servants and labourers fled. One day Dee persuaded two farmers to come for dinner with him, but their meal was interrupted by another appearance of the cavorting ghost. In a fury Dee threw his knife, which went straight through the spirit and stuck in the wall, but made no difference to the antics. When a field of hay was due to be cut a hundred spectators turned up, hoping to see some spectral activity. The ghost did not disappoint, but its dance of death terrified the people, who fled.

An Anglican clergyman came to exorcise the perturbed spirit, without success. Dee's neighbours suggested that he ask the catholic priest at Little Malvern Court, who went to the pond, summoned Mrs Dee to appear in the name of God, and read the service of exorcism. He then forbade her to appear as long as the light burned before the blessed sacrament at Little Malvern Court.

For a time no more was seen of the ghost, but then it appeared again, no longer dancing, but sitting, head on hands, on a great stone near the farm which came to be called Mrs Dee's Rock. Repairs in the chapel at Little Malvern Court meant that the light had been extinguished. The priest again came to conduct an exorcism, this time bidding the ghost to show itself again before the day of judgement. He then threw the candles he was holding into the pool, and Mrs Dee's ghost has not been seen since. In 1911 *Berrow's Worcester Journal* ran an item on the ghost which mentioned the late Mrs Parsons of Stuart Lodge, Malvern Wells, who 'was personally acquainted with the daughter of Mrs Dee, who had seen the apparition of her mother so often'.

The ghost of a reputed murderer haunted a house in Beoley for some time until in about 1800 a conclave of clergymen subdued it and chained it to the bed of the Red Sea (a favoured confinement), but only for 50 years. Once the term had elapsed odd things began to happen again in the house. Doors slammed, and something could be heard running about above the ceilings. Sceptics suggested rats as being responsible for the latter, but some people—notably the parish beadle—refused to enter the house during the hours of darkness.

An unsuccessful exorcism was carried out in the 1870s at Childswickham House, where a blue lady was often seen at one of the bedroom windows. Twelve parsons gathered with bell, book and candle, and for some reason agreed that if one of them were to die within the year their attempt at exorcising the ghost would fail. One of them did die, and the blue lady resumed her appearances.

The story of Black Harry, told by A.C. Smith of Great Comberton in 1932, concerns a bad-tempered farmer, always anxious to check that his boundaries were not being infringed, who often rode about on a little white pony. One morning he was found dead in bed, murdered. Soon after the funeral, Black Harry and the white pony rode again. A priest tried to exorcise the spirit, and failed. A second priest offered to make another attempt, on condition that he should be entirely alone. He, too, failed, but then discovered that a servant girl had breached his privacy by peeping through the curtains of her window. He claimed success at the third time of asking; otherwise, he said, the unlighted candle which he threw in a bottle into a pond would have surfaced again, alight. An alternative outcome involves twelve parsons from twelve parishes round Bredon Hill, each of whom held a lighted candle and said a prayer. Eleven of the candles went out; the twelfth burned on, with a blue flame. The twelfth parson repeated his prayer: Black Harry and his white pony were seen no more.

Fairies

Martha Sherwood—famous in Victorian times for her series of novels, *The History of the Fairchild Family* (published 1814-47)—was born at Stanford-on-Teme in 1775. She looked back with great affection to the stories she heard there as a child from her father's curate, Robert Nash, who was also a relative:

> Oh! it was a happy day when he was seen coming across the park, in his great bushy wig, his shovel hat, his cravat tied like a King William's bib, his great drab coat, and his worsted splatter-dashes [leggings]. ... As soon as it was dark, in a winter evening, I took my place on his knee, and calling him Uncle Robert, begged for a story. Again and again I heard the same, but the old tale never tired. He told of dogs which were supposed to have been spirits, and which were always seen in certain rooms when any of the family were about to die, and other marvels of like description.

Miss Clarke (aged 91) of Little Witley, in 1932 with some of the children to whom she told fairy stories

Mrs Sherwood mentions the title of two tales told by Uncle Robert—*Robert and the Owl* and *Henry Milner*—but I have not been able to trace them. She also saw as a child fairy rings in the woods near Stanford.

When she died (in 1887) some adults in Worcestershire still believed in fairies. At the end of the century 'an intelligent working man, just past middle age' gave E.J. Latchbury 'many anecdotes about them':

> When a lad he lived with his father, a small farmer, on the edge of the
> Forest of Wyre, and went out with the horses. His bedroom was over the
> pantry, and near the stable. He declared that at night things were thrown
> about in the pantry, crockery rattled violently, etc., but that in the
> morning everything was in its proper place. He scorned the suggestion of
> rats. The horses used to rush wildly about in the stable, and one night,
> when he went down to look at them, he found them with tails plaited up
> and 'all of a lather' as if they had been ridden at great pace. The stable
> door was fastened, and nothing was to be seen but some 'short straws'
> into which, he was convinced, the fairies had 'turned themselves' on the
> sound of a mortal footstep.

Similar treatment of horses is also ascribed to witches (see below).

Mildred Berkeley described in 1932 how 'an old inhabitant of the Wyre
Forest' told her that she remembered going to look for fairies in the orchard
'and finding their clay pipes; and that it was the custom to leave a few apples
on the trees for elfin use, and then in return the elves would bless the tree and
provide a good crop in the coming year'.

According to 'a Worcestershire Lady' writing in the *Worcester Journal* in
1892, Penrice of the Commandry—a mansion at Crowle now gone, whose
name survives in that of a farm—'had a beautiful daughter, said to have a fairy
god-mother, who, through her spells, caused the lovely Mildred Penrice to be
beautiful for ever, although she lived to a very old age':

> This fairy godmother used to meet her goddaughter at the 'Fairy Spring' at
> Cawdy Well, and commanded her to leave her bed before sunrise on nine
> mornings in May before the young May moon was at the full—being the
> first new moon in May—and wash her face in the May dew. Her beauty
> would then surpass all others, but she was not to let the rays of the sun
> touch the dew before she washed her face, or the spell would be broken.

People tried hard to befriend the fairies. A labourer at Upton Snodsbury
heard one of the little creatures crying over a broken seat. He mended it, and the
fairy fed him in return on biscuits and wine. Everything he did afterwards turned
out well, and he prospered. A similar tale was told at Alfrick, where a man and
a boy were ploughing when they heard lamentations coming from a copse. They
went over, and found a fairy grieving over a lost pickaxe. They managed to find
it, and were rewarded by bread, cheese and cider. The man ate and drank but the
boy was too frightened to do so. Another example of fairy benevolence was the
belief in Lulsley that if a woman broke her peel—the flat tool used for moving
bread into and out of the oven—the fairies would mend it if she left it in a cave
(the Fairies Cave) by Osebury Rock, near the River Teme.

On the other hand, as with the ploughing boy, the fairies could inspire fear.
They were able to spoil butter, to steal babies and substitute changelings, to

inveigle people into accompanying them for what seems a few minutes or hours and turned out to be years.

Little is now heard of fairies outside films and stories for children. However, they remain in the names of fields and landscape features, sometimes in the form of Puck, Hob or Dob—all beneficent and occasionally mischievous spirits. Such names include Hobacre (Frankley), Hob's Hole (Offenham), Hob Moor (Chaddesley Corbett), Little Dobbin's Hill (Berrow), Puck Meadow (Hallow), Puck Hill (Himbleton), Puck Croft and Pixies' Ham (Powick), Puck Pit (Abberton), Puck's Piece (Abbot's Lench), Puxton (Wolverley) and Cob's Piece (Dodderhill).

The Devil

In the popular imagination the devil was often linked with sinister or spectacular places. A deep dingle between Dodenham and Martley is called the Devil's Leap. The Devil's Den is the name of a dark wood near Stanford-on-Teme. One spot in the wood is called Hell Hole, and a plant called Devil's Bit (*Succisa pratensis*) grows there. This was once used to heal deadly wounds, and when the devil saw how many were being saved he bit off the roots, but the plant appears to grow without any. Near Stourbridge is Hell Bank, and at Upton Warren, Hell Patch. Inkberrow has a Devil's Bowling Green, and Leigh, a Devil's Pig Trough. At Aldington are Devil's Dyke and Devil's Punchbowl.

Comforting stories illustrated how easily the devil could be outwitted. 'The devil and the farmer' was told to Jesse Salisbury as a boy 'by a thresher man while at work in a barn':

> The devil once called on a farmer at Little Comberton and asked if he could give him a job. 'What con'st do?' said the farmer.
> 'Oh, anything about a farm', said the devil.
> 'Well, I wants a mon to help me to thresh a mow o' whate', says the farmer.
> 'All right', says the devil, 'I'm yer mon'.
> When they got to the barn the farmer said to the devil, 'Which 'ould thee do, thresh or throw down?'
> 'Thresh', said the devil. So the farmer got o' top o' the mow and begun to throw down the sheaves of whate on to the barn floor, but as fast as he could throw 'em down the devil with one stroke of his nile [flail] knocked all the corn out on 'em, and sent the sheaves flying out the barn door. The farmer thought he had got a queer sort of a threshermon, and as he couldn't throw down fast enough for 'im, he says to 'im, 'Thee come and throw down'.
> 'All right', says the devil. So the farmer gets down off the mow by the ladder but the devil he just gives a lep up from the barn floor to the top o' the mow, athout waiting to go up the ladder.

'Be you ready?' says the devil. 'Iss', says the farmer. With that the devil sticks his shuppick [pitchfork] into as many sheaves as 'ould cover the barn floor, and throws 'em down. 'That'll do for a bit', says the farmer, so the devil sat down and waited till the farmer'd threshed that lot, and when a was ready again, he throwed down another floor full; and afore night they'd finished the whole o' the mow o' whate.

The farmer couldn't help thinking a good deal about his new mon, for he'd never sin such a one before. (He didn't know it was the devil, thee knowest, 'cause he took care not to let the farmer see his cloven foot). So in the morning he got up early and went and spoke to a cunning mon about it. The cunning mon said it must be the devil as had come to him, and as he had asked him in he couldn't get shut on him without he could give him as job as he couldn't do.

Soon after the farmer got wum [home] again his new mon wanted to know what he was to do that day, and the farmer thought he'd give him a teaser; so he says, 'Go into the barn, look, and count the number of corns there be in that heap o' whate as we threshed out yesterday'.

'All right', says Old Nick, an off he went. In a few minutes he comes back and says, 'Master, there be so many' (naming ever so many thousands or millions and odd, I don't know how many).

'Bist sure thee's counted 'em all?' says the farmer.

'Every corn', says Satan. Then the farmer ordered him to go and fill a hogshead barrel full of water with a sieve. So off he shoots again but soon comes back and tells the farmer he'd done it; and sure enough a had; and every job the farmer set him to do was the same. The poor farmer didn't know what to make on it, for though he was getting his work done up so quick, he didn't like his new mon's company.

However, the farmer thought he'd have another try to trick him, and told the devil he wanted him to go with him a-mowing next morning. 'All right', says the old un, 'I'll be there, master'. But as soon as it was night the farmer went to the field and in the part the devil was to mow he drove a lot of harrow tines into the ground amongst the grass. In the morning they got to the field in smartish time and began to mow. The farmer he took his side and told the devil to begin o' the t'other, where he'd stuck in the harrow tines, thee knowst.

Well, as it went the devil—who but he?—he soon got in amongst the stuck up harrow tines; but they made no odds, his scythe went through'em all, and the only notice on 'em he took was to say to the farmer every time he'd cut one through, 'A burdock, master'; and kept on just the same. The poor farmer he got so frightened at last he throwed down his scythe and left the devil to finish the field.

As luck would have it sooner after a got wum a gipsy woman called at the farm house, and seeing the farmer was in trouble asked him what was the matter. So he up and told her all about it. 'You a-got the devil in your house sure enough and you can only get shut on him by giving him summat to do as a can't manage'.

'Well, woman', says the farmer, 'what's the use o' telling me that? I a-tried everything I can think on but I darned if I can find him any job as a can't do'.

'I'll tell you what to do', says the gipsy woman. 'When a comes wum you get the missis to give him one of her curly hairs, and then send him to the blacksmith's shop to straighten him on the blacksmith's anvil. He'll find a can't do that and he'll get so wild over it he'll never come back to you again'.

The farmer was very thankful to the gipsy woman and said he'd try her plan. So bye and bye in comes the old fellow and says 'I a finished the mowing, master. What else a you got for me to do?'

'Well, I can't think of another job just now', says the farmer, 'but I thinks the missis got a little job for thee'. So he called the missis and her gave the devil a curly hair lapped up in a bit o' paper, and told him to go to the blacksmith's shop an 'ommer that hair straight, and when a was straight to bring him back to her. 'All right, missis', says the devil, and off a shot. When he got to the blacksmith's shop he 'ommered and 'ommered at that there hair on the anvil but the more he 'ommered the crookeder the hair got. So at last he throwed down the 'ommer and the hair and bolted, and never went back to the farmer again.

By contrast, various alarming tales continued to circulate. In about 1800, according to Jabez Allies, an old fiddler called Pengree (or Pingrie), was on his way home to Old Storridge from a wake at Knightsford Bridge Inn when he had to pass a place in Alfrick called Hell Garden. 'Well, I'll give "The Devil's Dream"', he exclaimed, and struck up the tune on his fiddle. No sooner had he done so when 150 strange female figures came and danced round him in pattens. He ignominiously stopped playing and ran away.

'A Worcestershire Lady' wrote in 1892 of the tradition at Naunton Beauchamp Court, seven miles east of Worcester, that on St Bartholomew's

Naunton Beauchamp Court

Artist's impression of the victim of the Hagley Wood murder

The graffito on the obelisk

Eve (23 August), Urso d'Abitot rode along the Ghost Walk from 1 a.m. until daybreak in a gold chariot dawn by three white bears and driven by Satan. Unless he wore a cross any person encountering Urso would be torn to pieces by the bears. (Urso, who came over with William the Conqueror, was renowned both for his Herculean strength and size, and for the many bears he kept).

As late as the 1940s a bizarre murder which came to light at Hagley, between Halesowen and Kidderminster, led to suggestions of satanism or witchcraft. In April 1943 two boys out birds' nesting in Hagley Wood who clambered up a wych elm and peered into its hollow inside saw a human skull and fragments of clothing. Bones and more clothes were then found nearby. A leading pathologist, Professor J.M. Webster, concluded that the remains were those of a woman, five feet tall, and aged between 25 and 40. An inquest delivered a verdict of murder. Despite strenuous efforts, neither victim nor killer was ever identified. One theory held that the dead woman was a German spy, or a double agent. Margaret Murray, egyptologist and witchcraft expert, believed that devil worshippers must have been involved. A tremendous stir resulted when an obelisk (just off the present A456 road) was found to have been inscribed by unknown hands with the words 'Who put Bella in the wych elm?' The painting seems to have been periodically renewed, and in 2003 Simon Holt became so deeply affected that he wrote the words and music of an opera on the subject, which was performed both in Aldeburgh and London. The mystery remains.

Witches

In 1542 witchcraft became a crime under English law for the first time. Indictments in Worcestershire seem to have been limited to the seventeenth century, but patchy court records mean that sentences (if any) are often unknown. After the repeal of the Witchcraft Act in 1736, although the offence ceased to exist in law fear of alleged witched lingered until perhaps the twentieth century.

Malicious accusations against women—to gratify spite, to avoid a debt, or simply to make mischief—were by no means unknown. In 1601 John Genifer laid charges of witchcraft against a midwife at Worcester—he said she 'had deserved burning seven years sithence'—when she asked for the return of money lent him by her husband, Edward Buckland. For good measure, Genifer added of Mrs Buckland that 'being a midwide she was unfit to bring a dog to bed much less a woman'.

One test applied to a suspected witch was to bind the woman's limbs and throw her into water. The innocent sank; the guilty 'swam', or floated. Either way the experience was unpleasant, and could even be fatal.

According to the diary of a magistrate, Henry Townsend of Elmley Lovett, four witches—'one Widow Robinson and her two daughters and a man'—were brought to gaol in Worcester from Kidderminster. The older daughter, speaking of the restoration to the throne of Charles II, remarked:

> if they had not been taken the king should never have come into England, and though he now doth come yet he shall not live long, but shall die as ill a death as they.

Despite this, Townsend observed that since little was proved against the witches 'they were put to the ducking in the River'—they would probably have been held in the cells under the Guildhall, and taken down Cooken (later Copenhagen) Street to the Severn—'and they would not sink but swam aloft'. To the guilty sign of floating in the water was added the discovery that 'the man had five teats, the mother three, and the eldest daughter had one': imperfections in the skin which proved insensitive to the pricking of a pin, or did not bleed—birthmarks, scars, warts and any other protrusions or malformations—were regarded as nipples for the feeding of familiars or devil marks. The fate of the Kidderminster Four is not known.

Townsend recorded in the same year that Joan Bibb of Rushock, near Elmley Castle, on suspicion of being a witch was 'tyed and throwen into a poole ... to see whether she could swim'. She must have been a woman of rare

Abbot's Morton

spirit, for 'she did bringe her Act'n ag'st Mr Shaw the Parson' — who instigated the proceedings — 'and Recov'rd 10 lb [£] Damadges and 10 lb for costes'. In 1687 an Oldswinford nailer called Jospeph Orford was indicated as 'a common disturber' for boasting that 'he could have Barnes and his wife duckt for witches, and would procure one John Johnson, a drummer, to be present at the doing of it, to make the more sport'.

In 1716 a Worcester JP, John Goodere, was removed from the bench not so much for attending the 'swimming' of an alleged witch, but afterwards for stripping off and jumping into the water himself: 'he swam about it on his back, exposing his nakedness to the Men and Women who were present'. Then he pulled on his breeches 'before several women that were present and asked which of them would be kn---kt' (knocked).

The typical victim of a witch-hunt was an old woman living alone, as in the case of Ann Bellett, a widow of Stacy Morton (an old name for Abbot's Morton), who was accused in 1633 by three Inkberrow men of 'evil art' in the form of 'the jugling trick of the sire and sheves [scythe and shears] to find out goods lost and using the names of Peter and Paule therein in profane manner being saide to be founded on that sleight and cunning trick'. Finding lost or stolen goods was one of the standard functions of a village wise man or woman.

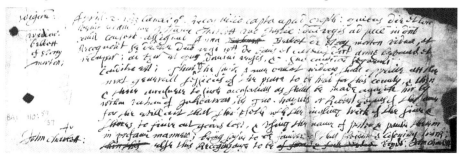

The indictment against Ann Bellett

A fine line divided it from witchcraft. Charming away disease or misfortune was usually acceptable, but not bringing them on by spells or curses.

In 1660 Elinor Burt was accused at Worcester of healing the sick by the laying on of hands. She claimed 'a gifte from God' which indeed enabled her to cure 'by good prayers and laying her hands upon ... heads or faces'. The outcome of this case is not recorded.

According to Nash, four women, Margaret Landis, Susan Cook, Rebecca West and Rose Holybred, were tried and executed at Worcester in 1649 for the 'supposed offence' of witchcraft. Strangely for the meticulous Nash, this seems to be a howler, since these women lived in Essex, where in 1645 one died 'by visitation of God', two were condemned for witchcraft (and presumably executed), and the fourth was acquitted.

Attempts to deprive Joyce Dovey or Dovie of Bewdley of her property during the early 1640s may have caused the fits which came on her at prayer time. However, her state was attributed to demonic intervention, and the case described in a pamphlet, *A strange and true Relation of a Young Woman possest with the Devill ... with a particular of her actions, & how the evill Spirit speakes within her ....* published in 1647.

In 1661 a Defford woman, Ursula Corbett, a bride of three weeks, was found guilty of burning her husband and burnt at the stake as a witch. The following year Elizabeth Ranford of Great Comberton laid information before the magistrates

> that she heard Joane Willis, wife of Thomas Willis of Great Comberton, say that shee will take her oathe that shee, the said informant, is a witch, and bewitched to death one Ths. Right's wife, and one Robert Price's child, both of Comberton. That she behegged one of the said Joan Willis her children: likewise the said informant informeth that shee, the said informant, was going to one Mgt. Willis her house in Comberton about her business, and the said Jane Willis came violently upon her and gave her several blows with a staffe, and ripped her quaife [coif] of her head, and profanely did swear, blood and wounds she would kill her.

Joan Willis's accusation of witchcraft against Elizabeth Ranford could have had serious consequences, and the latter was understandably anxious to clear her name. If a woman acquired the reputation of dabbling in witchcraft she would find it hard to shake off.

Martha Farmer of Astley claimed in 1698 that Margaret Hill of Shrawley had called at her house when she was out and asked her young daughter for some oatmeal. When the child refused Margaret bent her finger and made it bleed. Next morning the child fell ill and remained so for some days till Margaret came and prayed over her. Then she relapsed, and Margaret came a second time, but only after Martha had threatened that 'if the child died she would have life for life'. In addition, Margaret 'called her [Martha] a Judas b---, and told her that she would not be well whilst she lived, whereupon she fell lame'. Another party, Mary Wall, swore that 'Margaret Hill came to her house and begged for buttermilk, but she had none, and the same afternoon the cow fell ill, and they sent for a man skilled in distempered cattle, who told her the cow was bewitched'. Mary's husband went to a wise man at Worcester, who told him the cow would be dead by the time he got home, which proved to be so. Two more women added their complaints about Margaret Hill, but there is no record of any outcome to the case.

Strange Powers

Long after the judicial pursuit of witches ceased, belief in their extraordinary abilities continued. Master Fidkin, the Hartlebury wizard (for whom, see also page 58) put people under a spell which made them wander the village all night—or so they thought.

At Worcester two old women could halt carts in the mud of Salt Lane (now Castle Street) or free them from it. Waggoners learned to offer sixpence, so that their carts could go on their way. On one occasion a horseman happened to see straw lying across his horse's back, and cut it with a knife. Immediately one of the women fell dead. The other survived, to turn a troop of tax-gathering soldiers into the stones of the Tything. The full story was told by Edward Corbett in 1912.

The Tything Witches

Once upon a time—and it were a very long time ago—there was a little house in the Tything at Worcester, and in it lived two old women. They was witches, and what they didn't know the devil had kept to himself. They sold charms and spellings, and sent things, and they'd cure warts and toothaches and find anything as was lost; but they would have made a poor living of it if it wasn't for the carts. Because every now and again a cart as it was passing by their house would stick in the mud, and all for whatever the horses and men could do that cart couldn't go on.

Then one of these here old women would come out of the house, and the men would give her sixpence, and she'd say 'God bless the cart', and then the horses would start away with it as easy as if it weren't loaded. Folks didn't like it but nobody never said anything to the old women about it. For one thing they never meddled with carts that belonged to the town—it was mostly the salt carts as was stopped—and for another thing it wasn't reckoned gain to cross them.

Well, this here went on a long time, and at last a salt cart came along and stuck afore the house, and out comes the old woman. The man as the cart belonged to had been stuck a good many times before and he was going to pay the money; but he had a new man with him, one as knew something himself, and he says: 'Wait a minute, master. Don't you give her nothing yet. Just you talk to her while I has a look'.

So he goes round the team and sees a long straw lying across the wheel-horse's back. He outs with his knife and cuts it in two, and the horses screamed and started on, and away went the cart; and there in the road lay the other old woman cut clean in two, and the blood running round about.

After that the old woman as was left didn't stop no more carts, and she got very poor. One day she was coming out of the town with a loaf as she had been to buy, and in the road she meets a big regiment of soldiers on horses that had come to see about the taxes. In front of them a very brave gentleman was riding, and he pulls up to talk to her.

'Good day, old woman', he says. 'Where did you get that loaf?'

'In Worcester', she says, a-bobbing.

'How much did you give for it?', he says, and she says, 'A penny, captain'.

'Ho', says he, 'by the time I've done with the town you won't be able to get a loaf there for a penny, nor for sixpence neither'. And all his men laughed.

Then the old woman was very angry. 'Worcester?' says she. 'You'll never get to the town, and you'll never be done with it'.

They all laughed again, and the captain says, 'Never get to town, old woman? Why, we'm nigh there already. There's the gate'. And they all laughs again.

'Yes', says she, 'you'll get to the gate and no furder. Stone you are, all the lot of you, and stones you'll be to Judgement Day', she says. And she pointed her finger at them and away she goes.

So they rode on and came to the gate, and as soon as ever the captain's horse camc to it, it fell down and turned to a stone, and so did the captain and all his men and horses; and there they lay by the road-side, a long heap of grey stones. And the old woman laid a word on them that they should stay stones till someone would come by the light of a new moon and put a loaf on each of them and say the Lord's Prayer over it. Nobody did it, and after a while she died.

The stones lay a long time by the side of the road and nobody durst cross the old woman's word, but at last there was a brave man—but he were a gallus random lad—as said he would do it for the sake of the poor soldiers like. So he went in the new moon and he put a loaf on every stone and said his prayer over it. But when he came to the last stone but one, as soon as he had said the prayer it started up into a live horse in the light of the moon. And he were that afeard that he dropped the last loaf and ran away and never finished it; and nobody else ever darst do it. So the stones lay there by the roadside for ever and ever, and it is because of them that the Tything is called Whitestones.

Hounds kept by a Mr John Spooner at Hopton Court, Leigh, would always start unseen game in a particular field at Leigh Sinton called the Oak and Crab Tree Ground. The dogs would pursue the quarry but invariably lose it on

Crumpton Hill to the west of the village by a cottage belonging to an old woman called Cofield. 'They've been after old witch Cofield again', Spooner would say. Prior to one hunt, Spooner sent his huntsman, James Bayliss, ahead to watch the cottage to see what happened. Bayliss saw the hounds going straight as an arrow towards the cottage, over the hedge and into the garden, but then wheel away. Strangely, this was just after the black cat which they had been pursuing bounded on to the roof of a shed and then through the old woman's bedroom window.

There is an animal connection, too, with Becky Swan, the last Worcestershire witch to be widely known. She was a healer and recoverer of stolen property who lived in Worcester Street, Kidderminster, and died in 1850. One day a huge black cat came walking down the street, and dogs took to their heels before it. The cat scratched at Becky's door; she opened it, and turned pale. The cat went in. For three days it roamed the locality, then no more. Becky, too, failed to appear, so the neighbours broke down the door. The cat, which they found sitting on the hearthrug, dashed up the chimney and was not seen again. Becky's body lay on the floor, reduced to ashes, though nothing else in the room was even singed, and there was no smell of smoke. 'This story', wrote Corbett, 'was told me within twenty years of the alleged event'.

The matted locks of a horse's mane were known as witches' stirrups, from the belief that witches rode by night. John C., Arthur Savory's shepherd at Aldington, said of some colts kept in a distant set of buildings that "'Old P.G."—an ancient dame in a neighbouring cottage with a reputation for witch-craft—had been a-ridin' of 'em on moonlight nights'. The so-called 'Witch of the Lenches' was remembered in the 1930s for her ability to ride on a hurdle and to stop a team of horses in their tracks without speaking to them. Rev. Chafy speculated:

> Perhaps it was a descendant of the same weird woman who ... was asked, as the oldest inhabitant, to settle a dispute between Ab Lench and Sheriff's Lench about a boundary. She was taken to the spot and swore a solemn oath that she was standing on Ab Lench soil, but it was later discovered that she had put the soil in her boots. The field is still called Sworn Lies.

Sarah Brown, another with power over horses, lived in a hut somewhere between Button Oak (near Bewdley) and the River Severn. One day she asked a young carter to bring her some logs. He refused. 'All right', she said. 'Thee'll bide outside my lodge till I tells thee to go'. He laughed at her, but when the horses reached the old woman's house on their return journey they would not go past it. After two hours, Sarah released them. After relating the story Brian Waters added (in 1949):

I believe that there is substance of truth in this tale that has been told to me by several people, including a man at Far Forest. He was completely sceptical about witchcraft and, indeed, anything supernatural; but he recalled how his own father, and several others, were only prevailed upon with much difficulty to carry the coffin to Callow Hill of a woman reputed to be a witch.

Finally, as late as 1994 an Overbury resident told Brian Hoggard of Old Mother Darky, a witch who turned children into hounds and used them to hunt on Bredon Hill. They could be heard giving tongue when the hill was enveloped in mist. The children were returned to their parents after a year but after their experience they would never leave the hill.

Precautions

Some people carried charms to counteract spells. A court at Stourbridge in the nineteenth century was shown a small bag of black silk containing pieces cut from a prayer book and Bible, together with some hairs from a cat's back. Its purpose was to cancel a spell of paralysis laid on one woman by another, and its use had been advised by a local wise woman.

Other objects were often kept in the home or farm to repel witches. A horse-shoe was fastened over doors or bedsteads. The coloured glass walking sticks made at Stourbridge—now kept purely as a pleasing nicknack—were once thought to protect a house against witchcraft. Another possibility was to draw a neat border of white chalk round a doorstep after it had been scrubbed, then

Anti-witch markings at the Fleece Inn, Bretforton

to mark nine Xs in a row inside. The ancient Fleece Inn at Bretforton has an elaborate pattern of white lines painted on the floor of one room for the same reason. The Fleece suffered a disastrous fire in 2004. The careful restoration by its owner, the National Trust, reinstate meticulously the appropriate anti-witch patterns. In 1995 a Women's Institute member recalled that at Queenhill, near Upton-on-Severn, 'We knew an old lady who actually whitened the lines between flagstones to keep witches out'.

Various plants were also deemed to be effective. These included vervain (*Verbena officinalis*) and St John's Wort (*Hypericaum perforatum*), both best picked in the morning of St John's Eve (23 June) when they were still wet with dew. A house leek (*Sempervivum tectorum*) growing on a roof or wall was considered particularly good against witches—and also lightning. Twigs of wych elm or wych hazel—the latter ideally in bundles of nine—were also used, though their names are not in fact connected with witches since wych means pliant.

The fruits of the famous Whitty Pear (see chapter 4) in the Wyre Forest were carefully kept as another form of protection. The mountain ash or rowan was another anti-witch tree. The red berries of the rowan were thought a good protection in themselves against evil. Elder was unlucky to cut or burn, but a branch might be nailed over a door to keep witches out. A piece of the wood was often let into churns to prevent witches from spoiling the butter.

Since water left after christenings might be used in witchcraft the lids of

Vervain

St John's Wort

Fruits of the Whitty Pear, after the drawing in Nash's Worcestershire *(1781)*

fonts were at one time secured. At Shrawley the staples in which padlocks could be inserted can still be seen, and staple holes can be found at Dormston.

Near Little Shelsley in Worcestershire on the hillside above the River Teme is a hollow called Witchery Hole. According to local tradition witches were burned there in mediaeval times, and it is said that nothing of value will grow at the spot. When a cold wind blows strongly from the north, villagers say that it comes from Witchery Hole.

Font at Shrawley, showing staples on the left and, partially, far right

CHAPTER 6

Work

The metal trades and mining were important in Worcestershire, especially in some of the towns such as Dudley, Halesowen and Stourbridge which ceased to be part of the county after the boundary reorganisation of 1974. Museums at Avoncroft, near Bromsgrove (nailers and chainmakers), Hartlebury (scythe-makers) and Redditch (needle-makers) commemorate some of them. The long-established trade of carpetmaking continues, albeit in much reduced form, at Kidderminster, where there is also a relevant museum. Agriculture, long a staple feature of Worcestershire, remains, though hugely changed in the half century after the Second World War. The customs and practices of farming in the past are still a source of fascination, and country life of the present draws a perennial audience to the fictional Ambridge of *The Archers*, which is widely identified with Inkberrow.

Needle-makers and Nailers

The word, needler, was first recorded in 1362. According to a Redditch archae-ologist, George White, the Cistercian monks of Bordesley Abbey brought needle-making to Worcestershire. John Leland, who toured England in the 1530s and '40s, remarked that Astwood Bank 'stands by needles'. The earliest identifiable needle-makers in Redditch were the Shewards, who built a Quaker meeting house there in 1702. Some 80 years on there were 400 needle-makers in the town and 2,000 in villages round about such as Alvechurch.

Pedlars hawked the needles in country and town. One of them, known as Redditch Needle Jack, was frequently to be seen dancing and singing in Birmingham's High Street during the 1840s:

> (Chorus)
> All sorts of needles, oh!
> The best of Redditch needles, oh!

Here's a needle for to sew your gown,
Here's one to sew the flounces round.

When your Sunday coat is torn
Here's one will mend it in a rap;
This will all your stockings darn,
This will hem your cambric cap.

He then broke off to run through his wares—'Here's a stocking needle, darning needle, sewing needle, hemming needle', and so on—before finishing with a last chorus of his song.

Needle-making, originally done by hand in small, independent workshops, progressively moved into factories where specialisation and mechanisation could be introduced. In 1830 a party of workers downed tools and marched with fife and drum to Tardebigge, where they attacked 'the machinery and house of Mr Baylis [the owner] ..., but were interrupted by the arrival of the constabulary from Redditch'. Six men were later imprisoned for a year in Worcester Gaol. Others, thrown out of work, sought sympathy and support by selling ballads such as 'The Needle Makers' Lamentation' and 'Red-ditch, in Worcestershire'. Both of these are straightforward attempts to raise funds. The first begins:

Good people all attend awhile,
And lend an ear I pray,
While we unfold the reason why,
We're wandering here today.

NEEDLE FISH HOOK & TACKLE MANUFACTORY,
ABLE WORKS EDWARD STREET, REDDITCH WORCESTERSHIRE
ESTABLISHED 1849

It is because we're out of work,
And bread we can't procure;
To see our children pine for food,
What parents can e'er endure

The workers must have been some way from home, or they would not have needed to explain, in a note appended to the ballad: 'The bearers hereof are a party of Needle makers from Redditch, Worcestershire, who have been thrown out of employment by the rapid improvement of machinery, as two men and three boys can do the work of ten men, and this has caused the deepest depression in our trade'. The sheet bears no printer's name, but 'Red-ditch, in

Forge Mill Needle Museum, Redditch

A Redditch pointer

Worcestershire' was printed by J. Hill of Lambeth in London, which may explain the peculiar spelling of the town. Presumably the needle-makers, on tramp as far as London, paid for Hill (who was in business from 1837) to produce the sheets, which were left at houses to advertise the later arrival of 'two unfortunate brothers, W. and T. Needham and families' with 'some Needles of the best quality' for sale.

Men who sharpened the points of needles on grindstones were called pointers. Their working life was often shortened by a fatal disease, pointers' rot, caused by inhaling the steel dust raised during grinding: the 150 pointers at Redditch in 1839 averaged under 28 years of age. Ebenezer Elliott wrote:

> There draws the grinder his laborious breath,
> There, coughing at his deadly trade, he bends,
> Born to die young, he fears no man, nor death,
> Scorning the future, what he earns he spends.

Needleworkers outside A. Showell's factory in Red Lion Street, Redditch in 1936

Red-ditch, in Worcestershire.

FOR the MASTER or MISTRESS.

We Needle Makers ask pardon for the liberty we have taken, in calling upon you, but our master having the misfortune to fail in business, was obliged to discharge us, and many more besides; our trade being so bad we could not obtain employ from any other master, and our Parish was so overburthened, that we could obtain but little relief; but we now trust to the Lady or Gentleman, (with the Lord's assistance and their benevolence,) that they will purchase some Needles of the best quality, of two unfortunate brothers, W. and T. Newman and families, for it is the only support we have at present, until the Lord assists us with some employ.

COPY OF VERSES.

We Needle-makers are in great distress,
  Employ we cannot find,
Thousands are by want compell'd,
  To leave their friends behind.

The oldest man now on the earth,
  Or living in the land,
Can ne'er remember trade so bad,
  Nor work at such a stand.

The mother she sat weeping,
  She raves and tears her hair,
When she beholds her children dear,
  For they were all her care.

Their altered looks she does behold,
  Like death appears in view,

With weeping eyes to heaven she cries,
  Good Lord, what shall we do.

Our visit now to you, kind friends,
  We hope you will excuse,
And as we have explained our cause
  We hope you'll not refuse.

And when we saw one in distress
  We join'd to help him thro'
But now we cannot help ourselves,
  For we have no work to do.

For he that giveth to the poor,
  But lendeth to the Lord,
So now, kind friends, on us bestow
  Whate'er you can afford.

There are more than Four Hundred out of Employ at the present time.

This Bill will be called for.

Printed by J. HILL, (late Taylor) 14, Waterloo Road, near the Victoria Theatre, Lambeth.

'Redditch and its surrounding area', wrote Peter Havins, 'gained a notoriety for drunken rioting, the only respite from the drudgery of the mill and the spectre of an early death from grinder's disease'. Pointers nevertheless resisted—and even, in 1846, went on strike against—the introduction of fans to extract the lethal dust, since they feared a subsequent reduction in wages.

By the 1860s, according to Elihu Burritt, the American consul in Birmingham, each fortnight in Redditch and district 200 million needles were being produced, enough to supply every man, woman and child in the world with one apiece. Every needle passed through 70 pairs of hands before reaching its user. In addition to all kinds of needles, Redditch, Feckenham and elsewhere made a huge quantity and variety of fish hooks. Girls and women were welcomed into the factories because of the nimble fingers needed for some of the processes.

The making of nails, like that of needles, has a long history in Worcestershire. John Hygesley of Dudley, 'naylor', is mentioned in the records of the 1420s. Nailers turn up at Pershore and Worcester in 1550, and at Belbroughton in 1596 ('Thomas Wheler, sonne of John Wheler, a naylor'). The quarter session papers between 1591 and 1643 include nailers from Alvechurch,

A nailmakers' shop, by Harold Piffard, 1896

Bedwardine (St John's), Claines, Elmley Lovett, Hagley, Stourbridge and Whitstones (in Worcester).

By the time of the 1831 census nailers were spread from Evesham to Tenbury, with a big concentration—1,169—in Bromsgrove. There, 30 years later, together with the neighbouring villages of Alvechurch, Belbroughton, Bentley, Clent, Cofton Hackett, Frankley, Hagley, Pedmore, Redditch, Romsley and Stoke Prior, 20% of all nailers in the county were to be found.

Strictly speaking, apart from his basic raw materials, iron rods, a nailer needed only a pair of bellows, a hammer and an anvil, hence the rhyme:

> Yo' gets a piece of wire,
> Yo' puts it in the fire,
> Yo' teks it out,
> Yo' gis it a clout,
> Yo' yods it,
> Yo' got a nayul.

As another verse showed, earnings were low:

> 'Ommer, 'ommer, 'ommer, clink, clink, clink,
> Work all day without any drink;
> Pudding on a Friday without any fat:
> Poor old nailers can't buy that.

Part of the problem lay with 'foggers', middlemen who supplied nailers with rods and paid for the finished nails. They used, it was said, three pairs of scales: one, weighing light, for the iron; a second, weighing heavy, for the nails; a third, accurate, in case of a visit by an inspector of weights and measures. Foggers, especially during the mid-nineteenth century, paid partly in tokens which could only be used in their own shop or tavern, where inflated prices obtained.

Like the needlemakers, nailers had a turbulent history. They are credited with the invention of the 'tiswas', a four-spiked nail which always landed with one spike pointing up when it was thrown under the hooves of cavalrymen's horses when they mustered against striking nailers. One of a whole series of strikes took place in 1852, when a party of nailers marched from Halesowen to Bromsgrove, pulling a ton of coal donated by a wellwisher for sale in aid of the strike fund. Their song owed much to the language of the Bible:

> Oh, I wish could see all nail dealers
> Draw such a load as we poor nailers,
> And to feel such punishment and such smarts,
> That it may soften their hard, stony hearts.

So as the nailers do suffer such smarts,
I hope it will soften Pharoah's heart;
Let every nailer tell to his son
The labours that we for just rights have done.

The musical predilections of nailers were often mentioned. In Bengeworth many in the 1860s and '70s 'posed as no mean authorities on vocal and instrumental music', played in the Evesham Rifle Volunteer Band, or belonged to the choir of the Old Church.

The Bengeworth nail merchants expected 45 lbs of nails from 56 lbs of rods, with any additional wastage charged to a man or woman's earnings. The last nailer there was a woman, Elizabeth Williams, who carried baskets of nails down to the wharves on the River Avon for transport to Gloucester. She died in 1919.

Robert Sherard, the biographer of Emile Zola, visited Bromsgrove in 1896 when he was writing a series of articles entitled *The White Slaves of England*. He found the town 'bright and sweet and clean, with many picturesque old houses and a fine, old church, and all round it, within two minutes' walk from the long, principal street, some of the of the prettiest country in the Midlands'. However, he described the nail trade as 'one of the cruellest industrial tragedies in England'. Pay was very low. Sherard met one man of 85 who had given up work after 77 years in the trade because he could earn only one shilling a week for six or seven hours a day.

The problem was compounded by what Sherard with heavy irony called 'a pleasant little custom of the trade': 'a thousand nails, between master and man, are twelve hundred nails, but only eight hundred (especially in the matter of hobnails), as between master and customer. Result, four hundred nails gratis to the warehouse'. No wonder that until living memory there was a saying in Worcestershire 'As busy as a nailer'.

Nevertheless Sherard noted:

> The last sound I heard as I left Bromsgrove was the voice of a poor old woman, bowed and almost blind, who was working at her forge. She was singing in an enthusiasm of hope and fervour, 'The Lord will provide'.

Both nailers and chainmakers used an 'Oliver', 'a heavy hammer worked by a treadle, and restored to its upright position by a simple system of leverage'. The name comes from:

> Cromwell, the heavy hammer-man; ... Oliver the Democrat, whose name, by the exquisite irony of things, is now attached to an implement used by slaves most degraded, by starved mothers fighting in sweat and anguish and rags, for the sop of the weazened bairns, who in the fiery sparks grovel in the mire of these shameful workshops.

'The hand-made nail trade, underpaid and sweated in the vain struggle to compete against imports and machine-made nails, finally collapsed', wrote L.T.C. Rolt in 1949, but nevertheless met an old nailer still working at Catshill, near Bromsgrove—a Mr Weaver, who sturdily remarked: 'Easy money doesn't come sweet'. In the same village a Women's Institute member recalled in 1995 how children worked with their parents in the nailshop, their staple diet a thin, meatless soup, sometimes supplemented by a rabbit or a fowl. The fogger's shop where nailers were forced to buy groceries at inflated prices, transformed into a normal corner shop, closed down only in the 1980s.

> Each Sunday morning the nailers collected their orders and iron rod from one of the three warehouses. ... The nailer, assisted by his wife and children, from as young as the age of seven, produced thousands of nails each week. This work was undertaken with great skill ... They worked very long hours from early in the morning till late at night, especially if there were older children to take over when father or mother stopped for a break. After the decline of nailing, those nailers who did not go to work at Longbridge [car works] took up market gardening.

Others turned to hand chain-making, though this ceased in the Black Country some 30 years ago. One of its last practitioners was Lucy Woodall of Old Hill, who died in 1979. She started work in 1912 at the age of 13. 'I left school on the Friday and I started on the Monday. Four shillin' a week. Seven o'clock till seven o'clock. Two o'clock on a Saturday'. Sixty years later she still remembered the practical jokes played on her. Workmates would send her to fetch a left-hand spanner, or pass her a pair of tongs of which the handles had been heated enough to give an unpleasant surprise. Yet her recollections were pleasurable. 'Them days were happier—tougher, but happier'. When the boss was safely out of the way Lucy and her workmates would sing in the chainshop. 'Rosemary Lane' was one of her favourites; another, 'My Chainmaker Lad':

Lucy Woodall

Chainmaking, Oak Street, Old Hill, Dudley c.1910

My chainmaker lad he's a masher, he's allus a-smokin' his pipe.
He's allus a' whistlin' the wenches, especially on Saturday night.
Saturday night is my delight, Sunday morning too;
Monday morning, off to school, he's allus after me.
Collier boys, collier boys, come in;
Down the road as black as coal but they're the chaps for me.

Carpet Weavers

After centuries of cloth weaving in the town, carpet manufacture came to Kidderminster in 1735. By the end of the century the place had become the main centre for the trade not only in Britain but perhaps the world. However, in the 1820s competition from Scotland and Yorkshire led to difficulties, and in 1828 the manufacturers decided to reduce weavers' pay by twopence a yard, from 1s. to 10d. The workers were willing to take a cut, but not that much, and 2,000 of them 'turned-out' on strike. A bitter, five-month struggle ensued.

A series of street ballads sought to hearten the strikers and gain support for them. For example, 'The Carpet Weaver's Lamentation' begins:

> Break off that yoke that binds you down,
> And let your enemies see,
> Although we've been to misery doom'd,
> We'll have our liberty.
> (Chorus)
> Then rise like men in bravery

> To gain the cause or die,
> We will be free of slavery,
> And have our liberty.

The mood in 'A Weaver's Song' is more relaxed:

> Come all you jovial tradesmen that delight in a song,
> And listen to these few lines, they'll not engage you long,
> It's of the carpet weavers, who in Kidderminster dwelt,
> They've struck for their Wages, and all with one consent.
>
> The looms are all now standing, the men are all at play,
> The Gentlemen are crying the trade is going away,
> Our carriages we now must sell, our servants all dismiss,
> Our country seats the lawyers have, to pay the mortgages.

As the dispute continued, bitterness inevitably increased, particularly when the employers brought in strike-breakers. Even so, a certain playfulness remains in the irony of 'The Funny Rigs of Good and Tender-hearted Masters in the Happy Town of Kidderminster':

> Of old and steady workmen, late,
> Our masters sadly tired,
> Search'd England through and through & then
> Some new ones briskly hired.
>
> The muse will not attempt to paint
> These new and untried men:
> Which l regret; for sure their like
> Will ne'er be seen again.
>
> Lean-flesh'd and lowly, scant of clothes
> Almost as when first born,
> Cook'd meat they never could have seen,
> Nor smelt John Barleycorn.
>
> We wonder'd much; some ask'd, how long
> Unhandcuff'd they had been?
> And other some, if ever they
> A Carpet Loom had seen?

In an imaginative passage, the writer depicts the looms themselves as being resentful of the blacklegs (or knobsticks, as they would have been called at the time):

However, into Looms they got,
And to work they tried their best;
And Masters and their Foremen too,
Thought they could do the rest.

But here, events unthought of rose,
To baffle such design;
What animals were set to work,
The Looms could not divine!

The lishes, treddles, sword and all
Danc'd to such crazy tune;
That each Loom thought its Master turn'd,
Into a crazy loon.

His senses too seem'd lost outright;
Aye, all now gone to pot!
Till the poor Loom now wish'd himself
Consum'd by the dry rot.

A Kidderminster carpet loom

The Shuttle vow'd, whene'er he stirr'd,
He always went astray;
And almost swore, that he'd not been
Once right throughout the day.

The Draw Boys, too (God bless the lads
And keep them from all evil!),
Wish'd the strange medley any where
Perchance, but at the devil.

Rev. Humphrey Price

Two pseudonymous poems, 'The Complaint of a Kidderminster Weaver's Wife to her Infant' and 'A Kidderminster Weaver's Wife's Dream', squarely placed the blame for the dispute on the masters, who were enraged to discover that the writer was a clergyman, Rev. Humphrey Price of Christ's Church, Needwood (near Lichfield), and a native of Kidderminster, who had attended the town's grammar school with some of those he attacked.

The strike ended in August 1828, with the weavers starved back to work. Seven months later, Rev. Price was tried at Hereford for criminal libel and sentenced to a year in prison. He returned to his parish afterwards, ill, embittered, but defiant: he became a convinced Chartist. Decades of struggle lay before the weavers.

The handloom carpet weavers of the nineteenth century were much given to drink and rough sports like dog and cock fighting. They delighted in fairs, and kept up local customs such as Heaving and the Lawless Hour (see chapter 10). They also kept St Monday, the practice of taking Mondays off—and sometimes Tuesdays too. Thus their independence was asserted but the price involved working longer and harder for the rest of the week:

Dingle, dangle.
Play all day,
Work by candle.

Carpets are still made in Kidderminster. Now it is probably true to say, though, that the attitudes and practices of carpet weavers differ little from those of other workers.

Farm Workers

At the beginning of the twentieth century a working life on the land began, as it had for generations before, with patrolling the fields to keep birds off the crops. Children, sent out for three or four pence a day, more to keep up their own spirits than to frighten the birds, sang or chanted such verses as:

> Shoo all ye birds!
> Shoo all ye birds!
> I'll up with the clappers
> And knock ye down back'ards.
> Shoo all ye birds!

This was heard at Upton-on-Severn; and at Evesham:

> Ah! You nasty black-a-top,
> Get off my master's radish tops;
> He is coming with his long gun:
> You must fly and I must run.
> Oh you hallo!
> Eh you hallo!
> Eh you hallo!
> Hallo, hallo, hallo, ay.

John Hall, having started as a part-time bird scarer, moved on to help with the harvest by laying out the bands ready for tying the shcaves. This was in 1904 during the school holidays, when he was nine. 'I received sixpence a day, and worked from half past six in the morning till seven at night. After the first week I laid bands for two men and got eightpence a day'.

Henry Pheysey (1869-1961) vividly recalled beginning full-time work at Areley Kings:

> When I left school I started farming in earnest ... For about three months I got up at five o'clock and went with the carter who passed at that time. In those days there was no half day on the farm. They worked from six until six, with half an hour for breakfast and an hour for dinner. They were not paid until 6 p.m. on Saturdays, and after this they walked to their homes, and then some more miles to town for their shopping. ... After three months I started to live in, so I could get up a little later, but I still had to be in time to fill the men's cider bottles for them to collect at six. At harvest time there was hardly any limit. If any man was late finishing a job, it was 'Just draw so-and-so a cup of cider'. I think that satisfied any overtime. Every man had his own little wooden barrel which he carried about with him—a bit of leather or hide for a handle.

Haymaking at Norton, near Evesham before 1913

Wages varied slightly. In the years before the First World War, near Redditch for a 72-hour week labourers received 12s., shepherds, cowmen and waggoners 13s. and 16s. plus a house. 'Of course', one of them wryly commented, 'one could not dress like a lord on that wage; it usually meant a clean pair of trousers for Sundays'.

The waggoner (horseman) would start earlier and finish later than the rest since he had his team to look after. He was the top man on the farm, and would deputise for the farmer in his absence. He was expected to work in all weathers save the absolutely impossible; a drenching downpour was wryly called 'waggoner's rain'. An acre's ploughing was considered a fair day's work, and

Sowing, from a misericord at Ripple

207

in accomplishing it with their single-furrow plough the waggoner and his team would walk thirteen miles.

Such work was a source of immense pride. The sentiment is expressed in 'We're All Jolly Fellows', which was amongst the best known of country songs. This version was sung to me in 1966 by Joe Gardiner, a farm worker from Hinton-on-the-Green:

> The cocks was a-crowin', 'twas break of day;
> Our master came to us and this he did say:
> 'Come, rise my good laddies, come rise with goodwill,
> For your horses want something their bellies to fill'.
>
> The clock strikes four and so up we then rise
> And into the stable so merrily flies;
> With rubbin' and scrubbin' our horses I'll vow
> You're all jolly fellows that follows the plough.
>
> Then seven o'clock comes and away we then go,
> And over the plains, boys, as nimble as does;
> For when we get there so jolly and bold
> To see which of us a straight furrow can hold.
>
> Our master came to us and this he did say:
> 'What have you been doing, boys, all this long day?
> For you've not ploughed an acre, I'll swear and I'll vow,
> And you're not jolly fellows that follows the plough'.
>
> Then I steps up to him and I made this reply:
> 'We've all ploughed an acre. Why tell such a lie?
> We've all ploughed an acre, I'll swear and I'll vow,
> And we're all jolly fellows that follows the plough'.
>
> Then he turns himself round and he laughs at the joke:
> 'It's past three o'clock, boys. It's time to unyoke.
> Unharness your horses and rub them down well,
> And I'll give you a jug of my bonny brown ale'.
>
> So now all you fellows whoever you be,
> Come take this advice and be ruled by me,
> And never fear your master, I'll swear and I'll vow,
> For you're all jolly fellows that follows the plough.

In caring for the horses waggoners employed many traditional cures and recipes. Cobwebs were used to staunch bleeding, and for this reason the chaff-house roof was never swept. The dosages and ingredients for some potions were closely kept secrets. A horse tonic was supplied by dried and powdered oxberry root, otherwise known as black bryony (*Tamus communis*). Human urine was used to moisten the animal's bait if the appetite needed stimulating. Tobacco rubbed each day on his bit kept him free of worms, and a pinch of blue vitriol (copper sulphate) made him lively enough to 'jump through his collar'.

Horses' names were chosen from a select, traditional list. The most popular were: Bert, Blackbird, Bonny, Bounce, Bowler, Boxer, Brandy, Captain, Charlie, Darby, Diamond (always pronounced Diament), Dobbin, Dragon, Duke, Flower, Gilbert, Jerry, Jolly, Lion, Lively, Short, Smiler, Snip, Spanker, Surly and Tommy.

Waggoners had their superstitions. Fears of horses 'hag-ridden' overnight by fairies or witches were mentioned in chapter 5. Mr Stanley Yapp of St Michael's, near Tenbury, told me that an old waggoner would never take a wagon into a hay-field unless the men were ready to start filling it immediately: otherwise rain might come to interrupt the work or even to prevent its ever being successfully concluded. To avoid this he would simply park the empty vehicle in an adjacent field until the right moment.

Other farm workers also had their role: the scythemen, for example, who at one time cut all the corn and hay. In Worcestershire the scythe was called an Isaac, after Isaac Nash, the Belbroughton maker. (Nash, who died in 1887, is featured in the museum of rural life at Hartlebury. His works at Belbroughton closed down in 1968).

A team of three or four men would contract to mow for so much an acre. They would work in echelon, the leader—known as the lord—setting the pace. The saying went 'You whet when the lord whets'. A rhyme on scythe sharpening ran:

> Wet it to whet, wet it to whet. The mower be too lazy.
> Give 'im a pint to make 'im work. A quart will make 'im 'azy.

'I knows more but it be too vulgar', said the farm labourer who gave this to Lavender Jones.

Apples and Cider

Until the First World War labourers had an allowance of cider, usually two quarts a day. The drink was decanted from barrels in the farm cellar each morning and lunchtime into small wooden kegs called costrels by a boy like Henry Pheysey who had to whistle at his task to show that he was not drinking. The men drank from their own cow-horn mugs. In the fields they would always take care to pour a small quantity on the ground as an offering to the gods or, as one Worcestershireman put it, 'a drap to the owd mon'. A mug would always be passed round in a clockwise direction, 'with the sun', and never against it.

*Cider mill from Birlingham, now in
Hartlebury Castle Museum*

According to R.H. Lloyd, General Sir Francis Davies of Elmley Castle asked two of his workers how much cider they drank in a day. They replied: 'Sometimes we drink sixteen pints, and sometimes we drink a lot if we can get it'. Even so, these volumes are modest compared with those quoted well over a century earlier by Kenrick Watson: 'The quantities which some individuals in Herefordshire and Worcestershire will drink in harvest must surprise persons in other counties; eight, ten or twelve quarts a day is a very common quantity; and in one instance a man drank twenty quarts of cider and pitched twenty loads of hay in about fourteen hours'. Arthur Savory's bailiff at Aldington succinctly said 'that sixpennyworth of cider would do more work than a shilling in cash'. Savory himself remarked that 'after quite a small allowance of cider on the farm the open-hearted man would become lively, the reserved man taciturn, the crabbed man argumentative; but the work went with a will and a spirit that were not so noticeable when no "tots" were going round'.

Cidermaking at Wood Farm, Shrawley

The tots were undoubtedly valued. When an 'old lady farmer in the neighbourhood' began watering the cider, one of the men, 'having discovered the dilution, arrived after the first day with two jars. Asked the reason for the second jar, he answered that he would prefer to have his cider and water separate'.

Many farms made their own cider. Apples were gathered from August to December, depending on variety, of which there are several hundred. Worcestershire preferred Badger Whelp, Bittersweet, Cherry Norman, Italies, Kingston Black, Norman White (or White Norman), Redstreak, Roughthorn and Wilding.

Well over a hundred perry pear trees have been established at the Three Counties Showground, near Malvern. The sixty varieties, some of them extremely rare, include Judge Amphlett (named after a Worcestershire man), Moorcroft (aso known as Malvern Pear or Malvern Hills), Newbridge (which came from Berrow), and Rock (which originated at Pendock in the early nineteenth century.

When collecting began, those apples which had not fallen to the ground were shaken or knocked down with long ash poles with hooks. Women picked up the fruit and put it into sacks to be taken to the press. The old stone mills were superseded by the scratter or scratcher mill driven by a small but noisy engine. The pomace (pulp) so produced was put between hairs (coconut matting; originally horsehair) and pressed. Spent pomace could be fed to stock, before it had time to ferment.

The juice—at first muddy brown, then golden—was put into hogsheads to ferment. Some preferred if possible to add blood, beef, bacon or rabbit skins, wheat or barley—all useful for adding nitrogen to feed the yeasts in the fermenting juice—but, contrary to popular belief, not rats. The finished product contained a hefty amount of alcohol, between 5 and 10%. Apart from being drunk, cider was used to wet apple-tree grafts: indeed it was believed that they would not survive without it.

In recent years there has been a tremendous revival in cider making and drinking. Old-established firms have been joined by Dunkertons (founded in 1981) and many small enterprises.

*Sampling the finished product
at Dodderhill in 1958*

Unfortunately the revival was not able to save the Plough at Elmley Castle, the only public house in England where cider had been made on the premises for generations. The same family ran the place for 135 years until the last landlord and his wife retired in 1991. Previously 150 tons of Vale of Evesham apples had been pulped and processed each year in a shed behind the pub. The resulting cider had an alcohol content of 8%. Traditionally, anyone falling into the village ditch on the way home would be dubbed Mayor of Elmley until the next person made the same mistake. The turnover was rapid. There is still a cider house, though, in Defford.

Hops and Hop-pickers
Hops are still an important part of agriculture in Worcestershire, though the picking is now mechanised. For many generations—until the 1960s—picking was done almost entirely by hand. The workers—mainly women, accompanied by their children—were brought in from Birmingham, the Black Country and South Wales. Kathleen Dayus (born in 1903) remembered being brought all the way from Birmingham by horse and wagon but most travelled on special trains arranged by the farmers. George Dunn (1887-1975) recalled:

> When th' 'op pickin' season come, about the beginnin' o' September or the latter end of August we'd sometimes be away for six weeks. The train was 'ired an' if you were 'ired you 'ad a ticket of th' agent. That was goin' from Cradley [Heath] to Worcester, an' went on to Leigh Court an' Tenbury an' Knightwick, Suckley, Leigh Sinton, Bromyard, Pershore. There's not many I 'aven't bin to. I used to love the 'op fields. We stayed in the barns, all the stables an' cowsheds an' that, just accordin' to the amount o' pickers they wanted. The animals were taken out and the stables white-washed and plenty o' new straw put in.

Hop picking at Holt in 1912

Hop picking at Holt Fleet in 1912

The work was exacting, pay (by the bushel) modest and conditions spartan. Dorothy Vintner wrote of a hundred or so pickers who lodged in the barn opposite Court Farm at Stockton-on-Teme. They were paid one shilling for five or six bushels of hops, together with a ration of potatoes and cider given out on Sunday mornings. 'They used to raid any nearby orchard or garden, and every walnut tree was invariably stripped'. Groups of bines called 'houses'—ten bines from each of two rows—were picked in turn. The cut bine would be dragged to a crib—a wooden frame supporting a piece of sacking nine feet long and four deep—and picked into it with a downward motion of the fingers. Small children used inverted umbrellas.

Twice a day, at noon and late in the afternoon, the busheller, preceded by the shout of 'Clear 'em up!', which warned pickers to remove any leaves and stalks, came round to measure the hops gathered. As he did so, the busheller called out to the tallyman, who noted the quantities and entered them on the picker's 'book', a folded card. The shout of 'Pick no more bines!' signalled the end of the day. Lavender Jones has written:

> There was a kind of magic about hop-picking: the misty early autumn morning—real 'oppickin' weather; the strong heady smell of the hops; the bitter taste of food eaten with hop-stained fingers, washed down with smoky tea brewed over a stick fire; and the camaraderie and sense of being in a little world apart—all these combined to produce an atmosphere which was unique.

There was plenty of banter and also singing. As George Dunn told me:

> Lovely in th' 'opyard. Everybody was a-singin'. You sung while you were pullin' the 'ops off. We 'ad sing-songs round the fire. I've 'ad some good times down the 'opyards. I 'ardly missed a year. It was the best o' my days.

The sentiments were echoed by thousands of other pickers.

By ancient tradition any stranger wandering into a hopyard would be 'cribbed', which Jesse Salisbury described as 'a custom (happily falling into disuse) by which female pickers seized upon, lifted into a crib, and half smothered with hops and kisses, any strange man who entered the hop-yard'. The victim was also expected to give money for drink.

At the end of the season as the last bines were pulled down for picking, the pole-pullers took hold of any unmarried woman and dropped her into a crib. Photographs give a fairly sedate impression of what in fact was vigorous horse-play with clear sexual overtones. The women would sometimes band together to retaliate by up-ending the binman or busheller into a crib and covering him with bines. In earlier times a woman would be thrown in with him too, thus enacting a kind of fertility rite meant to ensure a good harvest the following year.

Another custom was described in the *Worcester Journal* in 1956:

> On some farms, the last day of picking had its age-old ceremony of hoisting the last and best pole of hops, saved specially for the occasion. The pullers' caps and hats were decorated with rosettes, dahlias and asters and sprays of hops. Then a procession was formed, making its way to the farmhouse, headed by the busheller beating his metal measure to a drum, and followed by the pole-pullers, sack-holders and the pickers. At the farmhouse a feast was prepared and the farmer and his wife were toasted.

A pale echo of such vivid ceremonies is the practice still followed of displaying hop bines at harvest festivals or using them to decorate rooms in public houses.

Hop picking at Mrs Fisher's Farm, Hallow, in 1912

Farm Wisdom and Custom

A great deal of lore was transmitted in the form of memorable axioms and rhymes. For crops of grain the conventional advice used to be four seeds in each hole:

> One for the rook, one for the crow,
> One to rot and one to grow.

Wheat should be sown in the dirt (moist soil), and rye in the dust. In earlier times the aim was that 'At Michaelmas Fair [29 September] the wheat should hide a hare'. All seeds were set as the moon waxed, roots as it waned. Pigs were killed at the moon's waxing, otherwise—it was believed—the bacon would waste away with the moon. Every pig has four small holes in the skin inside the front ankle, and it was believed that this showed where Old Nick entered the Gadarene swine. Conversely, the black cross on the back of every donkey is a reminder of Christ's journey to Jerusalem.

A donkey was kept with cows in the belief that it would ensure that they never aborted. In the days when farmers took a lantern to visit their cowsheds at night it was considered that on no account should they put it on the table when returning to the house or a cow would lose her calf. In Worcestershire the Christmas mistletoe bough was fed to the first cow to calve in the New Year, and was thought to bring good luck.

For a horse to have three white feet was very unlucky; hence the rhyme, 'One buy, two try, three don't go nigh'; and also:

> One white foot, buy him;
> Two white feet, try him.
> Three white feet, doubt him;
> Four white feet, do without him.

As to the animal's treatment:

> Up the hill press me not;
> Down the hill trot me not.
> On the level spare me not;
> In a stable forget me not.

It was thought unlucky to keep sheep in the same field for two Sundays running, so before they heard the church bells on the second Sunday they should be moved to fresh pasture. When any animal was sold a little of the purchase price was returned by the seller to the buyer as luck money, a custom still widely followed, and even extended to motor vehicles.

Corn was once measured by the bushel, the size of which varied from place to place. The tod (28 pounds) was employed for wool. In hedging and ditching until relatively recently the rod, pole or perch (five and a half yards) and the chain (22 yards) were used. The latter still applies to cricket pitches.

Farm tenancies ran from Candlemas (2 February) or Lady Day (25 March), and the latter is still the date on which many farm rents fall due. A tenant destined to move into a farm at Candlemas had the right of access to plough land from the previous 1 November, together with stabling for two horses and a room for a ploughman. Similarly, a tenant leaving at Candlemas could keep his cattle on the pasture and retain the use of the house and some of the buildings until 1 May. It was customary when a young couple took possession of their first tenancy for neighbouring farmers to help them establish themselves during the first season.

The 'Evesham custom' gave the right to an outgoing tenant to nominate a successor whom the landlord was obliged to accept if his credentials were satisfactory. If the landlord wished to choose his own tenant he had to compensate the old at a valuation far exceeding the norm, and often greater than the freehold worth of the land. The unique arrangement gave great incentive to a tenant to maintain a high standard of cultivation.

A different custom, current at least until the 1930s on big Worcestershire farms, required that on the birth of the family's heir a brew of beer was made and kept to be drunk on his 21st birthday. Later children merely received the piece of fine china on which their christening feast was served.

Various seasonal rituals and calendar customs were observed on farms. Every year on Ascension Day the master gardeners of Evesham gave their workpeople a treat of baked peas, both white and grey, with pork. Generosity was similarly demonstrated at Hanbury where, until the 1930s at least it was the custom for all farmers to give milk to any who asked for it on Whitsun Eve. No milk was sold on that day since it was considered that ill luck would befall anyone doing so. As a result of the farmer's largesse everyone ate baked custard on Whit Sunday.

Harvest was—as it still is—the climax of the farming year. The last few stalks of the last field were called the mare. The reapers tried to cut it by throwing their hooks or sickles at it. The one who succeeded had the mare, and either plaited it himself or gave it to the mistress of the farm to do so. The plait would be hung with the bush burned in the early hours of New Year's Day (see chapter 10) in the farm kitchen to bring luck. Other plaited corn dollies were fastened to the thatch of ricks or used to adorn harvest suppers or harvest festivals in church. The art of making them dates back to mediaeval times, and is still widely practised. The dollies, which symbolised the harvest spirit, were carefully kept through the winter and ploughed in during the following spring.

The arrival in the stackyard of the last load of sheaves was greeted with due ceremony. Until the 1890s in Worcestershire men and boys shouted:

Up, up, up, up, harvest home.
We have sowed and we have mowed,
And we have carried the last load home.
Up, up, up, up, harvest home.

The wording at Elmley Castle was:

Well ploughed, well mown,
Well reaped, well sown.
Never a load overthrown.
Harvest home, hurrah!

There, a celebratory dinner provided by the farmer for his workers and their families was served in a marquee after a service in the church. 'A necessary adjunct' to such a meal, wrote Salisbury in 1893, consisted of 'singing, dancing (sometimes) and cider drinking without stint. Much merriment prevailed, and (it must be admitted) some drunkenness. The festival was frequently kept up until daylight the next morning; when the young men of the party would perhaps be seen, gallantly escorting the women to their respective homes, by the light (in addition to that of broad day) of a lantern and candle'. His conclusion is some-what acid: 'It can scarcely be denied that the change which has taken place in the manner of celebrating harvest-home in most parishes is for the better'.

A farm feast at Leigh for hop-pickers was described in 1930 in the *Worcester Journal*:

The long hop-room, gaily decorated with brilliant streamers, its walls and windows draped with softer hues, is the scene of the annual feast. The fare is all prepared in the Great House kitchen, or in the cookhouse whose furnace boils the Christmas pudding and whose 'stick-oven' roasts the great joint of beef. The master, his light-grey suit protected by a blue-striped apron, carves, and the wide plates circle to receive from busy helpers potatoes, creamed swedes, brussels sprouts and gravy (such gravy, founded on boiled goose and stuffed fowls).

Each guest, and there are at least seventy, is supposed to bring his own eating tools, but a pile is available for novices and the forgetful. Plum pudding and rum sauce are the second course, and mammoth jugs of beer and cider pass freely round the long trestle tables. When no-one can eat any more, the tables vanish and the fun waxes warm.

The guests are of both sexes and all ages and sizes; there are grandfa-thers and babies in arms, great strapping lads and bonny well-built lasses, and a host of small fry who scramble for the nuts, sweets and biscuits thrown to them. A professional entertainer with song and speech and dance performs on the dais, but the company furnish their own contribu-tions too. The same songs, the same pieces are clamoured for each year.

Harvest suppers continue in many villages but they now tend to be a kind of community celebration organised by volunteers, with participants paying their own way. For example, the village harvest suppers instituted at Wichenford in the 1970s have continued to the present time.

After the corn had been carried from the fields gleaners were normally allowed into the stubble to pick up any loose ears for their own use. Some farmers moved poultry houses into the fields so that their hens could glean for themselves. Arthur Savory, after pointing out that in Worcestershire gleaning was invariably called leasing, wrote:

Gleaning in south Worcestershire in the 1880s

> The 'leasings' would be thrashed by husband or brother with the old flail, in one of my barns, to be then ground at the village mill, and lastly baked into fragrant loaves of home-made bread ... One good old soul brought me every week, while the 'leased corn' lasted, a small loaf called a 'batch cake' ....; her loaves were some of the best and sweetest bread I have ever tasted.

Savory also described a kind of gleaning carried out elsewhere:

> When the pickers had gathered the crop, by an ancient custom all the village children were allowed to invade the orchards for the purpose of getting for themselves any apples overlooked. The practice is called 'scragging', but it is a custom that would perhaps be better honoured in the breach than in the observance, for hob nails do not agree with the tender bark or young trees. ... it is nevertheless a pleasant old custom, and seems to give the children huge delight.

Farm workers, both male and female, indoor and out, were hired on an annual basis at 'mop' fairs held in Worcestershire in the autumn. At Evesham the event took place on the Friday before Old Michaelmas Day. In its issue of 11 October 1862, which also noticed the holding of Pershore Mop on the Wednesday, the *Evesham Journal* reported:

The day was fine and the attendance large, but not so numerous we think as that of last year, and as compared with the mops of past days, it showed a considerable diminution. There were the usual number of exhibitions containing 'all the wonders of the earth', and one of more than ordinary pretensions and merit being an exhibition of Wax Work models, which was stationed in the High Street. All these seemed extensively patronised, as did also the noisy 'round abouts' and 'swing boats', which with their freights of juveniles turned one almost giddy to look at. Rifle galleries and photographic establishments were made prominent by the noisy solicitations of their proprietors to 'have your portrait taken, glass, frame, and all for sixpence!' and 'fire away lads, 40 in the middle', which saluted the ears of every passerby. There were no distinctive features to notice; the hiring, though apparently conducted to some extent, was evidently not the principal business of the day, the meeting of friends and the pleasure thus occasioned, and the enjoyment of the sights seemed to take the first thoughts of the majority of those present. Good servants asked high wages, and there were but few of those for hire, for many who were present had been previously engaged. The masters and mistresses on the look out for servants mustered pretty strongly, but only a comparative few seemed to make engagements.

The following year an editorial in the same newspaper reflected on the 'year by year' decrease in hiring at the mop, while recording the institution's value as 'a day of relaxation and amusement; of the renewing of the domestic ties and the enjoyment of the society of those nearest and dearest to one another'. At the same time the writer regretted 'the attraction of those low-class and debasing spectacles which annually, at Mop-time, crowd our Market-square'. A report in the same issue (10 October 1863) described some of the 'spectacles':

The amusements were of the ordinary character, and the temptations held out to 'John and Mary' to spend their hard-earned wages were numerous in the extreme. 'Cheap Jack' held out as many showy and plausible inducements as ever, and business appeared to thrive with him; while the puffers and hawkers of cheap jewellery, gold and silver watches ('duffers' of course) and other such trash, plied their avocation with success. The 'Great Medicine Man', who offered a remedy for every disease, very readily found applicants for his nostrums. The photographic 'studies' (?) &c., were also present in numbers, affording strong temptations to the damsels to obtain fac-similes of their smiling faces for presentation to their swains. Of gingerbread-stalls and toy-stalls there were plenty; while other attractions were to be found in a tolerably good peep-sow, a circus (!), the real wild boar 'All alive, O', the tent cabalistic, &c. Shooting-galleries, turn em-rounds, swing-boats, and other sources of fun for all were also to be found. The morris-dancers, itinerant songsters, roving ballad-singers, maimed colliers, and sailors shorn of one or more limbs, and other applicants for a 'trifle', almost inundated the town.

The 'hurry-skurry' at Evesham Mop

At St John's, just outside Worcester, those seeking work gathered on St John's Green (the lower part of Bransford Road), where, the *Worcester Herald* reported on 12 October 1861:

Yesterday was the anniversary of this noted statute for the hiring of agricultural servants generally. The attendance of robust, sturdy servants was very numerous, particularly females, and although in a business point of view it might have struck the spectator on gazing at the throng, that few employers were about, still that would have been no criterion in these days of anti-mop tendencies of the absolute engagements entered into. Unlike former gatherings, the amusement seeker could find nothing at all attractive beyond the enjoyment of an airing on a remarkably balmy dry sunshiny afternoon.

Ten years later, Mrs Todherty, a character in 'Going to the Mop', one of Mrs Henry Wood's *Johnny Ludlow* stories, visits the statute fair at St John's to hire a new dairymaid. By this time, though, Mr Chipp, Police Superintendent at Worcester, had become distinctly hostile:

After the Mop is over drinking, cursing and swearing, and fighting are carried on to a fearful extent, and I have many times been called out to quell the disturbances. When night comes on, there is scarcely a place in the parish in which couples are not seen elated with drink. In many cases the females are easily taken advantage of. I have known young women entrapped by procuresses, and have often been employed by their distracted friends to find and restore them. But when they have once been tainted they often break out again. Mops are calculated to bring trouble and misery, without producing the least benefit to society.

An agency called the Worcester Servants' Registration Society was set up, and by the late 1870s hiring had ceased at St John's Mop, though a pleasure fair continued. The mop at Bromsgrove, held on the Wednesday before Old Michaelmas Day (10 October), was described in 1879 by W.A. Cotton:

the servants assembled in front of the George Inn and near the Town Hall, for the purpose of obtaining hire or situations, their several occupations being indicated by badges, thus:- the carter exhibited a piece of whip cord on his hat, the cowman had a lock of cow hair in his; and the dairymaid was similarly distinquished. The time of hiring was usually for the understood twelve months. These statutes were of frequent occurrence in this district, as the villages of Alvechurch and Belbroughton once had their statute fairs; that of Hanbury is the largest in the neighbourhood that I know of.

Bromsgrove's mop ended in 1914, after 137 years of existence; Bewdley's lasted until the 1920s, for hiring, that is.

Memories remained. As a boy on Stanley Farm at Ashton-under-Hill, Fred Archer (born 1915) saw the bothy where 'not so long ago the single chaps slept,

Evesham Mop Fair in 1913

hired hands from Evesham or Tewksbury Mop Fair'. The carter, Ralph, who had been hired in his youth at Evesham Mop, told Fred 'of the hard times on the land when boys were given cider sop (bread soaked in cider) for breakfast; when hired by a farmer they had to stay one year, from one Michaelmas to the next'. ('Work was his life', added Archer, 'and the horses his interest, apart from bell ringing and singing at concerts. When the work went well he sang or whistled'.)

Others remembered how 'each man had to carry his clean Sunday smock on his arm, to show he possessed one, or no good master would engage him'. When a bargain was struck the farmer would give a shilling, known as earnest money, to seal it. Normally, both sides would respect it.

A story of master and man unconnected with hiring, comes from Tenbury Wells. A very rich farmer there was excessively mean. Any animals—cows, sheep, poultry—which started to ail were quickly killed and dressed, either to be sold for meat or cooked for the workman's dinner. One morning the postman called at the farm and found the workman packing up ready to leave. On asking the reason why he was told: 'Everything that is about to die is dressed and put out for dinner. Well, this morning the gaffer died, so I'm off'.

Similarly wry humour is revealed in the anecdote which Savory relates about his farm bailiff, William Bell: 'Bell happened to pass one day when I was talking to the vicar [of Badsey]. "Hello, Bell", said he, "hard at work as usual; nothing like hard work, is there?" "No, sir", said Bell; "I suppose that's why you chose the one-day-a week job!"'

Another climactic time was New Year's Day. Some farms roasted their finest ox to be eaten by their workers on 1 January. Few people in any case can have been fit for work on New Year's Day after the celebrations of the early morning.

Nor did they work on Plough Monday—the first Monday after Twelfth Night—which traditionally marked the resumption of farm work after Christmas. In Worcestershire 30 of 40 men would turn out to drag a plough by long ropes round local houses and farms. Their hats and white shirts would be bedecked with ribbons and emblems. A boy or young man dressed in women's clothes—and known as the Bessy—carried a collecting box. In return for a contribution the ploughboys brought luck; in default of it they would wreak some mischief by way of reprisal. On the same day if by rising very early indeed a ploughman could place his whip, plough staff or hatchet by the fireside before the maid could get her kettle on the fire she would in due course have to surrender her Shrovetide cockerel to him.

CHAPTER 7

Music

Fiddler's Knap is a sharp little hill above Elmley Castle. Fred Archer thought the name might be connected with the Whitsun sports and revels held on Bredon Hill. The story is surely lost, though it would no doubt have helped to illustrate the importance attached to music both in public and in private life.

Minstrels, first mentioned in Worcestershire in a document of 1293, were employed by various lords and prelates until well into the sixteenth century to play for their own pleasure and on certain public occasions. Overlapping with them were the waits, musicians in municipal service. Individual instrumentalists also appear in the records, sometimes because of falling foul of laws or regulations.

Singing, too, played an important part in popular culture. Singers made up their own songs or drew on the printed ballads sold in the streets, which covered a great range of topics, including sport, work, crime, war, politics, and love. The ballad printers, of which there were several in Worcester, both reflected and affected the oral tradition of song which flourished in towns and villages across the county several decades into the twentieth century. This has now largely gone, except perhaps in the case of children's playground songs, but the old tradition of song and instrumental music still flourishes in pub sessions, folk song clubs and concert venues.

Minstrels and Waits

Between 1293-4 and 1534-5 frequent payments to minstrels, by which was meant instrumentalists, not vocalists, are recorded in the accounts of Worcester's monastery. The musicians are often identified as 'belonging' to grandees, who hired them out, so as to spread the cost of liveries, instruments and wages. Churchmen—the abbots of Gloucester and Evesham, and the bishop of Durham—are mentioned on a few occasions, but members of the royal family and nobility predominate as sponsors of groups of minstrels. The musicians of Henry VI, Edward IV, Henry VII, Henry VIII and Elizabeth I all

Angel musicians shown in a window at Malvern Priory Church

played at Worcester, as did those of a dozen noblemen from the earl of Arundel to the duke of York.

The accounts often list payments without giving details of why minstrels were performing. One assumes that at times the prior's guests were being entertained at one of the monastery's manor houses of Battenhall, Crowle or Grimley. In some cases it is clear that minstrels played for events such as Epiphany, Lady Day (25 March), Easter, Rogationtide, Whitsun, Trinity Sunday, Mary's nativity (8 September), Advent and Christmas. The installation of a new prior also called for music, for example, in 1338-9.

Most minstrels are anonymous in the records, their instruments unspecified, their music unknown. Perhaps the first musicians ever named as performing in Worcestershire were Henricus and Giraldus, German fiddlers in the service of Edward I, who received the large sum of 13s. 4d. apiece for playing at Kempsey in 1300. The series of *citharedi* and then *citherazatori* engaged between 1337-8 and 1446-7 played the harp. Named lutenists played in Worcester in the 1340s, including John at Lee. Almost two centuries later, 'William the lewter' received 4s. (in 1520-1) 'for his syngyng & pleyng in the cristmas wycke' and 'for pleyng & syngyng in the halydays be fore me'. The 'me' is William More (real name: Peres, Pears or Peers; on taking office, as was customary, he took the name of his birthplace), Prior of Worcester from 1518 until 1535 or early '36, and the last to hold the full office before the Dissolution. There is a tradition that he was buried at Crowle, but the Alveston (Warwickshire) parish register has the entry: 'William More sometyme Prior of Worcester was buried the xvj[th] of September [1552]'.

More enjoyed good living, sport and drama (see chapter 8), as well as music. His accounts feature not only 'William the lewter' but 'a blynd harper', 'John harper Mynstrell' and 'Philip the harper'. 'Wyett & his son Mynstrelles' appear in 1518-19. Wyett (either father or son) crops up until 1533-4, when he performed at Crowle alongside 'the Kynges Mynstrelles his shambulles' (shawms, rather like oboes). More also delighted in singing, judging by payments 'to syngares of carralles at cristmas day at nygth [night]' (1518-19), 'to syngers of carrlles Apon Neweyeres day' and 'to syngares of the towne' (1519-20), 'for caralles on cristmas day dyner' and 'to carroldes A pon seynt Iohnsday [24 June]' (1520-1), 'to William synger' (1522-3), 'caralles on cristmas day fryday & seynt sthevens day' (1523-4), 'to the yong Men of Crowle for singyng on Maij day in the Morenyng' and 'to the Maydens of Crowle for syngyng on holyrowde day [14 September] toward our lady lyght' (1531-2), 'to Iohn Acton & Iohn Tylor for syng at batnall on Maij Morenyng' (1532-3), and 'to iiij syngyng men crafesmen of Wurceter upon seynt Georges day in the morenyng at Crowle' and to 'vj maydes at Crowle that did syng in the morenyng on Seynt philip & Iacob[us: St James the Less] day [1 May]' (1533-4). This is only a selection from the entries for singers, and it is interesting to see More's willingness to pay out for May Day singing.

Minstrels were paid alongside singers on many of these occasions. The sum of 12d. given in 1447-8 to *Minstrell ville wygornie* (minstrels of the city of Worcester) may be an early allusion to the waits. However, the city's own accounts refer to musicians' liveries only in 1568-9; and the first unequivocal entry on the waits occurs only in 1585-6, when an agreement is recorded with 'Thomas Wheeler the musysian ... for playinge the waytes of this Cyttye yearly ffrom the ffeast of Saint Michaell [29 September] untill the ffeast day of the puryficacion of the blessed virgin Marye [2 February]'. An entry of 1598-9 records the decision that 'the Comitors [comet players] or Musicions ... be allowed the Waighes or Musicions for this Citty'; and there is a further reference the following year to 'the waite plaiers'.

Unidentified waits, perhaps those of Worcester, played at Bewdley 'at the coming of the Lorde Zowche' in 1604; and the Worcester men undoubtedly performed at Coventry in 1613, 1623 and 1631. However, in 1642 their own authorities ordered that 'John Browne & his companie of musicians called the waites be suppressed from playing their instruments about the Citty in the morning'.

The waits must have continued, though, because one of the lay clerks in the cathedral, Roger Fosbrooke, was in trouble in 1684 for attaching himself to the 'town musick' which played at public festivities and also in taverns. Eventually he was given the alternative of leaving the waits or resigning his place as lay clerk. Future clerks were required to give a bond of £100 to the dean and chapter as surety that neither they nor their wives 'shall keep any tavern, alehouse, or victualling house' nor 'accept or perform any service in any publick musick, nor at any time playe in any public house whatsoever'.

During the eighteenth century the Worcester waits still played on public occasions, wearing their livery of cocked hats and blue coats or cloaks. Unfortunately, no pictures seem to have survived. By the end of the century they had become a drum and fife band. They still existed in some form in the 1850s, when John Noake commented that 'their operations are confined to an early serenading of the citizens with soft music a few mornings in the Christmas time', though a few lines later he wrote that 'at the approach of Christmas they salute us with their nocturnal concerts'.

More Musicians
Some households well below the ranks of the nobility had performers or possessed musical instruments. William Sheldon, dyer, of the famous tapestry-making family at Beoley, bequeathed in 1571-2 to 'every one of my five musy-cians foure pounds to be paid with in two yeres after my dethe'. Under the terms of another will, of 1576-7, Harry Smyllie of Worcester left 'unto my boyes all my Instruments boths vyalls [viols] & Recorders & theyr boks', worth a total of £6. Edward Crosby, a Worcester draper, left in his will of 1559-60 a 'lute praysed at ixs. iiijd.' In 1618 Edward Archbold, who lived within the precinct of Worcester Cathedral, bequeathed to his daughter, Mary, 'ye virginalls usuallie placed in ye Parlour'. In the same year the cathedral accounts record the payment of 20s. to 'Goodman Stanton the Musician for playinge on the Cornetts in the Quyre'.

Musicians feature rather less creditably in several recorded cases which came before the church authorities. Thomas Parker, alias Tinker, of Stockton-on-Teme, having confessed in 1572-3 to playing the tabor (presumably in service time) was obliged to do penance in the church at Eastham one Sunday and at Lindridge the next. In 1606 Francis Downe of Doddenham faced the charge that he 'keepeth A Common Alehowse without licence...', and that

> He hireth one Bruton A lewde and Bad persone to play there Holiedayes and the sabboth dayes in prayer tymes, y^t cawseth mens Sonnes & servauntes ffrom theyer good Busines.

As so often happens, the outcome of the case is not known. However, when George Farse, alias Barber, failed to appear in 1613 at Great Malvern to answer 'ffor playenge on his drum in service time to drawe the youth from Church to the offence of the minister and the better disposed of the parishe' he was excommunicated (that is, forbidden to receive the sacraments of the church: communion, marriage or burial).

Singers, too, caused resentment at times by what they sang. Indeed, some set out deliberately to provoke. The 'ballet [ballad] caled come Downe ffor all your shaven crowne', written in 1546 by John Davis, does not sound very complimentary.

In the Swan Inn at Evesham in December 1605 a group of townspeople set out to make a ballad on a local squire, George Hawkins, who, they alleged, had fathered a bastard child. They were unable to write it down, so they enlisted the help of three travelling salesmen from Coventry who happened to be staying at the inn. The finished ballad was sung in the Swan; then copies were made and sent round all the other Evesham inns. Hawkins took one of the authors to the Star Chamber court, thanks to which a copy of the ballad has survived in the records, where it was discovered by Adam Fox:

> I canne noe more
> This is the whore,
> Of cowardye George Hawkins.
> He gott with childe,
> In a place moste wilde,
> Which for to name yt is a shame.
> Yet for your satysfactione,
> I will make relatione,
> It was in a privey,
> A place most filthy.
> As gent you may judge,
> Yet nothinge to bade,
> For a knave and a drabbe,
> And soe they praye goe trudge.

A ballad on similar lines circulated only orally, in 1611, and it did not survive. This was 'The Parson and his Mare', directed against the vicar of Belbroughton, Thomas Tristram, and sung by John Penne, husbandman, 'with a lowde and high voice ... not only [at] great fayres and other great assemblies and concourses of people but also in publique tavernes and alehowses'. This may help to explain why the dean and chapter of Worcester Cathedral did not want their lay clerks to go singing in such places.

As well as home-made material of this kind, singers could acquire the printed ballads sold in the streets (see below). In 1622 the authorities in Worcester decided

> That noe person whatsoever shall henceforth be tollerated or suffered to bringe to this Cyttie uppon the market days or any other days aney ballettes & within this Cyttie & liberties of the same to singe the same whereuppon much damage & prejudice may ensure to maney of the Kinges maiesties lege people.

Some 20 years later (in 1640-1) the prohibition was repeated. Further orders followed during the Civil War and Commonwealth:

> We do order and ordain that all ballet singers shall be put out by the heels. (1649)

> It is ordered that to suppress all ballat singers, their ballats shall be burnt
> and themselves imprisoned by the space of three days. (1653)
> That ballad singers be put in the stocks. (1659)

Three hundred years later one writer, J. Kyrle Fletcher, was asking whether any ballad singers remained in country towns, or whether they had all gone 'in this age of jazz to join the old men who wore smocks and billycock hats, and spoke with the slow, rich speech of the border country'. From his boyhood in Worcester during the 1880s he remembered the singers who came round on market and fair days:

> The best remembered of these was an elderly blind man with a concertina who had a regular stand on the Cornmarket. He was a big stout man with a large white face fringed with grey whiskers. His sight-less eyes were closed and he had a perpetual smile, a most unpleasant grin I should better describe it. He was led about by a small boy who carried a number of printed ballads still wet from the printing press, and as the old man sang he moved through the crowd selling the ballads at one penny each. We called this blind ballad singer The Welshman, but anyone who came from west of Malvern Hills was usually called Welsh, even those who spoke with the broad Hereford accent.

Instrumental street music was provided by wandering players such as the man encountered in about 1789 by Martha Sherwood's father, who was rector of Kidderminster at the time:

> One day ... there was a poor blind fiddler passing through the town, and by some accident he was knocked down, and his violin broken to atoms. My father, not having any cash about him, could not bear to see this scene of distress unrelieved; he went into his field and caused a tree to be cut down, which he sold, for the benefit and consolation of the poor itin-erant musician.

Such players continued to perform in the Shambles at Worcester until the 1930s. In the 1980s they re-appeared in the pedestrianised High Street and are still there.

Although he belonged only to a low echelon of a prestigious family, Rowland Berkeley, who lived at Ripple, was socially well above the level of an itinerant fiddler. We cannot be sure that he even played the fiddle, but his manuscript music book clearly points that way. He mislaid or abandoned the book at his brother Thomas's house in Aston-on-Carrant, four and a half miles from Ripple by way of lanes, footpaths and a ferry over the Severn at Twyning. Rowland died in 1829 at the age of 36; the book, with some tunes unfinished and some pages with a title but no music, is dated 6 July 1813. Most of the

The celebration at Aston-on-Carrant in 1995 at the house where Rowland Berkeley's book came to light

Tombstone in Ripple churchyard of William Berkeley and 'Rowland son of the above'

completed items, some 20 in number, are marches, quick steps (not to be confused with the modern quicksteps) and minuets, and clearly intended for dancing. Some—'Astley's Ride', 'Bath Minuet', 'March of the 15th Regiment', 'The Recovery', 'The Sylph'—turn up in other collections; others date from specific events and people—'Belleisle March' (after the battle of 1761) and 'Prince of Brunswick's Minuet' (after the Prussian soldier who died in 1806). Two are local: 'Tewkesbury Assembly' and the somewhat enigmatic 'Black March of the view on Brockrige Common' (which refers to Brockeridge Common, close to Ripple). Only in the 1990s did the book come to light, in the wall of Thomas Berkeley's house. During a celebratory party songs, tunes and dances were given their first airing for well over 150 years.

Printed Ballads
Most early street ballads seem to have been printed in London. Some of them make reference to provincial places but have no real connection apart from the mention of a name.

This would hold true for Martin Parker's ballad of 1663, 'A Fayre Portion for a Fayre Mayd: Or, The Thriftie Mayd of Worstersheere, and for The Valiant Virgin: Or, Philip and Mary' of about 1671 which tells how a 'young Gentlewoman of Worcestershire (a Rich Gentleman's Daughter), being in love with a Farmer's Son, which her Father despising, because he was poore, caus'd him to be Prest to Sea; And how she disguised herself in Man's apparel and followed him'.

Other sheets issued in London genuinely dealt with provincial events but are now lost. The background remains obscure to three lost ballads of 1564-5 which appear to concern the Malvern Hills. Their titles are 'An Answere to the Dystruction yat Men agaynste thayre Willes beynge answered by thayr Wyves muste Digge downe Malbroue hilles'; 'An newe Instruction to Men of such Willes that are so Redy to Dygge up Malbron hilles'; and 'A Seconde Destruction agaynste Malborne y hylles sett fourth by us Wyves consente of our Wylles'.

The killing of a man by his brother was the subject in 1577 of 'A lamentable Songe of a cruell Murder Donne in Worcester' but we have only the title of the ballad. Details are also lacking on 'A Doleful Ballad of a Cruel Murther in Worcestershire' (1605) but a sheet issued the following year must refer to some of those involved in the Gunpowder Plot: 'A Ballett Declaring the Arraignment and Execucon of the Traytors late executed at Worcester'.

One ballad which did survive concerns a woman (originally from Beckford) sentenced to death for poisoning her husband, an Evesham maltster. Since she was pregnant the execution was delayed, until she was 'delivered of a male child (which happily died)':

THE LAST DYING SPEECH, CONFESSION, CHARACTER, and BEHAVIOUR of
ELIZABETH MORTON, alias Owen, Who was first strangled and afterwards burnt
at EVESHAM on Friday, the 10th of August, 1744, for poisoning her husband ...

All you who have a patient Heart,
A word or two pray hear,
While I a Murder do impart,
That of a Husband dear.

It was not far from Evesham town,
A damsel there was bred,
Her parents but of small renown,
But virtuous lives they led.

Now I in youth being very fair,
The comfort of mother's life,
My sweethearts soon they did appear,
And I made one a wife.

But ere that 8 months they were gone,
And I a wife had been,
My heart did quickly prompt me on,
To do a heinous sin.

A Husband now I cri'd I hate,
And want to take away his life,
Oh! Poison soon shall be his fate,
To free me from the name of wife.

This cruel wish I soon attain'd,
And had its full desire,
For which I am now arrain'd,
And condemn'd to die by Fire.

Learn I pray who ere you are
O prize your Husband's Life,
And let true love be all your care
To make a happy wife.

Wedlock is a blessed state
When Man and Wife agree,
And may it be your happy fate,
To live in Unity.

Printing started in Worcester as early as 1549, when John Oswen received a licence to produce religious works there, but another two centuries elapsed before ballads were produced. The city's first ballad printer appears to have been John Butler, who was in business in the High Street from 1750 until 1793, then until his death in 1796 near the Packhorse Inn at 14 Garden Market (later called St Nicholas Street). He was succeeded by Sarah Butler (probably his daughter), who carried on the business until at least 1835.

From his High Street premises John Butler advertised that 'Country Dealers and Travellers may be supplied with Histories, Old and New Songs, Patters, Carols, Godly Books, &c'. He also announced that his publications could be obtained from Mr Hazell in Bolt Lane, Gloucester, from Mr J. Cooper in Kidderminster, and from A. Gamidge, J. Grundy and G. Lewis in Worcester (see below).

Butler's output was therefore probably large, but only a score or so items seem to have survived. These include four out of five of the eight-page book-lets entitled 'A Collection of Carols', of which the first, for example, contains 'God's dear Son without Beginning', 'God rest you merry Gentlemen' and 'Oh! Fair Jerusalem!' Butler also issued collections of 'new' songs (some of them far from new) in the same format; one of them contains 'Saunder's Ghost', 'The

Golden Glove', 'The Banks of the Dee', 'Plato's Advice' and 'A Hunting Song'. The same overall heading was given to single sheets bearing medleys of songs printed in three columns. One of these includes 'A favourite Scotch song, sung by Mrs Hillier, at the Theatre in Worcester', 'The Damsel's Wish that the Wars were all over', 'Labour in Vain', 'Contentment' and 'The Frisky Girls':

> I'll lay a groat unto a shilling,
> I'll lay a guinea to a crown,
> There's never a girl in Covent Garden
> That shall pull my courage down.
>> We'll be there at the fair;
>> If you meet a girl that's frisky,
>> Stick a fairing in her hair.
>
> Give my service to the young man
> That is cloathed all in black;
> Tell him that I will be with him,
> For his name is Paddy Whack.
>> We'll be there, &c.
>
> Give my service to the young man
> That is cloathed all in red;
> If that I was queen of England
> He should have my maidenhead.
>> We'll be there, &c.
>
> Here's your buy-men [buz-men: pickpockets] from St Giles's,
> Here's your flash-men [pimps] from Fleet-Lane,
> Here's your flashy girls of all sizes,
> They are fit for the game.
>> We'll be there, &c.
>
> Tell me, tell me, tell me truly,
> Tell me all you girls that know,
> If a girl is fit for kissing
> She must wear the ribbon bow'd.
>> We'll be there, &c.
>
> I kiss'd her once, I kiss'd her twice,
> I kiss'd her three times in a day;
> I kiss'd her once, I kiss'd her twice,
> I kiss'd her maidenhead away.
>> We'll be there, &c.

Clearly, this is imported from London, but Butler also printed items with greater local interest. 'The Twenty-Ninth of May: Or, The Restoration of King Charles II' could well have been issued for one of the annual commemorations at Worcester's Guildhall; and 'Robin Hood's Hill' celebrates the charms of a beauty spot not too far distant, near Gloucester (and now called Robinswood Hill).

None of Butler's 'histories' have survived; nor have those of Samuel Gamidge, but at least we have lists of the latter's, which include potted versions of *Gulliver's Travels*, *Robinson Crusoe* and *Moll Flanders*, the lives of Dick Whittington, Guy of Warwick, Robin Hood and pirates such as Captain John Deane, and also information such as lists of fairs, ways of interpreting moles and dreams, prophecies, fortune telling, cookery, riddles. Other chapbooks (eight-page booklets) issued by Gamidge featured sometimes a single ballad, some-times several. Crime and disaster were perennial attractions, with such titles as 'The Garland of Trials', 'A Mournful Tragedy', 'The Oxfordshire Tragedy' and 'The Somersetshire Tragedy'. (The subtitle of the last — 'The Unnatural Mother' — reminds us that child abuse has a long history). Gamidge's political sympathies — or those of his readers — may have been signalled by his publishing a ballad on the radical, John Wilkes: 'A New Song on Alderman Wilkes, Member of Parliament for Middlesex, Sung by the true Sons of Liberty'. On the other hand, he also sold from 'his warehouse' in Leech Street 'Britannia's Charter', a garland with five songs of which the first was 'Rule Britannia'.

Some of the items Gamidge published — 'The Baffled Knight', 'The Beggar of Bethnal Green', 'Children in the Wood', 'The Cuckoo's Nest' — remained in oral tradition until the twentieth century.

The Baffled KNIGHT;

Or, The LADY's Policy.

WORCESTER: *Printed for* S. Gamidge; *and Sold by Mr.* Taylor, *in* Kidderminster; *Mr.* Harward, *in* Tewkesbury; *Mr.* Hemming, *in* Alcester; *Mr.* Rowney, *in* Evesham; *Mr.* Well, *in* Stourbridge; *and Mrs.* Ball, *in* Bromyard.

There was a Knight was drunk with wine,
    A riding along the way, sir,
And there he did meet with a lady fine,
    And among the cocks of hay, sir.
One favour he did crave of her,
    And ask'd her to lay her down, sir,
But he had neither cloth nor sheet,
    To keep her from the ground, sir.
There is a great dew upon the grass,
    And if you should lay me down, sir,
You would spoil my gay cloathing,
    Which has cost me many a pound, sir.
I have a cloak of scarlet red,
    I'll lay it under thee, love,
So you will grant me the request,
    That I shall ask of you, love.
And if you'll go to my father's hall,
    That is moated round about, sir,
There you shall have your will of me,
    Within, sir, or without, sir.
On yonder stands my milk-white steed,
    And among the cocks of hay, sir,
If the king's penner [pinder] should chance to come
    He'll take away my steed, sir.
I have a ring upon my finger,
    It is made of the finest gold, love,
And it shall serve to fetch your steed
    Out of the penner's fold, love.
And if you'll go to my father's house,
    Round which is many a tree, sir,
There you shall have your chamber free
    And your chamberlain I'll be, sir.
He sat her on a milk-white steed,
    And himself upon another,
And then they rode along the way,
    Like sister and like brother.
But when she came to her father's house,
    Which was moated round about, sir,
She slip herself within the gate,
    And locked the Knight without, sir.
I thank you, kind Knight, for seeing me here,
    And bringing me home a maid, sir,
But you shall have two of my father's men,
    For to see you as far back again, sir.
He drew his sword out of the scabbard,
    And whet it upon his sleeve, sir,

Saying, Cursed be every man,
    That will a maid believe, sir.
She drew a handkerchief out of her pocket,
    And threw it upon the ground, sir
Saying, Thrice cursed be every maid,
    Who will believe a man, sir.
We have a tree in our garden,
    Some call it rosemary, sir;
There's crowing cocks in our town
    That will make a capon of you, sir.
We have a flower in our garden,
    Some call it a marygold, sir,
And he that would not when he might,
    He shall not when he would, sir.
And if you chance to meet a maid,
    A little below the town, sir,
You must not fear her gay cloathing,
    Nor wrinkling of her gown, sir.
And if you chance to meet a maid
    A little below the hill, sir,
You need not fear her creeking out,
    For she quickly will lie still, sir.

Gamidge was not himself a printer. In 1754 when he published Valentine Green's *Survey of the City of Worcester* 'at the Prior's Head' the printing was done by J. Butler, who may have performed the same office for Gamidge's chapbooks. These typically have the notice: 'WORCESTER: *Printed for* S. Gamidge; *and Sold by Mr.* Taylor, *in* Kidderminster; *Mr.* Hemming, *in* Alcester; *Mr.* Rowney, *in* Evesham; *Mr.* West, *in* Stourbridge; *and Mrs.* Ball, *in* Bromyard'. Gamidge also had agents in Cleobury Mortimer (W. Lloyd), Hereford (John Green, of Capuchin Lane), Ledbury (Mr Yarnold), Leominster (John Berrow and Philip Travis), Tewkesbury (Mr Harward) and even Taunton (Mr Daw, cutler). In addition, his 'Collection of New Songs. Num. VIII' was sold by Robert Martin of Mount Pleasant, Birmingham, himself a printer who had been apprenticed to the famous, Worcestershire-born John Baskerville, and in business from 1768 until his death in 1796.

Gamidge was at Leech Street (now gone, beneath the Giffard Hotel, and formerly called Lich Street, since it led to the cathedral's lichgate) from 1754 until 1768, when he moved to premises in the High Street near the Guildhall. After his death in 1777 his widow, Ann, took over the business and moved to 46 Sidbury, where she remained until 1798. She probably continued with the old stock, and may have sold some on because a copy of 'The Garland of Trials. Printed for S. Gamidge, at his Warehouse, Leech Street, Worcester', preserved in Worcestershire Record Office, bears the manuscript annotation:

*Lich Street, Worcester,
home of Gamidge's business*

'Elizabeth Oakley September 24th 1808'.

The same name appears on a sheet entitled 'George Ryley', printed by J. Grundy. This was James Grundy, junior, printing at 10 Goose Lane (now St Swithin's Street) from 1770 until 1792-3, and then at 4 Silver Street until 1811. He published single sheet ballads, usually in single column, and also advertised 'books circulated on the lowest terms'. The 20 or so of his sheets which have survived include 'Jack Tar's Frolic':

JACK TAR'S
FROLIC.

—

J. Grundy, Painter, Silver Street, Worcester.

—

Come all ye ranting boys,
That delight in failors noife,
  We'll compare it to nothing but laughter;
Jack Tar he came on fhore
With his gold and filver ftore,
  No one could get rid of it fafter.

The firft thing Jack did crave,
Was a parlour fine and brave,
  With good liquor of every fort;
And a pretty girl likewife,
With two black and rolling eyes,
  Then Jack Tar was pleas'd to the life.

236

Then bold Jack he kept on
Till all his money was gone,
  And the old bawd began for to frown;
With a nafty fneering eye,
And her nofe ftood all awry,
  Says fhe, failor, 'tis time to begone.

Then Jack he wink'd his eye,
Candlefticks to her let fly,
  Which put the old bawd in a rage;
The old beldam in her fright
Call'd the watchman of the night,
  Saying, bundle him away to the cage.

Then Jack he did underftand
A fhip was to be mann'd,
  Unto the Weft Indies 'twas bound;
With a fweet and pleafant gale,
Jack hoifted aloft his top fail,
  And bid adieu to all girls on the town.

   Printers were usually in a small way of business, producing jobbing work as well as ballads, and supplementing their incomes by selling stationery and medicines, binding books and running lending libraries which people paid small sums to join. Some traded only for short periods, others for decades. The work of Thomas Hayes is represented by a single ballad, 'Devil and Bonaparte. New Song to the tune of "Derry Down"'. Hayes, a bookseller and stationer at 56 Broad Street, Worcester, from 1819-21, continued as a printer at least until 1839. His neighbour, Thomas Lewis operated at 69 Broad Street as a stationer from 1795 until 1840. His only venture into ballad printing seems to have been 'Jim Crow's Visit to Worcester', an adaptation of 'Jump Jim Crow'. This song, which reached England from America in 1836, became enormously popular, and gave rise to a string of adaptations, including 'Jim Crow's Description of the London Lasses' and 'Jim Crow's Visit to Newcastle'. The Worcester version would seem to have been sung in the theatre, as well as in the streets.

Jim Crow's Visit to Worcester
with additional Verses, As sung by Mr. Hughes

    I leave the gay Metropolis,
    To Worcester then I go,
    To see the country people
    And to jump Jim Crow.
       Wheel about, turn about, Do just so;
       Every time you turn about
       Jump Jim Crow.

I came down by the Sovereign [stage coach],
The Coachman Master Dennick,
He drive me to the Star Hotel,
And then I go to Henwick.

To Henwick then I go
To see the Porto Bello,
Then I drink and smoke my pipe
Like a jolly fellow.

I went to the Athenaeum,
A little while ago,
And there I saw the clever fleas
Jump Jim Crow.

In Foregate-street they're building
The new County Court;
But they spent all their money
And that spoilt their sport.

Down in Copenhagen-street
I saw Saint Andrew's spire,
I think there's one at Coventry
Stands a great deal higher.

The Severn Navigation
Is a very useful thing;
But the cunning knaves at Gloucester
Will stop it if they can.

They did not like to be opposed,
In their own canal we know,
But when Worcester sends to Parliament
They jump Jim Crow.

ENCORE
I'm sorry I don't please you,
And dat is very plain,
I sing my song so very bad,
You call me back again.

There's a pretty lady yonder
Sitting on the third row,
For a husband now she'd wheel about
And jump Jim Crow.

At All Saints they pull houses down,
To shew the Church more plain,
They ought to have left the rubbish there
To fill the hole again.

At last I went to the theatre,
I sat in the first row,
There I saw little Master Hughes
Jump Jim Crow.

I'm sure I could jump better,
To Massa Bennett's I will go,
And get engaged to wheel about,
And jump Jim Crow.

I'm getting almost tir'd,
I pray let me go,
I'll come again another time,
And jump Jim Crow.

By contrast with the output of Hayes and Lewis, over 30 ballads with the imprint of Richard Houghton survive, which makes him one of the most prolific of the Worcester printers. He was in business from 1829 until 1834 at the General Printing Office, 5 Merry Vale (now gone; formerly near All Saints' and St Andrew's churches) where he advertised that 'Hawkers & Shopkeepers' could be 'supplied on moderate terms'. The material includes a high proportion of traditional songs such as 'All Round My Hat', 'Bonny Blue Handkerchief', 'Dame Durden', 'Fair Phoebe and her Dark-eyed Sailor', 'Female Drummer', 'Gosport Beach', 'The Indian Lass', 'Lord Marlborough', 'The Pretty Ploughboy', 'Thorney Moor Woods', 'The True Lovers, or, the King's Command', 'Van Dieman's Land', 'The Wealthy Farmer's Son' and 'The Young Sailor Bold'.

At least one new song is cast very much in a traditional mould. 'The Lamentation of James & Joseph Carter' must have done well, for it was issued twice by Houghton, paired once with 'The Blind Beggar's Daughter' and once with 'My Village Fair':

Come all you wild and wicked youths, wherever you may be,
An example take while you have time to shun bad company,
Refrain from all your former sins, reform & take good ways,
Then you'll be blest with sweet content, live and see happy days.

(Chorus)
Take advice young men all,
And think of our downfall.

We was brought up near Bewdley town, all in fair Worcestershire,
Where our parents now reside in sorrow, grief, & care,
When from them last we took our leave, the tears flow'd from their eyes,
Desiring to take good ways, we heeded not their cries.

Soon after we left our parents dear, employment we did gain,
But being prone to wretched vice, not long we did remain,
For in lewd harlots company, we spent each night and day,
And to maintain this wretched set we robbed on the highway.

In eighteen hundred & thirty-three, Feb. the 7th day,
We did attack one Mr. Jones, all on the king's highway
We robbed him of his property, and also beat him sore,
Dispersed and left him on the ground weltering in his gore.

But soon we apprehended were & unto Worcester sent,
Within strong prison walls to dwell in grief & discontent,
And at the last assizes we were guilty found and cast,
And then the awful sentence of the law was on us past.

Now with strong bars we are confin'd in a dismal cell,
And soon upon the fatal drop must bid this world farewel,
Ah! young men all we little thought of this any more than you,
That we should meet our fate so soon & bid this world adieu.

So all young men a warning take who hath sweet liberty
And for two dying sinners sake, shun harlots company,
For they will soon your pleasure blast, and prove your overthrow,
And then like us you will get launch'd into a gulph of woe.

The facts behind the ballad are straightforward. On 7 February 1833 a farmer called Jones from the village of Rock went to Kidderminster Market and on the way home spent the evening in public houses at Bewdley. In the last of these, the Union, he was spotted by James Carter (aged 22) and his brother, Joseph (30). Jones left at about 10 p.m. to walk home. The Carters followed, and outside the town they knocked him into a ditch and took his money, a few shillings. He was not seriously hurt but the Carters' smock frocks—which, incidentally, point to their having been agricultural labourers—were spattered with blood. Part of the proceeds of the robbery was devoted to buying new frocks in Broad Street, Worcester. The old ones were left with the shopkeeper who handed them to the police a day or two later. The Carters further drew attention by booking a night's lodging in Angel Street, then failing to turn up.

They seem to have been very amateurish criminals. At their trial in Worcester they were inevitably found guilty of robbing Jones, and also of stealing on the same day a Kidderminster five pound note. Despite being 'given a good character' they were sentenced to death. On 22 March 1833 they were hanged in front of Worcester Gaol. As a contemporary account put it:

> Both men met death with firmness, but without bravado; and Joseph Carter addressed the populace from the scaffolding, warning them to avoid Sabbath breaking, drunkeness, and bad women. The crowd on this occasion behaved with unusual decorum, and seem really to have been impressed with a feeling of sadness at seeing two persons hurried out of life so early.

The Carters were buried at Ribbesford. A curious notion arose that their coffins were in fact filled with stones, and that their bodies were elsewhere. Rev. John Walcot eventually became so exasperated that he obtained the necessary authority to have coffins and contents examined. The remains of the Carters were there after all.

Then, as now, crime, a major preoccupation, received sensationalist treatment in the popular press. The last public execution in Worcester was covered in a lavish sheet issued by the last ballad printer in the city, H.F. Sefton. Henry Francis Sefton combined the occupations of bookbinder, bookseller, lending library proprietor, stationer and printer. From 1829 for perhaps twenty years he was at 41 Broad Street, where he advertised that 'travellers may be supplied at reasonable rates' from his 'Wholesale and Retail Warehouse'. By 1849 he had moved to the Britannia Office, 33 Broad Street, where he remained active until at least 1856 when, at the end of the Crimean War, he issued 'A New Song on the Proclamation of Peace between the Allied Powers and Russia'.

Considering the length of time he was in business the number of his sheets extant, about 40, indicates either that his output of ballads was low or that only a small proportion of them has survived. We know that Sefton acted as an agent for ballads printed in Birmingham, and this might well have been more prof-

Worcester Gaol, which closed in 1922

itable than producing his own. Those he issued favoured traditional titles such as 'Banks of Sweet Primroses', 'Farewell to Your Judges and Juries', 'Gallant Poachers', 'Honest Ploughman', 'The King and the Tinker', 'Plains of Waterloo' and 'Lovely Nancy'. He also issued popular or sentimental songs like 'Isle of Beauty', 'Lass of Richmond Hill' and 'Rory o' More'.

'Tiddlewinkie! Or, "Allowed to be Drunk on the Premises"' is a welcome to the liberalising Beer Act of 1830, to the tune of 'Drops of Brandy':

> Good people pray how do you stop,
> I own I'm a little bit blinkey;
> Because I've been taking a drop,
> Just by at a tiddlewinkie;
> And drink I will all day long,
> In spite of your threats and your menaces,
> For the golden rule's over the door,
> Allow'd to be drunk on the premises.
> > Rum te iddite iddite &c.

The song, of five verses with four more for the encore, was 'Written by MR. DOBBS, and sung by him, and MR. BLAND, At the THEATRE-ROYAL, WORCESTER'. James Dobbs (1781-1837) of Birmingham was what we now call a singer-songwriter. One of his songs, 'I Can't Find Brummagem' (1828), was well enough known in Worcestershire for an adaptation featuring Chaddesley Corbett:

> Full fifteen months and more have passed,
> Since I was in Chaddesley.
> To it I'm com'd again at last.
> Lord! How changed is Chaddesley!
>
> I'm grieved so much that tears I've shed,
> I thought that most of the folks were dead,
> For I couldn't see a body's head
> Peeping out in Chaddesley.

The last extant sheet of Sefton's is very large, measuring 16 inches by 11½. It has the comprehensive heading: 'Life and Career of Robert Pulley Who was Executed in front of Worcester County Gaol, on Monday, March the 26th, 1849, for the Wilful Murder of Mary Ann Staight, aged 15, in Windmill-Hill Lane, near the "Sister Elms" (which stand on each side of the London Road, about 6 miles from Worcester) at Broughton, Near Pershore, Wednesday, December the 5th, 1848'. There is an engraving of a gaol, showing a hanged man. Extensive prose passages report the man's trial, the verdict, sentence of death, confession, and 'awful execution'. Finally, though in a prominent position, comes the time-honoured 'Copy of Verses' with the inevitable moral:

Now may this fate a warning be, to all both far and near,
And shun such deeds as he has done, when his sad fate you hear!
There's scarcely one will pity him, he better should have known,
He was not like a thoughtless youth, he was to manhood grown.

I will conclude this mournful song, may every mother take
This copy to their children, for Robert Pulley's sake;
To instruct them in their early days, to shun all murderous ways,
And he that reigns and dwells above, will bless their fleeting days.

The frontispiece of The British Orpheus

The printers of street ballads included only texts. George Nicholson (1760-1825) of Stourport issued songbooks with both music and words, as well as other publications. He worked as a printer, publisher and book-seller in Bridge Street at Stourport from 1897 until his death, when his wife, Mary, took over the business. He was a workaholic, a vegetarian, and a fierce opponent of blood sports and slavery. He published not only the work of others—poetry, literary miscellanies, educational and travel books (including Mary Southall's *Description of Malvern* in 1822)—but his own writings on subjects as diverse as shorthand and healthy eating. In addition he edited collections entitled *Songs and Ballads* (1810), which I have not seen, and *The British Orpheus* (1819). The latter, a selection of 270 songs and tunes, used innovatory moveable type for the music instead of the then-customary engraving. The contents are divided into amatory, moral, rural, elegaic, baccha-nalian, humourous, sea and patriotic. Many items are by well known composers, with the conspicuous exception of a few traditional ballads such as 'Lord Thomas and Fair Annet'. On what were Nicholson's premises, at the corner of Bridge Street and Raven Street in Stourport, the faded words can still be seen: 'PRINTING OFFICE'.

The Oral Tradition

Although there are plenty of references of singers and singing it is unusual to see details of songs. Broadside ballads and songbooks give a good indication of what could have been sung locally at given periods, but texts with known oral provenance are another matter. A very rare record is that of 'The Red Herring', taken down in 1831 from a manuscript copy with the note: 'This Song used generally to be sung by Mr Alderman Slayney, Hatter, at The Bailiff's Feast, in Bewdley':

> As I was Walking Down by the Sea Side
> I saw a Red Herring was forty foor Wide
> he was forty foot wide & fiftey foot Square
> if that beant a Lie I wil Come no more thear.

> (Chorus)
> Hark how thou liest Why Marry thou Liest
> Why Marry thou mights have told Mee so
> Yes Marry So I do—Sing I O lantre lo Larl lal Larriel I O

> And wat Do you think I maid of my Joley Red herrings
> Head as good an Oven as Ever Baked Bread
> Oven & Baker and every thing
> Don't you think I maid wel of my Joley Red Herring
> And wat Do you think I maid of my Red Herrings hears
> forty pair of Taylors & fiftey Pare of Sheers
> Needles & Thimbles & every thing
> Don't you think I mad wel of my Joley Red Herring

> And wat Do you think I maid of my Red hearrings Eys
> forty pare of fesants & fifty pare of flies
> fesants & flies & Everey thing
> Dont you think I maid wel of my Joley Red Hering
> And wat Do you [think] I maid of my Red Hearrings Nose
> forty pair of Stockins & fiftey pare of Showse
> Stockings & Shows, Buckles & garters & Everey thing
> Dont you think I maid wel of my Joley Red herring

from The Aldermans
Cop.
Nov 1834.

This Song used generally to be sung by Mr Alderman Slayney, Walker,
at The Bailiffs Feast, in Bewdley.

As I was a Walking Down by the Sea Side
I saw a Red Herring was forty foot Wide
he was forty foot wide & fifty foot Square.
if that beant a lie Round Come no more thear.
Hark how thou Liest why Marry thou Liest *chorus*
why Marry thou mights have told Mee So
yes Marry So I do - Sing I O bantre lo Larl lal lamiel I O

And wat Dee you think I maid of my Joley Red Herring
Head as good an Oven as Ever Baked Bread
Oven & Baker and every thing
Dont you think I maid wel of my Joley Red Herring

And wat Do you think I maid of my Red Herrings heart
forty pair of Taylors & fifty Pare of Sheers
Needles & Thimbles & Every Thing
Dont you think I mad wel of my Joley Red Herring

And wat Do you think I maid of my Red herrings Eys
forty pare of fesants & fifty pare of flies
fesants & flies & Every thing
Dont you think I maid wel of my Joley Red Herring

And wat De you I maid of my Red Hearrings Nose.
forty pare of Stockins & fifty pare of Showse
Stockings & Shows, Buckles & Garters & Every thing
Dont you think I maid wel of my Joley Red herring

And wat Do you think I maid of my Red Hearrings Skin
As good a Ship as Ever did Swan
Ship Men Mass Pole and Every thing
Dont you think I maid wel of my Joley Red hearring

And wat do you think I maid of my Red Hearrings Guts
forty pare of Morkins, & fifty Pare of Slubs
Morkins & Slubs and Every thing
Dont you think I maid wel of my Joley Red herring.

And wat Do you think I maid of my Red Herrings Tail
As good a Windmill as ever had Sale
Windmill & Miller, Toal Dish & Every thing
Dont you think I made wel of My Joley Red hearring

And wat Do you think I maid of my Red herrings Ribs
Saint Pauls Chuerch Steeple & London Bridge.
Steeple & People & Every thing
Dont you think I maid wel of my Joley Red herring.

Manuscript of 'The Red Herring'

And wat Do you think I maid of my Red Hearrings Skin
As good a Ship as Ever did swim
Ship Men Mast Pole and Everey thing
Dont you think I maid wel of my Joley Red hearring
And wat Do you think I maid of my Red herrings Ribs
Saint Pauls Church Steeple & London Bridge
Steeple & People & Everey thing
Don't you think I maid wel of my Joley Red herring

And wat Do you think I maid of my Red Hearrings Guts
forty pair of Morkins [scarecrows], and fifty Pare of Sluts
Morkins & Sluts and Evereything
Dont you think I maid wel of my Joley Red herring.
And wat Do you think I maid of my Red Herrings Tail
As good a Windmill as ever had Sale
Windmill & Miller, To al [?] Dish & Everey thing
Dont you think I made wel of My Joley Red hearring

This is the earliest known record of the song in question.

George Jorden (1783-1871) of Bewdley made a collection of songs and ballads which unfortunately has not survived. However in the diary which he kept from 1822 until 1866 he quoted from an election song of 1802 'composed and sung by Mr Moreton who was an excellent singer. He always accompanied Mr Andrews at the Bailiff's feasts and elections'. He also took down 'The Battle of Waterloo' ('a most popular song ... sung probably by greater numbers of people than any other) and 'Our Snug Little Island'.

Jorden noted only words; those involved in a revival of interest in traditional song towards the end of the nineteenth century also wanted tunes. When Lucy Broadwood (1858-1929), a well-to-do member of the piano-making family, appealed to friends and contacts throughout the country to send her songs, she received several responses from Worcestershire. As a result her book, *English County Songs* (1893) included two children's game-songs from Upton-on-Severn, sent by Mrs Emily Lawson, and a version of 'Sweet William' contributed by a Mrs Harley of Bewdley, with the note: 'This song is a great favourite with the boys of Bewdley. They can give no account of it, except that "there was an old man as used to sing it". The best singer, when he has ended the song, always turns to the audience, remarking emphatically, "Till apples grows on an orange tree!" [that is, repeating the last line] — probably the usual custom of the old ballad singers'.

Mrs Harley also sent the tune of a maypole dance (see chapter 10); several songs, including 'Good King Arthur', 'A Lady once loved her swine' and 'Ramso was no sailor'; and a *cantefable*:

Oh, yes I saw something

After the late French war, when the army was disbanded, a soldier who was making his way home through an out of the way part of the country near Bewdley knocked at the door of a farm house to ask for food. The farmer's wife who had never seen a soldier was so dazzled at the splendour of his appearance that she took him for an angel. She welcomed him with much awe and hastened to get dinner ready for him. Presently she ventured to ask where he had come from. 'From Paris', he answered. 'From Paradise! Then you will have seen my first husband, John Jones', said she, adding some particulars of John Jones' appearance. The soldier recollected everything that was expected of him. He said that John Jones was very comfortable in heaven, only rather tired of having nothing to do, and that he wanted a little money to set up a peppermill. 'Ah', said the old woman, 'that is so like my poor dear John Jones! He would always be making a bit of money'. Then she gave the soldier twenty guineas out of an old stocking hanging in the chimney corner, and an old grey mare to turn the peppermill.

Soon after the soldier had gone the farmer came in, and was very angry when he heard of his wife's visitor. He set out in pursuit forthwith, and soon met a shepherd, of whom he asked tidings of the soldier and the grey mare. But the shepherd who had been bribed by the soldier replied:

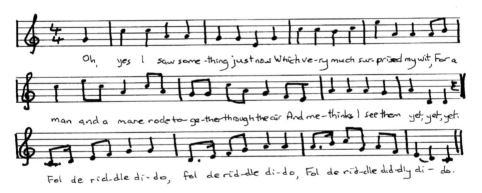

Then the old man lay down on his back
And into the elements he did stare,
To try whether he could discern or not
The young man on his bob-tailed mare.

Other correspondents of Broadwood's included Lady Mary Lygon, daughter of Earl Beauchamp of Madresfield Court, and Winifred Norbury, a friend of Elgar, 'W.N.' in his *Enigma Variations*, and the daughter of a landed gentleman. Norbury took a particular interest in traditional carols, and she would notate a tune from a singer, then invite him or her or write out the words. Two items came from workers on the Norbury estate at Sherridge, near Leigh

Norbury family and retainers at Sherridge, near Leigh Sinton.
William Phillips is in the back row (extreme left),
Winifred Norbury is seated (far right)

Country carol seller, drawn by Cuthbert Bede in 1869

Sinton: William Phillips's 'The Saviour's Love' of 1899, and a Mr Gallett's 'The Angel Gabriel' of 1902; learned 60 years earlier at Hanley Castle. 'The Moon Shines Bright' (no provenance indicated) ends with the typical carol singer's verse:

> My song is done, I must be gone,
> I can no longer stay here,
> God bless you all both great and small,
> And send you a joyful New Year.

Rev. Edward White of Eckington sent Broadwood in 1907 the text from a blind man, William Price, of a carol beginning, 'When Mary in the morning to the sepulchre came' ('sung by men & accompanied with an accordion, generally after a preliminary visit to the inn'), together with the words and tune of 'How grand and how bright', from Alfred White, whose son noted:

> This carol ... my father says has been sung as far back as he can remember. (He is nearly eighty). It is sung by children, usually only by those who do not know any other, & is rather despised by them. It is sung rapidly & generally gabbled through & its singing has been for that reason discouraged. ... Eckington children invariably sing ... 'O grandad O bright'. About 25 years ago there was an old wheelwright of the name of Bright living in the village & that may have caused the corruption.

The text in fact derives from an eight-page booklet, 'The True Christian's Real Comfort. A Choice Collection of Christmas Carols', issued in the mid-nineteenth century by the Birmingham ballad printer, William Pratt, where it appears as 'The Worcestershire Christmas Carol' (for which see overleaf).

By contrast, another clergyman, Rev. W.K. Clay of Hartlebury, was taking in interest in secular songs. In 1908 he noted from William Millicheap 'The Green Mossy Banks of the Lea' ('Sung by him at Harvest Homes and learnt when a boy'), and from Mary Hayes, 'Cold Blows the Wind', 'Three Gypsies betrayed her' and 'Spare me the Life of Georgie' (the last 'learnt ... from a dairy maid in Upton Warren Parish fifty-seven years before').

THE WORCESTERSHIRE
CHRISTMAS CAROL.

How grand and how bright
That wonderful night,
When angels to Bethlehem came !
They burst forth like fires,
They struck their gold lyres,
And mingled their sound with the flame.

The shepherds were 'maz'd,
The pretty lambs gaz'd
At darkness thus turn'd into light ;
No voice was there heard
From man, beast or bird,
So sudden and solemn the sight.

And then when the sound
He echoed around,
The hills and the dales all awoke ;
The moon and the stars
Stopt their fiery cars,
And listen'd while Gabriel spoke.

I bring you, said he,
From the glorious three,
A message both gladsome and good ;
The Saviour is come
To the world as his home,
But he lies in a manger of wood.

At mention of this,
The source of all bliss,
The angels sung loudly and long ;
They soared to the sky,
Beyond mortal eye,
But left us the words of their song.

All glory to God,
Who laid by his rod,
To smile on the world through his Son ;
And peace be on earth,
For this wonderful birth,
Most wonderful conquests has won.

And good-will to man,
Though his life's but a span,
And his soul all sinful and vile ;
Then pray, Christians, pray,
And let Christmas Day
Have a tear as well as a smile.

During the years 1906-1908 *Evesham Notes & Queries* printed for local contributors a series of song texts including 'General Wolfe', 'The One, O, or the Twelve Apostles' and 'The Bitter Withy'. At the same period Cecil Sharp (1859-1924) made a series of visits from London and noted morris dance tunes at Redditch (see next chapter), together with songs such as 'The Holly Twig' at Hunnington and 'Mary of the Silvery Tide', 'The Outlandish Knight', 'Plains of Waterloo', 'Rosetta [and her Gay Ploughboy]', 'Rude Boreas' and 'Young Henry the Poacher' at Evesham (where his informant, Mr Gibbs, aged 74, may have been the person of the same name who supplied some of the items to *Evesham Notes & Queries*). Sharp also took down songs in various places such as Armscote and Shipston-on-Stour which in 1930 transferred to Warwickshire.

Another song-hunter, H.E.D. Hammond (1866-1910), found that his land-lady at Bath in 1906—a Mrs Webb—was a Worcestershire woman who had lived at King's Norton and Malvern. She knew 17 songs, all of which she had learned from old singers in her native county. According to Mrs Webb, her father-in-law had said that his great-grandmother had known one of these songs, 'The Dairymaid' (better known as 'When spring comes in'). She remembered only one verse, the second, and the first has been added from else-where:

When spring comes in the birds will sing,
The lambs will play and bells will ring,
And we shall enjoy their glorious charm,
So lovely and so gay.

Where primroses grow and cowslips too,
And violets in their sweet attire,
And daffodils show through every briar
While daisies fade away.

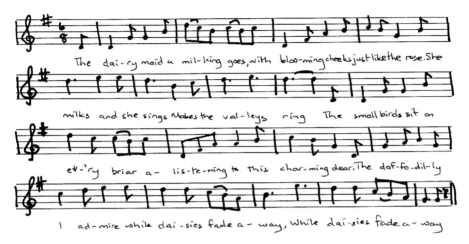

Julius Harrison (1885-1963), like other composers of classical music such as E.J. Moeran and Ralph Vaughan Williams, took an interest in traditional song. Harrison, born in Stourport, went to Queen Elizabeth School, Hartlebury, then studied music at the Birmingham and Midland Institute. From 1905 he was the organist at Hartlebury and left for London three years later. One wonders whether he knew of Rev. W.K. Clay's song collecting. Harrison revisited Stourport in 1917, and as a result wrote his *Worcestershire Suite* (first performed in a piano version in 1919). Three of its four themes, 'Pershore Plums', 'Redstone Rock' and 'Shrawley Round' (the last inspired by a recollection of children seen dancing at Shrawley), were his own; the fourth, 'The Ledbury Parson', came from oral tradition, and was dedicated 'To the memory of those two inimitable artists, Bob and Abel Spragg [singer and fiddler respectively], who could be heard interpreting this Worcestershire song over many glasses of beer, every Saturday evening in the [eighteen-] nineties, at the Bridge Inn, Stourport'. (Purists will claim the song in fact for Herefordshire, since it is based on events which took place in Ledbury, but it obviously took root in Worcestershire, too).

When *The Worcestershire Suite* was performed at the Three Choirs Festival in Worcester in 1920 Elgar expressed his admiration. Harrison went on to write a *Severn Suite* (1927) in which he used tunes heard in the Wyre Inn (now gone) at Shrawley, where the ferry crossing over the river was much used by Ombersley men who went over for the music and dancing. In 1940 Harrison became director of music at Malvern College, and remained in post until the establishment temporarily moved to Harrow in 1942. In 1941 he wrote a suite

*The Bridge Inn, Stourport, where Bob and Abel Spragg
played and sang in the 1890s*

for violin and orchestra, *Bredon Hill*. Few, if any, of his works are now available on disc, though a 1920 recording of the *Worcestershire Suite* was re-issued on LP in 1982.

It was in the late 1920s or early '30s that the first sound recordings of traditional songs in Worcestershire were made, thanks to an American academic, James M. Carpenter (1888-1984), using a dictaphone powered by a 6 volt car battery. The recordings, now in the Library of Congress in Washington, include children's songs, sea shanties and some items ('The Pretty Ploughboy', 'The Gallant Poachers') from unidentified singers. From John Morris of Broadway, Carpenter recorded 'Jones's Ale' and 'Old King Cole'; and from two brothers at South Littleton, Charles and Jack Rose, 'Gaffer Gray'; 'The girl I left behind me', 'I am a rover', 'The Miller's Three Sons', 'The One, O' and 'The Unquiet Grave':

Thanks to a revival of interest in traditional song after the Second World War, further songs carne to light. In the 1960s I recorded at Hinton-on-the-Green the Easter carol, 'Christ is born in Bethlehem', from George Freeman (aged 57), a factory worker; and from Joe Gardiner (aged 64), a farm worker, 'We're all jolly fellows that follow the plough' (see above, p.208), 'Buttercup Joe' and 'Jim the carter's lad'. From Hubert Bradley (aged 59) of Mamble in 1972 I recorded 'The Old Sow' and 'The Parson with a wooden leg'. Some of the same songs were found in the 1970s by Gwilym Davies at Ashton-under-Hill (from Stan Cope) and Birtsmorton (from Harry Dawe). For Charles Menteith, 'Buster' Mustoe, landlord of the Round of Grass at Badsey, sang 'Bill the Weaver', 'Buttercup Joe', 'The Tree on the Hill' and 'Wassail Song'. In the Pershore area in the 1970s, and again in Malvern in 1999, Charles Menteith heard 'Evesham Cider', of which the words are in fact adapted from the poem of 1930 by E.V. Knox, 'Hell in Herefordshire':

In spite of church and chapel, ungodly folk there be,
Who pluck the cider apple from the cider apple tree.
They crush it in their presses till the golden juice runs out
At various addresses that no bugger talks about.

Unspeakable carouses, at least so it is claimed,
Take place in various houses that cannot here be named
Black timber and white plaster hide secret drinking dens,
Where be-elzebub is master of the cider drinking men.

Then, maddened by their orgies on that infernal brew,
They slit each other's gorges — according to the few,
Till Hampton is a shambles and Bengeworth runs with blood
Of gamblers who've disturbed a cider-drinking mob.

I've travelled many places but before my days are done
I'll go back and see them faces at dear old Eve-e-sham.
I'll watch that golden sunset behind them Malvern Hills,
For I know it does me more good than all them bloody pills.

CHAPTER 8

Dance & Drama

Passion for dance and drama is a remarkable feature of popular cultural history. A spontaneous, joyous feeling is communicated by observations such as that of Mrs Margaret Cheshire of Ashton-under-Hill, in 1950: 'Our older inhabitants can remember the broom dance held in the village street when the travelling threshing machine arrived and all the villagers brought their small stocks of grain to be threshed'. Some 60 years earlier Jesse Salisbury, writing on south-east Worcestershire, recalled dancing on the green as a youth:

> He has seen staid dames, as well as lads and lasses of the village, taking their places in the sets and footing it right heartily—and that, too, after having done a day's work on the farm or in their own houses. The orchestra usually consisted of a fiddle, with the addition, perhaps, of one or two flutes and occasionally also of a bass viol.

Similar gatherings can be traced back through generations who, depending on fluctuating orthodoxies, danced sometimes with the blessing of church and state, sometimes despite their malediction. One form of dancing, the morris, still has dedicated adherents whose appearances remain a familiar feature of many public occasions. Country dancing also continues, often in the context of fund-raising events for clubs and societies. Bands which are the descendants of Jesse Salisbury's 'orchestras' play on.

Popular drama has an equally lengthy story, going at least as far back as the morality plays, known as pageants, of mediaeval Worcester. These disappeared after the Reformation, together with village plays of various kinds. Drama returned with the Restoration. As early as 1717 a shack in the yard shared by the King's Head and the Golden Lion at Worcester saw performances of *Oedipus, King of Thebes*, and also the stage debut of Sarah Siddons. The Theatre Royal opened in Angel Street in 1781 and survived three re-buildings before closing in 1955.

Travelling players or 'barnstormers' once toured the county. In 1949 Sidney Knight memorably evoked the visit to Broadway, half a century earlier, of Hemingway's Travelling Theatre:

> The wagons and caravans arrived, drawn by horses, and a structure of wooden sections was erected at the back of an inn. ... admission money ... was 3d. in the gallery (a rickety tier of planks extending right up to the roof), 6d. in the pit, and 1s. in one row of seats in front for those of high degree. We gazed with awe at the leading man, a tall, handsome figure of about thirty years of age with melancholy features, when he heard that he was receiving the enormous salary of 25s. a week. ...
>
> Practically the whole population of Chipping Campden walked down Broadway Hill to see the *Campden Wonder*, but *Sweeney Todd, the Demon Barber of Fleet Street* ran it close. The womenfolk sobbed as they watched *East Lynne*, and *The Murder of Maria Marten in the Red Barn* brought the worked-up audience to its feet as they booed and hissed the rascally villain who was responsible for Maria's betrayal and untimely death.
>
> We had to go early to ensure a seat on Saturday night, when the singing competition was held for men only; the prize was a young pig held under the competitor's arm as he sang a popular song of the day, preferably comic, with a straight face. This was an uproarious performance lasting until midnight. Slimmy Robinson, the village baker, was a popular visitor on one occasion. He sang 'Dear Louise, I'm waiting in the moonlight', his face as expressionless as a lump of his own dough, while the pig squealed and fought to break loose.

Traditional drama—first recorded in Worcestershire in the mid-nineteenth century but undoubtedly existing earlier—survived in the form of Christmas mumming plays featuring stylised combat, knockabout comedy and lively singing. The performers, all village people, sometimes doubled as morris men: both dancers and actors looked to their appearances as useful sources of funds when opportunities for work out of doors were curtailed in hard winters. The words, 'In comes I', nevertheless signalled the return of a well-loved seasonal celebration.

Early Dancers: 'rude Ruffions and drunken Companions'
In the time of Prior More (see previous chapter) of Worcester small payments were frequently made to dancers at religious events. For example, the sum of twenty pence was given 'to vij dawnceres of Claynes on trinite Sonday' on at least three occasions between 1524-5 and 1533-4. Dancers were rewarded during Rogation Week in 1525-6, and four years later for unspecified reasons 'the dauncers of seynt sewthans [Swithun's]' received twelve pence.

By contrast, in the next century another churchman showed a very different attitude. Archdeacon John Johnson of Worcester sternly enquired in 1609:

'Whether any Dauncers players of Enterludes or such like, or any other doe Daunce play or use any unseemly parts or games ... in the church or churchyard ... during service time'. Where such offences were reported, ecclesiastical courts cited the culprits. At Bradley, near Feckenham, Thomas Paddy, John and William Sale, Humfrey Foukes and William Lewe were accused in 1617-18 of 'daunsenge uppon whitsontewsdaye in time of devine service'. In 1611 at Crowle Richard Chaundler 'ffor playeinge on his fiddle one hour Sundaye last tempore divinorum' and Richard Auster, John Horniblow, Jordan Dyson, John Davies and Humfrey Bowling, for dancing at that time, were ordered to perform '*canonicam penitenciam in consuetis vestibus*' (penance in due form in the usual clothing). Penance (see also page 110) was also required from George Heming of Grafton Flyford for 'setting & suffering daunsenge in his new barne floore the 18 daye of Iune 1615 at time of devine service'. His wife, Alice, and others present, confessed their error and were dismissed, after being admonished, as was Thomas Dugard, the musician who played for them. The same rap on the knuckles was administered in 1616 for 'daunsenge the morris uppon the Lordes day' at Ribbesford to Thomas Weaver, John Budd, William Lake, William Sparrie, Thomas Nashe, Edward Parker, Thomas Lucas, junior, Thomas Hayward, junior, and John Briggs.

Much more serious penalties could by imposed by the secular courts. William Jeffreys, the Longdon constable, complained to the Worcestershire magistrates in 1617 that

> the Inhabitantes and youth of Longdon, Have every yeare, upon the Saboth daie, in the sommer time used to sport drunken Companions, have used to sport themselves with maygames, Morrices, and dawncinges, by reason whereof many rude Ruffions, and drunken Companions, have comen thither, from other townes adioyneinge, to the said sportes, and have made much quarrellinge, redye to murther one an other.

In 1614, he said, 'some of ffortingtons [Forthampton's] men ... gave one a broken heade', and the following year 'some of Elsfildes [Eldersfield's] men ... made an affray upon the Smithes man of longdon'. Then in 1616 'there was much sport made in longdon, by morrices, and dawncinges, and because at evening prayers the same day, they were forced to cease their sportes, some of the youth of longdon, procured a poore woman then beinge excommunicated, to goe into the Church in service time, ... hopeing thereby to put an end of godes service, That soe they might againe retorne to their sportes'. Then, on Trinity Sunday when the constable tried to arrest 'the Minstrell there playinge ... one of the dawncinge Companie strake up your petitioners heeles and said he would breake your petitioners necke down the stayers there if I departed not from them, and lett them alone. Whereby your peticioner beinge thus terrified by them departed'.

At Broadwas in 1624 Robert Price, victualler, not only sold ale 'att the tyme of prayers on Sondaye last 13th June' but permitted 'disorders in his house [such] as daunceing'. In addition, 'ffloris Serman musician' was in trouble for 'playing upon his musick' on the same occasion. In the same year the extreme views of some were exemplified by the Eldersfield parson, a Mr Prior, whose unhappiness with James I's toleration for sports and dancing after evening prayer on Sundays caused him, allegedly, to make 'scandalous speeches towards the Kinge' and to pray before his sermon for 'god to turne the Kinges harte from profanes[s]'.

Despite such references to dancing there is no precise information on which dances Worcestershire people favoured at the time. It is just possible that 'Worcester Braules' could have been an exception. This was a tune written or arranged by Thomas Tomkins, and included in a collection of keyboard music known as the Fitzwilliam Virginal Book, compiled between 1609 and 1619. A 'braule' or 'brawl' was a French dance popular in Elizabethan England. The Welsh composer, Tomkins (1572-1656), was the organist at Worcester Cathedral in 1596, and in the following year he married the widow of his predecessor, Alice Hussard. The pair then moved to London, but returned to Worcester in 1642, when Tomkins again became involved in music at the cathedral. In 1646 services here were discontinued because of the Civil War but he was allowed, despite being a strong Royalist, to continue in accommodation there until 1654, when he retired to Martin Court at Martin Hussingtree.

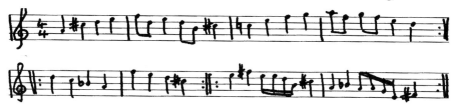

Music for 'Worcester Braule'

Pageants and Interludes

Early drama had a similar trajectory to that of dance, with even more abundant records of its part in civic and church activities. In the fifteenth and sixteenth centuries the monks of Worcester Priory in various accounts—those of almoner, cellarer, prior and sacristan—listed payments to actors (all men at the time), for whom the term, player, was used in English, *famulus* (servant), *histrio*, *ludens*, *lusor*, or *mimus* in Latin. As with minstrels (see chapter 7), many magnates from the monarch downwards had in their service actors who went on tour and were paid by their hosts. Different cities, including Worcester, and even particular churches, also sponsored groups or troupes of actors. These are some examples:

Sacristan's Account Roll, 1423-4
In dono ludentibus die Corpus Christi iijs. iiijd.
(In gift to the players on the day of Corpus Christi 3s. 4d.)

Prior's Account Roll, 1445-6
Item *diversis ludentibus ville in nocte Epiphanie vjs. viijd.*
(Item to various players of the town on the night of Epiphany 6s. 8d.)

Cellarer's Accounts, 1449-50
Item *in donis datis mimis & histrionibus ville Wygomie ad festum Natale domini xijd.*
(Item in gifts given to mimes and actors of the town of Worcester at the feast of the nativity of the lord 12d.)

Civic Ordinances, 1466
diversis ludentibus apud Claynes Aston & Poywyke hoc anno iijs.
(to various actors at Claines Aston and Powick in this year 3s.)

Prior's Accounts, 1463-4
In donis datis diversis ffamulis domini Regis et Ministrallis eiudem ad diversas vices hoc Anno una cum donis datis diversis famulis ducum Comitum et aliorum magnatum hoc Anno viijli. xixs. ijd.
(In gifts given to the servants of the lord King and Minstrels of the same at various times in this year together with gifts given to various servants of dukes earls and other magnates this year £8 19s. 2d.)

Cellarer, *c.*1470-80
Et datis lusoribus Ecclesiarum omnium Sanctorum Sancte Elene Sancti Swithuni Sancti Albani sancti Petri & sancti Michaelis in Wigornia videlicet cuilibet Ecclesie vijd. vjs. Et datis lusoribus Iohannis Yonge vice comiti pro labore suo ...
(And given to the players of the churches of All Saints, St Helen, St Swithun, St Alban, St Peter & St Michael in Worcester that is to each church 7d. 6s. And given to the players of John Young sheriff for their work ...)

Performances were closely linked to the church and its calendar. Parish fundraising explains the payments made to the churches of Clent (St Kenelm's) and Martley (St Peter's) in 1520-1 and 1518-19 respectively. In Worcester several parishes benefitted from contributions, including St Michael's (1518-19) and St Peter's (1519-20 and 1534-5). In 1532-3 Prior More gave 6s. 8d.

In rewardes to alhaland [All Saints] churche at the play holden at hynwyckes hull [Henwick Hall, in the parish of Hallow] synt Thomas even [20 December] beyng sonday & on seynt Tomas day beyng Monday, whiche play was kept to the profett of alhaland churche.

Top: Old St Michael's (demolished in 1840), near Worcester Cathedral and bottom: St Peter's, Worcester (demolished in the 1970s), off Sidbury, both churches that benefitted from Prior More's contributions towards the costs of performances by players

In the following year he donated to the 'sheowes' of St Helen's, St Swithun's and St Andrew's Churches.

The priory's accounts in the single year of 1521-2 included 19 payments to players for performances, among others, on Shrove Tuesday, Palm Sunday, at Easter, Rogationtide, and on Whit Sunday. Advent, Christmas, New Year and Epiphany were marked by similar expenditures in other years. In 1529-30 'iiij pleyeres of wurceter on seynt Wlstansday' (19 January) were paid 3s. 4d., or 10d. apiece.

The high point of the year in terms of spectacle was the elaborate processions and plays, known as pageants, on themes from the bible and apocrypha, which took place on Trinity Sunday (the first after Whitsun), Corpus Christi (the Thursday after Trinity) and the following Sunday. The pageants—well known in Coventry and York, where some texts have survived—were first recorded in Worcester in 1466, and continued for over a century. The dissolution of craft guilds in 1547-8 under Edward VI put an end to the processions, which they had organised, though these were revived for a time under Queen Mary. The pageants survived, with some sequences later excised which were deemed unacceptable to Protestants. In August 1575 when Queen Elizabeth, 'rydyng upon her Palfrey', arrived in Worcester for a week's stay, two pageants were specially put on for her on stages erected at the Grass Cross (now simply known as 'the Cross') and 'in Saint Albons streete end at Saynt Ellyns Churche'. The total cost amounted to the very large sum of £173 8s. 4d.

In the year after Elizabeth's visit the will of Henry Smythe mentions 'pleyers geare', valued at 40s., and in 1576-7 an inventory of property in the cathedral reveals what the actors wore:

> A gowne of freres [friars]
> gyrdles
> A womans gowne
> A kings cloke of Tyshew [tissue: rich cloth, interwoven with gold or silver]
> A lytill cloke of tysshew
> A Ierkin of greene
> A Ierkin and a payer of breeches
> A gowne of silk
> 2 Cappes and the devils apparrell

The last of these pageants in Worcester seems to have been in 1583-4. They were rehearsed in the Pageant House, which stood just off the Cornmarket in New Street. Its lease—no doubt for other purposes—is mentioned in documents of 1605-6 and 1659.

Alongside its public place drama had a role in private gatherings. Prior More paid 3s. 4d. to 'iiij pleyeres of glowceter' who entertained 'A pon sonday when the balyffes & the xxiiij^{ti} [bailiffs and the 24 (councillors)] dyned with me in the grete hall' at Worcester (some time between 30 December and 5

January, 1520-1). The relaxed nature of the occasion can be gauged from the expenses at a similar event at Battenhall eight years later, when the prior paid the 'pleyeres of coventrie' the standard fee, but more than twice that—7s. 10d.—for 'mawemesey [Malmsey] red & claret'.

We do not know what was performed for the prior and his guests: perhaps interludes (see below); but Robin Hood plays were undoubtedly secular, though tolerated by liberal clerics. When Hugh Latimer was bishop of Worcester (1535-9) he visited a village in his diocese one Sunday morning, to find no one in church because of 'Robin hoodes day', and later told the story in a sermon preached before Edward VI. The accounts of Worcester Priory provide further evidence of the popularity of such plays. In 1528-9 'certen yong men of seynt Elens that pleyd Robyn Whod' were rewarded with 12d. On Trinity Sunday in 1529-30 Prior More put a similar sum in 'the [collection] box of Robyn hood'. Later in the same year 'Robin Whot' is mentioned again, together with 'Mayde Marian'; and in 1533-4 'Robyn Whod & Litle Iohn of Ombursley' appear.

The many travelling companies which visited Worcester—and also towns such as Bewdley—are likely to have provided secular plays. John English '&

other the Kynges pleyeres' performed at Grimley in October 1524-5 and again in August-September four years later. John or William Slye (possibly ancestors of the William Sly who was a fellow-actor of Shakespeare's) came several times with the King's Men between 1526-7 and 1533-4.

The first mention of a play's title in surviving documents in Worcestershire seems to be John Lyly's play, written in 1589-90, *The Comedie of Midas*. The listing of a copy in the will of Richard Evans of Bredon, drawn up in 1594, shows that it was prized, but does not necessarily indicate that it had been performed locally.

When Lord Chandos's Men visited Worcestershire in 1596-7 one of the company, Robert Armin, played a clown called Grumball. Armin (1563-1615), a goldsmith turned actor, singer, mimic, dancer and comic writer, had been encouraged by Queen Elizabeth's jester

Robert Armin as the clown, Blue John, from the title page of his play, History of the two Maids of More-clacke *(1609)*

and player, Richard Tarlton. He succeeded Will Kemp in the Lord Chamberlain's Men, and played a series of Shakespeare's characters, including Dogberry in *Much Ado*, Touchstone in *As You Like It*, Feste in *Twelfth Night* and the fool in *King Lear*. Armin's own writings include *Foole upon Foole*, or *Sixe Sortes of Sottes* (1600), which describes six professional fools in the service of the nobility of gentry. For one of these, Jack Miller of Evesham, Armin seems to have gathered material in 1596-7 when he performed with Chandos's Men at Pershore and Upton-on-Severn.

Attitudes to plays and players soon changed radically. Although in 1600 Francis Walker received payment 'for making a playe in the church' at Tenbury, as early as seven years afterwards Bishop Gervase Babington of Worcester was making enquiries as to whether his clergy had 'suffered ... any playes, feastes, banquets, Church-ales, Drinkings, or any other profane usages, to be kept in your Church, Chappels, or churchyard'. In 1611 John Butcher was taken to task merely for 'proclayminge a playe in the Church one the Saboath daye' at Beoley. In the same year John Browning of Leigh stood accused of 'being presente at a playe made in a howse at service tyme one a Saboath day', and Edward Bartlemere of 'plaing an interlude with divers others at the time of divine service'. Interludes, short moralistic dramas with a single episode, were performed by professional actors for wealthy patrons, including perhaps Prior More, but were also favoured by village players, much like those in *A Midsummer Night's Dream* who put on 'Pyramus and Thisbe'. At Alvechurch those involved in the 'stagge play uppon the Saboath daye and uppon St Peters daye', in addition to Bartlemere, were Randolph and John Lyddiat, John Lilley, Richard Davis and William More.

John George and others faced a similar charge at Pershore in 1612-13; and at Rock the following year, even 'for acting a stage plaie upon a Sundaie after Evening praier', Thomas Monday was excommunicated and members of the audience, having confessed their error, had to do penance for a day in the parish church. At Martin Hussingtree in 1617 Griffin Glynn was charged with 'causing a puppett playe to be in the Chauncell' on 17 December. John Jones, formerly of St Michael's in Bedwardine parish, devised his own method for authorising performances: he forged a licence from the Master of the Revels, Sir Henry Herbert, permitting him 'To sett forth and shew a Motion with dyvers storyes in ytt Also tumbleing vaulteing sleight of hand and other such like feates of Activety'. Somehow, Jones was rumbled at Upton 'super Sabrinam' (on Severn), and indicted at the Worcester Quarter Sessions. His fate is not known.

In Worcester the civic authorities came to the firm decision in 1622:

> that noe playes bee had or made in the upper end of the Twonehall [town hall] of this Cyttie and Councell Chamber used by anie players whatso-ever, And that noe playes bee had or made in Yeald be nyght tyme, And

> yf anie players bee admytted to play in the Yeald hall [Guild hall] to bee
> admytted to play in the lower end onelie uppon paine of xls. to be payd.

Four years later the prohibition was repeated with regard to the Trinity Hall
in Trinity Street (which was sold in 1796 and pulled down in 1890). Even the
'Kinges maiesties players' were turned away in 1630, ostensibly 'for feare of
infeccion', and given 12s. 4d. for not performing. Similar bans were repeated
through the decade. Meanwhile, actors' costumes owned by the city were
ordered to be burned, in 1634.

The puritan, Richard Baxter, preacher at St Mary's Church, Kidderminster,
from 1641 until 1660, heartily disliked the town's yearly 'shew, in which they
brought forth ye painted formes of Gyants & such like foolery, to walk about
ye streets with'. The Civil War brought to an end Kidderminster's 'Shews &
wakes & Stage playes'.

Morris

Dance and drama re-emerged after the Civil War. However, so far as the record
is concerned in Worcestershire, the morris seems to have gone unnoticed for a
considerable period. Then in the nineteenth century, sightings recur. Dancers
were seen at Kidderminster in the 1830s and '40s; then in 1847 an eye-witness
at Droitwich reported: 'On the 27th of June, a large party of Morris Dancers
still continue to parade the town and neighbourhood, it is said, in commemoration of a discovery of some extensive salt mines'. (This was probably to do
with the St Richard celebrations, for which, see chapters 3 and 10). The regular
appearance of a team at Hanbury was mentioned in 1850.

According to John Noake, writing in 1856:

> Morris dancing is still resorted to by the boatmen on the Severn and the
> canals, whenever the frost interrupts their ordinary occupations, on
> which occasion small parties of them, dressed up fantastically with
> ribbons, and carrying short sticks, which they strike together in time with
> parts of the dance, perform in the streets, soliciting alms.

Similar activity continued until at least the 1930s, and possibly even later.
Lavender Jones was told by a 50-year-old woman at Claines in 1961 that she
remembered being taken by her mother to see boatmen dancing outside the
Pheasant Inn at Lowesmoor, Worcester, when ice on the canal made it impossible for them to move their boats.

In the winter of 1890 or '91 boatmen from Ombersley who were out of work
because the waterways were frozen went round morris dancing, dressed in
white, wearing baldricks, and carrying sticks. Until about 1920 up to 40 out of
work fishermen and boatmen from Upton-on-Severn danced at Christmastime
to raise money. They divided into parties and went round to grand houses such

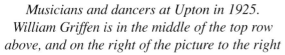

Musicians and dancers at Upton in 1925.
William Griffen is in the middle of the top row
above, and on the right of the picture to the right

as Madresfield Court. Some even walked as far as Tewkesbury or Cheltenham. In 1925 William Griffen got a group together to demonstrate a stick and a hand-kerchief dance to Maud Karpeles, Cecil Sharp's associate. A photograph of the occasion includes Griffen's daughter, Edith Hill, who (unusually) made up the numbers when male dancers were lacking.

Evesham had its own stick and handkerchief dances, done in the streets in the late nineteenth century, and taken down from the side's musician, George Collins, in 1940. Pershore, too, had a stick dance, performed from the 1840s until the Second World War. Dancers went out for ten days at Christmas time, accompanied by a musician and Tom Fool, the latter with blacked face, a feature of the get-up of all the dancers from neighbouring Drakes Broughton and Peopleton.

Bill Scarrett of Pershore, who died in 1986, came from a fairground family which settled in the town after their equipment was destroyed by a flood in the Weir Meadow. He was a fiddler and dancer for 30 years, starting at the age of eight, two years before he left school. 'We went out before the First World War as youngsters; after the war as real dancers'.

The side would get down to practice each October so as to be ready for the Christmas season, of which the high point was Boxing Day. The men went on foot to places like Malvern or Ledbury. 'We used to walk ... As you came to a village, so you danced'. At night they put up if need be at a lodging house. One of Bill Scarrett's memories—told to Dave Jones—was dancing for two hours at Worcester in the old market opposite the cathedral. On another occasion the Pershore men went to Ross-on-Wye, pushing a handcart with their sticks and other equipment, and taking turns to ride on a tandem.

Members of the side included 'brickies, carpenters, plumbers, ordinary working fellows, fellows off the ground'. Competition for a place was lively because 'there wasn't the work about at that time of year'. Eight men usually danced. In addition there were two musicians—playing fiddle and concertina usually, but also at different times piccolo, tin whistle, triangle, tambourine and bones—together with the all-important collector, the person responsible for going round with the hat.

The favourite dance was 'The Black Boy' which went to the tune of 'Not for Joe'. This in turn gave the name to this style of dancing of Not for Joeing. It was not, of course, confined to Pershore—I have seen an account of something very similar from Oxfordshire—but it certainly occurred there. As well as having the tune played instrumentally the dancers from time to time would break into a snatch of the words:

> Not for Joe, not for Joe,
> Not for Joseph if he knows it;
> Not for Joe, not for Joe,
> Stick him in the garden, let him grow.

The original song was a composition—which sold 80,000 copies—by Albert Lloyd, a music hall singer of the 1860s and '70s, whose other works

'Bluff King Hal'

'Heel and Toe' (resembling 'Belle Isle March').
Two morris dances taken down in Redditch by Cecil Sharp in June 1906

include 'Married to a Mermaid', 'The Street Musician', 'The Organ Grinder' and 'Policeman 92X'. To the delight of Bill Scarrett, Dave Jones was able from his descriptions to reconstruct the costumes, steps and figures of the dances. Two Not-for-Joes, George Collins and Sam Dufty, lived on into the twenty-first century. They were interviewed in 2001 by visiting morris men from Vancouver, Canada, who had adopted their dances.

Other towns and villages had their own traditions. According to W.G. Leadbetter, six or eight men regularly danced in May at Bromsgrove, bedecked with coloured ribbons and silver paper, wearing 'a garter with little bells' round the leg or ankles, and clashing 'be-ribboned batons'. He does not give a date. Even the small settlement of White Ladies Aston had six or eight men who performed most winters, and in one severe season continued from Christmas until Candlemas (2 February). In 1906 Cecil Sharp travelled from London to see them and note their tunes and dances; a few months earlier he had been to Redditch on a similar errand.

The practice of dancing during bad weather also applied at Malvern. During the severe winter of 1893-4 A.R. Williams, then a boy of five, saw in Albert Road a spectacle which remained so vividly in his mind that he was able to describe it over 40 years later (in 1937) to Maud Karpeles of the English Folk Dance and Song Society. Twelve men—perhaps from a village outside Malvern, since there is no record of a team based in the town—danced with staves to 'a lively jig measure' played on a concertina:

The Faithful City Morris Men from Worcester dancing at the Talbot Inn, Knightwick, on St George's Day, 2002

They wore heavy boots, breeches, thick grey stockings or gaiters. Most had a second waistcoat on too with sleeves instead of a jacket, of knitted brightly coloured wools, striped flannel or moleskin. Woollen wrappers round their neck. Some had hard hats, others slouched felt. Two or three had short, drab-tailed coats. Round their ankles, knees, wrists and hats they wore bands of coloured ribbons with strings of bells round ankles and legs. The short sticks had ribbons on the middle.

Their dancing seems to have been particularly vigorous, and Williams described it as a 'display of masculine bellicosity'.

Morris continues in Malvern. In December 2004 seventy dancers were in the town for a weekend which included dancing on the Worcestershire Beacon as well as at the Brewer's Arms in West Malvern. The event was organised by Mike Salter of the Old Meg Morris group. The Faithful City Morris Men from Worcester dance on many occasions through the year, including Plough Monday and St George's Day (see below).

Pebworth Morris Men and musicians at the Three Kings,
Hanley Castle, in 2004

Mumming

Village drama in the form of Robin Hood plays staged as parish fundraisers is recorded in Worcestershire as early as the 1470s. It is possible that Christmas mumming plays were also on the go at the time. Some claim that their central theme of death and resurrection is connected with the death of the old year and the birth of the new. Yet no example of such a play was recorded until 1738.

A misericord thought to show mummers' face masks in Great Malvern Priory Church (on the south side of the choir stalls)

The earliest text from Worcestershire was taken down by Cuthbert Bede (Rev. Edward Bradley) over the Christmas season of 1856-7. He saw 'several performances of a set of mummers who lived in the hamlets of Upper and Lower Howsell in the parish of Leigh ...; and went the round of the Malvern district with their masque'. Their version, he says, was 'handed down by oral tradition; and had been taught to the boys by their elder relatives, who had learnt it from the dictation of their seniors'. He continues:

> The lads were well up in their parts, and were spirited performers. The Valiant Soldier wore a real soldier's coat; Old Father Christmas carried holly; the Turkish Knight had a turban; and all of them were decked out with ribbons and scarves, and had their faces painted. Little Devil-doubt had a black face, and carried a money-box, a besom, and a bladder; with the bladder he thwacked the performer whose turn it was to speak—a proceeding that reminds us of Mr Lemuel Gulliver and the philosophers of Laputa. Little Devil-doubt having brushed away the snow and cleared a space, the performers ranged themselves in a semicircle, and the play began.

A performance recorded by the BBC at Great Malvern in 1946 seems to have been a revival, using the Great and Little Howsell text of 90 years earlier.

Plays were given in town streets and on village greens, in public houses, farms and (by invitation) mansions. The actors—always male—stood in a line or semi-circle, stepping forward with the formulaic 'In comes I'. Speeches were delivered with due solemnity punctuated by comic relief and even horse-play, especially where the doctor's part was concerned. The series of stylised combats and deaths, followed by rapid restoration to life, was the essential

St George's play at Knightwick in 2002

point of the play. Its text—perhaps one should say texts, for there are many variations, all very similar—might not read very well on the page but both for actors and audience was (and still can be) very satisfying in performance.

Versions of the play have been recorded from Upper and Lower Howsell (1856), Evesham (*c.*1870), Broadway (*c.*1874), Shrawley (*c.*1880), Pershore (1890s) and Great Malvern (1923 and 1946). Some of these were performed in more than one place, so exposure was much wider than the list would seem to indicate. In the 1970s further texts came to light which had been noted 40 years earlier by J.M. Carpenter at Bretforton (two versions), Broadway, Cleeve Prior and South Littleton. A completely new play, albeit retaining the ritual combats and the intervention of a quack doctor, *George and Dragon—The Final Conflict*, by Nick Hurt, was presented, not at Christmas but on St George's Day at the Talbot Inn, Knightwick, in 2002. This chapter concludes, though, with the traditional texts from Broadway and Bretforton respectively.

Broadway

Taken down in 1909 by Helen Dorrill of St. Louis, Missouri, from her father who had been one of the performers in Broadway, Worcestershire, some 35 years previously. The players ranged in age from 14 to 21. They toured farmhouses, asking permission to perform: 'Would you like to hear the mummers tonight?' They were usually invited into the front kitchen. Old Father Christmas wore a fur cap and gloves, a long red coat and topboots. He had a wig and beard of long white hair, and the end of his nose was reddened. Beelzebub carried a club and wore a big black hat and long black coat. The doctor wore a top hat and swallow-tail coat. The soldier had a blue uniform and military cap. Little Dick Nip had a hat with a wide brim, a short coat, and carried a long stick, with a pig's bladder tied to the end. St George wore a small hat with a feather, a dark red coat, knee-breeches and low shoes. After the play the performers were usually given hot spiced ale or cider and bread and cheese, together with from two to five shillings.

Characters

Father Christmas, Beelzebub, St George, Turkish Knight, King of Spain, Soldier, Italian Doctor, Sweet Moll, Little Dick Nip.

FATHER CHRISTMAS	In comes I, Old Christmas. Christmas or Christmas not, I hope Old Father Christmas will never be forgot. Christmas comes but once a year, And when it comes it brings good cheer. Roast beef, plum pudding, and mince pie, There's no Old Father Christmas loves better than I.
BEELZEBUB	A room, a room, brave gallant boys, And give us room to reign, For we have come to show our bold activity, Here on a merry Christmas time. Activity of youth, activity of age, The like was never acted upon any stage. If you don't believe what I say, Enter in, St George, and clear the way.
ST GEORGE	St George, that man of courage bold, With sword and spear all by my side, Hoping to gain the twelve crowns of gold. 'Twas I who slew the fiery dragon, And brought him to the slaughter, And by those fiery means I hope To gain the Queen of Egypt's daughter. Seven long years I was kept in a close cave Where I made my sad and grievous mourn. I have led the fair Sarepta from the snake, Which neither man nor mortal would undertake. I brought them all most couragely, And still I gain the victory. Show me the man who dare me.
TURKISH KNIGHT	I am the man who dare fight thee, The Turkish Knight, Come from my own Turkish land to fight. I will fight St George, that man of courage bold.

	If his blood is hot I will quickly made it cold.
	(They fight)
(dropping on one knee)	Hold, hold, St George. Another word
	From thee I have to crave.
	Spare me this time and I will arise
	To be thy Turkish slave.
ST GEORGE	Arise, arise, thou Turkish Knight.
	Go over to thine own Turkish lands and fight.
	Tell them there the champions grow in England.
	Tell them the wonders I have done:
	I have slain ten thousand for thy one.
TURKISH KNIGHT	No, rather than tell them that,
	I cut thee, hew thee small as flies,
	And send thee to Jamaica to make mince pies.
ST GEORGE	Mince pies I do not like;
	But another battle, then, and I will fight.
	(He kills the knight)
BEELZEBUB	A room a room, and let the prudent King of
	Spain come in.
KING OF SPAIN	In comes the prudent King of Spain.
	All with my glittering sword
	I have cut and slain St George
ST GEORGE	Thou prudent King of Spain,
	Hast thou come here to fight?
KING OF SPAIN	Yes, bold champion, and I think it is my right;
	And with thee I have come to fight.
ST GEORGE	Firstly, thou hast challenged me, king.
	Secondly, thou hast challenged me.
	Stand forth, thou figure of a tree,
	And see who gains the victory.
	(He kills the king)
BEELZEBUB	A room a room,
	And let the valiant soldier in.
SOLDIER	In comes the valiant soldier.
	Cut and Slasher is my name,
	All from the fiery wars of Spain.
	'Twas I and seven more
	Who slew eleven score,
	And could have slain twelve thousand more,
	All brave marching men of war.
	Many a battle have I been in,
	And still fight St George, that noble king.

(Soldier kills St George)

BEELZEBUB	A room, a room, a gallant room,
	And let the little Italian Doctor walk in.
ITALIAN DOCTOR	In comes the little Italian Doctor
	Lately come from Rome, France, and Spain.
	I carry a little vial bottle
	In the waist of my break, with which I can cure.
BEELZEBUB	What canst thou cure?
ITALIAN DOCTOR	What thou canst not cure, old dad.
BEELZEBUB	Old dad, what's that?
ITALIAN DOCTOR	Rheumatic gout,
	Pains within and pains without.
	Bring me an old woman
	Of three score years and ten
	With the knuckle of her little toe broke,
	And I can set it again.
BEELZEBUB	Set it, then.
ITALIAN DOCTOR	Drop on thy brow,
(who goes round slain,	Drop on thy heart.
who lie on the floor,	Arise up, Jack,
and says over each)	And take thy part.

(All arise. Sweet Moll enters)

ST GEORGE *(sings)*	Sweet Moll, Sweet Moll, where art thou going
	So early and so soon?
	I have something to say to thee
	If yet that thou canst stay.

Sweet Moll, sweet Moll, where art thou going & ear-ly and so soon? I've some - thing to say (to thee) If yet thou canst - stay. —

SWEET MOLL *(sings)*	What hast thou got to say?
	Pray tell it to me now,
	For I am spending all my time
	In what I can't tell how.
ST GEORGE *(sings)*	Thy parents and mine had well agreed
	That married we should be,
	So pull down thy lofty looks
	And fix thy love on me.

SWEET MOLL *(sings)*   But I must have a little boy
Who speaks a peevish tongue,
A pair of silver buckles
That ladies oft have on;
And I must have some butcher's meat
Of every sort and kind;
And in the morn a cup of tea,
At night a glass of wine.

ST GEORGE *(sings)*   Won't bacon serve thy turn, Sweet Moll,
Some good fat powder puffs?
And in the morn a cup of tea,
And that's the farmer's cut.
Sweet Moll, thou hast no cause
To talk of silver things,
For thou wast not brought up in palaces
Amongst lords, dukes and kings.
And the little thou hast learnt
Thou hast almost forgot;
And if thou wilt not marry me,
Then thou canst go to rot.

LITTLE DICK NIP   In comes I, Little Dick Nip,
With my big head and my little wit.
My head is so big and my body so small,
Yet I am the biggest rogue of all.
My forehead is lined with brass,
My head is lined with steel;
My trousers touch my ankle bones,
Pray, doctor, come and feel.

DOCTOR   Yes, yes.

ST GEORGE   A room, a room, a gallant room,
And let old Beelzebub in.

BEELZEBUB   In comes old Beelzebub.
On my shoulder I carry a club,
In my hand my dripping pan.
Don't you think I'm a jolly old man?
A mug of good ale will make us merry and sing,
And a few of your half-crowns and five-shilling
     pieces
In our pockets would be a very fine thing.
(They collect, dance and sing a carol)

ALL   Here's health to her stock,
Likewise to his flock.

> We'll take this small cup
> And we'll drink it all up;
> And then there's enough to fill it again.

(The tune for St George and Moll's song comes from Mrs Webb—for whom see chapter 7).

Bretforton

Taken down in the late 1920s or early '30s by James M. Carpenter from Stanley Archer and Charles Fowles, who learned the play 20 years earlier from Harry Haines of Bretforton, who later moved to the inn at Callow End, near Worcester.

Characters
Hind Before, Aunt Sally, King George, Doctor John Finney, Jack,
French Daummer, Belzebub, Happy Jack

HIND BEFORE	In comes I, old Hind Before,
	I comes fust to open the door.
	A room, a room; a rout about,
	I brought a broom to sweep your house.
	(Brings in broom, begins sweeping).
	I hope you won't be angry nor take in offence,
	For if you do, I shall quickly go hence.
	Room, room, I say, that I can bring old Aunt Sally this way.
	Walk in, Aunt Sally, and act thy part,
	An' show the ladies an' gentlemen thy gallant 'art.
	Walk in, Aunt Sally.
AUNT SALLY	Room, room, give me room to rhyme,
	That I may show you some festivity
	This merry Christmastime.
	Bring to me the man who bids me stand;
	An' says he'll cut me with his audacious hand.
	I'll cut 'im and hew 'im as small as a fly,
	An' see what he'll do to make his mince pies.
HIND BEFORE	Walk in, King George.
KING GEORGE	In comes King George, a man with courage bold.
(Like a royal prince, with sword, etc.)	With my sword an' shield I've won three crowns of gold.
	I've fought the fiery dragon, I've brought him to the slaughter,
	I saved our beautiful king and queen of England's daughter.

My mind is high, my mind is bold,
If thy blood is hot I'll make it cold.
Sword to guard your life; sir!
Or pull out your purse an' pay;
For you an' me this battle shall try,
To see which on the floor shall lie.

(They fight; Aunt Sally falls wounded)

HIND BEFORE	What' st done, now!
KING GEORGE	That's what I come in to do,
	What dost think?
HIND BEFORE	Oh if a doctor could be found
	As could cure Aunt Sally as lies bleedin' in the ground.
DOCTOR	*(speaking outside)* Yure is the doctor!
HIND BEFORE	Walk in, Jack Finney.
DOCTOR JACK	My name is not Jack Finney.
	My name is Mr John Finney, a man of great request.
HIND BEFORE	Walk in, Mr John Finney, an' work thy will.

DOCTOR JOHN FINNEY *(comes riding in on broomstick; wagging tail, accompanied by a boy named Jack)* 'Old me 'oss, Jack!

JACK	'Owld 'im theeself
DOCTOR	What's that?
JACK	I've got 'im, sir, fast be the tayel.
DOCTOR	Mind 'e don't kick yer. If 'e don't kick, 'e don't bite.
	Take 'im into the stable an' give 'im a bucket o' ashes to eat,
	Rub 'im down wi' a broomstick.
JACK	Do it theeself
DOCTOR	What's that?
JACK	I've done it, sir!

(Leaves Aunt Sally there, bleedin' on the ground)

DOCTOR	Well, Jack, as I was a-goin' up yonder hill,
	Neither runnin', walkin'; nor stood I still;
	I stood still to see what was the matter
	An' I heard nineteen bells a-going without a clapper.
JACK	An' so did I!
DOCTOR	I went on a little furder an' I met a wagon load o' apples
	With a millstun on top to keep 'em from smashin.
JACK	An' so did I:
DOCTOR	An' I went a little furder an' I met a pigstye built wi' apple dumplin's an' thatched wi' pancakes.
JACK	An' so did I.
DOCTOR	An' I went a little furder an' I met a man on horseback

underneath a mare's belly, with a glowworm stuck in her tayel to light 'er the way. I ast 'im the road to Mr Broadgate's. He said follow thee nose, an' keep to thee two left elbows an' you'll come to a large red brick house, built wi' pebbles an' styuns, brass steps an' stwun knocker. So followed me nose an' me two left elbows, an' I come to a large red-brick house, built wi' pebbles an' stwuns, brass steps an' stwun knocker. I knocked at the maid an' out come the door. I ast if Mr Broadgate was in: 'Er said no, he'd be yure in about ten or five minutes. Would I sit down in 'is old arm chair an' 'ave a cup o' cider to eat an' some bread an' cheese to drink. I says No thank ye, yes if ye please, I never denies by any means. So I sat down in 'is old arm chair an 'ad a cup o' bread an' cheese to drink an' a piece o' cider to eat. An' in about ten or five minutes I siz Mr Broadgate come rollin' from the neck o' a glass-bottle. He says good marnin' to he; an' I says good marnin' to me. He says I got one o' the funniest sights down in my back cellar you ever zee. A little kid, stripped stark naked with all his clothes on, threshin' bacca. He gied sich tremendous blows that 'e knocked a empty sack bag full o' barley carn through a nine-inch wall an' kill a jud dog t'other side as wuzent thure. I 'eard 'im come 'owlin' up our street late last night early this marnin'.
(Turns to old lady with shop tongs and animal tooth, etc.)
Now, Jack, what's the matter of this old lady?
(Jack goes and looks at her)

JACK	Only a slight touch o' the tuthache, sir!
DOCTOR	What's a good cure for the tuthache, Jack?
JACK	Pull the old un out an' put a new un in.
DOCTOR	All right, Jack, where's my medecine bag, Jack?
JACK	Lost un.
DOCTOR	What's that?
JACK	I got un, sir!
DOCTOR	*(opens bag)* Where are my spectacles, Jack?
JACK	Broke 'em, sir.
DOCTOR	What's that?
JACK	Broke 'em tumblin' under that shart stump of a little stile las' night, tumbled under un an' broke 'em.
DOCTOR	Never mind, Jack. Fetch me five o' the strongest hosses you can find; We must 'ave this tuth out o' Aunt Sally's.

JACK	Do it theeself.
DOCTOR	What's that?
JACK	I've got 'em, sir.

(Brings in five mummers—form a chain, doctor first. Start heaving—all fall)

DOCTOR	Not this time, Jack. Try it again. *(Aunt Sally groans)*
	Have another try, and pull it out. *(Hold up to show company)*
	Ladies an' gentlemen, a very large tusk indeed. More like a helephant's tuth nor a human bein's, started two yurs afore her fifty-second granny was barn.
HIND BEFORE	Walk in, French Drummer.

FRENCH DRUMMER In comes French, uv [with] all 'is art,

(old-bucket for drum) I 'opes Mr Doctor 'ave done 'is part,

	An' done it with a free goodwill.
	But Mr John Finney's the best man still
HIND BEFORE	Walk in, old Belzebub!
BELZEBUB	In come I, old Belzebub.

(club in his hand an In me 'and I carry a club,

old drippin' pan On my 'ead a drippin' pan,

on his head) I think meself a jolly ole man.

HIND BEFORE	Walk in, 'Appy Jack!
HAPPY JACK	In comes I; old 'Appy Jack,

(humped back with With all me family on me back.

pillow stuffed up I've got noyen [nine] left out' seven,

back, hobbled with All t'others are gone to heaven.

a stick; stick with Christmas comes but once a yure,

pig's bladder on An' when it comes it brings good cheer.

end thrown over Roast biff, plum puddin' an' mince pies;

his shoulder) Who likes that any better than I? *(Smacks lips)*

Me father killed a good fat pig,

An' that you plainly see.

I've got 'is bladder yure to make

A hurdy-gurdy gee! *(They start thumping each other)*

Good dog, good dog, lie down thy bones

An' riddle 'em through thy wrists,

An' merry Peg stretch up thy leg

An' dance an Irish jig.

What song will you 'ave, ladies an' gentlemen?

The ran-tan tinder box or Jack up the Archard?

(Sing two songs)

CHAPTER 9

Sport & Play

The early years of the twenty-first century saw impassioned debate on the subject of hunting with dogs. Some two hundred years earlier a similar controversy over blood sports ended with the outlawing of bull baiting and cock fighting. Subsequently, bare-knuckle boxing had to accept rules to temper its ferocity, though by one of the quirks of history it is apparently once more gaining in (clandestine) popularity.

Fairs were once among the principal events in the calendar. People calculated the passage of the year by them, and a saying widespread in Worcestershire held that 'You never hear the cuckoo before Tenbury Fair [20 April] or after Pershore Fair [26 June]'. Alternatively, 'The cuckoo goes to Bromsgrove Fair [24 June] to buy him a horse and to Pershore Fair to buy him a saddle, and then he flies away'. People also added: 'There is always a thunderstorm at Bromsgrove Fair'. The original reason for fairs was to provide opportunities for buying and selling goods and animals, but the elements of pleasure and entertainment which they attracted eventually came to dominate. Very large numbers of people attended, like Old Tricker, one of Arthur Savory's labourers at Aldington in the 1890s, who 'was fond of fairs, wakes and "mops" ... and he would often beg a day off for such outings'. Wakes, originally religious occasions (see chapter 3), and mops (hiring fairs, see chapter 6), came, like fairs, to be mainly places for fun and relaxation, as they are now.

Various town carnivals and village fetes have to be added to the catalogue of merrymaking. Stourport Carnival, with some gaps, has been held every September for 80 years. The Three Counties Show claims a pedigree dating back to 1797, though the separate agricultural societies of Gloucestershire, Herefordshire and Worcestershire came together only in 1922. The show moved round different grounds until 1958, when a permanent site was adopted near Malvern. In addition to the main annual show, the ground is used for events throughout the year and attracts very large attendances. The ancient conjunction of open-air trading and entertainment thus retains its place in the calendar.

'The Bear Bites Back', by Henry Alken (1785-1851)

Blood Sports

Bear baiting, recorded at Droitwich in 1522, is mentioned more than once in the Worcester Priory accounts during the time of Prior More. The king's bear-ward came at Easter to Worcester in 1524-5 and to Battenhall 'havyng ij bears there' in 1528-9. In the 1530s various bearwards were paid, usually 20d. a time, at Worcester, Crowle, Grimley and again at Battenhall. As late as 1606-8 in Bewdley the town paid 'xiijs. vjd. For the beare at my lordes cumming'.

In the same place expenses 'for pavenge at the bohynge' (bull ring) were recorded in 1575-7. Four years earlier William Phillips was in trouble at Bayton for being 'present at bull baiting *die dominico*' (on the Lord's day). The event at Rock regularly took place after morning service on Mondays outside the churchyard wall. The stocks also stood there until a man confined for drunk-enness walked away with them and after extricating himself threw them in the brook. They are now kept in the church.

As late as 1818 a bull was baited at the Pitchcroft in Worcester: that is, it was tethered and then subjected to attacks by dogs. 'The poor animal was most barbarously mangled', wrote an eye-witness, 'and, after the "sport" was driven through the principal streets to the slaughter house, writhing in torture'. Similar spectacles must have taken place in the bull rings at St John's and at Kidderminster, where street signs bearing those words can still be seen. William Avery (1832-99), drawing on his father's notes on the history of his town, wrote:

The bull breaks loose

One of the principal amusements was bull baiting, which took place in various parts of Redditch and neighbourhood. In the town, the favourite localities were behind old Ben Carr's house (where Mr Turner's steam mill now is), and at the back of the Tanhouse, where my father has often pointed out to me the post and ring to which the bull was fastened. In a meadow near the Star and Garter, Crabbs Cross, there is yet to be seen another such post and ring; and here George Wells was 'berrod' [bear-ward] and looked to the interest of the bull, and saw fair play. The bull was fastened to the ring by a cord several yards long, and then the dogs were loosed at him. The true bull-dog made straight for his nose, and if he caught in any other place would keep changing his grip till he got hold of the desired point: but other dogs would rush at the nearest part, tail or nose being a matter of indifference to them. Often times the dog would be sent by the bull whirling through the air, and then all hands would run to the rescue and catch him ere he fell. Sometimes the bull would inflict great injuries on the dogs, in fact, it was unusual to see a good dog with all his bones in their normal condition. One of the best dogs was Jim Wright's 'Kit', but there were many favourites. The bull would generally be baited all day, and when he was tired the 'berrod' would throw a bucket of water over him to refresh him. At the end, the best appreciated part comes in, the 'smut'. This was when all the dogs were set on the poor bull at one time. Occasionally, at this time, the bull was 'accidentally' let loose, and then a general stampede finished up the sport.

Despite the popularity of bull baiting, Parliament passed the Cruelty of Animals Act in 1835 and within a few years the sport came to an end. The same Act put paid to cock fighting, though this continued in secret and has still not completely disappeared. Innkeepers often promoted it. The Pheasant in New Street and the Star and Garter in Foregate Street at Worcester were well known venues. The Crown at Upper Arley attracted boatmen from as far away as Bristol to its contests, and the appropriately-named Three Cocks Inn, just outside Offenham, staged matches between the cocks of rival villages.

As well as working people, 'gentlemen' took a keen interest. Lord Plymouth, who lived at Hewell Grange, Tardebigge, in the late eighteenth century, had a cock pit at Barnt Green. This could have been an elaborate, purpose-built structure, with circular tiers of seating and a space in the centre for the fights, of the kind which can be seen in the Avoncroft Museum of Buildings, near Bromsgrove; or simply a conical pit dug in the ground. Even more rudimentary was the arrangement described by William Avery:

> The most celebrated cock-pit was one kept by Joseph Lewis, at Crabbs Cross. It was made of gorse kids [faggots], with the sods turned up for the ring. People came from all parts to see the 'mains' fought in this pit, and as many as five hundred persons at a time would pay their penny entrance to witness the 'sport'. There were three ways of fighting: the 'long main', which generally continued for a week; the 'short main', which was finished in a day or two; and the 'battle royal', in which all the cocks were down at once, and the last cock left was the victor.

The birds were very carefully trained, and also fed: hence the saying, 'to feed like fighting cocks'. Bets were placed on their success, and the contests were taken with all the seriousness of a modern boxing match. A typical advertisement appeared in the *Worcester Herald* on 29 March 1805:

This is to give Notice,

THAT at John Moore's, at the White-Hart in Bromsgrove, will be a Main of Cocks fought between the Gentlemen of Kidderminster, and the Gentlemen of Bromsgrove; to weigh on July 1, and fight the two following Days; each Party to shew and weigh 21 Cocks in the Main, for Four Guineas a Battle, and Twenty the Odd Battle; and each Party to shew and weigh 20 Cocks for Bye Battles, for Two Guineas each Battle.

Notice in the Birmingham Gazette, *22 June 1752*

COCKING: A main of cocks will be fought at the house of Mr. John Lloyd, the sign of the Pheasant, New Street, Worcester, between the gentlemen of Worcestershire and the gentlemen of Gloucestershire, to show and weigh thirty-one cocks on each side in the main, for four guineas a battle and fifty guineas the odd battle; and twenty cocks on each side in the byes, for two guineas a battle. To weigh on Saturday the 18th of April, 1805, and fight on Monday, Tuesday, and Wednesday, the following week, being Easter week.   FEEDERS, {GOSLING, W.
{HAYNES, G.

Prize-fighting

The gentry passionately followed prize-fighting, too. Fights took place in the open air, with rounds lasting until a man was knocked down, and contests ending only when one of the combatants could no longer come up to scratch. At Redditch contests took place in the 1820s in the Pound Meadow, on the Green, at Crabbs Cross, Mappleborough Green, and at the Old White Hart, Headless Cross. Many needle-makers enjoyed fighting, and the pointers enjoyed the reputation of being the toughest of them all. One of their number, Tom Paddock, beat a good many fighters before being matched with William Perry (better known as 'the Tipton Slasher') for the championship of England. They met at Woking in 1850 but Paddock was disqualified in the twenty-seventh round for a foul blow.

Tom Paddock

It was customary at the time for ballads to be issued with round by round—sometimes even blow by blow—versified accounts of important contests. 'The Great Fight between Paddock and the Tipton Slasher' curiously fails to mention the foul. Its last verse runs:

Now to conclude and make an end
Of this my simple rhyme.
Success unto bold Tipton
When he does fight again.
And may he prove the Champion
Of the British ring,
Like Ward, or bold Bendigo,
Or the veteran Tom Spring.

THE GREAT FIGHT BETWEEN
PADDOCK
AND THE
TIPTON SLASHER.

Ye sporting blades of England,
  Come listen to my song,
And if you'll pay attention,
  I'll not detain you long,
It is concerning a gallant fight,
  The truth I will unfold,
In the prize ring of England
  For £200 in gold.

CHORUS.

So here's success to Tipton Slasher
  He has shown him British play,
And he has beat bold Paddock,
  And bore the prize away.

On the Seventeenth of December,
  These men came into the ring,
They toss'd up for the choice of ground
  And Tipton he did win,
Then time being call'd these men did
  And Paddock he did say,   [strip,
I will bet twenty pounds,
  That I will take the prize away.

These men they then came to the
  Being eager of the game,   [scratch
Tipton let fly with his right,
  Paddock stopp'd it like a man,
Then they let fly both right and left,
  To each other they did stand,
After a tremendous struggle,
  Both men came to the ground.

At the commencement of the second
  round,
  These men they both look'd shy,
But Paddock he shot out his left
  And cut the Slashers eye,

Then Slasher hit out right and left,
  And the people round the ring,
Bet three to one on Tipton
  For they was sure that he would win

When Tipton came to the scratch again
  For mischief he was bent,
Paddock was not for to be gull'd,
  At him left and right he went,
Paddock hit out and got away,
  They cried its all a hoax,
Tipton with a tremendous blow
  Cut Paddock's knowledge box.

These men they fac'd each other,
  With courage stout and true,
Tipton with a well aimed blow,
  Bold Paddock's claret drew,
Paddock returned the compliment,
  With all speed so free,
With a left handed blow
  On Tipton's box of ivory.

When Paddock he came up again,
  He was weak and nearly done,
Tipton went in both right and left,
  Broke Paddock's collar bone
Paddock he did try his best,
  Bold Tipton for fling,
But Tipton with a heavy blow,
  Knock'd Paddock out of time.

Then time being call'd
  He was deaf unto their cry,
The referees they did declare,
  Tipton had won the day,
Then the ring it was broken in,
  The crowd did shout and sing,
Hurrah for brave Tipton
  He his the Champion.

Now to conclude and make an end,
  Of this my simple rhyme,
Success unto bold Tipton
  When he does fight again,
And may he prove the Champion!
  Of the British ring,
Like Ward, or bold Bendigo,
  Or the veteran Tom Spring.

Ballad sheet probably printed by W. Wright of Birmingham

The last of those mentioned fought a challenger, John Langan, at Worcester in January 1824. According to a contemporary account:

> The great fight between Spring and Langan for the championship, which is to be found commemorated by a print hanging up in almost every inn and public house in England, took place in Pitchcroft, the ring being formed just opposite to the Grand Stand. Considerably more than 150 guineas were paid to the managers of the fight to ensure its taking place at Worcester. The stakes were 300 guineas a side; and the betting two to one on Spring, who was a native of Warwickshire [in fact, Herefordshire]; while Langan was an Irishman.
>
> Not less than 40,000 people thronged Pitchcroft as spectators, many being perched upon sheds and booths, erected temporarily, and let out at standing places at considerable prices. During the second round one of these erections gave way, and a number of persons were precipitated to the ground, a distance of twenty feet, amidst the broken timber, and trampling upon each other. At least thirty people were carried to the Infirmary with serious fractures of limbs or ribs, and one unfortunate fellow died of a compound fracture of the leg.
>
> Spring came on the ground at half-past twelve, but Langan could not be found for some time. He was, in fact, making off, and his backers brought him back with some difficulty. Lord Deerhurst and Sir James Musgrave kept time; and Colonel Berkeley acted as umpire. Spring was exceedingly cautious, and Langan impetuous, and the greater part of the rounds ended in wrestling, in which Langan often succeeded in throwing his antagonist. By the eighteenth round the ring was broken in by the crushing of the mob, and not ten square feet of space was left for the men to fight in. After an hour and a half's fighting the affair seemed as little near conclusion as at its commencement.
>
> At the eightieth round, Langan planted a tremendous blow on Spring's head; but, at the eighty-fourth, Spring knocked Langan down with such terrific hits, that he fell as weak as a child. The cry then

A print of the fight at the Pitchcroft. Some spectators seem to be sitting on the yards of ships moored in the river

became general to take him away, but although covered in his gore, he refused to give in, and was at last only removed by force. The battle lasted two hours and thirty-two minutes—a most unheard of length of time. At the next assizes Mr. Justice Park, in his charge to the grand jury, administered a severe rebuke to the county and city magistracy for winking at, and permitting, this affair.

The 'affair' was celebrated in street ballads printed all over the country, in places as far apart as Bristol and Gateshead. One of these ended:

> You boxers all now drink a health
> To Spring upon the stage, sir,
> And if any other man comes forth
> He will soon be engaged, sir;
> To lose the fame of England
> We then should think it hard, sir,
> But while we have such men as Spring
> We defy the world at large, sir.
> [Chorus]
> For Englishmen will not be bet [beat]
> By any other nation,
> For if they will fight man to man
> They're sure of a good thrashing.

Fairs

The earliest Worcestershire charter for an annual fair seems to have been that granted by King John in the first year of his reign (1199-1200) to Bromsgrove. Wigorn (Worcester) followed 18 years later under Henry III, who also gave charters to Tenbury and Feckenham. Over the centuries, the list expanded, with fairs lasting up to five days, and invariably starting on the eve or day of saints' feasts: nativities, translations, and in one case, a decollation (beheading)—that of St John the Baptist (29 August, at Broadway). Even small villages such as Elmley Castle (Feast and morrow of St Lawrence, 10 and 11 August), Holt (St Mary Magdalene, 22 July), Rock (St Margaret, 20 July, 3 days) and Severn Stoke (St Faith, 6 October, 3 days) had their fairs, though these may have disappeared by the time W. Pitt compiled the details given in his book, *General View of the Agriculture of the County of Worcester*, published in 1813. Places which I have preceded by an asterisk are now in other counties.

Alvechurch, April 22, August 10, for cattle, sheep and lambs.
Belbroughton, first Monday in April; Monday before St Luke's (October 18), for horned cattle, horses, and cheese.
Bewdley, April 23, for horned cattle, horses, cheese, linen and woollen cloth; December 10, for hogs only; 11, for horned cattle, cheese, horses, linen and woollen cloth.

*Blockley, Tuesday after Easter week, for a few cattle; October 20, a mop, or statute, for hiring servants.

Bromsgrove, June 24, October 1, for linen cloth, cheese, horses, and cattle.

Droitwich, Good Friday, October 28, December 21, for linen, cloth, and hats.

*Dudley, May 8, for cattle, wool, and cheese; Aug. 5, for sheep, lambs, and cattle; October 2, for horses, cattle, wool, and cheese.

Evesham, February 2, Monday after Easter week, Whit-Monday, September 21, for cattle and horses.

Feckenham, March 26, September 30, for cattle.

Kidderminster, Holy Thursday, and three weeks after, September 4, for cattle, horses, cheese, linen and woollen cloth.

*King's Norton, April 25, September 5, for all sorts of cattle.

Pershore, Easter Tuesday, June 26, Tuesday before All Saints; November 1, for cattle and horses.

Redditch, first Monday in August, for all sorts of cattle.

*Shipston, June 22, Tuesday after October 10, for horses, cows, and sheep.

*Stourbridge, March 29, for horses (very noted) and other cattle; September 8, for all sorts of cattle and sheep.

Stourport, weekly, on Wednesdays, from September to Christmas, for hops.

Tenbury, April 26, July 18, September 26, for horned cattle, horses, and sheep.

Upton, Midlent Sunday, Whitsun-Thursday, for horses, cattle, sheep; July 10, Thursday before St Matthew (September 21), for horses, cattle, sheep, and leather.

Worcester, Saturday before Palm Sunday, Saturday in Easter week, for
horses and linen cloth; August 15, September 19, for cattle, horses,
cheese, lambs, linen, and hops.

Fairs were important civic events, which called for due ceremony. At
Bromsgrove the town bellman made this proclamation:

*Bromsgrove Horse Fair,
from a card postmarked 1906*

O yes! O yes! O yes! -----
High Bailiff of Bromsgrove to
the ----- Lord of the Manor of
Bromsgrove, doth charge and
command all persons that are
here this day, that they do not
bear, or wear any unlawful
weapon, or make any assault,
riot, or rout, in disturbance of
the presence of God and our
Sovereign Lord (or Lady), the
King (or Queen), but as far as
in them lies preserve the same,
and that all sellers of cattle,
sheep, pigs, and horses, do pay
to the toll gatherers the accus-
tomed tolls, and that all sellers
of wool do place the same in
the place appointed for that
purpose and that they do pay
to the toll gatherers the accus-
tomed tolls, immemorably
collected, or they will answer
the contrary to their peril. God
save the King (or Queen), the
Lord and Lady of the Manor,
the Bailiff of Bromsgrove, and
all loyal subjects.

W.G. Leadbetter, writing in the 1940s, described the scene in Bromsgrove:

In far-off days the crowded High Street, the stalls on the side walks, the
concourse of visitors, the multitude of all kinds of vehicles, the trotting
and racing of decorated horses, the lowing of cattle, the many farmers in
their customary white smocks with their wives riding pillion, the antics
of tinselled acrobats and quack medicine vendors, the music and songs
of the minstrels, the swarthy gipsies in colourful costume and their
trickery in ringing the changes and pretensions to fortune telling—all

The revived court of pie powder at St John's in 1914

combined to make the Midsummer Fair the most sensational day of the year. Probably the most attractive feature for the mass of merrymakers, next to the foaming tankard of beer, was the sale of the wild Welsh ponies as they were herded near the old Tithe Barn at the bottom of Holy Lane, and later in the Rack-field.

The mayor and aldermen of Worcester walked in procession over the river to St John's Fair on the Friday before Palm Sunday; they were said to be fetching their own fair, which began the next day. The mayor presided in Church House (which later became the Bell Inn) at St John's and dispensed summary justice to offending fair-goers in what was known as a Court of Pie Powder (the last two words a corruption of the French, *pieds poudreux*). The fair came to an end in the 1830s when St John's became part of the city of Worcester. However, both fair and court of pie powder were revived in about 1910. Tenbury had a similar court at its April and September fairs. Even little Hanley Castle, according to the local historian, Pamela Hurle, had its own toll booth and pie powder court, near where Gilbert's End Lane, Robert's End Street and the main Upton–Worcester road meet.

Fairs were by no means universally popular. Henry Sherwin in the *Worcestershire Mirror* bitterly attacked in 1831 the ancient gathering in the grounds of Pershore Abbey:

How degrading to human nature are those disgraceful amusements which come under the denomination of Pershore Fair; can any person, without a shudder, witness them in consecrated ground, disturbing the ashes of the slumbering dead? Scarcely was the Sabbath worship concluded when the Sacred Gates were thrown open, and the churchyard was presently filled with the very scum of society, who, regardless of that solemnity which, in the heart of every christian, accompanies the thought of the Lord's Day, began erecting Booths, Stalls and Stages for the ensuing fair. Instead of that deathlike silence, that gentle calm which ought to mark the spot, particularly on the Sabbath Day, where our departed friends are reposing, the noisy hammer and the loud shouts of a gathering multitude are heard.

On the following day ... instead of the awe-inspiring appearance of a Burying ground I was greeted with all the noise and bustle of a country fair: a large caravan of Wild Beasts in one part, Giants and Dwarfs in another, stages of Dancing Girls, all resting upon the scattered graves, endeavouring to outbawl each other, giving utterance to low and filthy jests, and stunning every spectator with a discord of grating instruments. In other parts were stalls of various articles, ginger-bread, nuts and toys. Tombstones, which religious love, and weeping affection had placed over the mouldering ashes of departed friends were converted into the backs of bowling alleys, over which the most dreadful imprecations were constantly being uttered, mocking the inscriptions which said 'Sacred to the memory'.

Some of the townsfolk evidently shared Sherwin's views. One year, according to a story which may be apocryphal, they barred the gates to the abbey but the fair people dragged them open with an elephant. In 1836, though, the showmen accepted a cash payment to move to Broad Street, and the fair stayed there until its suspension during the Second World War, and 'retained some of its old exuberance', wrote D.P. Grant-Adamson. The day before the fair people were kept back from Broad Street until 8 p.m., 'when the local police inspector

Pershore Horse Fair in 1909

dropped his arm as a signal and there was a fierce and uninhibited rush for the best pitches'. After the war the fair moved to the outskirts of the town.

Another case of a fair's being too popular for some tastes occurred at Dover's Hill, in Gloucestershire but less than a dozen miles from Pershore. Both the hill and the games held there took their name from the lawyer, Robert Dover, who moved to Saintbury in 1611 and plunged into organising the local Whitsuntide sports. Some 200 years later, a newspaper reported: 'It is still a great holiday for all the lads and lasses within ten or fifteen miles of the place, and is attended by numbers of gentry and people of respectability in the neighbourhood'. Then things went downhill. During the 1840s Mrs Ann Stratton, landlady of the Plough and Harrow at Evesham, regularly supplied refreshments for people attending. Her son later wrote:

> My mother used to go to Dover's Hill each year, taking a large tent, a good supply of ale, cider, wine, spirits, and eatables to sell during the gaming week. She made a good sum of money, and the surroundings were so alarming that as fast as her silver changed into gold she would drop the sovereigns into the large barrels of ale or cider through the bung-hole (this was her safety bank). She also had a couple of loaded revolvers under her serving table ready for use. She never left the tent day or night until the festivities were over, and no one was safe from the lawlessness of the cardsharpers, thimble-riggers, pick-pockets, thieves, confidence-men, vagrants, and criminals of the deepest dye, the riffraff of society. During the daytime the turmoil was terrible, but all night long it was a perfect pandemonium. Cries of murder were often heard, and disorder and rapine held full sway. If the shadow of a person showed through the sheeting of a tent at night he would be almost sure to be struck with a heavy bludgeon from without, and the miscreant would crawl underneath and rob his victim. One year every stall and tent (except my mother's) was levelled to the town and their contents pillaged. Scores of persons, nut sellers and others, found a safe asylum in my mother's tent. The scenes, she said, were indeed terrible. Yet my mother went there every year with her serving-maids and her men, and with eatables and drinkables for sale, and was never molested or robbed.

Mrs Stratton later discovered the reason for her immunity: her husband had once helped a man who turned out to be 'a sort of leader of the lawless band who attended Dover's Hill'. It was he who quietly organised protection.

Local middle class people were not amused that the games had become 'the trysting place of all the lowest scum of the population which lived in the districts lying between Birmingham and Oxford'. Canon G.D. Bourne, rector of Weston Subedge, managed to have the land included in a Parliamentary Enclosure Act, and the last games, held in 1853, attracted 30,000 people— possibly including Mrs Stratton of Evesham, with her serving maids and men.

Even half a century later, the mild C.R. Ashbee could write:

> To have the scum and refuse of the nearest great factory towns shot annually into [Chipping] Campden for a week's camping in tents on Dover's Hill, two or three thousand at a time, with unlimited beer from unlimited booths and hooligans ... ; to have ... the pleasant valleys of Saintbury and Weston tramped by armed bands of Birmingham yahoos was not a thing to be desired.

Less spectacular fairs continued, and were held in affection by many. Wilfred Byford-Jones described the scene at Bewdley in the 1930s:

> I went to the fairground ... with a mental picture of what the old fair would be like when the merchants from Bristol and Gloucester came up the Severn in trows to make merry, and when hundreds of people came overnight on horseback from all over the Midlands. ... On a small patch of ground, brilliantly lighted by coloured electric globes, which swung in the breeze, were hundreds of girls and youths drunk with excitement. There as one contrivance on which about forty little motor cars filled with big-boned farm labourers, servants and milkmaids, who, for twopence, had the pleasure of shattering every section and sub-section of the Road Traffic Act. The cars crashed into each other amid the screams of the girls, the lusty shouts of youths intoned more for controlling horses than motors, and the toot-toot of horns. Above all this was the blaring music of the mechanical organ, the cries of sellers of pills and powders, the clang of wood balls on the iron sheeting of coconut shies,

Whitsun Fair on Malvern Link Common in the 1890s

and the dull 'phut' of air-rifles. People who have only seen a town fair would have difficulty in imagining the sheer abandonment of joy of these country lads and lassies on their night off.

Byford-Jones adds that after leaving the fair by way of a footpath through a meadow to the Severn he passed an avenue of trees where he could hear 'the giggles of girls and the low voices of youth'. 'Love-making among these visitors to Bewdley from the outside villages', he concluded, 'has a certain primitive quality which is not altogether crude'.

As late as the 1990s Women's Institute members related nostalgic memories of fairs such as that which stretched all over Malvern Link Common and 'swarmed with fairground and Romany people'; or the Hop and Cheese Fair held each year at Worcester on 19 September:

> Packets of hops were sold in the Worcester Hopmarket and farmers brought their cheeses for sale. Stalls were set up in both Angel Place and Angel Street on which were displayed goodies to delight the eyes of children who were eager to buy a 'fairing'. The sweet stall had kai suckers, gobstoppers, liquorice laces and scented cachous. There were toys galore: ticklers, trumpets, rattles and drums, the noisier the better. Dolls of all sizes were for sale, from cut-out paper ones to the lovely jointed dolls. The brandy snap stall was well patronised and the hand-operated roundabout did very good business. In the evening, kerosene flares cast a bright but flickering light on the noisy, happy, jostling crowd who had gathered to join in the annual delight of Fair Day.

This latter account is from a woman born in 1905.

Angel Street, Worcester, as seen on the city's Hop Fair Day in 1935

Wakes

Church wakes, originally vigils for prayer (see chapter 3), in time were transformed either into genteel fetes or turned into events which became indistinguishable from pleasure fairs. The word wakes was also applied to gatherings
to pick or sell fruit, such at the Bilberry Wake at Lickey of the 1860s, after
which those involved repaired to the Old Rose and Crown or the Plough and
Harrow. 'The subsequent rowdyism, intoxication and licentiousness', wrote
W.G. Leadbetter, 'made the event a blot on the landscape'. At Dodford's
Strawberry Wake, until about 1900, after the main crop had been harvested
visitors were allowed into the fields, on payment of a small sum, to pick or eat
as much fruit as they could.

Some wakes became noted for violent sport. A local moralist, John Lacy,
wrote in 1778 of the villages of Sidemoor and Catshill, near Bromsgrove:

> The third Sunday in July a Wake (a rabbleing kind of wake) [is held] at
> Sythemore and also at a small village called Catshill about two miles
> north of the town where Bull baiting, bowling, Wrestling, Cock-fighting
> and such other Disagreeable and Cruel sports are used, to the disgrace of
> humanity, scandal of Christianity and shame of our officers who suffer
> such shameful things to be done in their parish.

During the early nineteenth century a series of Sunday wakes took place in
July and August in villages round Kidderminster, including Franche,
Hoobrook, Broadwaters and Blakebrook. Competitions such as eating hot rolls
and treacle, dancing for pumps and climbing a greasy pole for a leg of mutton
took place, and, until they were outlawed in 1835, bull baiting and dog fighting.
Many publicans also organised Monday wakes with such games as apple
bobbing, foot racing, jumping in bags, catching a soaped pig and grinning

---

CHERRY WAKE,
HEADLESS CROSS,
MONDAY NEXT, JULY 15th, 1867.

MR. GEORGE WALKER,
WHITE HART INN,

BEGS respectfully to inform his friends and the
public that he will have a SHEEP ROASTED
upon the above occasion.

N.B.—A Quadrille Band is engaged for Dancing.

---

through a horse's collar. 'For many people', wrote L. Smith, 'the season of wakes and fairs represented the annual holiday, even though it was interspersed with working days'.

Bull baiting also featured at Stourport's Mitton Wake, in front of the Red Lion (now Steps House), though the day began with a decorous church service with visiting choir and charity sermon. Dancing for pumps (plimsolls) and corduroy trousers took place on a low cart, to the music of an ensemble consisting of fiddle, flute and double bass. Donkey races started at the Red Lion and went over the bridge and back. Other competitors tried with hands tied behind their backs to take bites out of a sticky treacle roll hanging from a string.

At Stoulton, between Pershore and Worcester, the wake took place on Ascension Day, with fiddling and dancing, wrestling, backswording, dipping for oranges, grinning through horse collars, jumping in sacks, and racing with wheelbarrows. Vendors of gingerbread, Banbury cakes, peppermint humbugs, rice-pennies and whim-whams stood between St Edmund's Church and the Somers Arms Inn. Professional wrestlers and backsworders who went from wake to wake would fight after the ritual challenge: 'O iss! O iss! This is to gi'e notice that a belt ull be wrustled for at Stoulton Wake, by two strong men and true. No booty works. No kickin''.

Despite the popularity of such occasions, farmers and landowners began to withdraw support. Stoulton's Victorian vicar re-introduced a church service on Ascension Day to emphasise the wake's Christian origins, and Lady Henry

Part of the green where wakes were held at Stoulton

Somerset, an ardent temperance advocate, closed the Somers Arms, thus dealing a final blow.

Similar pressures, no doubt, were brought to bear on the Whitsuntide sports held near Parsons Folly on Bredon Hill. (The name, by the way, comes not from a cleric but from Squire Parsons, who in about 1795 built the tower, 40 feet in height, to raise the hill from 960 to 1,000 feet, thus making it, he thought, into a mountain). Sports there included wrestling, shin-kicking (also favoured at Dover's Games), quarterstaff fighting and bare-fist boxing. Among the sideshows were swingboats and coconut shies. 'The story of the coconuts being rolled down the hill past the Banbury Stone', wrote Fred Archer, 'is just one of Uncle Jim's tales. The stall holder tried to do a Tibblestone man out of his change; but he paid for his crookedness as he watched his coconuts roll down the hill'.

Farmers failed in an attempt to stop the wake at Badsey after the Enclosure Acts of 1802 and 1817. 'It was formerly', wrote A.H. Savory, 'a time of much cider-drinking, a meeting-day for friends and relations, and for various trials of strength and skill, though I believe the carousals outlasted the sports by many years'. In the 1870s the wake, on St James's Day (25 July) was a sedate social occasion, starting with a church service, and followed by a procession with banners to a field near the vicarage where 500 people sat down to tea. Brass bands played, then came a programme including races for donkeys, for men over 60, and for choirboys (the last, over 100 yards, with prizes of a hat, a silk tie and a knife). Twenty years later the wake had gone, replaced by a flower show.

At Shrawley the annual wake took place on 6 November at the Wyre Inn which stood by a ford over the Severn. The inn went, many years ago, pulled down as a haunt of poachers. The wake became an August bank holiday fete. Hardebury Wake lingered until the mid-nineteenth century on the first Sunday after 25 July, 'suffered rather than encouraged'. At Offenham the wake took place on 29 May on the village street between the maypole (see chapter 10) and the church, but later transferred to the recreation ground. Upton Snodsbury's, recorded as early as 1618, was lively enough to attract visitors from Worcester. Eckington's even generated a local rhyme:

> Whitsuntide early, Whitsuntide late,
> The week after Whitsuntide's Eckington Wake.

Some wakes retained their vigour. Wake Sunday (24 June) at Feckenham was in Victorian times reckoned to be second only to Christmas in the importance people attached to it. A Mr C.F. Stratton—surely related to the Mrs Stratton of Dover's Games—ran Cropthorne Wake from the New Inn for over 40 years, starting in 1836. His son wrote this account of the events in 1908:

First, the game of back-sword or single-stick, with which the combatants would strike at each other, and the first who drew blood would be adjudged the victor. I have known some of the combatants to prepare themselves by drinking a mixture of gunpowder and vinegar, to prevent the flow of blood. This battle was a favourite pastime with the country folk. Some few men would put off their differences until Cropthorne Wake. There they would settle them in a determined contest with bare fists, afterwards toasting each other in a jug of old barleycorn.

Shin-kicking: each combatant would take hold of the other's shoulders and would kick his bare legs until one or the other cried enough. Wrestling or tripping was another favourite contest. This would test the strength and prowess of the contestants. For the juveniles a tun of water would be provided, into which several oranges would be thrown. The boys' hands would be tied behind their backs, and they would have to fish the oranges out of the water with their teeth. Another shallow tub would be filled with flour, into which coins were dropped. These would have to be secured in the same manner. Bobbing for buns or rolls covered with treacle: a rope would be secured to two posts or trees a distance apart. Strings would be suspended from this at short distances apart; to these would be secured the buns and rolls covered with treacle. The boys would have their hands tied behind them; two boys would be placed opposite each bun, which they would try to eat. Of course, they would smother each other's faces with treacle. A man at the end of the rope would occasionally jerk it, and another would replenish the strings with fresh buns and treacle. This was a treat for the youths, who thoroughly enjoyed the fun; likewise the spectators.

Then there would be a wheelbarrow race for men and boys. The barrows would be placed in a line, and each competitor would be blind-folded. At the sound of a pistol they would all start; some would go pretty straight, some would get mixed up, others would turn round and go in an opposite direction. Sack race: men would be put into sack bags; these would be tied over their shoulders; they would have to race a hundred yards or more. Some would come into contact with each other and fall; these would commence to roll the distance or try to get upright and run or walk. Others would place a toe in each corner of the bag and run along pretty well, if not tripped by the others. This race caused lots of fun.

Climbing a greasy pole, generally for a leg of mutton. A tall pole was fixed in the ground, at the top of which was placed a bunch of flowers, which had to be secured in order to win the prize. The pole was well greased, and the feat of climbing was a difficult matter to accomplish; many would nearly reach the top and would suddenly slip down to the bottom again; but eventually the prize would be won. Pig race: a small pig would be selected, one without a tail if possible. The pig would be greased all over and then let loose, and whoever caught the pig and held him was adjudged the winner.

Then there was the old men's race, old women's race, boys' and girls' races; old men and women would dance for prizes of tea, tobacco, hats, or gown pieces; high and wide jumping, hornpipe and country jigs, blind man's buff, kiss-in-the-ring, scrambling for nuts and oranges and hot coppers. Quoit pitching contests; also skittles and ninepins; the prize in this contest would generally be a copper teapot or a kettle. Various other sports would be carried out, accompanied with music of the fiddle, flute, and tambourine. Prizes of some sort would be given for each event, and the merrymaking would end far into the night, each one seemingly well pleased with the day's sports. Some of course would have broken heads, black eyes, bruised shins, and stiff joints; others would indulge in the juice of the grape or John Barleycorn, so that a wheelbarrow or a neighbour's support would be required to land them at their respective houses. Yet, withal, those were the good old days of fun and friendship.

The same would have undoubtedly been true of Broadway Wake. Sid Knight, who remembered this as the greatest event in the calendar during his boyhood, and saved up all the year for it, wrote a loving description in his book, *Cotswold Lad*. A woman still living in the 1990s remembered saving her pennies for Broadway Wake 'held on Whit Wednesday and Thursday on Broadway Green and the Lower Green below the Swan Inn. There were ginny horses, the cake walk, the dodgems, the Noah's Ark, swinging boats, coconut shies and lots of stalls selling home-made rock, nougat and mouthwatering brandy snaps. The proprietors of these amusements were Curtis's in the early days, then later R. Edwards & Sons from Swindon and then, following them, Mr Billy Kimberley, the local showman from Evesham'.

Another woman was born on Wake Day, 12 July, in 1926 at Chaddesley Corbett, which turned out to be the last time the traditional event took place. Previously it was a day for family reunions, with ducks and green peas traditionally served for lunch. Attractions included a maypole (despite the month) set up on a triangular grass patch opposite the vicarage. Stalls, swings, roundabouts and booths were set up in the village street. Bennett and Patch's theatre sometimes attended. The Talbot and the Swan served drinks. After 1926 fetes replaced the wakes, though in May 1988, a wake was again held over two days to raise money for the maintenance of St Cassian's Church. There were steel, brass and jazz bands, falconry displays, side shows, police dog demonstrations, maypole dancing, 'Miss Wake' (junior and senior), a Bavarian jamboree, a parade of veteran military vehicles, pig roasts, dog shows, an 'It's a Knockout' competition, and also a giant marquee with a grand market in the grounds of Brockencote Hall. Shin-kicking was a notable absentee but even so 'fun and friendship' undoubtedly prevailed.

CHAPTER 10

Seasons

Calendar customs marking the passing of the year and its seasons have a tenacious hold on people's affections and emotions. Many of those relating to churches and farms have been considered in chapters 3 and 6 respectively; others feature here.

Although they may give the feeling of dating from time immemorial, few rituals have an unbroken history of any length, and some are of recent creation. The custom of decorating the Guildhall at Worcester on Oak Apple Day (29 May) has died and been brought back to life more than once. There seems to be a current fashion, which must respond to a profound emotional need, for reviving calendar customs in particular and folk culture in general. Plough Monday events, renewed interest in St George's Day, and well dressing for May Day, are examples. The proliferation of parties with all the appropriate gear at Hallowe'en is a new and growing phenomenon.

Commercial motives may play a part, and also civic pride or the desire to promote tourism. In other cases the joy and satisfaction generated are their own reward. For whatever reason, the celebration of turning points in the year is deeply ingrained, and one can safely predict that in one form or another it is destined to continue.

January
New Year's Day
The desire to greet the New Year now leads some people to assemble in the centre of Worcester.

In private houses many still prefer the first caller of the year to be a dark-haired male. Such a person used to be invited to enter by the front door and leave by the back, contrary to normal superstition which held that a caller should enter and leave by the same door so as not to take the luck away from a house. The first footers at Bromsgrove greeted the occupants with this rhyme:

Good master and good mistress and everybody here,
We wish you a merry Christmas and a happy New Year;
A pocket full of money and a cellar full of beer,
And a good fat bacon pig for to last all the year.

Then those concerned, usually boys, would knock at the door at say: 'Open the door and think of the poor, and let the New Year in, the old un out, and the new un in'. At Castlemorton and also (until the 1950s) at Longdon boys and girls would go gifting—asking for a gift or tip—round the farmhouses on New Year's Day and say, all in one breath:

Bud well, bear well,
God send you fare well.
Every sprig and every spray,
A bushel of apples on New Year's Day.
Morning, master and mistress,
A happy New Year,
A pocket full of money,
A cellar full of beer.
Please to give me a New Year's gift.

It was considered unlucky for a house to be without mistletoe, so a small sprig was kept throughout the year, to be thrown out and replaced by another on 1 January. Until at least the 1930s Worcestershire people believed that clothes should not be washed on New Year's Day, or the person they belonged to would be dead before 12 months.

The ceremony of bush burning was performed in the first hours of New Year's Day, though some areas preferred Twelfth Night (see below). The custom survived at Malvern until 1900; and in 1932 a Knighton-on-Teme woman described how 'you bake a piece of blackthorn plaited like a crown, and burn it in the field, then scatter the ashes over the ridges of the first sown, or last sown, wheat'. A new bush—normally a sort of hollow globe of twisted shoots of hawthorn or blackthorn—would then have been placed in the farm kitchen to replace the old, and to stay in place for a year.

Twelfth Night
Twelfth Night (5 January) and Twelfth Day (6 January) are otherwise known as the Vigil and Feast of the Epiphany. By Act of Parliament the calendar was changed in 1752 from the Julian to the Gregorian. Eleven days were omitted in the first year, but from then on many country people insisted on sticking to the old dates, at least for certain important occasions. As well as being Twelfth Night, 5 January was therefore Old Christmas Eve. We are told that until the middle of the nineteenth century Old Christmas was observed in

Worcestershire 'as much as Christmas Day itself'. According to T.J. Packer, writing in 1902, Old Christmas Day was 'still celebrated' at Ashton-under-Hill 'and a general holiday observed'.

Half a century earlier, John Noake described this version of the fire-purification ceremony:

> On the confines of Worcestershire, towards Ledbury, it was some years ago the custom, on Twelfth Night, for the farmers to make twelve fires on the head (east side) of one of their wheat fields. One of these fires was larger than the others, which they called 'Old Meg', and around this the farm servants, with their families and friends, congregated to drink warm cider, with plum-cake toasted in it, and with loud hurrahs wishing success to the master and his crops; then they proceeded to the cow-house, which had been nicely cleaned for the occasion, and the cows had also been cleaned and tied up, being allowed a good supply of their best provender. A large plum-cake, bound round with tape, was stuck on the horns of the best cow, and buckets of cider with plum cake were carried in. Each person present then drank to the health of the cow, using this doggrel [*sic*]:
>
> > Here's to thee, Ball, and to thy white horn;
> > Pray God send thy master a good crop of corn,
> > Of wheat, rye, and barley, and all sorts of grain,
> > And at this time twelve months we meet here again.
> > > The leaves they are green,
> > > The nuts they are brown,
> > > They all hang so high
> > > That they cannot come down.
> > They cannot come down until the next year,
> > So thee eat thy oats and we'll drink our beer (or cider, as the
> > > case may be).
>
> Then the cowman went up to the cow, and caused her by one movement to shake her head, and if the cake tumbled over in front of her it belonged to the cowman; if it fell behind, it became the property of the dairymaid. The party then retired to the house, and made the evening jolly, never concluding the festivity without a dance.

Writing some 20 years later than Noake, Edwin Lees gave a description of wassailing in the valley of the Teme, where on Twelfth Night or Old Christmas Eve a farmer and his neighbours would go

> To an elevated wheat field, where twelve small fires were lighted, and a large one in the centre, these fires generally being considered as representative of our Saviour and the twelve apostles, though in some places they have the vulgar appelation of Old Meg and her daughters. Jugs of prime old cider having been brought, healths are joyously drunk with

abundant hurrahing from a circle formed round the central fire. The party afterwards adjourn to an orchard, and there encircling one of the best bearing trees, and not forgetting cider, sprinkle the tree, while one of the party carols forth the following verse:

> Here's to thee, old apple tree,
> Whence thou may'st bud, and whence thou may'st blow,
> And whence thou may'st bear apples enow.
> > Hats full and caps full,
> > Bushels full and sacks full,
> And my pockets full too.

A chorus of obstreperous huzzahs follows ..., and the whole party then return to the farmhouse, where a bountiful supper with libations of cider, the result of former wassailing, awaits them. That this observance is not yet given up in some secluded places is evident from what I have heard of an old farmer, who stated to a visitor that his neglect of wassailing one year caused the failure of his crop of apples.

The blooming of the Holy Thorn provided a further attraction for Twelfth Night. The thorn (in fact a variety, *Crataegus monogyna*, of the common hawthorn which flowered both in winter and in summer) was thought to derive from an original at Glastonbury in Somerset believed to have grown from a staff stuck into the ground by Joseph of Arimathea. In Worcestershire examples were recorded during the twentieth century at Hampton (near the remains of the churchyard cross), Newland (in the hedge of the Swan Inn garden), Tardebigge (in the churchyard) and Ripple (at the Grove). Of the last *Berrow's Worcester Journal* wrote:

The Swan, Newland

The tree is in an open glade. It is twelve minutes to twelve. ... The thorn tree stands alone casting a long black shadow. ... Suddenly the silence is broken by the far-off chimes of the village church. Twelve solemn strokes. ... By the uncertain light of the moon the little white buds of the thom tree are seen. Slowly, weirdly, the buds unfold and in half an hour the holy tree is white and glistening as a hawthorn tree in main moon-light. The people kneel on the cold ground. The place and hour are sacred. But one woman, too bold, breaks off a spray of the silver blossom, and lo, the petals drop and she is holding a bare winter twig. Until one o'clock the tree remains in bloom, then softly the petals drop like white snowflakes and the tree is black and gaunt and common once more. The old folk silently depart, overawed.

Plough Monday

On this day, the first Monday after Twelfth Night, ploughmen in clean white shirts, with ribbons in their hats, would ceremonially drag a plough along the streets or lanes, accompanied by morris dancers, a fool or perhaps a Bessy—a man or boy dressed as a woman. If a farm's ploughman could insinuate himself into the kitchen and sit by the fireside with whip, plough staff or hatchet before the maid had put her kettle on, then she would later have to surrender her perquisite of a Shrovetide cockerel to him. After their tour and collection the ploughmen would cut the first furrow of the New Year.

The Victorians instituted a church service the day before Plough Monday, on what became known as Plough Sunday. A plough was taken in to be blessed, together with other of implements including milk churns and spades. The tradition was revived in 2005 at the Talbot Inn at Knightwick, with a service conducted by Rev. Peter Lawrence of Malvern, during the weekly farmers' market. 'It helps to start the farming year off', said Jean Clift of the Talbot. On the same day representatives from Young Farmers' Clubs all over the county met at Shires Farm, Hawford, just north of Worcester, for a ceremony when a plough, bags of soil and a milk churn were given a blessing by a clergyman.

February

On 3 February in former times the woolcombers of Kidderminster commemorated the feast day of their patron saint, Bishop Blaise. A lavish procession through the town feature the woolcombers, led by an orator, Jason with the Golden Fleece, a shepherd and shepherdess, and Bishop Blaise himself, attended by two pages. Bands played and drink flowed.

Country people believed that on St Valentine's Day (14 February) every bird chose a mate. 'Since the establishment of the penny postage system and the cheapening of paper and print', wrote Noake in 1856, 'the custom of sending Valentines has been much on the increase, some of our Worcester booksellers having found the trade sufficiently important to warrant the insertion of advertisements in the newspapers announcing a varied stock of these little missives on hand'. He would perhaps have been surprised to discover the practice even more widespread, some 150 years on.

Depending on the date of Easter, Lent begins on a Wednesday between 3 February and 9 March. The previous day is Shrove Tuesday, which used to be the occasion for horseplay, mischief-making and cruel sports such as (at Bewdley, Bromsgrove and Worcester) throwing sticks at tethered cockerels. A Jack-a-Lent is mentioned in Worcester's chamberlain's accounts for 1653 as part of the Shrovetide procession. The figure, of straw and cast-off clothes, was dragged through the streets and then either burned or shot to pieces. It was thought to stand for Judas, but may originally have represented the old year.

The pancake bell once gave the signal to begin frying pancakes. Upton-on-Severn had a bell at 11 a.m. for 'pans on' and another at noon for 'pans off'. A Worcestershire rhyme ran:

> Hark I hear the pancake bell,
> And fritters make a gallant smell.

George Jorden noted in 1827 at Bewdley: 'Shrove-tide or Shrove Tuesday, gray pease and pancakes eaten today, two bells are tolled at 11 o'clock, an old custom. The first two bells cry "pot on at one", the other two bells toll "pot off pan on"'. The custom of making pancakes on Shrove Tuesday now seems to be waning—but one makes such comments at one's peril.

Like Valentine's Day, Mothering Sunday—now called Mother's Day—is heavily commercialised. The earliest reference to the occasion seems to be from the diary for 1644 of a Royalist officer: 'Every Mid-Lent Sunday is a great day at Worcester, when all the children and god-children meet at the head and chief of the family and have a feast. They call it the Mothering-day'. Curiously, something similar still takes place, usually on the premises of a hospitable public house.

As late as 1932 a Mrs Oakley of Romney Green remembered that at Beoley on Mothering Sunday her parents had always eaten roast veal, followed by cheese cakes made with rennet. Veal was also the preferred dish at Bromsgrove, where special 'mothering cakes' were also cooked. During church services held at Inkberrow posies were presented by the vicar to the children, who passed them on to their parents.

March

Easter Day is a moveable feast depending on the moon and falling between 21 March and 25 April. Good Friday was thought to be a particularly auspicious day for planting, especially for the seeds of stocks; if these were set as the sun went down their flowers would be double. Bread or hot-cross buns baked on

Good Friday might be saved and hung up for good luck. After being kept until the following Easter they could be grated into a liquid which was then drunk to ease stomach-ache. Hot-cross buns were once baked only on a Good Friday but now they are on sale in some bakers' shops and supermarkets for many weeks.

Bakers themselves kept some buns, reminding people of the belief that as Christ was on his way to be crucified a washerwoman threw some dirty water over him whereupon a woman carrying newly baked bread wiped him dry and gave him a loaf. Christ then said 'From henceforth blessed be the baker and cursed be the washer'. It follows that washing clothes should be avoided on Good Friday, a belief which lingered until the 1940s at Broadwas, Offenham and no doubt elsewhere. It was even considered unlucky to leave suds in a tub or boiler over Good Friday.

Writing in the early years of the twentieth century, F.T. Spackman described the traditional Good Friday activity at Whittington, close by what is now the M5:

> So long as I can remember there has always been, once a year, a great concourse of Worcester people on Crookbarrow Hill, with swings, roundabouts and other accessories for merrymaking, to the very great inconvenience of the occupiers of the estate in which the barrow is situated. This annual exodus of citizens occurs on Good Friday—perhaps the most sacred of all the fasts observed by the church. So firmly established is the custom, so great are the throngs of people who attend, that in spite of all the inconvenience suffered by the tenants, no opposition, so far as I know, has ever been offered to the merrymaking.

Whittington Fair in 1910

The fair seems gradually to have faded but until the Second World War Worcester people kept up the custom of walking to the top of the hill and picnicking on Good Friday. In May 1900 their predecessors celebrated the relief of Mafeking by burning Kruger in effigy on the top.

A favoured Easter diversion was heaving. Originally this had a religious significance to symbolise Christ's rising from the dead, but it became a secular celebration.

At Alvechurch, Bromsgrove, and Hartlebury, for example — women were lifted on the Monday; at other places — Kidderminster and Worcester — on the Tuesday. At Hartlebury farmers' wives believed that if their maidservants were heaved

Heaving in the eighteenth century

they would break no crockery during the ensuing year.

Heaving continued at Worcester until the 1850s, its last outposts being the slum areas of Birdport and Dolday (which were later cleared of houses). At Kidderminster the women, gaily dressed for the occasion, would bedeck a chair with ribbons and stretch a rope across the street. Any man then passing — and one wonders how many men did pass by accident — was seized, put in the chair, raised aloft, and turned three times. After being returned to earth he was kissed by all the women and released on making a contribution towards an evening of drinking and dancing. Next day it was the men's turn to take the active role. In 1834 the custom was adapted to political campaigning: the popular M.P., Richard Godson, was heaved by women at 47 public houses and given — it was calculated — 2,160 kisses. Ebenezer Guest of Kidderminster, writing in 1906, recalled that, confronted with the choice of paying a fine or kissing 'the leader of a party of thirsty amazons', men opted to do both. Heaving lasted longer than anywhere else in the factories and pubs of Kidderminster, but even there it was only a memory by the turn of the nineteenth century.

April

All Fools' Day (1 April) continues to have an appeal, though it is far from being a major festival. On St Richard's Day (3 April) a ceremony is held each year by the saint's statue in Vines Park at Droitwich (see chapter 3). Tenbury Fair is held on 22 April, the traditional date when the cuckoo is expected to be first heard there. St George's Day (23 April) is assuming increasing importance in the calendar, with morris dancing, the promotion of traditional fare, and even discos. Rogationtide—Rogation Sunday, the fifth after Easter, can fall in April or May—was the classic time for beating parish bounds (see chapter 3). In the last days of the month at Malvern some 20 wells and water features are dressed with flowers for an annual competition which is judged during the May Day celebrations.

May

May Day
This was once one of the highlights of the year. After the Restoration some of its customs gravitated to 29 May but others remained. In Worcestershire it was known as Robin Hood's Day.

In 1908 G.M. Stratton described the May Day, 'one of the greatest festivals of the year', half a century earlier:

> Evesham upon that day was en fete. The streets were crowded, and a number of sweeps issued from the Bewdley (the part of the town where they principally resided), dressed in fantastic attire, made of gaily coloured ribbons, paper, etc., hats of various shapes; also carrying various instruments of their craft, accompanied with a gaily-decorated vehicle, in which was seated the Queen of the May and the Little Boy Sweep. There were many master sweeps, journeymen and juvenile sweeps, playing on various instruments, jumping, dancing, and gyrating about with wands gaily dressed with flowers, ribbon, and May blossoms, and each vying with the other to celebrate the festival in a happy, joyous manner. Hundreds of people from the surrounding villages would assemble in the good old borough of Evesham upon that day to see the sights and do homage to the Queen of the May.

Earlier still, William Timings painted an idyllic picture in his *Guide to the Clent Hills* of 1835:

> May day is observed as an holiday in Clent and Hagley for the juvenile part of both sexes, who are wont to rise a little after midnight, and go to the neighbouring woods, where they cut off the branches of the oak, and adorn them with nosegays, crowns of flowers, and ribbons of various

May Day meeting on Worcester's Pitchcroft in 1911

colours. When this is done they return with their booty homeward about the rising of the sun, and make their doors and windows to triumph in the flowery spoil. There formerly was a large May-pole erected in the village, and a Queen of May appointed, but this custom is now discontinued.

In 1880 a correspondent writing under the pseudonym of 'Vigorn' added these remarks, in the periodical, *Notes and Queries*:

> The custom of going to the woods for oak boughs on May Day has quite died out in Clent, in fact, in Timmings's time (died 1850, aged 78) it was not observed with much spirit; birch boughs, indeed, were in as much request as oak for garlands. Timmings [in fact, Timings], who owned a small estate in the parish, was an ardent lover of old customs, and in one of his fields he set up a maypole, which is mentioned in his *Guide*. The

Elmley Castle May Day in 1910

308

Clent children are now satisfied with hawthorn branches cut from the nearest hedge, and the dirty ribbons and dingy finery with which they decorate them would certainly be no ornament to cottage doors. About the beginning of this century, at the Temple of Theseus, one of the ornamental buildings near Hagley Park, as soon as it was light on May morning, crowds of people would congregate and four or five bands be in attendance. This could not have been a long-established custom, since the Temple was built by the first Lord Lyttleton about 1760, and the usage probably came to an end in 1826, when the public were stopped from going when they liked to Hagley Park. Besides May Day, Clent people, young and old, went to the woods again on May 29, and fetched oak enough to decorate the church tower, so much being used that the tower seemed to terminate in an oak tree instead of a weathercock, while the villagers universally wore oak-balls about their persons, and decorated their houses with oak boughs. This custom, also, is now entirely abandoned, and I think perhaps Timmings has been confusing the two days; the latter day was considered the greater holiday of the two, and several clubs met and walked in procession about the village.

Some villages had permanent maypoles: Bayton (until 1868) and Hartlebury (until the 1850s), for example. Offenham's 55-foot column is the only one left in the county. It has been replaced on various occasions, including

Offenham's maypole in 2004

in about 1850 when its predecessor blew down in a gale. The cost of maintenance is borne by the village wake committee, which regularly takes down the pole to repair and repaint it and to re-gild the weathercock. Formerly the pole was garlanded with flowers and greenery on May Day each year. People danced on the surrounding green to the music of fiddle, viol and bassoon, pausing to take refreshment at the adjacent Maypole Inn. The last vestige of green was removed in 1938, and the inn is now a private house.

May Day, as the passages from Timings and 'Vigorn' show, was primarily an adult festival, but as time passed it became a children's event. From the three parishes of Longdon, Bushley and Queenhill the children met at Pull Court to choose a May

309

king and queen. 'Then we went down to Moss Green, headed by the Bushley band, where we spent the day dancing round the maypole, singing and making merry'. Mildred Berkeley noted, unfortunately without tunes, a number of songs sung on such occasions:

> All round the maypole, tret tret trot,
> See what a maypole we have got.
> Garlands above and garlands below,
> See what a maypole we can show.
>
> The cock flew up in the yew tree,
> The hen came cackling by,
> Good morning, missus and master,
> Please to give me a mince pie.
>
> The roads are very dirty, my shoes are very thin,
> And I've got a pocket to pop a penny in.
> If you haven't a penny a ha'penny will do
> If you haven't a ha'penny God bless you.
>
> I wish you health, I wish you wealth,
> I wish you money in store.
> I wish you heaven when you die,
> What could I wish you more?

Below is a version of the May song given by Jesse Salisbury in 1893:

All round the may-pole we will trot, See what a may-pole we have got,

Gar-lands a-bove and gar-lands be-low – See what a pretty may-pole we can show.

Revivals of such activities naturally tended to be for children, though at Hallow in 1951 on the eve of May Day there was a parade of local organisations including the Mothers' Union, Women's Institute, British Legion and the Free Foresters, followed by a service in the church, which happens to be dedicated to St Philip and St James, whose festival is on 1 May. On May Day itself children danced round a maypole on the green, and the May queen and her attendants drove round the village before attending a concert in the village hall. Since 1992 Malvern has regularly staged May Day events for both adults and children, including a procession, music, a mystery play, exhibitions and stalls. 'May Day meets Narnia' was one summation of the atmosphere.

Oak Apple Day

After the battle of Worcester in 1651 the future Charles II eluded pursuing Parliamentary soldiers by hiding in an oak tree at Boscobel House in Shropshire; birds—one version says an owl—perching in the tree remained undisturbed, and flew off only at the approach of the troopers who concluded that no one could be hiding there. When Charles was formally restored to the throne on 29 May (in 1660) this date, combined with commemorative oak leaves and sprays, came to be regarded in many places as the real May Day.

Charles II never returned to the 'Faithful City', but every year on 29 May the cathedral clergy kindled a huge commemorative bonfire in the close. During the Stuart rebellion of 1715 and 1745, though, the city was strongly Whig and Hanoverian, and such celebrations lapsed. In the 1790s the Tory faction revived the practice of decking the Guildhall with oak boughs and holding processions on 29 May. The latter lasted until the 1860s, and the day was taken as a good opportunity by the people of Dolday. 'Gangs of "largesse" gatherers perambulated the adjoining streets, some of the males wearing exaggerated crinolines—if it be possible to exaggerate a fashionable garment of that description, but as there was little more drunkenness or rioting than is usual, it is inferred that the contributions were limited'.

In 1934 the custom of decorating the the Guildhall was revived, and four years later *Berrow's Worcester Journal* carried this account of a rather restrained event:

Worcester Guildhall decorated on 29 May 1935

Oak Apple Day fell on Sunday, but though only formally on this occasion, Worcester remembered to commemorate the birthday of King Charles II. In accordance with custom—revived a few years ago after a considerable lapse—the gates and main entrance of the Guildhall were decorated with boughs from oak on Lord Coventry's estate at Croome. It being Sunday, only the Mayor (Dr E.W. Moore Ede) and the Town Clerk (Mr C.H. Digby-Seymour) and a few passers-by noted the little ceremony. A bough was fixed to the gate by the Mayor, and he and the Town Clerk placed a sprig of oak with an oak-apple attached in their button-holes, following which the Town Clerk called in a loud voice 'God save the king'. So did Worcester continue to show its traditional loyalty and faithfulness to the crown.

The custom again lapsed at the end of the twentieth century.

Oak Apple Day at Elmley Castle in 1954

At Alvechurch oak boughs were placed over the doors and windows of houses, and a big branch was set up in the church, or so old people remembered in 1915. Until about 30 years earlier any boys or girls failing to display oak sprigs or oak apples ran the risk of being pinched. At Kidderminster, Malvern and elsewhere, boys would 'nettle' those not sporting oak; as Arthur Savory put it, 'a spray of oak or an oak-apple is in some villages worn as a badge of loyalty, the penalty for non-observance being a stroke on the hands with a stinging nettle'.

In the early nineteenth century boys at a school at Chadwich, near Rubery, traditionally appealed for a holiday by chanting:

> Hurray, hurray, hurray
> For the twenty-ninth of May!
> The twenty-ninth of May is oak-ball day;
> If you don't give us a holiday we'll all run away,
> And if we run away we shan't come back again,
> So let us have a holiday and leave our book and pen.
> Hurray, hurray, hurray
> For the twenty-ninth of May.

At Clent, Offenham and Upton-on-Severn dancing round the maypole on 29 May remained popular until about 1870. In Evesham and round about the custom lingered until the 1930s:

> On May-pole day, the 29th of May, the children, assisted by their parents, decorate a pole with may-blossom and with flowers ... The May-pole is carried from house to house by two or three strong lads and, at intervals, is set up and held in an upright position ... while the children join hands and dance round it, singing:

All around the May-pole we will trot,
See what a May-pole we have got;
Garlands above and garlands below,
See what a pretty May-pole we can show.

An identical verse was sung at Elmley Castle, both early in the twentieth century and in the course of a revival in the 1950s.

Another Oak Apple Day revival takes place at Upton-on-Severn, where on the nearest Saturday to 29 May the town crier starts proceedings at 10.15 a.m. In addition to a fair, archery, skittles, a pig roast and a barn dance, there is processional dancing from Old Street, through High Street, Dunns Lane and Waterside. People wear seventeenth-century dress. Morris dancers and street entertainers perform. Charitable agencies raise funds at a multitude of stalls. The whole event is organised by the Upton-on-Severn Tourist Association.

Oak Apple Day at Upton-on-Severn in 1930

Club Walks

Before the advent of state welfare schemes, and, indeed, overlapping with them, benefit clubs for a small weekly subscription offered sickness payments and assistance with funeral expenses. Most were for men, though an exception,

At the Upton Festival in 1990

the Society of Females, based at the White Lion at Stourport, remained in existence until 1974. Bewdley had three (for men), followed respectively in 1808 (the Friendly Society), 1823 (the Union Club) and 1825 (the White Sheaf Club).

Some of the clubs held processions on Oak Apple Day, in conjunction with church services, feasts for members and relatives, and fair-style entertainments. The small village of Hanley Castle alone had two clubs, based respectively at the Quay public house (now gone) on the river at the bottom of Quay Lane, and the Three Kings. The former paraded on 29 May, the latter on Whit Monday. At Ombersley sick club members marched to church behind a brass band before having a meal at the King's Arms. Rustic sports followed in the afternoon.

Many clubs were lodges of national organisations such as the Oddfellows and the Foresters. Miss Margaret Gibbons recalled in 1950 that the Foresters at Hartlebury met at the Mitre Public House and paraded through the village with the principal officers dressed as Robin Hood, Maid Marian and Friar Tuck. A maypole was erected on the green outside the public house. In Stourport Foresters' processions provided a lavish spectacle which thrilled I.L. Wedley as a boy in the 1880s:

> About eleven in the morning the thud of the drum was heard, followed by the strains of 'Auld Lang Syne', as the band marched down Holborn, and along Lombard Street to the fete ground. But the band was not the chief item, the Foresters' procession which followed took principal place, especially in the hearts of the youngsters.
>
> First came Will Scarlett and a band of the archers with bows and arrows, then Friar Tuck, a jovial monk remarkable for his rotundity, he being followed by Little John, a local barber of some sixteen stone in weight, riding a steed that matched the rider. But to us youngsters the great feature of the processions was our boys' hero, Bold Robin Hood (whom we believed always helped the poor at the expense of the rich), and his sweetheart, Maid Marian. Side by side they rode, Robin Hood on a black horse and Maid Marian on a beautiful white steed. Robin Hood

Foresters' Fete at the Mitre Oak in 1911

looked every inch a Forester with his doublet of Lincoln green, and his cap with a long feather, jauntily placed on his head, while Maid Marian, in a white dress and beautiful hair falling luxuriously over her shoulders, was indeed a sweetheart to fight for. ...

These were followed by a long procession of Kidderminster and Stourport Foresters, some with green aprons, others with coloured sashes across their chests, but those were nothing to us, our hero and heroine had passed by. This was my introduction to Forestry.

Some clubs preferred to walk at Whitsuntide, or later in the year.

Flyford Flavel Foresters' Fete in 1912

June

Whit Sunday, seven weeks after Easter, could fall between 9 May and 13 June. On Whit Wednesday at Broadway both wake and walk were held. Members of the Coach and Horses sick and dividend club, adorned with rosettes and streamers, and carrying red, white and blue staves topped with heraldic devices, paraded behind the village brass band to the new church. 'Two stalwarts marched in front', wrote Sid Knight, 'proudly supporting between them a huge colourful banner on which was painted the story surmounted by the title, THE GOOD SAMARITAN, each tall elm pole resting in a leather socket'. After a service the procession formed up again to march back to the Coach and Horses' orchard, where in a big marquee 'a sumptuous repast prepared by mine host, William Roberts, was enjoyed by all', and washed down by specially brewed Whitsun ale.

Club Day at Harvington was on Whit Thursday. On the Monday people from Grafton and other villages round Bredon gathered on top of the hill to socialise and to take part in games and competitions. The event may once have been connected with meetings of the Court Leet held on the hill summit until the nineteenth century.

Upton Snodsbury's Foresters held their Club Sunday in June. People came from miles around, and men with banners walked in procession from the

315

Coventry Arms to the church for a service. One the following day, writes Jane Tomlinson, 'Hot meals were served outside the Coventry Arms, while the fete itself spread into the fields opposite, where there were roundabouts and stalls with brandy snaps, a band and dancing, sports—and a good deal of match-making, to judge by the number of weddings that followed in the year'. The event, well-attended and popular though it was, came to an end in 1914 and did not return at the end of the war.

Until 1850 'Ditching the Mayor of Bewdley Street' took place at Evesham during Whit Week. The man chosen as a kind of mock mayor was taken down the street on a cart. If he could hang on when the crowd tried to dislodge him he was taken back for more drinks until such time as he could cling to the cart no longer and was tipped into a ditch at the bottom of the street.

On Midsummer Eve (23 June) the people of Church Street in Kidderminster enjoyed their Feast of Peace and Good Neighbourhood which is claimed to date from time immemorial. Funds have been periodically topped up by legacies such as the £150 left for investment in 1776 by a local bachelor, John Brecknell. The items provided are a farthing loaf and a twopenny plum cake for every child and unmarried person born in Church Street; a piece of cake for all residents; and pipes, tobacco and ale for all the men living there. Great quantities of beer were drunk round a bonfire. In some form the custom has continued to the present day. Not so in Worcester, where there was once a procession on St John's Day (24 June) of trade guilds, waits, morris dancers, and also the figures of giants and dragons. Bonfires were lit, both in Worcester and on high

The Street of Peace and Good Neighbourhood, Kidderminster

Distribution of cakes and farthing loaves in Kidderminster in 1953

places such as Midsummer Hill in the Malvern range.

Midsummer Day was the occasion for Bromsgrove's horse and pleasure fair, once known as 'the blessed fair'. The horse sales lapsed in the early twentieth century but the pleasure fair continues. So does the Court Leet which meets on the Saturday after 24 June, though its high bailiff, ale-taster and the like now have only ceremonial functions.

Pershore Fair is held on 26 June (the Feast of St Edburga) and the two days following. By ancient custom anyone hanging out a bush (or bough, or even a cabbage) had the right to sell beer during the fair, until the magistrates intervened in 1865 and declared the practice illegal.

Some of the functions of the old fairs and wakes are now filled by agricultural events such as the enormous Three Counties Show held near Malvern in mid-June.

July

On the second Sunday of July it was the custom at Chaddesley Corbett to put any stranger 'through the whoop'. The procedure followed is unclear since those in the village who remembered it were reticent about giving details. Presumably it was a way of demanding largesse.

Wakes and fairs continued in July. Fairs of the month include Hartlebury (the first Sunday after 25 July; now gone) and Clent (28 July, St Kenelm's Day; see chapter 3).

On the Monday after the second Sunday in July members of the Foresters' Club at Chaddesley Corbett proceeded round the village, led by a band. The main officers, dressed as Robin Hood, Friar Tuck and the like, paid courtesy calls at important houses, then the whole assembly sat down to a meal at the Talbot Inn. Sports and sideshows in an adjacent field followed in the afternoon.

Shrawley Foresters preferred the second Tuesday in July. Dressed in full regalia, they assembled at the New Inn for a march through the village led by a band, usually from Stourport. After a service in the church and refreshments at Church Farm they returned to enjoy the fun of the fair on the meadow (now occupied by houses) behind the inn. Special club cakes supplied by a Worcester baker were sold for a halfpenny each. Music for dancing on the green was

Crowle Foresters' Fete in July 1923

provided for many years by two local men, Abel and Bob Spragg (for whom see also chapter 7). Hanley Swan Foresters and Eckington Oddfellows held similar events in July.

Pupils at Wilden All Saints' First School on the outskirts of Stourport make a progress with flowers on St Swithin's Day (15 July) to the grave of Thomas Jones, who died in 1899 and left a field to be sold to provide an annual treat. Jones, aged 79, an illiterate cowman earning 12s. a week and living in a garret, caused a considerable stir by bequeathing £385 in cash, together with the field. The sale of the field produced £300, the interest on which initially gave the children an outing and a picnic. As the years passed, this became an outing only, then just an ice-cream. Now, £13 a year is added to funds supporting the school's swimming programme. Nevertheless, the homage to Thomas Jones continues every year, on his birthday.

Hanley Swan Foresters' Anniversary Day, July 1909

Shrawley Foresters' Fete in July 1914

August

On Lammas Day (1 August) common land which had been fenced off while hay grew was thrown open again for pasture. The Ham at Upton-on-Severn was common land in which plots, marked by mere (boundary) stones, reallocated each year by lot, were thrown open to all at Lammas.

On St Lawrence's Day (10 August), the day of the church's dedication at Alvechurch, there was until the first half of the nineteenth century a fair, with ox-roasting. Until some 50 years later the Foresters' Club at Alfrick held its annual walk in August. On a Sunday in the month the West Malvern Oddfellows had a procession led by a blue and silver uniformed band, which

Guarding the Lammas bread, the first made from the grain of the new harvest. From a misericord at Ripple

replaced an earlier drum and fife ensemble. Rather unusually, according to Miss E.M. Knight, mummers joined in the entertainment, led by the intriguingly-named 'Crack' Bethel, otherwise known as 'Old Crack'.

The modern August Bank Holiday (last Monday in the month) has been dubbed Plum Day at Pershore. Plum stones are used to identify varieties, trees are for sale together with other produce, and an exhibition is devoted to the history of plum growing in the area.

September

Until the middle of the nineteenth century the Lawless Hour was kept up at Kidderminster on the first Monday after Michaelmas Day (29 September). The understanding was that the high bailiff left office at noon but his successor did not take over till 1 p.m. With no one formally in charge of the town, officers could make no arrests for damage to property nor, within limits, for personal injury. The ringing of the town bell at noon unleashed, to the ritual cry of 'kellums, kellums', volleys of old shoes, cabbage stalks and other missiles in a bout of good-natured strife. At times the battle became unduly violent but when magistrates attempted in 1822 to curtail the festivities a serious riot ensued, as a result of which three men were sent to prison. The town authorities continued to support the custom, and provided large quantities of apples which were thrown to the crowd.

A Kidderminster woman, signing herself 'H.M.', wrote to William Hone in 1826 with a lively, first-hand account of the custom:

> The magistrate and other officers of the town are annually elected, and the first Monday after Michaelmas-day is the day of their inauguration, in celebration of which, they each of them cause to be thrown to the populace (who assemble to the amount of some thousands), from the windows of their houses, or sometimes from the town-hall, a large quantity of apples, in the whole often amounting to twenty or thirty pots (baskets containing five pecks each). This practice occasions, of course, a kind of prescriptive holiday in the town, and anyone having the temerity to refuse his apprentice or servant leave to attend the 'apple-throwing' would most probably have cause to repent such an invasion of right. A rude concourse therefore fills the streets which are the scenes of action; and as a sort of 'safety valve', if I may 'compare great things with small', recourse is had by the crowd to the flinging about of old shoes, cabbage stalks, and almost every accessible kind of missile; till at length the sashes are raised, and the gifts of pomona begin to shower down upon the heads of the multitude. Woe be to the unlucky wight who may chance to ride through the town during the introductory part of this custom; no sooner does he appear, than a thousand aims are taken at him and his horse, or carriage, and the poor benighted rider 'sees, or dreams

he sees' (if ignorant of the practice) the inhabitants of a whole town raised to oppose his single progress, without being able to form the most distant idea of their motive for so doing.

In due course a more firmly disciplined population combined with more sophisticated notions of entertainment put an end to the lawless hour in Kidderminster.

Broxash Oddfellows' Fete in September 1909

October
This was one of the classic months for mops (see chapter 6).

Hallowe'en (31 October) was feared rather than celebrated in the past, but parties are a fairly common occurrence now. However, they seldom include the attempts at divining a future husband which used to be made on the day by young women (see chapter 4). Some children have taken to going round in fancy dress, knocking on doors and demanding a 'trick or treat'. The practice has been condemned as an import from America but it originally travelled there from this country. Some people complained of feeling intimidated into giving treats, and in 2004 leaflets requesting no trick or treaters were produced for display by Malvern householders who wished to opt out. The sale of devils' tridents, witches' hats and brooms, ghost and skeleton outfits now brings in £100 million annually for Tesco alone, with a third of all Hallowe'en gear being bought for adult use—a curious reversal of the tendency for calendar customs to pass to children.

November
Guy Fawkes Night (5 November) is still a lively, popular festival, though some of the rhymes and chants associated with it have fallen out of use. In Worcestershire gangs of men and boys went round houses asking for fuel for

their fire. They thumped on the ground with sticks for emphasis, particularly on the words *plot*, *forgot* and *faggit*. The last couplet is as clear a threat as today's trick or treat:

> O don't you remember the fifth of November
> Is gunpowder, trayson and plot?
> I don't see the rayson why gunpowder trayson
> Should ever be forgot.
> A stick and a stake for Queen Victoria's sake,
> I pray, master, give us a faggit;
> If you don't give us one we'll take two,
> The better for us and the wuss for you.

Until the twentieth century an even more elaborate song was sung:

> Guy Fawkes and his companions did contrive
> To blow the Houses of Parliament up alive,
> With three-score barrels of powder below
> To prove old England's wicked overthrow;
> But by God's mercy all of them got catched
> With their dark lanterns and their lighted match.
> Ladies and gentlemen sitting by the fire,
> Please put hands in pocket and give us our desire;
> While you can drink one glass we can drink two,
> The better for we and the worse for you.
> Rumour, rumour, pump-a-derry,
> Prick his heart and burn his body,
> And send his soul to Purgatory.

Preliminaries to the Court Leet meeting at Feckenham in November 1909. A Court or Manorial Leet dealt in medieval times with petty offences such as common nuisance and highway or ditch repair, as well as electing a constable, ale taster, pinder and other minor officials. In modern times the proceedings became largely ceremonial

Miss Lillian Allen recalled in 1950 that on Bonfire Night at Newland the village blacksmith took his anvil to the common. He charged the hole in it with gunpowder, which he set off with a loud report.

On St Martin's Day (11 November) until at least the 1980s a squad of infantry paraded colours through the ruins of St Stephen's Without at Worcester. The original troop was recruited by Colonel Montagu of Pershore for Wellington's march on Badajoz in 1812. Opposite the church seven felons were gibbeted in 1704, and some who go near on February evenings experience a feeling of dread.

St Clement's Day (23 November) is followed two days later by St Catherine's Day. The former was one of the ancient quarter days. The Dean and Chapter of Worcester Cathedral used to close their audit on the latter, marking the occasion by a distribution of spiced wine in the 'Cattern Bowl' to residents in the college precincts.

Worcestershire children went round singing on both days. As early as 1826 a correspondent, 'Selitis', wrote to William Hone about a celebration common in his native Worcestershire:

> On the afternoon of St Clement's day, a number of boys collected together in a body, and went from house to house; and at the door of each house, one, or sometimes more, would recite, or chaunt, the following lines -

> Catherine and Clement, be here, be here;
> Some of your apples, and some of your beer;
> Some for Peter, and some for Paul,
> And some for him that made us all.
> Clement was a good old man,
> For his sake give us some;
> Not of the worst, but some of the best,
> And God will send your soul to rest.

> Some would say,

> And God will send *you a good night's rest.*

> Sometimes grown men would go in like manner, and, to such, the people of the house would give ale or cider; but to the boys they gave apples, or, if they had none to spare, a few halfpence. Having collected a good store of apples, which they seldom failed to do, the boys repaired to some of their houses, where they roasted and ate the apples; and frequently the old would join the young, and large vessels of ale or cider would be brought in, and some of the roasted apples thrown hot into it, and the evening would then be spent with much mirth and innocent amusement; such as, I sorrow to think, have departed never to return.

Yet the custom did continue at Alvechurch, for example, until 1900. Just a few years earlier this account came from Hartlebury:

> 'Catten and Clementing', by the youths of this parish and the adjoining parish of Chaddesley, is still indulged in on the night of 23rd. November, by the lads going round to the principal houses and repeating the following verses, but the last verse is used in connection with the same at Hartlebury only: and the boys occasionally take with them a 'Hoberdy' lantern, that is a light placed within a hollow turnip, having eyes, nose and mouth cut therein, which gives them a weird appearance.

> Catherine and Clement come year by year,
> Some of your apples and some of your beer,
> Some for Peter, some for Paul,
> Some for the merry boys under your wall.
> Peter was a good old man,
> For his sake give us some;
> None of the worst, but some of the best,
> And pray God send your souls to rest.
> Butler, butler, fill the bowl,
> Dash it up against the wall;
> Up the ladder, and down the can,
> Give us a red apple and we'll be gone.
> A plum, a plum, a cherry, a cherry,
> A cup of perry will soon make us all merry.
> We go a Cattin, a Cattin we go,
> From Hitton to Titton, as soon you shall see;
> From Hitton to Pitton, Hartlebury all three,
> Round by old Kiddy, and good Hillintree;
> Then down to old Arley, Astley and Shrawley go nimbly,
> And finish up at Holt, Hallow and Grimley.

Some places—Harvington, Leigh, Offenham—preferred St Catherine's Day itself for their collecting. Despite its references to St Clement, this 'quaint carol', according to W.W.A. Tree, was sung in many villages in the county by boys and girls who 'used to go round to the farm houses on St Catherine's Day':

> Catt'n and Clement comes year by year,
> Some of your apples and some of your beer.
> Some for Peter and some for Paul,
> Some for him who made us all.
> Peter was a good old man,
> For his sake give us some.
> Some of the best and none of the worst,

And God will send your souls to roost.
Up the ladder and down with the can,
Give me red apples and I'll be gone.
St Clement's, St Clement's! a cat be the ear!
A good red apple, a pint of beer.
Some of your mutton, some o' your veal,
If it's good gi'e us a deal,
If it's naught gi'e us some salt.
Butler, butler, fill the bowl.
If you fill it of the best
God will send your soul to rest;
But if you fill it of the small
The devil take butler, bowl and all.

Tenbury holly and mistletoe sales in 2002

Tree adds that 'The custom of "going a Cattering" is said to have been observed in Worcester when Queen Elizabeth visited the city on St Catherine's Day'.

Since mid-Victorian times, pre-Christmas sales of mistletoe have taken place at Tenbury Wells. Latterly, Brightwells have conducted auctions on several Tuesdays in November and the first in December, each year. Mistletoe and also holly and Christmas trees, mainly from from Herefordshire, Shropshire and Worcester, but also from places farther afield such as Brittany, are sold in bulk. The sales of 2004 could be the last, after the market site at Tenbury was sold for re-development. A spokesman said: 'Brightwells are looking for somewhere else in the town. We don't want to lose the tradition because it's very popular'.

December

St Thomas's Day

Until the early years of the twentieth century various doles—hand-outs in modern parlance—helped to prepare the poor for the onset of the worst of the winter. On St Thomas's Day (21 December) the wives, mothers and children of all those who worked on the Beckford estate were expected to call on Mr King-Ross at Beckford Hall to be given 'a sixpenny piece' each which was solemnly produced from a leather bag. The recipients, some 40 in number, then went round to the back door to be given 'a steaming cup of hot coffee and plenty of bread, spread thickly with lovely farm butter'.

In some places legacies provided for assistance to the needy. Thanks to a bequest by Rev. John Dobyn, on St Thomas's Day the 'aged, widows and parents of large families' in the parishes of Beckford and Grafton received tickets which local tradesmen would exchange for supplies. At Alfrick twelve penny loaves were given to each of five poor people under the seventeenth-century will of Thomas Makam. Many such small legacies existed, though for the most part the amounts invested now produce only insignificant sums.

Where little or no formal provision for assistance existed, people had traditional licence to collect. The activity was called thomasing, gooding or mumping. Money received would be spent on useful things for the winter like boots or blankets. Food helped families to prepare for Christmas in particular or winter in general. Collectors sang to announce their presence:

> Bud well, bear well,
> God send spare well.
> A bushel of apples to give
> On St Thomas's morning.

At Stoulton the formula differed:

Christmas distribution of meat and bread to the tenantry at Croome Court
by Lord and Lady Coventry in 1908

> Well a day, well a day,
> St Thomas goes too soon away;
> Then your gooding we do pray,
> For the good time will not stay.
> St Thomas grey,
> St Thomas grey,
> The longest night and the shortest day,
> Please to remember St Thomas's Day.

Cuthbert Bede (Rev. E. Bradley) observed that 'at Harvington [near Stourport] it is the custom ... for persons, mostly children, to go round the village begging for apples, and singing':

> Wissal, Wassail, through the town,
> If you've got any apples throw them down,
> Up with the stocking and down with the shoe,
> If you've got no apples money will do.

Mrs Hilda Brazier of Harvington remembered as late as 1950 a version of the same rhyme:

> A wissal a wassal about the town: got any apples, throw them down.
> Jugs white, ale brown, this is the best house in our town.
> Holly and ivy and mistletoe bough, give me an apple and let me go.
> Up the ladder and down the wall, up the stocking and down the shoe.
> Got no apples, money'll do; got no apples, God bless you.

The request to throw apples 'down' seems to indicate that they were kept in lofts or attics; and the reference to 'the best house in our town' is a none-too-subtle piece of flattery. At Evesham the words were:

> A wissal, a wassal about the town:
> Got any apples, throw them down.
> Jug's white, ale's brown;
> This is the best house in the town.
> Holly and ivy and mistletoe bough,
> Give me an apple and let me go.
> Up the ladder and down the wall,
> Up the stocking and down the shoe.
> Got no apples, money'll do;
> Got no money, God bless you.

At Grafton, according to R.H. Lloyd, the old custom came to an end in 1925. However, the late Fred Archer claimed that a boy who may have been the last of the thomasers sang before dawn at Ashton-under-Hill in 1963:

> Here I come a-thomasin',
> A-thomasin', a-thomasin'.
> Here I come a-thomasin'
> So early in the morning.

The first words of the Evesham and Harvington songs are a corruption of 'wassail', a word of ancient pedigree meaning 'be well' or 'good health'. The wassail bowl typically contained lambs' wool—a mixture of hot ale, spices, sugar and roasted apples, to which eggs and thick cream were sometimes added. In some family gatherings during the festive season each person in turn took an apple from the bowl and ate it, then drank the health of the company.

Wassailers also toured houses and farms with their bowl, which might hold up to two gallons. A Worcestershire variant of their song begins:

> Wassail, wassail, all over the town,
> Our toast it is white and our ale it is brown.
> Our bowl is made of the white maple tree,
> With the wassailing bowl we'll drink to thee.

Christmas

On Christmas Eve at Alvechurch bees were thought to sing in the hive. At Tenbury the cows knelt in the byre at midnight (as oxen did elsewhere on Twelfth Night), and twelve fires were lit to bring twelve months of fruitfulness. The old mistletoe bough which had hung in the kitchen for a year was taken down and replaced with a new. Ivy and holly were brought in on Christmas Eve, holly especially being unlucky at any other time. There is an intriguing entry as early as 1529 in the accounts of the churchwardens of St Helen's, Worcester, to twopence spent on 'Holly and eyvy agenst Crestomas'. A visitor to the church at Ashton-under-Hill in 1865 was surprised to see 'suspended inside the tower a bough of mistletoe, which the venerable sexton led him to understand was an institution of the ringers'. The sexton explained that the mistletoe 'remained there all the year, and was supplanted by another on the following Christmas'. The Yule log would also be drawn to the fireplace on Christmas Eve. People were careful to retain some fragments of it for a year; among other things they warded off lightning.

For Fred Archer Christmas Day began at Ashton-under-Hill in the 1920s with singers coming round the village accompanied by the Tewkesbury fife and drum band, known as 'the tabber and tut [toot]' band. After just one carol, 'O come all ye faithful', they moved on.

At Bewdley on Christmas morning it was the custom to allow servants and apprentices to lie in bed while the mistress of the house got up to begin the work. The bellman (mentioned in a local rhyme quoted in chapter 1) went round the town to make known his request for a tip by singing:

> Arise, mistress, arise,
> And make your tarts and pies,
> And let you maids lie still;
> For if they should rise
> And spoil your pies
> You'd take it very ill.
> Whilst you are sleeping in your bed,
> I the cold wintry nights must tread.
> Past twelve o'clock. Ehe!

Then he called 'Good morning, masters and mistresses all. I wish you all a merry Christmas'. On Christmas Day the morris dancers or mummers (see chapter 8) might come round, or carol singers (see below). Boxing Day was once the time for shooting pigeons in Worcestershire. The same day at a farm between Hadzor and Oddingley was reserved for rabbiting. Ferrets flushed the holes; men with dogs and guns killed the rabbits. At midday the men ate home-cured bacon cooked on a fire of sticks, followed by mince pies and cheese, and drank cider. Fox hunters also favoured Boxing Day. In 2004, with legislation pending to outlaw hunting with dogs, a thousand people assembled at Pershore for the meet of the Croome and West Warwickshire Hunt, and a similar number supported the Clifton-on-Teme Hunt at Bromyard.

Carols Ancient and Modern

A collection of carols pre-dates John Alcock's time at Worcester, but was in his possession during his years as bishop, between 1476 and 1486. He later became joint Lord Chancellor of England, Master of the Rolls, and founder of Jesus College, Cambridge. He loved to have his rebus (a pictorial version of his name) wherever possible, and it is drawn on one of the carols, 'To the Virgin'.

The language of some of the carols is macaronic, a mixture of English and Latin, as in:

> Worshyp be the birth [child] of the[e],
> Quern portasti, Maria [Whom you bore, Maria],
> Both in boure and in cite [both in town and city];
> Ave domina [Hail, lady].

Or:

> A litil child ther is ibore,
> Ysprong owt of Jesse more [Jesse's stock]
> To save all us that were forlore;
> Gloria tibi, Domine [Glory to thee, O Lord].

Others are entirely in an English which is still largely comprehensible, over five hundred years later, especially when read aloud; for example, 'Good Day, Sir Christmas';

Godys Sone so moche of myght
From heven to erthe down is lyght
And borne ys of a mayde so bryght;
    Good day!

Heven and erthe and also helle,
And alle that ever in hem dwelle,
Of your comynge they beth ful snelle [glad];
    Good day!

Of your comynge this clerkys fynde:
Ye come to save al mankynde
And of here balys [troubles] hem unbynde:
    Good day!

Alle maner of merthes we wole make
And solas to oure hertys take,
My semely lorde, for your sake;
    Good day!

The carol may have been used in a ceremony during which a singer representing Christmas entered a hall during the festivities. Another, 'Speed the Plough', may have been intended for Plough Monday:

The mathe of alle this — lon — de Maketh the gode hys—
bon — de With er-ynge of — his plowe — :
[working]
I blessyd be Cris—tes son — de That hath — us
[message]
sent — in hon — de — Mathe and joye — y— nowe.

The plowe goth mony a gate,
Both erly and eke late,
   In wynter in the clay.

Aboute burly and whete,
That maketh men so swete,
   God spede the plowe al day!

Browne Morel [name of oxen] and gore [good]
Drawen the plowe ful sore
   Al in the morwenyne.

Ewarde hem therfore
With a shefe or more
   Alle in the evenyne.

Whan men bygynne to sowe,
Ful wel here come they knowe
   In the monnthe of May.

Howe ever Janyver blowe,
Whether hye or lowe,
   God spede the plowe allway!

Whan men bygynneth to wede
The thystle fro the sede,
   In somer whan they may:

God lete hem wel to spede
And longe gode lyfe to lede,
   All that for plowemen pray.

The opening verse has the ploughman singing at his work, but R.L. Greene suggests that the carol, together with others in the collection, would have been performed by choir-boys, specifically those of the Chapel of the Blessed Mary in the nave of Worcester Cathedral. On the other hand, some of the many singers of carols rewarded by Prior More (see chapter 7) may have been acquainted with the same repertoire.

The carols in the Worcester manuscript did not survive into modern oral tradition, but carol singing remained a perennial favourite. According to Jesse Salisbury singers went round from St Thomas's Day until Christmas; most continued until the New Year. At Christmas 1867 Cuthbert Bede heard children singing this, in an unnamed Worcestershire village:

> Here we come a-whistling, through the fields so green;
> Here we come a-singing, so far [?fair] to be seen.
>> God send you happy, God send you happy,
>> Pray God send you a happy New Year!
> The roads are very dirty, my boots are very thin,
> I have a little pocket to put a penny in.
>> God send you happy, &c.
> Bring out your little table and spread it with a cloth,
> Bring out some of your old ale, likewise your Christmas loaf
>> God send you happy, &c.
>> God bless the master of this house, likewise the mistress too;
> And all the little children that round the table strew.
>> God send you happy, &c
>
> The cock sat up in the yew tree,
> The hen came chuckling by,
> I wish you a merry Christmas,
> And a good fat pig in the stye.

It is possible that Bede misheard 'whistling' in the first verse for 'wassailing' (locally pronounced wazlin). The word clearly is 'wassailing' in the version recorded in 1974 by Gwilym and Carole Davies and Charles Menteith from 'Buster' Mustoe of Badsey. Inspired, perhaps, by seeing Bede's article in *Notes and Queries*, 'F.S.L.' wrote in on the subject of the 'religious ballads sung in the same way at Christmas', some 40 years earlier. 'Joseph was an old man' had been 'prohibited in the houses'—probably because it tells how Joseph declines to pick cherries for Mary and suggests that she ask the man that got her with child. (The composer, Ralph Vaughan Williams, took down a version from a Stourport singer called Davies in 1913.) 'Diverus and Lazarus', though, was known to 'every village child'; the writer quotes the full text from memory, 'As Sung by Carol-Singers at Christmas in Worcestershire, at Hagley and Hartlebury, 1829-1839':

SEASONS

As it fell out upon one day,
Rich Diverus he made a feast;
And he invited all his friends,
And gentry of the best.

And it fell out upon one day,
Poor Lazarus he was so poor,
He came and laid him down and down,
Ev'n down at Diverus' door.

So Lazarus laid him down and down,
Even down at Diverus' door;
'Some meat, some drink, brother Diverus,
Do bestow upon the poor'.

'Thou art none of mine, brother Lazarus,
Lying begging at my door;
No meat, no drink will I give thee,
Nor bestow upon the poor'.

Then Lazarus laid him down and down,
Even down at Diverus' wall:
'Some meat, some drink, brother Diverus,
Or surely starve I shall'.

'Thou art none of mine, brother Lazarus,
Lying begging at my wall;
No meat, no drink will I give thee,
And therefore starve thou shall'.

Then Lazarus laid him down and down,
Even down at Diverus' gate:
'Some meat, some drink, brother Diverus,
For Jesus Christ his sake'.

'Thou art none of mine, brother Lazarus,
Lying begging at my gate;
No meat, no drink will I give thee,
For Jesus Christ his sake'.

Then Diverus sent out his merry men all,
To whip poor Lazarus away;
They had not power to whip one whip,
But threw their whips away.

Then Diverus sent out his hungry dogs,
To bite poor Lazarus away;
They had not power to bite one bite,
But licked his sores away.

And it fell out upon one day,
Poor Lazarus he sickened and died;
There came two angels out of heaven,
His soul thereto to guide.

'Rise up, rise up, brother Lazarus,
And come along with me;
There is a place prepared in heaven,
For to sit upon an angel's knee'.

And it fell out upon one day,
Rich Diverus he sickened and died;
There came two serpents out of hell,
His soul thereto to guide.

'Rise up, rise up, brother Diverus,
And come along with me;
There is a place prepared in hell,
For to sit upon a serpent's knee'.

The contributor added: 'I once saw it (about 1833) on a hawker's broadsheet, but have never seen it since; and of late years the clergy have been discouraging carol-singing of this kind'. Even so, 'The Withy Carol' was reported from Evesham and Ashton-under-Hill, in the latter case in 1950. 'The Bewdley Carol', otherwise known as 'Genner's Anthem', and 'The Far Forest Carol' were noted as recently as the 1970s.

Large numbers of people remembered carol singers with affection. Fred Archer wrote in 1985 that his Uncle Jim walked all round Bredon Hill at Christmas time with his singing and melodeon and earned more 'than the squire paid him in a month'. In one village,

> There was a brass band and they always played carols at Christmas. The bandsmen were well-primed with home-made wine and plum-jerkum in particular, and on one occasion they played two carols outside what they thought was someone's cottage. It was only when they couldn't find the door that they realised the 'cottage' was a neatly thatched hay rick in a farmer's yard. It took them a long time to live that down.

The Inkberrow band, too, played in the village and visited outlying farms during the time between Christmas and the New Year when work was slack. They often included the tear-jerking 'Mistletoe Bough'. At each farm they were given money and treated to food and cider. They, too, fell into the error of playing at a hay rick—or perhaps this is just a local tale. Broadway band went round with carols at Christmas, 'mostly to the "posh" houses at the top of the village, where lived Madame de Navarro (Mary Andersen, the actress) and Lady Maud Bowes-Lyon'. Contributions seldom exceeded five shillings, 'even from the "toffs"'.

In 1995 a woman who had been a housemaid at Ombersley Court in the early years of the century still recalled Christmases with a warm glow:

> On Christmas Eve the vicar and choirboys from the village church came to sing carols. The staff collected in the gallery above to hear them. The vicar always gave an address afterwards. I remember one Christmas Eve as he was speaking he had to stop for breath for a moment. The parrot, whom everybody had forgotten, was in a cage nearby and suddenly shouted, 'Go on!' The choirboys were very much amused. They were always given hot drinks, cakes and oranges. Christmas Day was a wonderfully happy time there.

Bell ringers at Elmley Castle had their own carol:

> Now Christmas is come, let us honour the birth
> Of our great god of heaven and saviour on earth;
> With a peal of sweet bells we so joyfully ring
> All honour and praise to our heavenly king.
>
> We are Elmley ringers approached at your door.
> We'll handle our ropes and we'll ring you six score.
> Here's dodge, bob and single and likewise extreme,
> When the treble is leading the treble-man's name.
>
> Our eyes to the starting, our ears to the call,
> When the treble is leading then we must mind all.
> So I hope that our neighbours will not think it ill
> In asking one favour our bellies to fill.
>
> Here's mince pies and puddings and other fine cheer,
> For Christmas is still the best time of the year.
> Let's drink and be merry, cast sorrows away,
> Our saviour, Christ Jesus, was born on this day.

New Years' Eve

On New Year's Eve a farmer at Queenhill, near Upton-on-Severn, until the 1950s put out all his loose money on the grass in front of the house to bring him luck in the ensuing year. Farm workers in the county went into public houses to 'bury Old Tom'. There seems to be no full description of the proceedings in existence, but they involved a mock funeral followed by dancing, cider-drinking and singing. There were all kinds of songs, but this one was never missed out:

> We wish you a merry Christmas, a happy New Year,
> A pocket full of money and a cellar full of beer,
> And a good fat pig to serve you all the year.

In the closing minutes of the old year the Elmley ringers rang a muffled peal, followed as soon as midnight had struck, by a joyous peal. Then they joined friends in the village square to sing a carol which seems more appropriate to Christmas morning, yet remains traditional at Elmley at New Year:

> Behold the bounteous gift of heaven
> This day to all mankind is given;
> Oh, happy day, mankind rejoice
> And praise him with a cheerful voice.
>
> See our blessed saviour lay
> Within a manger filled with hay,
> While spotless innocence divine
> Did on his sacred temple shine.
>
> But now the great messiah reigns
> Where angels sing in heavenly strains,
> Where great Jehovah dwells on high
> Above the regions of the sky.

Bibliography

Abbreviations
FL: *Folklore*
FMJ: *Folk Music Journal*
nd: no date of publication shown
np: no place of publication shown
NQ: *Notes and Queries*
MS: manuscript
TBAS: *Transactions of Birmingham Archaeological Society*
TS: typescript
TWAS: *Transactions of the Worcestershire Archaeological Society*
TWNC: *Transactions of the Worcestershire Naturalists' Club*
WHC: Worcestershire History Centre
WWL: *Warwickshire and Worcestershire Life*
WWM: *Warwickshire and Worcestershire Magazine*
WRO: Worcestershire Record Office
Books are published in London unless otherwise stated.

Adlam, Brian *The Worcester Visitor* Buckingham, 1983
Allies, Jabez *On the Ancient British, Roman, and Saxon Antiquities and Folk-lore of Worcestershire* London and Worcester, 1852
Amphlett, Dorothy 'Worcestershire Folklore', in F.B. Andrews, *Memorials of Old Worcestershire*, 1911
Amphlett, John (transcr. and ed.) *The Churchwardens' Accounts of St Michael's in Bedwardine, Worcester, from 1539-1603*, Worcester, 1896
    A Short History of Clent, 1890
Anderton, Thomas *Letters from a Country House* [Hagley Hall], 1891
Andrews, Janet, *et al. Wichenford Village Record 2000*, Wichenford, 2000
Anon. *The Story of an Old English Hostelry* [The Lygon Arms], Broadway, 1914
Archer, Fred *Farmer's Son. A Cotswold Childhood in the 1920s,* 1984
    The Secrets of Bredon Hill, 1971
    The Tibblestone Hundred. Journey through an English Village, Stroud, 1996
    'Fred Archer recalls Christmas', WWL, 32:10 (Dec. 1985), 63
Atkin, Malcolm *The Civil War in Worcestershire,* Stroud, 1995
Avery, William *Old Redditch*, Redditch, 1999 (orig. 1887)
Baines, C.C. 'Children born with a caul', FL 61 (1950), 104
Baker, Charles H. 'Church Ales', *The Three Pears Magazine*, no. 4 (1929), 13
Baker, Eric C.M. *Claines and its History*, [Claines, *c*.1963]
Barnard, E.A.B. (transc.) *Churchwardens' Accounts of the Parish of South Littleton, Worcestershire, 1548-71*, np, nd (copy in WHC)
    (ed.) *Notes & Queries Concerning Evesham and the Four Shires*, Evesham, 3 vols, 1911-14
    The Tower and Bells of Evesham, Evesham, 1910
Barrand, A.G. (ed.) 'Morris at Malvern', in *Roy Dommett's Morris Notes,* vol.5, New York, 1986
Baxter, Richard *Reliquae Baxterianae*, 1696
Beable, W.H. *Epitaphs: Graveyard Humour and Eulogy,* 1925
Beach, A.J. and E.M. *The Story of Wichenford*, np, [*c*.1980]
Bede, Cuthbert [Edward Bradley] 'Anecdote of the Battle of Worcester', NQ, 10 (1854), 259-60
    'Modern Mumming', NQ 2 ser., 40 (1861), 271-2

'Proverbial Sayings', NQ, 2 ser. 1 (1856), 429

'Two unpublished Christmas Carols', NQ, 4 ser., 2 (1868), 551-2

'A Worcestershire Legend in Stone', NQ, 6 (1852), 216-7

Berington, William J.C. *Little Malvern Court, Worcestershire*, Malvern Wells, 1948

Berkeley, Mildred 'The Ferries of Worcestershire', TWAS, n.s., 8 (1932), 74-88

'The Romany in Worcestershire', TWAS, n.s. 13 (1937), 11-14

'Some Local Superstitions', *Reports and Papers of the Associated Architectural Societies*, 36:1 (1921),103-116

with C.E. Jenkins *A Worcestershire Book*, Worcester, 1932

Bethel, Hal 'Kinver's sand-castles', *Countryman*, 94, no.3 (1989), 69-73

Bird, Vivian 'One Man's Alvechurch', WWL 30:10 (Dec. 1983), 46-7 and 49

Blake, J.E.H. 'Bretforton', TWNC 7 (1920), 221-7

'Gravestones in Midland Churchyards', TBAS 51(1925-6)

Bond, Winifred L. *From Hamlet to Parish. The Story of Dodford, Worcestershire*, Dodford, 1972

Bradford, Anne *Stourport-on-Severn. A History of the Town and Local Villages*, ed. M.R. Kettle, Redditch, 2002

Bradley, A.G. *The Avon and Shakespeare's Country*, 1910

Worcestershire, 1909

Bradley-Birt, B. *A Worcestershire Anthology*, Kidderminster, 1934

Brassington, W. Salt *Historic Worcestershire*, Birmingham, Leicester, Leamington and London, nd [1894]

Bridges, Tim *Churches of Worcestershire*, Logaston, 2000 (repr. 2005)

Briggs, Katharine M. *A Dictionary of British Folk-tales,* 4 vols, 1970-1

Bradfield, E. *A Guide to Kidderminster*, Kidderminster, 1889

Bromsgrove Notes & Queries, vol.5, Bromsgrove, 1913-15

Brown, Raymond Lamont 'Graveyard Wit and Humour', WWL 13:1 (Mar. 1976), 56-7

'Harry Bentham's Ghost Journal', WWL 12:5 (Jul. 1975), 44-5

'A Supernatural Miscellany', WWL 27:10 (Dec. 1980), 38-9

'The Unexpected Spectres', WWL 14:10 (Dec. 1977), 46-7

Burne, Charlotte S. 'Souling, Clementing, and Catterning. Three November Customs in the Western Midlands', FL, 25 (1914),285-99

Burritt, Elihu *Walks in the Black Country and its Green Borderland*, Kineton, 1976 (orig. London, 1868)

Burton, J.R. 'Early Worcestershire Printers and Books', *Reports and papers of the Worcester Diocesan Architectural and Archaeological Society*, 24:1 (1897-8), 197-213

A History of Bewdley, 1883

A History of Kidderminster, 1890

Bushaway, Bob *By Rite. Custom, Ceremony and Community in England, 1700-1880*, 1982

Byford-Jones: see Quaestor

Canvey, Mollie *Reminiscences of Lower Moor*, np, 1972

Cash, J. Allan *Shakespeare's Avon*, 1949

Cave, E.L. 'The Burning of the Bush', *Transactions of the Woolhope Naturalists' Field Club* (1898), 5-8

Cawte, E.C. 'The Morris Dance in Herefordshire, Shropshire and Worcestershire', *Journal of the English Folk Dance and Song Society*, 9:4 (Dec. 1963), 197-212

Helm, Alex, and Peacock, N. *English Ritual Drama. A Geographical Index*, 1967

'C.B.' 'Mistletoe Superstition', 'New Year's Superstitions' and 'Spring Flowers' Folk Lore', NQ, 2 ser., 3 (1857), 343

Chafy, W.K.W. *A Short History of Rous Lench*, Evesham, 1901

The City of Worcester Official Guide, Worcester, 1964

Clay, W.K. (ed.) *Four Folk Songs from Hartlebury, Worcestershire,* Kidderminster, nd [?1900]

Conway-Jones, Hugh (comp.) *Working Life on Severn and Canal*, Stroud, 1990

Coombes, E.D. *The Parish Church of St Leonard, Beoley* [?Beoley], 1972 (2nd ed.)

Cooper, Audrey *George Nicholson: Printer at Stourport*, Stourport, 2001

Cooper, Margaret 'The Worcester Book Trade in the Eighteenth Century', *Worcester Historical Society Occasional Publication*, no.8, Worcester, 1997

Cooper, W. Sterry *Droitwich Mediaeval and Modern; with the Life of St Richard of Droitwich*, Droitwich, nd

Corbett, Edward F. [see also under Stroller] 'Some Notes of the Folklore of Worcestershire', TWNC, 5:2 (1912), 348-62
'Some Worcestershire Fairy Tales', TWAS, 2 (1943-5), 22-29

Cotton, John 'Local Folk-words, Expressions and Modes of Speech', *Notes and Queries for Bromgrove*, 5 (1913-15), 21-99

Cotton, W.A, *The Antiquities of Bromsgrove*, Bromsgrove, 1879
Bromsgrove Church: Its History and Antiquities, London and Bromsgrove, nd

Cox, Benjamin G. *Short History of the Parish of Offenham*, np, 1953

Cox, J. Charles *Churchwardens' Accounts*, 1913

Coxe, D.C. *Evesham Abbey and the Parish Churches*, Evesham, 1980
'Worcestershire', in C.R.J. Currie and C.P. Lewis, *English County Histories. A Guide*, Stroud 1994

Craze, William *Whittington. The History of the Village*, Whittington, [1977]

Darton, F.J. Harvey *The Life and Times of Mrs Sherwood (1775-1851)*, nd

Dauglish, Gertrude (ed.) *This Was My Village*, Worcester, 1950

Davenport, James *The Washbourne Family of Little Washbourne and Wichenford*, 1907

Davies, Gwilym 'Percy Grainger's Folk Music Research in Gloucestershire, Worcestershire and Warwickshire, 1907-1909', FMJ 6:3 (1992), 339-358

Davies, James 'Old Herefordshire Customs', *Transactions of the Woolhope Naturalists' Field Club* (1877-80), 22-30

Davies, Owen *Witchcraft, Magic and Culture, 1736-1951*, Manchester, 1999

Davies, Pat, and Sage, Lorna (comp.) *Alvechurch Past and Present* [?Alvechurch], 2002

Davies, R.R. *The Revolt of Owain Glyn Dwr*, Oxford, 1997 (orig. 1995)

Dayus, Kathleen *Her People* (1982)

Defoe, Daniel *A Tour through the Whole Island of Great Britain*, Harmondsworth, 1971; orig. London, 1724-26

Dick, Alastair Innes 'The Old House' [at Alvechurch], WWL 23:10 (Dec. 1976), 62-3

Dickins, Margaret *A Thousand Years in Tardebigge*, Birmingham, 1931

Doel, Fran and Geoff *The Green Man in Britain*, Stroud, 2001

Drake, Daphne *The Story of Malvern Link*, Malvern, 1989

Drayton, Michael *Poly-Olbion*, vol.4 of *The Works of Michael Drayton*, ed. J. William Heber, Oxford, 1933 (orig. pt 1, 1613; pt 2, 1622)

Dyer, Ian D. *The City of Worcester in the Sixteenth Century*, Leicester, 1973

Eaton, John *A Lad from Elmley,* Elmley Castle, 1997

Edminson, Vera L. *Ancient Misericords in the Priory Church, Great Malvern*, Worcester, nd

Edwards, Tudor 'A Thousand Years of Worcester cathedral', WWM 9:7 (Sept. 1962), 36-41

Elliott, Jannion S. *Concerning the Manor House, Dowles*, Dudley, nd [?1918]

English, Wilfrid Elliott *Alvechurch. 1200 Years of History*, Worcester, 1997

Evans, Tunstall *The History of Tenbury*, London and Tenbury, 1840

Farmer, David Hugh *The Oxford Dictionary of Saints*, Oxford, 1987 (2nd ed.)

Faulkner, Christine *Hops and Hop-pickers*, Brierley Hill, nd

Fegan, Ethel S. (ed.) *Journal of Prior William More*, Worcester, 1914

Field, John *English Field Names*, Stroud, 1989

Fleming, Joan *Shakespeare's Country*, 1960

Fletcher, W. *Eckington. The Story of a Parish*, 1933

Folk-Lore 'Worcestershire Folklore', *The Three Pears Magazine*, no. 4 (1929), 6-9

Fox, Adam *Oral and Literate Culture in England 1500-1700*, Oxford, 2000

Foxall, W. *Old Redditch Pubs*, Redditch, 2002

Fraser, Antonia *The Gunpowder Plot*, 2002 (orig. 1996)

Fraser, Maxwell *Companion into Worcestershire,* 1939

Friar, Stephen *A Companion to the English Parish Church*, Stroud, 1996

G., H.S, 'Worcestershire Badge', NQ 2 ser., 10 (1860), 127

Gardiner, Charles 'Dialect in a changing countryside', WWM 2:12 (Jan. 1956), 405-6
> 'Evesham Custom', *Countryman*, 37:2 (1948), 279-80

Garrett, John Henry *The Idyllic Avon*, New York and London, 1906

Gaunt, Peter *The Cromwellian Gazetteer*, Gloucester, 1987

Gaut, R.C. *Worcestershire Agriculture*, Worcester, 1939

Gissing, Algernon *Broadway. A Village of Middle England*, 1904
> *The Footpath Way in Gloucestershire*, 1924

Godden, William 'The old Bengeworth Nailmakers', *Evesham Journal* (30 Nov. 1912)

Gould, Mark 'Ghosts of sisters past', *Guardian 2* (22 Nov. 2004), 18-19

Grant, Jeremy Campbell *St Peter's School, Martley: A History*, Malvern, 2000

Grant-Adamson, D.P. 'Pershore Fair', WWM 1:3 (1952), 70

Gray, Edward F. 'Old Ripple', TWAS 13 (1937), 50-64
> and Diana *Ripple in the Past*, np, nd (copy in Malvern Library)

Green, Andrew 'Spectral Spectrum'', WWL 12:10 (Dec. 1975), 48-9

Green, Valentine *An Account of the Discovery of the Body of King John*, London and
> Worcester, 1797
> *The History and Antiquities of the City and Suburbs of Worcester*, 2 vols, 1796
> *A Survey of the City of Worcester*, Worcester, 1754

Greene, Richard Leighton *The Early English Carols*, Oxford, 1977 (2nd ed.; orig. 1935)

Grice, Frederick *Folk Tales of the West Midlands*, 1952

Griffith, George *Reminiscences and Records during Ten Years' Residence in the Midland
> Counties*, Bewdley and Madeley, 1880

Grigson, Geoffrey *The Englishman's Flora*, St Albans, 1975 (orig. London, 1958)

Grindrod, Charles F. *The Shadow of the Raggedstone*, 1888

Gwilliam, H.W. (Bill) *Old Worcester. People and Places*, Bromsgrove, 1993 (orig. Worcester,
> 1977)
> *Severn Ferries and Fords in Worcestershire*, np, 1982
> *Worcestershire's Hidden Past*, Bromsgrove, 1991
> 'A Gazetteer of Old Public Houses and Inns in Worcestershire', photocopy of TS in
> WHC
> 'Old Worcestershire Inns and Taverns', photocopy of TS in WHC

Habington, Thomas *A Survey of Worcestershire*, 1606-47, ed. John Amphlett, Oxford, 2 vols,
> 1895-9

Hall, John 'One Way to Independence', *Countryman*, 36:2 (1947), 296-7

Hamand, L.A. *The Ancient Windows of Great Malvern Priory Church*, St Albans, 1947
> *Malvern Priory Church*, St Albans, 1928

Hancock, C.V. *East and West of Severn*, 1956

Harris, David R. *A Short History of St Bartholomew's Church, Tardebigge*, np, 1977

Havins, Peter J. Neville 'The Daily Grind' [needlemaking], WWL 36:7 (Sept. 1989), 83
> *Portrait of Worcestershire*, 1974

Haynes, Clive R. *Worcester within the Walls*, Worcester, 1996

Hazlitt, W.C. *Dictionary of Faiths and Folklore,* 1905

Hickin, Norman E. *The Natural History of an English Forest. The Wild Life of Wyre*,

Shrewsbury, 1978

Hodges, Geoffrey *Owain Glyn Dwr and the War of Independence on the Welsh Borders*, Logaston, 1995

Hoggard, Brian *Bredon Hill*, Logaston, 1999

Hole, Christina *British Folk Customs*, 1976

    Witchcraft in England, 1977

Holloway, John (ed.) *The Oxford Book of Local Verses*, Oxford, 1987

Hone, William (ed.) *The Every-day Book and Table Book*, 3 vols, 1826-38

Hopkinson, Beatrice 'Huddington Court - an historic association with November 5th', WWM 2:10 (1955)

Humphreys, John *The Wyntours of Huddington and the Gunpowder Plot*, Birmingham, 1905

Hunt, Robert, and Jackson, Ruth *The Inkberrow Book*, Inkberrow, 1974

    Inkberrow Folk and Farms, Inkberrow, [1978]

    Inkberrow Ways, Inkberrow, [1982]

    More about Inkberrow, Inkberrow, 1976

Hurle, Pamela *Hanley Castle ... Heart of Malvern Chase*, London and Chichester, 1978

    Malvern Chase, Malvern, 2002 (4th ed.)

    Upton. Portrait of a Severnside Town, Chichester, 1988 (2nd ed.)

Husk, H. 'The Bells of St Helen's Church, Worcester', NQ 3 ser. 8 (1865), 204-5

Huskinson, A. 'Kellums or the Lawless Hour', *Worcestershire Countryside* 1:8 (1948), 201

Hutton, Ronald *The Rise and Fall of Merry England. The Ritual Year 1400-1700*, Oxford, 1994

    The Stations of the Sun. A History of the Ritual Year in Britain, Oxford, 1996

Jeffery, F. Ronald 'Gleanings from the Diary of a Bewdley Naturalist' [George Jorden], TWNC 7 (1921), 294-308

Johnson, Andrew, and Punter, Stephen *Aspects of Worcestershire,* Logaston, 1989

Jones, Dave *The Roots of Welsh Border Morris,* Putley, 1995 (orig. 1988)

Jones, Lavender *Contented with the Time*, Hanley Swan, 1992

    Customs and Folklore of Worcestershire, 1970

    'Folklore Notes, mainly Worcestershire', MS (*c.*1940-1970s) in my possession

    ''Oppickin', WWL 13:7 (Sept. 1976), 73

    'Some Worcestershire Calendar Customs', FL 72 (1961), 320-2

Jones, Mary Munslow *The Lookers-out of Worcestershire. Memoir of Edwin Lees*, Worcester, 1980

Jones, Maud *An Arley Childhood,* np, nd

Jorden, George 'Bewdley', MS formerly in Worcester City Library/Museum but now lost; photocopy in Kidderminster Library

Joyce, F. Wayland *Tenbury. Some Record of its History*, Oxford, 1931

Judge, Roy *The Jack-in-the-Green. A May Day Custom*, Cambridge, 1979

Kempsey Collection, Kempsey, 1984

Kidd, Joan *Through Time*, np, [1988]

Kings, B.U., and Cooper, Margaret *Glory Gone. The Story of Nailing in Bromsgrove*, Bromsgrove, 1989

Kissack, Keith *The River Severn*, Lavenham, 1982

Klausner, D. *Records of Early English Drama: Herefordshire, Worcestershire*, Toronto, 1990

Knight, E.M. (comp.) *The West Malvern Book, c.1959*, Malvern, 2001

Knight, Sidney E. (Sid) 'The Barnstormers', *Countryman*, 39:2 (1939), 319

    Cotswold Lad, 1960

L., F.S. 'A Worcestershire Carol' ['Diverus and Lazarus']. NQ 4 ser., 3 (1869),75-6

Ladbury, E.J. 'Worcestershire Superstitions', FL 6 (1895), 305

    and Burne, Charlotte S. 'Scraps of English Folklore, II. Worcestershire', FL 20

(1909), 342-9

Lane, B.A. *Severn Tanking*, Coleford, 1991

La Touche, J.D. *William J. Symonds, Rector of Pendock: a Sketch of his Life*, Gloucester, [1914]

Lawley, Gill *'Of the Parish Here and There'. The History of Martin Hussingtree*, Fernhill Heath, 2000

Lawson, Emily M. *The Nation in the Parish, or, Records of Upton-on-Severn*, 1884 (orig. 1869)

Lawson, Robert *Upton-on-Severn Words and Phrases*, 1884

Leadbetter, William G. *The Story of Bromsgrove*, Bromsgrove, [?1944]

Leatherbarrow, J.S. *Churchwardens' Presentments in the Diocese of Worcester, c.1660-1760*, Worcester, 1977

   Worcestershire, 1974

Lees, Edwin *The Forest and Chace of Malvern*, Worcester, 1877

   'The History and Folklore of the Apple and Pear', TWNC (1897), 264-70

   'The Oddingley Murders', *Worcestershire Miscellany*, no.5 (Mar. 1830), 181-216

   Pictures of Nature in the Silurian Region around the Malvern Hills and Vale of Severn, Malvern, 1856

   Scenery and Thought in Poetical Pictures of Various Landscape Scenes and Incidents, 1880

   (ed.) *A Worcestershire Miscellany*, Worcester, 1831

Leicester, Hubert A. *Forgotten Worcester*, Worcester, 1930

   Worcester Remembered, Worcester, 1935

Lewis, John *Three into One: The Three Counties Agricultural Society, 1797-1997*, [?Malvern], 1996

Lines, Charles 'A ghostly Tale or two', WWL 20:10 (Dec. 1973), 62-3

Little, Bryan 'Oak Apple Maying', WWM 2:2 (1954), 46

Lloyd, R.H. *Bredon Hill and its Villages*, Oxford, 1968 (3rd ed.)

Lones, T.E. 'Worcestershire Folklore', FL 25 (1914), 370; and FL 36 (1925), 85-93

Luty, John *Needle Making and the Forge Mill*, Redditch, 1981

M., H. 'Custom at Kidderminster', in Hone (see above), vol. 1, cols 1343-4

Marsh, Jean [pseud. for Evelyn Marshall] *Bewdley, a 15th Century Sanctuary Town*, Stourbridge, 1979

Massingham, H.J. *Shepherd's Country*, 1938

Matthews, William (ed.) *Charles II's Escape from Worcester*, Berkeley and Los Angeles, 1966

Mawer, A., Stenton, F.M., and Houghton, F.T.S. *The Place-names of Worcestershire*, Cambridge, 1927

May, George *A Descriptive History of the Town of Evesham*, Evesham, 1845

   The History of Evesham, Evesham, 1834

McCormick, Donald *Murder by Witchcraft. A Study of the Lower Quinton and Hagley Wood Murders*, 1968

McKay, James *The British Camp or Herefordshire Beacon*, Malvern, 1875

Mee, Arthur *Worcestershire*, 1938

Menefee, S.P. *Wives for Sale*, Oxford, 1981

Mocquereau, André *Antiphonaire Monastique de Worcester*, Tournai, 1922

Morgan, F.C. 'Misericords of Malvern, Ripple and Stratford-upon-Avon', TWNC 7 (1921), 330-4

Morsley, Clifford *News from the English Countryside, 1851-1950*, 1983

Mytton-Davies 'The Church in the Farmyard [Warndon]', *Worcestershire Magazine* 1:6 (Sept. 1964), 12-13

Nash, T. *Collections for the History of Worcestershire*, 2 vols, 1781

Negus, Tina 'Medieval Foliate Heads: A Photographic Study of Green Men and Green Beasts in Britain', FL 114 (2003), 245-70

Noake, John *Guide to Worcestershire*, 1868
    The Monastery and Cathedral of Worcester, London and Worcester, 1866
    Notes and Queries for Worcestershire, 1856
    The Rambler in Worcestershire, or, Stray Notes on Churches and Congregations vol. 1: Worcester, [1848]; vol.2: London, 1851; one-vol. edition, 1854
    'Superstitions of Worcestershire', *Gentleman's Magazine* 44, pt 2 (1855), 58-9 and 384-6
    Worcester in Olden Times, 1849
    'A Worcestershire Legend in Stone', NQ 2 ser. 6 (1852), 288-9
    Worcestershire Nuggets, 1889
    Worcestershire Relics, 1877
Noake, M.V. 'May Day at Hallow', *Worcestershire Countryside* 1 (1951), 197-8
Northall, G.F. *English Folk-rhymes*, 1892
Norton, John 'Mamble', WWL 29:4 (Jun. 1982), 38-9
Norton & Lenchwick The last one hundred years, ed. John Middleton, Norton, 2001
Nott, James *Malvern Priory Church*, Malvern, nd
    Some of the Antiquities of 'Moche Malverne', Malvern, 1885
Ollard Richard *The Escape of Charles II after the Battle of Worcester*, 1966
Opie, Iona and Peter *The Lore and Language of Schoolchildren*, Frogmore, 1977 (orig. Oxford, 1959)
Opie, Iona, and Tatem, Moira (eds) *A Dictionary of Superstitions*, Oxford, 1989
Osborne, Geoffrey *Going Gee-oh in Grafton Flyford*, np, 1996
Osborne, Bruce, and Weaver, Cora *Springs, Spouts, Fountains and Holy Wells of the Malvern Hills*, Malvern, 2001 (3rd ed.)
Packer, T.J. *Round Bredon Hill*, Cheltenham, 1902
Palfrey, H.E. 'Foleys of Stourbridge', TWAS n.s., 21 (1945), 11-15
Palmer, Roy *Britain's Living Folklore*, Felinfach, 1995 (orig. Newton Abbot, 1991)
    'Brother of the More famous George' [Algernon Gissing], *Cotswold Review* (May-June 2005), 15
    The Folklore of Hereford and Worcester, Logaston, 1992
    Folklore of Warwickshire, Stroud, 2004 (orig. London, 1976)
    'The Funny Rigs of Good and Tender-hearted Masters in the happy Town of Kidderminster. Anno 1828', TWAS 3 ser. 3 (1970-2),105-113
    Herefordshire Folklore, Logaston, 2002
    'Lavender Jones' [obituary], *Guardian* (2 May 1997), 19
    with Pam Bishop (eds) *Songs of the Midlands,* East Ardsley, 1972
    'Your dancing is simply glorious' [Lavender Jones], *English Dance and Song* 51:1 (Apr. May 1989), 2-3
Parker, Mrs J.F. 'Old Bewdley and its Industries', TWAS n.s. 9 (1933), 1-20
    'Some old Bewdley Recollections', TWAS ns 21 (1945), 16-21
Partridge, J.B.: see under Stanton, M.L.
Paton, Augusta 'The Whitty Pear', *Countryman* 62:2 (1965), 351-3
Peel, J.H.B. *Portrait of the Severn*, 1980 (orig. 1968)
Pevsner, Nikolaus *The Buildings of England. Worcestershire*, Harmondsworth, 1968
Pitt, W. *General View of the Agriculture of the County of Worcester*, 1813
Poulton-Smith, Anthony *Worcestershire Place-names*, Stroud, 2003
Price, F.C. 'The Oddingley Murders', WWL 21:5 (Jul. 1974), 40-1
Price, W.H. (transcr.), and Barnard, E.A.B. (ed.) *Churchwardens' Accounts of the Parish of Badsey*, Hampstead, 1913
Pugh, A.H. 'Recollections of a Forgotten Man' [George Griffith], WWM 4:10 (1957), 414-5
Purton, R.C. 'Collection for a History of Kempsey', MS of 1899 in Worcester Cathedral Library, Add. MSS 27

Quaestor [W. Byford Jones] *Both Sides of the Severn,* Birmingham, nd

Randall, John *The Severn Valley: A Series of Sketches, Descriptive and Pictorial, of the Course of the Severn*, London and Madeley, 1882

Rastall, Richard *The Heaven Singing. Music in Early English Religious Drama*, Cambridge, 1999 (orig. 1996)

Redgrave, Sam *Here lyeth the Body. A Look at Worcestershire Churchyards*, Bromsgrove, 1992

Reiss, F.A. *The History of Rock*, 1904

Richardson, John *The Local Historian's Encyclopedia*, New Barnet, 1974

Richardson, L. *The River Severn between Upper Arley and Gloucester*, Worcester, 1964

Roberts, H. 'Worcestershire Proverbs and Rhymes', *Worcestershire Countryside* 1:8 (1948), 207

Roberts, Michael '"Waiting upon Chance": English Hiring Fairs and their Meanings from the 14th to the 20th Century', *Journal of Historical Sociology* 1:2 (1988), 120-160

Roberts, Stephen K. 'Oliver Cromwell and the City of Worcester', TWAS 3 ser. 16 (1998), 169-175

Rollins, John G. *A History of Redditch*, Chichester, 1984

Rolt, L.T.C. *Worcestershire*, 1949

Roud, Steve *The Penguin Guide to the Superstitions of Britain and Ireland*, 2003

Rouse, W.H.D. 'Tokens of Death', FL 4 (1893), 258

S., E.L. 'Sir Edward Mason: The Worcester of 80 Years Ago', NQ 3 ser. 6 (1864), 254-5

Salisbury, Jesse *A Glossary of Words and Phrases used in S E. Worcestershire*, 1893

Salter, Mike *The Castles of Herefordshire and Worcestershire*, Wolverhampton, 1989

Samuel, Raphael *Miners, Quarrymen and Saltworkers*, 1977

Sanders, Thomas *Perspective Views of the Market Towns within the County of Worcester*, Worcester, [1779]

Sandys, William *Christmastide: its History, Festivities and Carols* [1852]

Savory, Arthur H. *Grain and Chaff from an English Manor* [Aldington], Oxford, 1920

Seaman, R.D.H., and Sparrow, T.C. *A Brief History of Badsey and Aldington,* Badsey, 1983 (2nd ed. By Sparrow alone: Badsey, 2002)

Self, Geoffrey *Julius Harrison and the Importunate Muse*, Aldershot, 1993

Selitis 'St Clement', in Hone (see above), vol.2, cols 1576-7

Sharp, Cecil *Cecil Sharp's Collection of English Folk Songs*, ed. Maud Karpeles 2 vols, 1974

Shawcross, H. *Historical Memories of Bretforton*, Evesham, 1890

Shawcross, J.P., and Barnard, E.A.B. *Bengeworth*, 1927

Sherard, Robert H. 'The White Slaves of England. II, The Nailmakers of Bromsgrove', *Pearson's Magazine* (1896), 167-173
   The White Slaves of England, 1897

Sherwood, Mary Martha *Life*, ed. Sophia Kelly 1862

Simpson, Jacqueline, and Roud, Steve *A Dictionary of English Folklore*, Oxford, 2000

Sinker, Edmund *Salwarpe*, Worcester, 1918

Simon, Joan 'The Winters of Huddington', WWL 17:9 (Nov. 1970), 36-7

Smith, A.C. 'Ghosts' [in Bredon Hill area], TS of 1932 in WRO, ref. 899:38BA3624

Smith, Brian S. *A History of Malvern*, Leicester, 1964

Smith, L.D. *The Carpet Weaver's Lament. Songs and Ballads of Kidderminster in the Industrial Revolution*, Kidderminster, 1979
   Carpet Weavers and Carpet Masters. The Hand Loom Carpet Weavers of Kidderminster, 1780-1850, Kidderminster, 1986

Snow, W.G. Sinclair *The Story of Elmley Castle Church,* Elmley Castle, nd

Southall Mary *Description of Malvern*, Stourport, 1822

Spackman, F.T. 'Some ancient flint instruments recently obtained from the county' TWNC 4 (1911), 2-11

Spicer, Tony *The Battle of Worcester, 1651*, Manchester, 2000

Stainer, John, *et al.* (ed.) *Sacred and Secular Songs: Early Bodleian Music*, 2 vols, 1901

Stanton, G.K. *Rambles and Researches among Worcestershire Churches*, 2 vols, London and Birmingham, 1884 and 1886

Stanton, M.L., and Partridge, J.B. 'Worcestershire Folklore', FL 26 (115), 94-7

Sanwa, Mary L. 'The Black Dog of Arden and other stories of Midland Ghosts and Phantoms', WWM 2:4 (1954-5), 107

Statham, Gillian 'Teme Spirit', WWL 12:7 Sept. 1975), 48-51

Stevens, Douglas 'The Cider Makers of Dodderhill Common', WWM 5:11 (1958), 404-5

Stroller, A [Edward F. Corbett] *Chaddesley Corbett*, Worcester, 1932
    Articles from the *Worcester Herald* and *Berrow's Worcester Journal*, 4 vols, photocopies in WHC

Symonds, WS. *Malvern Chase*, 1881

Tate, W.E. *The Parish Chest*, 1969 (orig. 1946)

Taylor, Antoinette 'An English Christmas Play' [from Broadway], *Journal of American Folklore* 22:86 (1909), 389-393

Taylor, Joan *Mary Martha* [Sherwood] *of Stanford*, np, 1975

Taylor, Walter H. 'The Nail Shop. Memories of Halesowen', *Black Country Bugle* (14 Feb. 1978)

Thomas, Keith *Religion and the Decline of Magic*, Harmondsworth, 1973 (orig. London, 1971)

Thomas, Sean 'What's happened to weird?' *Guardian 2* (14 Jun. 2004), 6-7

Thompson, E.P. *Customs in Common*, 1991

Thompson, Robert D. *Rock*, Kidderminster, 1981

Thompson, W.H. 'A Worcestershire Trilogy' TS of 1989 in WHC

Tiddy, R.J.E. *The Mummers' Play*, Oxford, 1923

Timings, William *A Guide to the Clent Hills*, Halesowen, 1835
    The History and Antiquities of Saint Kenelm's, Stourbridge, 1839

Tindal, William *The History and Antiquities of the Abbey and Borough of Evesham*, Evesham, 1794

Tomlinson, Jane *Upton Snodsbury. Some Village Reflections*, np, nd

Totten, Eileen 'The Cave Dwellers of Wolverley', WWL 20:7 (Sept. 1973), 74-5

Townsend, Henry *The Diary of Henry Townsend of Elmley Lovett, 1640-1663*, ed. J. W. Willis Bund, Worcester, 2 vols, 1920

Tree, W.W.A. 'Some old Worcestershire Customs', TWNC 5:2 (1912), 203-223

The Trial of Thomas Clewes, Farmer, charged with the Murder of Richard Heming, at Oddingley, Worcestershire, Worcester, 1830

Turberville, T.C. *Worcestershire in the Nineteenth Century*, 1852

Tyack, George S. *Lore and Legend of the English Church*, 1899

Underdown, David *Revel, Riot and Rebellion*, Oxford, 1985

Vaux, J. Edward *Church Folklore*, 1894

Vickery, Roy *A Dictionary of Plant Lore*, Oxford, 1995

Vigorn 'May Day in Worcestershire', NQ 6 ser., 1 (1880), 282

Vintner, Dorothy *Village Life in Stockton-on-Teme*, np, 1970

Warde, R.C. 'The Worcestershire Legends: The Devil's Spadeful. Legend of King Keder', NQ 2 ser., 6 (1858), 521

Waite, Vincent *Malvern Country*, 1968

Walker, R.O. (comp. and ed.) *Hartlebury: a Record of a Parish*, Hartlebury, 1987
    The Parish of Shrawley, Shrawley, 1982

Walters, H.B. 'The Church Bells of Worcestershire', TWAS n.s. 2 (1925), 1-58; 3 (1927), 11-59; 4 (1928), 148; 5 (1929), 110-147; 6 (1930), 1-67; 7 (1931), 140; 8 (1932), 1-38; 9 (1933), 30

Waters, Brian *Severn Stream*, 1949

Watkin, Ann 'Feckenham in Focus', WWL 33:8 (ct. 1986), 22-7

Watson, Kenrick *Parish of Hartlebury (Statistical and General History of Worcestershire, Fasciculus II)*, np, [?1840]

Weaver, Cora 'Shocking Murders in Malvern Chase', pp. 50-53 in *Malvern Writers' Circle - 50 Years,* Malvern, 1989

Wedley, I.L. *Bewdley and its Surroundings*, Kidderminster, 1914
    Kidderminster and its Borderland, Kidderminster, 1936

Westwood, Jennifer *Albion. A Guide to Legendary Britain*, 1987 (orig. 1985)

Whitehead, David *The Book of Worcester*, Chesham, 1976

Whitley, W.T. *The Story of Droitwich*, Droitwich, 1923

Williams, Alan, and Day, Leonard G. *The Nailmakers of Northfield,* Birmingham, nd

Willis Bund, J. W. (ed.) *Calendar of the Quarter Sessions Papers, 1561-1643*,
        Worcester, 2 vols, 1900
    'The Legendary History of Worcestershire', *Reports and Papers of the Associated Architectural Societies*, 31:2 (1912), 585-612
    'Legends of the Severn', TBAS 43 (1917), 87-107
    'The Siege of Worcester', TWNC 6 (1918), 294-313

Wilson, Robert N. *Beautiful Britain. Worcestershire*, Bristol, [1923]

Wiltshire, Les *Whittington, Worcestershire. A History of the Village*, Whittington, [2000]

Windsor, John 'The little church with the long history' [Little Malvern], WWL 29:5 (July 1982), 24-5

Wood, John *Quiestest under the Sun. Footways on the Severnside Hills*, 1944

Woodley, W.J. 'Some Worcestershire Epitaphs', *The Three Pears Magazine* no.6 (1931), 19-22
    'Worcestershire Bells', *The Three Pears Magazine*, no.4 (1929), 5-6

Woolrych, Austin *Britain in Revolution, 1625-1660*, Oxford, (2002)

Worcestershire Lady, A 'Traditions and Superstitions of old Court and Manor   Houses in this County', nos. 7 and 8, *Worcester Herald* (20 and 27 Feb. 1892)

Worcestershire within Living Memory, Newbury and Worcester, (1995)

Wright, A.R., and Lones, T.E. *British Calendar Customs: England*, London and Glasgow, 3 vols, (1936-40)

Index